The Palgrave Handbook of Spirituality and Business

The Palgrave Handbook of Spirituality and Business

Edited by

Luk Bouckaert

and

Laszlo Zsolnai

First published 2011 by
PALGRAVE MACMILLAN

Palgrave Macmillan in the UK is an imprint of Macmillan Publishers Limited,
registered in England, company number 785998, of Houndmills, Basingstoke,
Hampshire RG21 6XS.

Palgrave Macmillan in the US is a division of St Martin's Press LLC,
175 Fifth Avenue, New York, NY 10010.

Palgrave Macmillan is the global academic imprint of the above companies
and has companies and representatives throughout the world.

Palgrave® and Macmillan® are registered trademarks in the United States,
the United Kingdom, Europe and other countries.

ISBN 978–0–230–23831–2

This book is printed on paper suitable for recycling and made from fully
managed and sustained forest sources. Logging, pulping and manufacturing
processes are expected to conform to the environmental regulations of the
country of origin.

A catalogue record for this book is available from the British Library.

Library of Congress Cataloging-in-Publication Data

The Palgrave Handbook of spirituality and business / edited by
Luk Bouckaert and Laszlo Zsolnai.
    p. cm
Includes bibliographical references and index.
ISBN 978–0–230–23831–2 (alk. paper)
    1. Business – Religious aspects. 2. Business ethics. 3. Spiritual life.
I. Bouckaert, Luk, 1941– II. Zsolnai, Laszlo.
HF5388.H36 2011
201'.73—dc23   201101695

10 9 8 7 6 5 4 3 2 1
20 19 18 17 16 15 14 13 12 11

Printed and bound in the United States of America

Contents

Introduction

Part I   The Nature of Spirituality

Part II   Spiritually Inspired Economics

Part III   Socioeconomic Problems in Spiritual Perspective

Part IV Business Spirituality

Part V   Good Practices and Working Models

Tables and Figures

Tables

Figures

Acknowledgments

The preparation of this book was supported financially and intellectually by the European SPES Forum. We are grateful to our language editor, Doug Shokes, for his dedicated work on improving the English of the text. Last but not least, we thank all our colleagues who contributed to this handbook.

LUK BOUCKAERT
LASZLO ZSOLNAI

Preface

The *Handbook of Spirituality and Business* is a response to three developments that simultaneously challenge the "business as usual" mindset.

First, there is a growing interest from the academic as well as the entrepreneurial side in "spirituality" as the term is applied today in models of transformational leadership, in theories of social capital and in practices of values-driven management. What is the nature and origin of this interest? What are the main underlying theories and leading practices? Does it lead to a new discipline? One of the aims of our handbook is to explore the emerging field of business spirituality: its main concepts, models and practices.

Second, there is a growing awareness that the world is unsustainable without a strong commitment to frugality and self-restraint in managing global goods. Material resources such as clean air and water – as well as non-material resources such as trust, compassion and peace – are fragile. Our vital material resources cannot be managed successfully without good management of the spiritual resources of humankind. The transition from a market-driven capitalist economy towards a values-driven post-capitalist economy is linked to a new interest in spirituality as the art of managing the non-material resources of humankind. Therefore, the handbook aims to elucidate some of the conditions for a transformation towards a post-capitalist, values-driven global economy.

Third, although the interest in spirit-driven entrepreneurship and governance is increasing, spirituality remains a vague and confusing concept that needs intellectual clarification. There is a risk that without critical reflection, the "spiritual wave" in business practice and global governance will be reduced to an ambiguous discourse manipulating ethical and spiritual motivations for corporate or political purposes. Hence, the third aim of the handbook is to clarify the concept of spirituality in the fields of business and economics.

There are two types of handbook. Some handbooks are encyclopaedic in their style and content. They aim to give a complete overview of a well-established discipline. Other handbooks are more heuristic in their style and content. They aim to explore new ideas on the frontier of a discipline. Our handbook belongs to the second category. Therefore we invited the authors to write short essays on spiritually relevant themes that have emerged in their research or business practices. We were surprised to see the enthusiasm and the cooperation we got from all the authors. We are grateful for their effort.

The contributions are ordered in accordance with the following structure: Part I, The Nature of Spirituality; Part II, Spiritually Inspired Economics; Part III, Socioeconomic Problems in Spiritual Perspective; Part IV, Business Spirituality; and Part V, Good Practices and Working Models.

It is our hope that this handbook can stimulate creative researchers and progressive business leaders to realize the enormous potential of integrating spirituality into business and professional life.

LUK BOUCKAERT
LASZLO ZSOLNAI

Contributors

John Adams is Emeritus Professor of Organizational Systems, and was for many years the chair of the faculty and the chair of the organizational systems PhD program, at the Saybrook Graduate School, San Francisco. He was also a guest faculty member at the Bainbridge Island Graduate Institute in the MBA in sustainability program. Adams has been at the forefront of the organization development and transformation profession since 1969. His early articulation of issues facing organizations has provided a guiding light for the evolution of organization and change management consulting. He is currently on the board of directors of Prevention International: No Cervical Cancer (PINCC) and serves as administrative director for PINCC-India. His book *Thinking Today As If Tomorrow Mattered: The Rise of a Sustainable Consciousness* (1999) is the culmination of several years' research, speaking, and writing.

Robert Allinson is Professor of Philosophy at Soka University of America. He has been invited to be a visiting professor or fellow at Beijing University, Fudan University, Waseda University, Yale University, Cambridge University, the University of Canterbury, Oxford University, Copenhagen Business School, the Helsinki School of Economics and Business Administration, and the University of Hawaii. He is author or editor of seven books and more than 250 academic articles, including *Saving Human Lives: Lessons in Management Ethics* (2005), *Space, Time and the Ethical Foundations* (2002), and *Understanding the Chinese Mind* (2000). His works have been translated into Chinese, Japanese, Korean, French, German, and Italian.

Michael Bell is the founder and director of Inukshuk Management Consultants, a consulting firm specializing in community and organizational development. For the past twenty-five years he has worked in Inuit and Dene communities in the Canadian Arctic. He spent his early life in a Roman Catholic monastery and worked as a priest in American inner cities and in Paris. After leaving the priesthood in the late 1960s, he worked as a community organizer in Milwaukee, Wisconsin, and northern Canada. He has a special interest in building a conceptual and psychic bridge that links the traditional teachings of aboriginal elders with the insights of the new science and cosmology.

Paul de Blot SJ is professor honoris causa at the Nyenrode Business University, where he was appointed Professor in Business Spirituality in 2006. He joined the Allied Forces during the Second World War and was imprisoned for five years. In 1948 he became a Jesuit and completed his studies in Indonesia in Indonesian and Javanese language, Eastern cultures, philosophy, politology, and physics; and in theology, psychology, philosophy of science and culture, spirituality, and business administration in the Netherlands. He is the editor of *Business Spirituality* magazine.

Zsolt Boda is a senior research fellow at the Institute of Political Science, Hungarian Academy of Sciences, and an associate professor at the Business Ethics Center, Corvinus University of Budapest. He is also active in the Hungarian green movement and has worked as an expert for environmental NGOs. He has co-edited and written books in Hungarian on corporate ethics, political theory, and environmental politics and policy. He has published several papers in academic journals and books on international ethics involving the fair trade problematic, trade and environmental issues, and the politics of global environmentalism.

Margot Esther Borden maintains a private psychotherapy practice in Paris; teaches at Antioch McGregor University in the US; presents seminars and public lectures in Europe, India, and the US; and consults for multinational and Fortune 100 corporations. Her orientation is in the schools of transpersonal and integral psychology. She is trained in a variety of therapeutic techniques aimed at addressing human experience and potential from an integral perspective. She has a long-term dedication to exploring consciousness through psychological and spiritual traditions, experiential therapies, meditation, and yoga techniques. Borden developed IPM™, which involves qualitative and quantitative research methodologies backed by insight and intuition.

Luk Bouckaert is Emeritus Professor of Ethics at the Catholic University of Leuven. He is a philosopher and an economist by training. In 1987 he co-founded the interdisciplinary Centre for Economics and Ethics at Leuven. In 2000 he started the SPES (Spirituality in Economics and Society) Forum, and some years later the European SPES Forum. His research and publications fall within the fields of business ethics and spirituality. He has written several books in Dutch. Recent publications in English include *Spirituality as a Public Good* (2007, co-edited with Laszlo Zsolnai), *Frugality: Rebalancing Material and Spiritual Values in Economic Life* (2008, co-edited with H. Opdebeeck and L. Zsolnai),

Imagine Europe (2009, co-edited with J. Eynikel), and *Respect and Economic Democracy* (2010, co-edited with Pasquale Arena).

David Boyle is a fellow at the New Economics Foundation in London, and has been at the heart of the effort to develop co-production and introduce time banks to Britain as a critical element of public service reform. He is also the founder of the London Time Bank network and co-founder of Time Banking UK. He has been closely involved in the Clone Town Britain campaign and writes about the future of volunteering, cities, and business. His work on the future of money has also been covered in books and pamphlets such as *Why London Needs Its Own Currency* (2000), *Virtual Currencies* (2000), *The Money Changers: Currency Reform from Aristotle to e-Cash* (2002), *The Little Money Book* (2003), and *Money Matters* (2009).

Gerrit Broekstra worked for thirty years as Professor of Organization Behavior and Systems Science at the Rotterdam School of Management of the Erasmus University, at the Kellogg School of Management of Northwestern University, Chicago, and at the Nyenrode Business University. He was active in the systems movement, was president of the Dutch Systems Society for eight years, and served a four-year term as president of the IFSR, the International Federation for Systems Research in Vienna. He has also been a consultant for many Netherlands-based companies. His research interest is in applying systems thinking and complexity theory to organizational challenges of distributed leadership and radical decentralization. His most recent book, *Deep Leadership: The Secret of Right Action in Times of Uncertainty* (2009, in Dutch), attempts to integrate Western business rationality with Eastern humanistic philosophy.

Luigino Bruni is Associate Professor of Economics at the University of Milano-Bicocca. His primary fields of interest and publication are the history of thought, ethics, reciprocity, and the philosophy of economics. He has published *Civil Happiness* (2006) and *Economics and Happiness* (2005, co-edited with P. Porta).

Frans de Clerck is a co-founder of Triodos Bank Belgium and senior advisor to the executive board of Triodos Bank Group. He is chairman of the Institute of Social Banking, and a board member of Triodos's sustainable investment funds and of sustainable companies in Belgium and Luxembourg. He lectures on business ethics in finance at Vlerick Leuven Gent Management School and at the Institute for Social Banking. He worked as an advisor to the Council of Europe and the European

Commission on social cohesion and corporate social responsibility. He has been working in banking since 1968 and in ethical banking since 1983.

Eelco van den Dool is an associate researcher in the Centre for Social Innovation and a lecturer in the Department of Business Administration at the Ede Christian University of Applied Sciences in the Netherlands. He is working on a PhD project entitled "Spiritual Dynamics in Social Innovation," which focuses on the potential of Dorothee Soelle's liberation theology in innovative organizations. He is author or co-author of several books on business spirituality and ideals in organizations and a co-founder of Effective Ideals.

Veerle Draulans is Assistant Professor of Ethics at Tilburg University, where she teaches in the master's program on organization and cultural diversity and ethical competences. She is also Associate Professor of Gender Studies at the Catholic University of Leuven, where she coordinates the interfaculty course on gender studies. Her research focuses on values and religion in Europe, civil society and religion, health care and diversity, gender and leadership, and gender and science. She is a participant in the European Values Study Project and a member of the Belgian Advisory Committee on Bio-ethics, the scientific board of Kadoc (Documentation and Research Center for Religion, Culture and Society, Leuven), and the board of governors of Emmaus, which runs Christian-inspired care institutions and hospitals in Belgium.

John Drew is Jean Monnet Professor of European Business and Management at the European Business School, London, and the Institute of Contemporary European Studies, Regent's College. He is a former president of EUROTAS, the European Transpersonal Association. He has been head of the United Kingdom offices of the European Commission, a director of Rank Xerox, and Director of Marketing and Executive Programmes at the London Business School. He was a member of HM Diplomatic Service in Paris, Beirut, Kuwait, and Bucharest. He has also held academic positions at Templeton College, Oxford; Imperial College Business School, London; the Open University; and the University of Durham.

Kenneth E. Goodpaster taught philosophy at the University of Notre Dame throughout the 1970s before joining the Harvard Business School faculty in 1980. In 1989, he accepted the David and Barbara Koch Endowed Chair in Business Ethics at the University of St. Thomas. At Harvard, he taught MBA candidates and executives and developed the second-year elective course Ethical Aspects of Corporate Policy, as well as the first-year required module Managerial Decision Making and Ethical Values. He also authored two textbooks, *Ethics in Management* (1984) and *Policies and Persons: A Casebook in Business Ethics* (1985, 1991, 1998, and 2006). His latest book is *Conscience and Corporate Culture* (2007). Goodpaster sits on the editorial boards of several journals in the field of business ethics, and has been active with the Caux Round Table; the Minneapolis-based Center for Ethical Business Cultures; the International Society for Business, Economics, and Ethics; and the Better Business Bureau (BBB).

Tibor Héjj has run his own company, Proactive Management Consulting, since 2003. He was co-founder, and for ten years an executive vice president, of Műszertechnika, the most successful Hungarian computer and telecom company of its time, setting up and presiding over subsidiaries in Germany, Switzerland, the US, and Taiwan. He went into management consulting in 1994 when he joined the Boston Consulting Group's Munich office, and was transferred in 1997 to the new Budapest office, where he was promoted to manager. In early 2001 he switched to A.T. Kearney to lead its emerging local office and became an international vice president.

Carlos Hoevel is Professor of the History of Economic and Political Ideas, Business Ethics, and the Philosophy of Economics at the Catholic University of Argentina in Buenos Aires. He is also director of the University's Center for Studies in Economy and Culture and editor of the *Journal of Economic Culture*.

Knut Johannessen Ims is Professor of Business Ethics at the Norwegian School of Economics and Business Administration (NHH), Bergen. He has taught courses on ethics for more than a decade, and has also taught PhD courses in system development and information and management. He is a member of the Business Ethics Interfaculty Group of the Community of European Management Schools, and is chairman of the board of the Centre of Ethics and Economics at NHH.

Tim Kasser is Professor and Chair of Psychology at Knox College, Galesburg, Illinois. His interests include personality, dreaming, clinical and abnormal psychology, and alternatives to consumerism. He has been associate editor of the *Journal of Personality and Social Psychology: Personality Processes and Individual Differences*, and serves as consulting editor of *Psychological Inquiry*. His best-selling book is *The High Price of Materialism* (2002).

Feisal Khan is an associate professor of economics at Hobart and William Smith Colleges, New York. He has published extensively on Islamic banking and finance and on economic development, governance, and corruption in Pakistan. He is currently working on a book on the Pakistani experience with Islamic banking. His nonacademic professional experience includes a stint in the corporate banking division of the largest foreign bank in Pakistan, where he gained firsthand experience of Islamic banking.

Suzan Langenberg is director of Diversity bvba in Belgium and the Netherlands. Her main interest is the organizational position of communication related to ethical business problems. In 2008 she completed her PhD on "Criticism as De-organization: Business Ethics and Free Speech" at Radboud University Nijmegen, the Netherlands.

François Lépineux is a professor at ESC Rennes School of Business in Brittany, where he is in charge of the CANON Chair "Foresight and the Common Good" and head of the Centre for Responsible Business. He has conducted various research and consulting activities, and has co-edited two books with H.-C. de Bettignies: *Finance for a Better World: The Shift Toward Sustainability* (2009) and *Business, Globalization and the Common Good* (2009). He is co-author of the first handbook on corporate social responsibility in French.

Ronnie Lessem is a co-founder of TRANS4M (Four World Laboratory for Social and Economic Transformation) and a professor at the University of Buckingham. He previously taught at the City University in London, and has spent the past twenty-five years developing educational and research curricula and programs that lead to social and economic transformation. He is the author of more than twenty books on the development of self, business, and society.

Marjolein Lips-Wiersma is a former chair of the Management, Spirituality and Religion interest group of the Academy of Management. She researches workplace spirituality, existentialism, and ethics. Her current interests center on the role of spirituality and leadership in relation to meaningful work, the role of spiritual retreats in organizations, shadows of spirituality, spirituality and new forms of organizing, purpose beyond profit, and the interplay between notions of spirituality and various forms of power. She is associate editor of the *Journal of Management, Spirituality and Religion* and has published numerous papers on workplace spirituality.

T. Dean Maines is the president of the SAIP Institute at the University of St. Thomas, Minneapolis. Previously, Maines worked for sixteen years in various capacities for Cummins, Inc., including chief human resource executive for the firm's worldwide Power Generation Group and president of the Columbus Occupational Health Association, Inc. He was a Sloan Fellow at Stanford University's Graduate School of Business, where he earned an MS in management. He is pursuing an MA in theology at St. Paul School of Divinity, University of St. Thomas.

Domènec Melé is a professor at the IESE Business School, University of Navarra, and holds the Chair of Business Ethics at this institution. He has chaired the biennial International Symposium on Ethics, Business, and Society led by IESE since 1991. Over the past twenty-five years, he has taught and written extensively in his areas of specialization, which include economic and business ethics, international management ethics, corporate social responsibility, Christian ethics and spirituality in management, and philosophy of management. He is the author of more than sixty scientific articles and twenty case studies and has authored or edited a dozen books in these fields. His most recent book is *Business Ethics in Action: Seeking Human Excellence in Organizations* (2009).

Laurie Michaelis is a member of the Quaker Community in Bamford in the English Peak District. He coordinates Living Witness, a charity working with Quaker and other groups in Britain to develop understanding of and action for spirit-led sustainable living. From 1998 to 2002 he worked at the Oxford Centre for the Environment, Ethics and Society as research director for the Oxford Commission on Sustainable Consumption. Other projects have included a study for the European Environment Agency on consumption futures in Europe and an assessment of the policy implications of sustainable consumption research for the UK Sustainable Development Commission. He previously worked as a policy analyst at the Organization for Economic Co-operation and Development and as an analyst at the UK Energy Technology Support Unit. He has been lead author or convening lead author for several reports of the Intergovernmental Panel on Climate Change, including the Special Report on Emissions Scenarios.

Daniel A. Monti is the director of the Myrna Brind Center of Integrative Medicine, and Associate Professor of Emergency Medicine and Psychiatry at Thomas Jefferson University and Hospital, Philadelphia. He has completed groundbreaking research work on complementary medicine in chronic cancer care.

Lani Morris is an independent business advisor and lecturer with a particular focus on leadership, motivation, creativity, communication, and sustainability, and on how these interrelate in complex and systemic ways. She is also an award-winning artist. She is a co-founder of the Holistic Development Group and has an abiding interest in how we can continually bring profound inquiry into the workplace.

Sanjoy Mukherjee is an associate professor at the Rajiv Gandhi Indian Institute of Management, Shillong. He was previously associated with the Management Center for Human Values at the Indian Institute of Management, Calcutta, for fifteen years. For more than a decade he has been editor-in-chief of the *Journal of Human Values*. His research interests include wisdom leadership, the Indian model of management, spirituality and business, business ethics, and corporate social responsibility.

Sharda Nandram is an associate professor at the Center for Entrepreneurship, Nyenrode Business University. She is also Professor of Entrepreneurship at the HAN University of Applied Sciences in the Netherlands. She is the lead author of *The Spirit of Entrepreneurship* (2006) and co-editor and author of *Spirituality and Business: Exploring Possibilities for a New Management Paradigm* (2010). Her most recent book is about the relevance of *Kautilya's Arthashastra* (in Dutch).

Judi Neal is the director of the Tyson Center for Faith and Spirituality in the Workplace at the Sam M. Walton College of Business, University of Arkansas. She is also professor emeritus at the University of New Haven and academic director of the Master of Arts in Organizational Leadership program at the Graduate Institute. She was the founder of the International Center for Spirit at Work, and the International Spirit at Work Awards. Neal authored *Edgewalkers: People and Organizations That Take Risks, Build Bridges and Break New Ground* (2006). She co-founded the Management, Spirituality and Religion Interest Group at the Academy of Management and was the group's second chair. She is also a co-founder of the *Journal of Management, Spirituality, and Religion*. Neal has published widely in academic journals and has spoken about spirituality in the workplace at conferences around the world.

Andrew B. Newberg is Director of Research at the Myrna Brind Center of Integrative Medicine at Thomas Jefferson University and Hospital, Philadelphia. He is also a professor in the Departments of Emergency Medicine and Radiology at Thomas Jefferson University. Newberg has been particularly involved in the study of mystical and religious experiences as well as the more general mind–body relationship in both the clinical and research aspects of his career. Much of his research has focused on the relationship between brain function and various mystical and religious experiences. He has published numerous articles and chapters on brain function, brain imaging, and the study of religious and mystical experiences.

Henk Oosterling works in the Department of Philosophy of the Erasmus University, Rotterdam. He is secretary of the Dutch–Flemish Association for Intercultural Philosophy (NVVIF) and chairman of the Dutch Aesthetics Federation (DAF). He practiced martial arts from his early youth, and stayed in Japan in the early 1980s to study Japanese sword fighting (*kendo*). In 1985 he wrote an instruction book on *kendo*.

Hendrik Opdebeeck is Professor of Philosophy and Economics at the University of Antwerp, where he is affiliated to the Centre of Ethics. His research focus is the cultural-philosophical background and effects of globalization, with special attention to the role of spirituality and technology. In 2000, together with Luk Bouckaert, he founded the SPES (Spirituality in Economics and Society) Forum in Leuven.

Moses L. Pava is the Alvin Einbender Professor of Business Ethics and Professor of Accounting at the Sy Syms School of Business, Yeshiva University in New York. He is on the steering committee of the Jewish Ethics Association and lectures internationally on Jewish business ethics and leadership, spirituality in business, and corporate accountability. He has authored or edited fifteen books, including *Business Ethics: A Jewish Perspective* (1997), *Leading with Meaning* (2003), *The Jewish Ethics Workbook* (2005), *The Search for Meaning in Organizations* (1999), and *Jewish Ethics as Dialogue* (2009).

Peter Pruzan is professor emeritus at the Copenhagen Business School (CBS) and visiting professor at Sri Sathya Sai University in India. Among his organizational initiatives are co-founding, designing, or governing bachelor's and master's programs at CBS in mathematics and economics (1987) and in philosophy and economics (1996); the Institute of Social and Ethical AccountAbility in London (now AccountAbility, 1996); the Copenhagen Centre – New Partnerships for Social Responsibility (1998); the CBS Centre for Corporate Social Responsibility (2002); and the European Academy for Business in Society (Brussels, 2002). His most recent books are *Rational, Ethical and Spiritual Perspectives on Leadership: Selected Writings by Peter Pruzan* (2009) and, together with his wife, Kirsten, *Leading with Wisdom: Spiritual-Based Leadership in Business* (2007, 2010).

Jean-Jacques Rosé is a researcher at the Norbert Elias Center, EHESS–CNRS, Marseille. He was previously an associate professor at University Paris IV–Sorbonne and CEO of ID FORCE – FCA communications consulting. He is vice-president of the Association for the Development of Education and Research on Corporate Social Responsibility (ADERSE) and a member of the European SPES (Spirituality in Economics and Society) Forum. He is particularly interested in the application of lexical analysis methods to the literature on business ethics, corporate social responsibility, and sustainable development.

Alexander Schieffer is a co-founder of TRANS4M (Four World Laboratory for Social and Economic Transformation). He also lectures at the University of St. Gallen, Switzerland. After working in various industries in Europe and Asia (he runs his own publishing company in Singapore), he found his passion in turning education and research into vehicles for social and economic transformation and innovation. Together with Ronnie Lessem, he has published *Integral Research and Innovation* (2010), *Transformation Management: Towards the Integral Enterprise* (2009), and *Integral Economics* (2010).

Mike J. Thompson is Professor of Management Practice at China Europe International Business School (CEIBS) in Shanghai. He was previously CEO of GoodBrand, an international sustainable enterprise consultancy that provides services to major multinational clients. He has served on the boards of a number of profit and not-for-profit companies, including the UK's largest independent toy retailer. He has been active in the field of social enterprise, serving on the board of Young Enterprise UK and as a director of Hub King's Cross, London, a serviced office and members network for social entrepreneurs. Since 2004, he has served on the board of the European SPES (Spirituality in Economics and Society) Forum, based at the University of Leuven.

Jurjen Wiersma is Professor of Ethics and Philosophy at the Protestant Theological Faculty in Brussels. His areas of interest concern the life and work of Dietrich Bonhoeffer, the European Union as an ethico-theological challenge, war and peace, good and evil, and theological journalism. His most recent book, *Een wiel dat draait* (2007), deals with identity and identity (re)formation.

Olivier F. Williams is an associate professor and director of the Notre Dame Center for Ethics and Religious Values in Business in the Mendoza College of Business at the University of Notre Dame. He was recently appointed a member of the four-person board of directors of the

United Nations Global Compact Foundation. He is the editor or author of fourteen books and numerous journal articles on business ethics. His most recent book is *Peace through Commerce: Responsible Corporate Citizenship and the Ideals of the United Nations Global Compact* (2008).

Stefano Zamagni has been a professor at the University of Bologna since 1979, a visiting professor at the University of Bocconi, Milan, since 1985, and an adjunct professor at Johns Hopkins University (Bologna Center) since 1983. He was previously a professor at the University of Parma. Zamagni is the author of several books, including *Microeconomic Theory* (1997) and *Civil Economy and Paradoxes of Growth* (1997). He co-authored *History of Economic Thought* (with E. Screpanti, 1995 and 2005), *Living in the Global Society* (with R. Papini and A. Pavan, 1997), *Multiculturalism and Identity* (with C. Vigna, 2002), *Civil Economy* (with L. Bruni, 2004), *Markets, Money and History: Essays in Honour of Sir John Hicks* (with R. Scazzieri and A. Sen, 2008), and *Dictionary of Civil Economy* (with L. Bruni, 2009).

Laszlo Zsolnai is a professor and director of the Business Ethics Center at the Corvinus University of Budapest. He is chairman of the Business Ethics Faculty Group of the Community of European Management Schools. He serves as editor of the "Frontier of Business Ethics" book series. With Luk Bouckaert he co-founded the European SPES (Spirituality in Economics and Society) Forum in Leuven, Belgium. His most recent books include *Spirituality as a Public Good* (2007), *Frugality: Rebalancing Material and Spiritual Values in Economic Life* (2008), *Europe-Asia Dialogue on Business Spirituality* (2008), *Responsible Decision Making* (2008), *The Future International Manager: A Vision of the Roles and Duties of Management* (2009), and *The Collaborative Enterprise: Creating Values for a Sustainable World* (2010).

Introduction

1
Spirituality and Business

Luk Bouckaert and Laszlo Zsolnai

From business ethics to business spirituality[1]

Business ethics, as an academic discipline and a management practice related to corporate social responsibility (CSR), emerged in the late 1970s and the 1980s. It was a promising movement in the shadow of the globalization process. It started in the United States and followed five to ten years later in all industrialized countries, including those in Europe. Some companies developed their first codes of ethics, mission statements and charters of values at that time. Seminars were held for managers in order to look at ethical dilemmas and analyze ethical case studies. The Body Shop, the well-known cosmetics company, went a step further in the 1990s by launching a major social and ethical audit of its operations. Shell, in its famous report "People, Planet and Profits," applied the notion of sustainable entrepreneurship to a new sort of reporting, which measured and analyzed not only the company's financial goals and results, but also its ecological and social goals.

Within this context the pioneers of business ethics developed the so-called *stakeholder theory of the firm*. This theory introduced the ethical problems of fair distribution of profit, transparency and accountability as genuine *managerial problems* and not just as problems of social and political regulation. Business ethics introduced the idea of moral self-regulation in business. New management instruments were created, like mission statements, ethical codes, ethical audits, triple bottom line policies, stakeholder management schemes, etc. There was an animated, philosophical debate between the proponents of stakeholder theory and the defenders of conventional stockholder theory of the firm. The stakeholder–stockholder controversy or the "Freeman–Friedman twist," was illustrative for this phase of business ethics. It was the flourishing period of business ethics.

The sequel to the business ethics story during the 1990s continued along the path of the Kuhnian scientific cycle. After a period of new ideas, a period of normal science followed. During that period of normal science, researchers tried to solve concrete empirical puzzles. Business-ethics centres got funds for research projects with a strong empirical and policy-orientated perspective. The shift from philosophical to empirical research made business ethics attractive to other social scientists, to consultancy firms and to business schools. A feeling emerged that made business ethics more consumer-friendly and operational. The networks were growing. At the end of the 1990s business ethics was considered a key factor in building good reputations, gaining trust and motivating people. In its Green Paper, the European Union considered CSR a new instrument of social regulation (European Commission, 2001). However, the success of business ethics also had a downside. The easy talk of ethics worked at the same time as a dazzling narrative, creating the illusion that good ethics is good business and, just one step further, that good business is good ethics.

After 2000 we were first confronted by a wave of scandals related to the ICT sector (think of the cases of Enron, WorldCom, Parmalat, Ahold, Lernout and Hauspie). Then, in 2008, a second bubble burst and brought us the banking crisis, followed by an economic recession. Although there are some signs of a recovery, belief in business ethics as a system of moral self-regulation fuelling relations of trust and good reputation is no longer evident.

In this Handbook, most of the contributors assume that the crucial question is not "Do we need *more* business ethics?" but rather "Do we need *another type* of business ethics?" They refer in one way or another to the *crowding-out* mechanism in business ethics. "Crowding out" denotes the process by which the instrumental use of business ethics crowds out genuine moral commitment and substitutes it with rational cost-benefit calculations. For instance, by looking at business ethics as an efficient instrument to strengthen the good reputation of a brand, we shift our attention from good ethics to good business. After a time, we create the illusion that good ethics always pays and that good business equates with good ethics. Through the crowding-out effect business ethics loses its intrinsic status and its potential to criticize opportunistic tendencies within business.

Why focus on spirituality for solving the ethical deficit in business ethics? Because spirituality – as an inner experience of deep interconnectedness with all living beings – opens a space of distance from the pressures of the market and the routines of business-as-usual. This distance is a necessary condition for developing innovative ethical ideas and practices. It restores intrinsic motivation and provides a long time horizon. Unfortunately, spirituality is not yet a mainstream concept in academia and the business world, where instrumental and utilitarian rationality is still the dominant perspective, rather than spirituality, which is anchored in a deeper, noninstrumental and nonutilitarian experience of life.

For more than a decade we, the authors, have been involved in the effort of disclosing spirituality in business and economics. In 2001 we organized an international conference in Szeged, Hungary, which was probably the first European workshop on "Spirituality in Management." The papers from this workshop were published in the Kluwer Academic Series of Business Ethics (Zsolnai, 2004). After this workshop the cooperation among different European centers involved in business ethics resulted in setting up *The European SPES Forum* in 2004 in Leuven, Belgium (SPES, the Latin word for Hope, is also an acronym for "Spirituality in Economics and Society"). The aim of the Forum is to promote spirituality as a public good and as a source of noninstrumental reasoning in business. The European SPES Forum was just one among other new networks in the field of applied spirituality. The point here is to realize that business spirituality is embedded in a broader intercultural and intercontinental development.

The transition to a postcapitalist, values-driven economy

We believe that the case for business spirituality on a micro-level is embedded in a global evolution towards a postcapitalist, values-driven economy. Undoubtedly, this evolution is not yet fully visible, nor is there certainty that it will ever be completely realized. But as an opportunity for a better and more sustainable world, the idea is already present in the mindset of progressive organizations, and leaders who are aware of the limits of our planetary resources. It will not suffice to replace the existing technology with "green technology" without changing the incessant underlying drive towards "more and bigger." Green capitalism may be a step in the right direction, but it is not a sufficient one. The transformation of means must be embedded in a transformation of values and preferences. If we build green cars but, at the same time, stimulate the production and consumption of more cars, we will not stop the overexploitation of our planet.

The challenge of sustainability requires both the greening of our technology and the self-restricting of our needs. Therefore we use the term "postcapitalism." Whereas capitalist economies are ultimately driven by the highest return on financial capital and may support "green capitalism" as a profit opportunity, postcapitalist economies are driven by a complex balance of spiritual and material values and respect for the human condition of future generations. A postcapitalist economy requires an institutional environment that corrects unregulated market competition and promotes a more frugal and responsible ethic of consumption. This Handbook, dealing with spiritually inspired economics, illustrates how religions and moral philosophies disclose older forms of noncapitalist economic rationality that can inspire our postmodern striving for a combination of technical progress and meaning. The Handbook also explores a series of socioeconomic problems where spiritual factors play an important role. These problems are related to the management of global, common goods. It is important to define the new areas of common goods such as the use of oceans, rainforests, outer space and the non-material goods such as trust and peace.

Planetary resources are perceived and managed today as competitive goods with an expected high return on investment and not as common goods with a high degree of vulnerability. The lack of appropriate management of those global goods leads to the tragedy of the planetary common goods, which is already visible today in the form of climate change and other symptoms of ecological deterioration.

There is an area of common goods that deserves our particular interest: the area of *non-material or spiritual* goods such as silence, trust, respect, beauty, moral values, wisdom, etc. All these goods share the characteristics of common goods. They are not excludable. Silence and trust, for example, are values and practices open to everyone. They are free, not regulated by markets and cannot be enforced by law. But at the same time, they are vulnerable goods. Silence can only be maintained if others share it as a public good. If some persons do not respect it, silence will diminish. Trust is another example of a common good with a high degree of vulnerability. One's trust is dependent on other people's trust and implies a reciprocal commitment to be realized. Hence, as a common good, trust can only exist when it is carefully managed as a vulnerable and shared good. The ongoing worldwide financial crisis clearly illustrates the importance of trust as a common and vulnerable good that needs more than market regulation.

The authors of the Handbook, analyzing the contrast between a materialistic and a non-materialistic drive in economics, define the new values of the postcapitalist economy: frugality, deep ecology, trust, reciprocity, responsibility for future generations, and authenticity. Within this values-driven economy, profit and growth are no longer ultimate aims but elements in a wider set of values. In a similar way cost-benefit calculations are no longer the essence of good management but part of a broader concept of wisdom in leadership.

The concept of spirituality

We do not believe that spirituality can be captured in one standard definition. Moreover, if we want to keep the notion of experience-based spirituality, we have to accept that spirituality is a rich, intercultural and multilayered concept. Throughout the Handbook the reader will find an impressive list of inspiring and complementary definitions.

As a guideline we have used the working definition of the SPES Forum: Spirituality is people's multiform search for a deep meaning of life interconnecting them to all living beings and to "God" or "Ultimate Reality." Most definitions of spirituality share a number of common elements: reconnection to the inner self; a search for universal values that lifts the individual above egocentric strivings; deep empathy with all living beings; and finally, a desire to keep in touch with the source of life (whatever name we give it). In other words, spirituality is a search for inner identity, connectedness, and transcendence.

Whereas spirituality was for a long time an exclusive area of interest within the context of religions, today it clearly goes beyond the boundaries of institutional religions. For believers, and nonbelievers as well, spirituality functions:

1. as a suitable platform for *interreligious dialogue* beyond the clash of religions and cultures;
2. as a *public and vulnerable* good which requires an appropriate form of public management;
3. as a *profane* good that does not remove the spiritual to a separate level but integrates it as a component of political, social, economic, and scientific activities;
4. as an *experience-based* good that is accessible to each human being reflecting on his or her inner experiences of life; and
5. as a source of *inspiration* in the human and social quest for meaning.

The Handbook is an expression of the new development of spirituality as a social experience within and outside the context of institutionalized religions. It is focused on forms of *profane* and *applied* spirituality in the fields of business, economics, and social life.

Note

See Luk Bouckaert, "From Business Ethics to Business Spirituality: The Socratic Model of Leadership" and Laszlo Zsolnai, "Ethics Needs Spirituality" in Nandram, S.S. and Borden, M.E. (eds) 2010, pp. 73–93).

Literature

European Commission 2001. *Green Paper of the European Commission Promoting a European Framework for Corporate Social Responsibility* (July 2001).

Nandram, S.S. and Borden, M.E. (eds) 2010. *Spirituality and Business. Exploring Possibilities for a New Management Paradigm.* Heidelberg, Springer.

Zsolnai, L. (ed.) 2004. *Spirituality and Ethics in Management.* Dordrecht, Kluwer Academic Publisher.

Part I
The Nature of Spirituality

2
Religion and Spirituality

Paul de Blot

According to the Oxford English Dictionary the term *spirituality* relates to the soul or spirit and the term *religion* refers to the existence of a super-human controlling power, especially God or gods, usually expressed in worship. This is a simple definition of a very complex reality. Essentially, the difference between spirituality and religion is not clear because it is about examining the same reality in a different light.

The difference between religion and spirituality

A religion is a way of approaching the uncontrolled environment. In their struggle for life people experience a mysterious power that can-not be controlled. This Ultimate Reality is given different names: God, Yahweh, Zeus, Allah, Brahman, etc. In this context religion is an organ-ized approach to the supernatural reality through human activities, which are mostly spiritual and usually encompass a set of narratives, beliefs, and practices. By giving the supernatural reality a name, we create a relationship with Him or Her and attempt to take part in this supernatural power. In this way religion covers the ultimate meaning of our lives and expresses the ultimate values of society. *Religion* is used interchangeably with *faith* or *belief systems*. We observe that in modern Western societies, existing values are weakening, and religious inspira-tion is disappearing. This weakening of religious traditions is called sec-ularization. At the same time new religions are being born, for instance in Africa, where many self-proclaimed prophets are initiating religious movements.

Spirituality is related to the same Ultimate Reality but takes a more secular approach, while religion's point of view is more sacral. Religion speaks about the meaning of human life as a religious belief system activated by obeying the will of God or gods. Spirituality, on the other hand, is a multiform search for a transcendent meaning of life based on the reflection of our human experience on the level of being. On this level of our existence we are conscious of our connection with all beings and with the whole of creation. Spiritual consciousness is an awareness of the Ultimate Reality of our inspiration and energy, which is nowadays often called our "flow." Spirituality is also the theoretical approach and rational formulation of this spiritual experience.

In the Western context we are conscious of our human existence as a dualistic composition of body and soul. Our physical life is rooted in the material world and our spiritual life is centered on the spiritual reality. The spiritual approach reflects this dual nature of our human doing, including doing business. Spiritual activity takes place within both the temporal and eternal worlds and can also be realized by a nonreligious person. But in our inner experience this rational distinction is not clear. In many cultures everything is an expression of the will of God.

This difference between religion and spirituality can be a cause of conflict, mainly because spirituality does not imply a doctrinal belief whereas religion claims an awareness of God that is institutionalized and supported by a rational doctrine. If institutionalized religious belief creates disharmony with spiritual awareness, the two faces of the Ultimate Reality, the divine and human levels, will lose their mutual reinforcement. The spiritual experience of being will no longer be represented by the dogmatic guidelines of religious doing and thinking. Such a disconnected, dogmatized religious belief system will be denied by spiritual people. But we can avoid this disconnection by keeping religion in touch with spiritual experience. In this case, religion can function as a source of inspiration for spiritual people and can support the paradigm shift in business (from doing to being).

Spirituality and materiality

The fundamental challenge for spirituality is not the conflict between religion and spirituality, but rather, the conflict between spirituality and materiality. A spiritual guru from India with a theological background, the Jesuit Anthony de Mello, uses a parable to explain this difference between material and spiritual ways of doing business (Anthony de Mello, 1990). The egg of an eagle was adopted by a chicken. The little eagle grew up with the other chickens, living as a chicken. One day the eagle was looking up in the air and was amazed by a wonderful bird that was gracefully moving high in the sky with its golden wings. It is an eagle, the chickens told him;an eagle is a wonderful bird, the king of the air, and quite different from a chicken. A chicken lives and forages on earth, but an eagle is a much higher being because it flies through the skies. The chicken-eagle continued its life as a free-range chicken, scratching around to find worms and insects. The chicken wanted to be an eagle, but instead continued its life as a chicken and eventually died as a chicken.

With this story de Mello tries to help people working on the material, business level to become aware of their divine and spiritual nature and divine vocation. Spirituality is essentially an awakening and liberation process leading to human freedom, freedom from the blindness of a chicken to realize the dream of flying like a divine eagle. Strong dogmatic or ethical norms and institutional systems of regulation are the reason for the loss of the spiritual power of an organization. The blindness of the chicken can be compared to the dualistic nature of humans, who live simultaneously on a material and spiritual level, the two levels of being and doing. Human nature is a composition of matter and spirit, of body and soul. In all our activities on an individual or social level, and even on a religious level, we are living on two levels, on the level of doing and on the level of being. Doing business in a spiritual way constitutes a physical way of doing, that is supported by the energy of a spiritual way of being. This spiritual consciousness cannot be expressed in rational concepts, ethical norms or dogmatic guidelines. Reducing spirituality to rational guidelines means reducing its power and creative inspiration and falling down in a lifeless system without inner meaning, like the eagle living as a chicken on earth.

Spirituality in business

Doing business is a human activity in the temporal context, which is by definition outside the religious world. Spirituality in business is defined as a double-faced reality. It is a professional way of doing business on the level of doing, an activity that takes place in the secular world. At the same time it is something done by humans who are simultaneously working with spiritual energy and inspiration on the level of being. Doing business is an interaction, also called "conversation," between a *doing*-action focused on performance and a *being*-contemplation of the ultimate meaning of our activities. Doing business in a spiritual way is about getting in touch with the Ultimate Reality of being, which is also called God, Brahman or the YOU in capitals. The purpose is to engender an effective and successful way of doing business that conforms to the corporative spiritual power and inspiration of the company.

In the last decade a lot of spiritual trends have developed, including schools or communities devoted to yoga, Zen and other charismatic religious and philosophical movements, and they are developing very fast. All these movements operate primarily on the personal level of spiritual awareness and are not directly aimed at organizations and business innovation. For the corporate awareness of organizations and collective spirituality, a new approach using appropriate tools needs to be developed. The Nyenrode Business University in Breukelen, the Netherlands, founded a Business Spirituality chair for the development of tools on the corporate level of spirituality.

Corporate spiritual power can be found in every organization. The spiritual resources are initially created by the founder(s) of the organization; but in many cases, after some time, their spiritual power weakens and becomes lost. The awareness of this corporate spiritual life can be awakened by a reflection on the founding power of the organization. In family businesses the founders mostly get their inspiration from relevant family spirituality.

A religious model of organization

Most religions tell a story about the creation of the world, consisting of a transformation of the chaos into a cosmos. Such a story can be used for management inspiration. For example, the creation story in the book of Genesis, the first part of the Torah, is considered Holy Scripture by the three dominant world religions: Judaism, Islam, and Christianity. In this story we get a clear picture of the essential ingredients of a spiritually driven organization and the weakness of nonspiritual management. This story about man and the organization of the world is both a religious and a spiritual narrative. It stresses explicitly that mankind is created by God, without telling us who God is, because God is an enigma that escapes rational definition.

In the beginning there was only the divine spirit breathing in the emptiness. He created a wonderful structure with the sun and moon as time references. The formation of plants and flowers, beautiful birds in the sky, and fishes in the water was followed by the creation of man. He modeled a man out of earth and breathed his own spirit into his nose. A living human being was created, a semblance of God. This occurrence was the most relevant expression of human dignity. However, man was lonely and so God created different kinds of animals, living beings named by man to become his friends. But Adam was still alone. So God created from his side a complementary person, equal, and different.

They were happy together and happy in their paradise. God enjoyed his creation and decided to take a rest on the seventh day of his paradise production. The crux of this story is that a divine man was created by the spirit of God.

The key values of good organizational design are explicitly expressed in the Genesis story: (1) a basic structure of space, (2) a basic schedule of time management, (3) a decorative enrichment of the human environment, (4) a social interaction resulting in human love, and (5) the finishing touch of a peaceful rest. This prototypical organization can be realized in every management practice.

The paradise is a *Planet-orientated* organization designed to support human life. Its composition is *People-orientated*, with its summit in the creation of the human couple. Being the product of earth and divine spiritual breathing, the work is *Pneuma-orientated*. After finishing his creation, God saw that his product was meaningful and profitable for everyone. That is the meaning of a *Profit-orientated* creation of paradise.

The Genesis model of creation results in a peaceful day of rest to enjoy the production. This is the *eudaimonia* experience described by Plato, which includes beauty, happiness, inner peace, shalom, and other similar inner experiences of being. A good product has to be beautiful and give the creator(s) inner peace and happiness. Hence, we may add the fifth P – *Peace-orientated* organization – to the paradise model. People, Planet, Profit, Pneuma and Peace form the consistent ingredients of a religion-based model of economic governance.

On the seventh day of the creative production, God enjoyed his inner freedom. This inner freedom of the first people was an inner freedom to enjoy both a material and spiritual life. This divine freedom is the highest quality of human life. It implies the power to say Yes or No to God.

The Bible continues the paradise story with the tale of the freedom and the fall of the managers of paradise. This mental attitude of refusing the power and inspiration of our being can be experienced by every organization that refuses one or more of the five Ps of the organization: the pollution of the *Planet*, the degradation of the *People*, the weakening of the *Pneuma*, the spoiling of the *Product*, and the freezing of *Peace*.

Conclusion

Spirituality as inner evidence is the evidence of the heart, while rationality is an external form of evidence that can be obtained through our senses and rational power. In a crisis situation this external evidence is weakened and can be supported by strong evidence from within. The main product of spirituality is its *gratuity*. Our lives and everything in our lives is given to us free of charge, by coincidence. We do not buy it; we do not produce or create it. Philosophy speaks of a *"contingent"* or a coincidental occurrence, which is also referred to as *synchronicity*.

In a religious perspective, the search for spirituality coincides with the inner search for God. The famous philosopher and theologian Augustine was searching for God all his life, but he was disappointed because he did not succeed in finding God throughout all of his studies. At the very moment he gave up, he received spiritual illumination from within and wrote in his confessions: "My God, my God, I was looking for you everywhere, but I couldn't find you. At the end I found you in the deepest part of my heart." Ignatius de Loyola wrote in his *Autobiography* about this spiritual insight after a period of depression during his revelation: "At that moment the eyes of my reason opened. Everything was new for me. Everything was clear and I got the impression that I was also a quite different man, a new man, with different knowledge than before" (Autobiography nr. 30).

For religious people every spiritual movement is the result of a conversation with God on the deepest level of being. It is the creation of a historical process of interaction with God on a psychological, social, cultural, religious, and spiritual level, which culminates in contact with the Ultimate or Divine Reality. In Eastern cultures they say, God created the world and is dancing in the whole creation. Religious spirituality is a way of looking at the dance of creation and recognizing the dancer.

Literature

Beth Jones, Laurie (1995). *Jesus, CEO: Using Ancient Wisdom for Visionary Leadership.* New York: Hyperion.

Blot SJ, Paul de (2004). *Vernieuwing van organisaties in een chaotische omgeving door vernieuwing van de mens. Een organisatievisie van Ignatius de Loyola. Een case studie.* Breukelen: Nyenrode University Press.

Buber, Martin (1958). *I and Thou.* New York: Scribner.

Capra, F. (2002). *The Hidden Connection: Integrating the Biological, Cognitive, and Social Dimensions of Life into a Science of Sustainability.* New York: Doubleday.

The Encyclopedia of World Religions (1989, 1999, 2000), Word worth Editions/ Concord Reference Books, two vols.

Geiselhart, Helmut (1999). *Das Managementmodell der Jesuiten. EinErfolgkonzeptfür das 21.Jahrhundert,* Wiesbaden: Gabler.

Geus, A.P. De (1997). *The Living Company.* Cambridge, MA: Harvard Business School Press.

Greenleaf, R. (2003). *The Servant Leader Within. A Transformation Path.* Marwah, NJ: Paulist Press.

Hock, Dee (1999). *Birth of the Chaordic Age*. San Francisco: Berrett Koehler.

Ignatius of Loyola, Saint (1900). *The Autobiography of St. Ignatius*. New York: Benziger Brothers.

Jaworski, J. (1980). *Synchronicity*. San Francisco: Berrett Koehler.

Lowley, Chris (2003). *Heroic Leadership: Best Practices from a 450-years-old Company that Changed the World*. Chicago: Loyola Press.

Mello, Anthony de (1990). *Awareness*. Broadway: Doubleday.

Nonaka, I. and H. Takeuchi (1995). *The Knowledge Creating Company: How Japanese Companies Create the Dynamics of Innovation*. Oxford: Oxford University Press.

Obama, Barack (2004). *Dreams from My Father: A Story of Race and Inheritance*. California: Three Rivers Press.

Wilber, Ken (2006). *Integral Spirituality: A Startling New Role for Religion in the Modern and Postmodern World*. Boston & London: Integral Books.

Senge, Peter, C. Otto Scharmer, Joseph Jaworski and Betty Sue Flowers (2004). *Presence: Exploring Profound Change in People, Organizations and Society*, www.Solonline.org

3
Spirituality and Rationality

Luk Bouckaert

Rationalism gradually attained its dominant position in Western culture from the nineteenth century. By *rationalism* we mean a way of life dominated by positive science as the ultimate source of truth and/or by utility maximization and rational choice as the ultimate criteria for ethics and management. The consequences of this dominance of the rational in Western culture and business life are ambiguous. On the credit side we find growing prosperity and improved material conditions of life and life expectations. On the debit side are the collapse of communities and the overexploitation of our ecosystems, causing unprecedented problems.

Is *spirituality* – as a way of exploring the sources of our deeper selves and the ultimate purpose of life – a means to overcoming the deficits of modern rationalism? At least spirituality aims at discovering meta-scientific sources for truth, such as wisdom, tradition, introspection and meditation, and it cultivates meta-utilitarian sources for decision-making such as intrinsic motivation, emotions and intuitions, and spiritual discernment. However, we must remain careful not to overdo the argument. Neither rationality nor spirituality requires making one choice to the exclusion of the other. The challenge is to find the right priority. In the case of rationalism, spirituality is subordinate to rational knowledge. It is at best a private and subjective source of knowledge without any claim on scientific authority or public argument. In the case of spirituality, the rational is subservient to the spirit, which is considered a higher faculty of knowledge and discernment disclosing the intrinsic meaning and purpose of life. A spiritually based concept of rationality aims at restoring the priority of the spirit over the rational.

Our focus is not on general and philosophical discussion of spirituality and rationality, but on analysis of their particular manifestations in the fields of economics and business. Economics and business par excellence represent a mindset that analyzes social reality in terms of instrumental rationality. Nobel Prize winner Amartya Sen warns us that the economic obsession to explain everything in terms of instrumental rationality can transform rational actors into "rational fools" (Sen, 1982). Indeed, there is a point where rationality turns into irrationality: rationality needs a "beyond" to remain in balance. But this beyond cannot be expressed in the conventional language of the *homo rationalis*. We need an appropriate way of speaking about spirituality in economics without reducing spirituality to the format of rational self-interest.

To avoid the pitfall of "economizing" spirituality, we can make a distinction between the *economics of spirituality* and the search for *spirituality in economics* (Bouckaert, 2007). Economics of spirituality looks at phenomena such as trust, loyalty, connectedness and other nonmaterial values as new data and tools for rational actors. This is of course a legitimate and eye-opening approach but, in the end, it results in economics-as-usual, missing the genuine meaning of nonrational, spiritual commitment. To disclose spirituality in economics more is needed. We have to deconstruct the conventional mindset of rationality and explore the possibilities of an enlarged concept of rationality. This kind of reflection, on the edge of economic science and economic philosophy, is a search for a new understanding of economics and business wherein spirituality plays a crucial role.

In the next section we analyze the ethics management paradox that can only be well understood and "solved" by introducing a genuine notion of spirituality into the fields of business and management. In the section on Ethics needs spirituality we will use Bergson's theory of the two sources of religion and ethics to elucidate why a spiritually based theory of management and leadership is needed to guide business leaders and to solve the ethics management paradox. The final section on The rational and the spiritual self clarifies the distinction between the rational self and the spiritual self, as the anthropological foundation for a spiritually based economics.

The ethics management paradox in the field of business

The ethics management paradox is based on an observation in the field of business. Business ethics gained more and more attention in the eighties and nineties of the last century. One of the basic arguments in this rise of business ethics was that in the long run ethics pays, hence ethics is a good investment for the company and its stakeholders.

I have observed that some companies and organizations have launched ethics programs and used ethical language but, once confronted with a deeper financial or other crisis, react as if ethics never existed. An example of this is the case of the closing of a Renault plant in Brussels in 1997. Renault at that time had developed an ethos of participation and cooperation on the factory floor but, once it was confronted with a problem of long-term profitability, forgot completely about its stakeholder philosophy and fired more than three thousand employees without prior communication or negotiation. This is just one example of how business ethics on the factory floor has been subordinated to the competing logic of profit maximization for shareholders. The point is not that long-term profitability does not matter, because it matters a lot, but the fact that the noncommunication with other stakeholders was not seen as a moral issue, revealing a kind of selective moral blindness. The result of this controversial Belgian case was a growing distrust of managerial ethical discourse. Other business scandals in the late 1990s in the ICT business revealed the same phenomenon: more ethics management does not create more ethical commitment. Analogous to the happiness paradox in economics teaching us that more welfare does not create necessarily more human happiness (Easterlin, 1974), we see that more ethics management does not create more ethics in management. How can we explain this ethical deficit in business ethics? We can account for it by understanding the dual structure of ethics.

Ethics has simultaneous instrumental/rational and noninstrumental/intrinsic meanings. The instrumental use of ethics involves the introduction of ethics to external goals, such as better reputation, lower transaction costs, less regulation and, most of all, higher profitability. On the other hand, an intrinsic or spiritual approach to ethics is characterized by its openness to noninstrumental motivations. Social capital research restores to some extent the imbalance between instrumental and intrinsic uses of ethics, by paying attention to relations of trust and reciprocity. However, the danger is always there that once again we reduce trust to its instrumental effects. We have to realize that deep relations of trust and reciprocity imply an ultimate willingness to give without calculation, or to do one's duty without compensation. This willingness goes beyond the logic of preference maximization.

The argument is not that spiritual or intrinsic ethics excludes instrumental ethics, because this would be an unrealistic and counterproductive claim; the point is that we must fully recognize the tension between intrinsic and instrumental motivations and keep them in the right order. Prioritizing instrumental motivations and arguments over intrinsic ones is destructive: it leads to the already mentioned selective moral blindness, to the substitution of economic calculations for genuine moral commitment. Calling for more "spirit in business" or more "spirituality in economics" is an effort to restore the right order, that is, to give priority to intrinsic motivation and use instrumental considerations as a secondary motivation.

Ethics needs spirituality

In his book *Les deux sources de la morale et de la religion*, the French-Jewish philosopher Henri Bergson (1941) gives us another argument in favor of spirituality in business and economics identifying two distinct sources of ethics. The *first source* is social pressure. Societies or collective groups cannot survive if they do not put limits on the individual opportunism of their members. This is done by means of the development of social taboos, collective rules, internalized moral feelings such as guilt and honor, consultation processes, jurisprudence, etc. Often religion reinforces these moral rules and feelings by placing them within a perspective of eternity. Following Bergson's view, one can see business ethics as a form of group pressure and group control that occurs via ethical codes, moral feelings, and consultation processes. This is how the group survives in a free market.

But there is a *second source*, which Bergson calls *mysticism*: a concept that nicely overlaps what we call spirituality. Ethical values and rules that help consolidate the group may, under different circumstances, become a straitjacket that hinders adaptation to new situations. This gives rise to pressure to change, to reinterpret or revise fundamental principles. According to Bergson, such a process of renewal is not a rational one. For in times of crisis and transition, there is no consensus on the basic principles or on the interpretation of these principles. The situation is analogous to what Thomas Kuhn, much later, describes in his book *The Structure of Scientific Revolutions* (1962) as the prelude to a revolution in science. In such a situation, there is no longer any rational basis to justify the transition from one scientific paradigm to another, and this leads to much emotional and misguided discussion among groups of scientists, all of whom are convinced they alone are right.

In turbulent times, fundamental change occurs, in Bergson's view, through moral and religious geniuses/leaders/pioneers who succeed in developing a new way of life and lifestyle in response to a profound crisis. People then mobilize around this new way of life, and in turn spread and refine it. Spiritually driven leadership plays a key role in Bergson's dynamic conception of ethics. He criticizes the classic Kantian and utilitarian theories that claim to have a fixed norm for good and evil based on universal, unambiguous principles. According to Bergson, they overlook the role and example of moral leaders and pioneers. The latter create new interpretations of values and are motivated by three things: first, a keen sense of social frustration and crisis; second, the mystical sense of the "élan vital," the vital force in history; and, third, the ability to speak to and mobilize people.

Bergson's account creates a link among ethics, spirituality, and leadership. It is no coincidence that nowadays the subject of spirituality in business ethics comes up primarily in relation to innovative leadership and entrepreneurship. Conventional management literature has lost sight of the distinction between the quest for meaning (inspiration) and rational management (control). Or worse yet, managers think that meaning simply coincides with rational efficiency or rational management. It is remarkable, for instance, that books about entrepreneurship and management rarely stop to consider the question of the *meaning* of the enterprise – the *"why"* question – but focus almost exclusively on the *"how"* questions, that is, questions about process management, control systems, financial management, etc. The distinction between the rational manager and the spiritually driven entrepreneur can gain philosophical depth from Bergson's theory of the two sources of ethics.

Rational management is essential to every organization. No policy can succeed without a clear definition of its goals, without cost-saving use of resources, and without alertness to the opportunities for entering the market. But this language and these methods do not bring us to the original moment of meaning and creativity. On the contrary, they destroy the art of entrepreneurship, which is to bring about something new. An entrepreneur designs a product or service that can make life different and better and that, for this very reason, creates a new market or market segment. It is this moment of irreducible creativity that makes entrepreneurship an art, albeit an art that is practiced within the space of free and competitive markets. Those who prioritize rational management will be inclined to limit and control creativity in order to get a streamlined organization. Those giving priority to meaning will leave more space for a historical and spiritual dynamic. The difference between the rational and the spirit-driven styles of management is echoed in the emergence of business spirituality as a new discipline within the field of business ethics.

The rational and the spiritual self

The analysis of paradoxes in economic life unveils the dual nature of human happiness and business ethics. This duality (not *dualism*), in human activities and motivations, can be further explored by clarifying its anthropological structure. The dual nature of human activities and motivations goes back to the dual structure of the human self. As human subjects we do not coincide with ourselves. We are always trying to be ourselves but we observe a distance between the ego and the deeper self. Often this distance is represented as a conflict between a self-interested ego and an altruistic self or as an opposition between *homo economicus*, the archetype of self-interest, and *homo moralis*, the archetype of altruism.

Commonsense defines self-interest as ego-driven and selfish. It means prioritizing my interests over the interests of other people, while altruism means prioritizing others' interests over mine. I give precedence to my own happiness at the cost of other people's happiness. Many economists will oppose this commonsense representation of self-interest and altruism. They consider self-interest as maximizing one's preferences. If you are an altruist, you will have "altruist preferences." In this case, as a rational actor you will prioritize other's interest over yours and, by doing this, you will maximize your own "altruist preferences" and hence your own utility or happiness. In this sense altruism is a special case of rational self-interest. The commonsense *homo economicus* may be selfish, but the rational *homo economicus* is only maximizing his/her preferences, altruism occasionally being one of them.

Is there another and deeper layer of self-reference than the rational one that rational-choice economists have in mind? A quotation from Amartya Sen (from his well-known essay on "rational fools") may illustrate very well the distinction between a rational and a spiritual concept of self-interest: "If the knowledge of torture of others makes you sick, it is a case of sympathy. If it does not make you personally feel worse off, but you think it is wrong and you are ready to do something to stop it, it is a case of commitment" (Sen, 1982, p. 92). Sympathy in Sen's quotation is a product of my feelings and preferences. Having an aversion to torture, as a rational actor I will try to minimize these unpleasant feelings. However, genuine commitment is not based on those feelings of sympathy or aversion but on a prior experience of a sense of duty. Even if my sense of duty can be associated with a feeling of sympathy for "duty conforming behavior," it is important to realize that the origin of my sense of duty has another source. It has its origin in something that precedes my sympathies or my expectation of some benefit. In a Kantian perspective the origin of my commitment is respect for the categorical imperative revealing itself as part of my identity as a human being.

The *homo spiritualis* is not characterized by *having* preferences and striving for maximum utility but by the awareness of *being* related to the other. I am the other and the other is part of me, as it is nicely expressed in the title of a book by the French philosopher Paul Ricoeur: *Soi-même comme un autre* (1990). This *inter-esse* of the self and the other cannot be reduced to a shared group interest or a collective welfare function. We are interconnected on a level of being, prior to our acting within and making the world. The *spirit* in each of us is the point of awareness where we feel ourselves related to all other beings and to *Being* itself. This spiritual self-understanding is not a matter of abstract philosophical thinking but is instead a feeling of universal love and compassion that gives our lives and actions an inner purpose and drive. It transforms our active and rational ego into a responsible and compassionate self.

It is plain that the notion of self-interest has very different meanings in debates about egoism and altruism. On the level of common sense, self-interest is associated with selfishness. On the level of rational-choice theory, it is defined as the natural desire of an actor to realize his/her set of preferences. On the existential level, spiritual self-interest refers to the self as an interrelated being. This other-related definition of the self explains why, on the spiritual level, self-interest and altruism are not opposed. The statement that we have to love others as we love ourselves illustrates the inner connection. However, we have to keep in mind that this statement is only correctly understood if we take our relational self as the point of reference.

Conclusion

A paradox is a contradiction that can only be solved by transforming our way of looking at things. Rational economics and ethics will not suffice to solve the ethics management paradox. According to Bergson's theory of the two sources of religion and ethics, we need a spiritually based concept of leadership to overcome periods of deep change and transformation. In order to give this concept a solid anthropological underpinning, we presented the thesis of the "dual self" which distinguishes the spiritual from the rational self giving precedence to the spiritual over the rational. The spiritual self is not driven by maximizing preferences but by the awareness of being related to other beings and to Being itself. On a more practical level, this implies that economic performance cannot be reduced to a financial cost-benefit analysis but must be measured in terms of relational, ecological, and nonmaterial goods.

Literature

Bergson, H. 1941. *Les deux sources de la morale et de la religion*. Paris: Les Presses universitaires de France.

Bouckaert, L. 2006. "The Ethics Management Paradox." In: Zsolnai, L. (ed.), *Interdisciplinary Yearbook of Business Ethics*, Oxford: Peter Lang, 2006, pp. 199–202 and pp. 215–219.

Bouckaert, L. 2007. "Spirituality in Economics." In: Bouckaert L. and Zsolnai L. (eds), *Spirituality as a Public Good*, Antwerp: Garant, 2007, pp. 11–25.

Easterlin, R. 1974. "Does Economic Growth Improve the Human Lot? Some Empirical Evidence." In: Davis P.A. and Reder M.W. (eds), *Nation and Households in Economic Growth: Essays in Honor of Moses Abramowitz*. New York: Academic Press.

Kuhn, T.S. 1962. *The Structure of Scientific Revolutions*. Chicago.

Ricoeur, P. 1990. *Soi-même comme un autre*. Paris: Ed. du Seuil.

Sen, A. 1982. *Choice, Welfare and Measurement*. Oxford: Basil Blackwell.

Senge, P., Scharmer, C.O., Jaworski, J. and Flowers, B.S. 2007. *Presence: An Exploration of Profound Change in People, Organizations and Society*. New York: Currency Doubleday.

Zsolnai, L. (ed.) 2004. *Spirituality and Ethics in Management*. Dordrecht: Kluwer.

4
Neuroscience of Spirituality

Andrew B. Newberg and Daniel Monti

For a synthesis of neuroscience and spirituality to be successful, an understanding and preservation of the fundamentals of science must be merged with an analysis of the cognitive elements of religious and spiritual experiences. This requires an analysis, and perhaps even a definition, of religious and spiritual experience from a neurocognitive perspective. Once a working definition is considered, the cognitive and emotional elements of those experiences can be considered and evaluated on both a theoretical and potentially empirical basis. This can lead to the larger development of a neuroscience of spirituality.

Cognitive definitions of religion and spirituality

Until the late eighteenth century there was practically no attempt at defining religion per se from any perspective let alone a cognitive one. Consequently religions, particularly in the West, were defined by their dogmatic formulations. It was only with Friedrich Schleiermacher in the late eighteenth century that an attempt was made to define "religion" as such by switching from a doctrinal emphasis to a more cognitive, visceral, or intuitive one. Schleiermacher defined religion as a "feeling of absolute dependence." Since his day all attempts at a general definition of religion have relied heavily on emphasizing the intuitive, emotional, or visceral. This shift has important implications for bringing a neuroscientific approach to the study of religion. However, it also results in a neuroscientific approach to both religious and nonreligious spirituality and spiritual experiences. In fact, as the definitions have evolved, the distinction between spirituality and religiousness has become much more complicated.

Emile Durkheim, in his *The Elementary Forms of the Religious Life* (1926), describes religion as nothing more than a transformation of society. On the other hand Sigmund Freud viewed religious behaviors and spiritual feelings in terms of a projection of various intrapsychic dynamics, and psychologist B.F. Skinner described them in terms of hopes and expectations based on previous experiences. At the turn of the twentieth century, scholars began to devote themselves to the phenomenology of religious and spiritual experiences on their own terms. An example of such an approach has been to analyze religion in terms of an awareness of the "sacred" and the "holy." Rudolf Otto, in *The Idea of the Holy* (1970), defines the essence of religious awareness as awe, described as a mixture of fear and fascination before the divine and referred to as a *mysterium tremendum et fascinans*. Such an approach began to describe a dominant form of Western mysticism but was not so applicable to Eastern religions or to primitive ones.

A more recent attempt at defining religion and spirituality, specifically from a scientific perspective, was elaborated as part of a consensus conference of scientists studying the physical, psychological, and neuroscientific aspects of religion and spirituality (Larson, 1998). These were described in the form of criteria rather than of a true "definition." The criteria for spirituality were the subjective feelings, thoughts, experiences, and behaviors that arise from a search or quest for the sacred, in which "search" referred to attempts to identify, articulate, maintain, or transform, and "sacred" referred to what the individual perceives as a divine being, ultimate reality, or ultimate truth. The criteria for religion included the criteria for spirituality and/or included a search for nonsacred goals (such as identity, belonging, meaning, health, or wellness) in the context of spiritual criteria. In addition, a religion required that "the means and methods of the search receive general validation and support from within an identifiable group of people." These criteria were meant to be operationalized for scientific analysis such that religion and spiritual experience could be considered in an experimental paradigm while preserving the essential nature of the experiences. How successful any of these definitions ultimately may prove to be will depend on both the religious perspective of such definitions and how well scientific methods can actually be performed on the basis of such definitions. But it must also be remembered that definitions that rely on cognitive, emotional, and perceptual constructs may inherently miss what is truly spiritual. If spirituality indeed merges human beings with something supernatural, then the scientific approach may only be able to measure the effects of spirituality rather than spirituality itself.

Methods of attaining religious and spiritual experiences

In considering a neurocognitive approach to the study of religious and spiritual experiences, it is important to consider two major avenues towards attaining such experiences. These two methods are group ritual and individual contemplation or meditation. A phenomeno-logical analysis reveals that the two practices are similar in kind, if not intensity, along two dimensions: (1) intermittent emotional dis-charges involving the subjective sensations of awe, peace, tranquility, or ecstasy; and (2) varying degrees of unitary experience correlating with the emotional discharges just mentioned (d'Aquili and Newberg, 1999). These unitary experiences consist of a decreased awareness of the boundaries between the self and the external world. Such experi-ences can also lead to a sense of oneness with other perceived individ-uals, thereby generating a sense of community. At the extreme, unitary experiences can eventually lead to the abolition of all boundaries of discrete being, thus generating a state of absolute unity.

It should be noted that the experiences of group ritual and individual meditation or prayer practices have a certain degree of overlap, such that each may play a role in the other. In fact, it may be that human cere-monial ritual actually provides the "average" person access to spiritual or mystical experience ("average" in distinction from those who regularly practice intense contemplation such as highly religious monks or nuns).

With regard to human ceremonial ritual, it is a morally neutral technol-ogy. Therefore, depending on the doctrine in which it is imbedded and which it expresses, ritual can either promote or minimize the structural aspects of a society and promote or minimize overall aggressive behavior. Utilizing Victor Turner's concept of *communitas* (Turner, 1969) as the pow-erful unitary social experience usually arising out of ceremonial ritual, if an ideology or doctrine manifests its incarnation in a ritual that defines the unitary experience as applying only to the group or tribe, then the result is only the *communitas tribus*. It is certainly true that aggression within the group has been minimized or eliminated by the unifying experience generated by the ritual. However, this may only serve to emphasize the special cohesiveness of the group vis-à-vis other groups. The result may be an increase in intergroup aggression even though intra-group aggression is diminished. An ideology or doctrine and its embodying ritual may, of course, apply to all members of a religion, a nation-state, an ideology, all of humanity, or all of reality. As the scope of what is included in the unitary experience increases, the amount of overall aggressive behavior decreases. If indeed a ceremonial ritual were giving flesh to the concept of the unity of all being, then one would presumably experience brief senses of *communitas omnium*. Such a myth-ritual experience approaches meditative states such as Richard Bucke's cosmic consciousness (Bucke, 1961) or even Absolute Unitary Being (Newberg, d'Aquili, and Rause, 2001).

A neurocognitive perspective on spirituality

It appears that there is a variety of spiritual experiences that, although they seem to be fundamentally different, actually have a neurocognitive origin and therefore lie along a similar continuum. On one end of the spectrum are experiences such as those attained through a church liturgy or watching a sunset. These experiences carry with them a mild sense of being connected with something greater than the self and mild emotional responses. On the other end of the spectrum are the types of experiences usually described as mystical or transcendent, often associated with powerful emotions and life-altering effects. Such experiences may or may not be related to anything religious, in terms of a particular doctrine or belief. The unitary element – such as with others, nature, God, the universe, or anything outside of oneself – that is common to spiritual experiences should not be thought of as limiting the specific aspects and experiences associated with them. It simply appears to be the case that unitary feelings are a crucial part of spiritual experiences. Most scholars and researchers have focused on the more intense experiences because of ease of study and analysis – the most intense experiences provide the most robust responses that can be qualitatively and perhaps even quantitatively measured. For example, Frederick Streng, in his "Language and Mystical Awareness" (1978), describes the most intense types of spiritual experience as relating to a variety of phenomena including occult experience, trance, a vague sense of unaccountable uneasiness, sudden extraordinary visions and words of divine beings, or aesthetic sensitivity. Ninian Smart has argued that certain sects of Hinduism, Buddhism, and Taoism differ markedly from prophetic religions such as Judaism and Islam and from religions related to Christianity, in that the religious experience most characteristic of the former is "mystical" whereas that most characteristic of the latter is "numinous."

Somewhat similar to Smart's distinction between mystical and numinous experiences is that of Walter T. Stace (1961), who distinguishes between what he calls extrovertive mystical experiences and introvertive mystical experiences. Stace characterizes all mystical experiences as having the following characteristics: (1) a strong sense of the reality of the experience; (2) a feeling of blessedness or peace; (3) a feeling of interacting with the sacred or divine; (4) paradoxicality; and (5) ineffability. In addition, extrovertive mystical experiences are characterized by a unifying vision in which all things are one and the more concrete apprehension of the One as an inner subjectivity, or life, in all things. On the other hand, introvertive mystical experiences are characterized as a unitary or pure consciousness that is perceived as nonspatial and nontemporal. There is a clear similarity between Stace's extrovertive mystical experience and Smart's numinous experience and between Stace's introvertive mystical experiences and Smart's mystical experience proper.

A neurocognitive analysis of mysticism and other spiritual experiences might clarify some of the issues regarding mystical and spiritual experiences by allowing for a better typology of such experiences based on the underlying brain structures and their related cognitive functions. In terms of the effects of ceremonial ritual, rhythmicity in the environment (i.e. visual, auditory, or tactile) drives either the sympathetic nervous system, which is the basis of the fight or flight response as well as general levels of arousal, or the parasympathetic nervous system, which is the basis for relaxing the body and rejuvenating energy stores. Together, the sympathetic and parasympathetic systems comprise the autonomic nervous system that regulates many body functions such as heart rate, respiratory rate, blood pressure, and digestion. During spiritual experiences, there tends to be an intense activation of one of these systems, giving rise to either a profound sense of alertness and awareness (sympathetic) or oceanic blissfulness (parasympathetic).

For the most part, this neurophysiological activity occurs as the result of the rhythmic driving of ceremonial ritual. This rhythmic driving may also begin to affect neural information flow throughout the brain. The superior parietal lobe may be particularly relevant in this regard because an inhibition of sensory information may prevent this area from performing its usual function of helping to establish a sense of self and distinguishing discrete objects in the environment. The result of such an inhibition of sensory input could result in an increasing sense of wholeness, progressively dominating the sense of the multiplicity of baseline reality, as well as a progressive loss of the sense of self. Ceremonial ritual may be described as generating these spiritual experiences from a "bottom-up" approach, since it is the rhythmic sounds and behaviors of the ritual that eventually drive the sympathetic and parasympathetic systems, and ultimately, the higher-order processing centers in the brain. It should also be mentioned that the particular system initially activated depends upon the type of ritual. For example, rituals might be divided into "slow" or "fast" ritual. Slow rituals would involve calm, peaceful music, and soft chanting to generate a sense of quiescence via the parasympathetic system. Fast rituals would utilize rapid or frenzied dancing to generate a sense of heightened arousal via the sympathetic system.

Individual practices such as prayer or meditation may access similar neuronal pathways, but through more of a "top-down" mechanism. In such a practice, as the person focuses on an object or phrase of spiritual significance, they might activate their prefrontal cortex, which is normally activated during attention-focusing tasks. The continuous fixation on the object begins to stimulate the limbic system, which is primarily involved in emotional processing and memory. Several scholars have implicated this area as critical for religious and spiritual experiences because of its ability to label experiences as profound or real and also because certain pathological conditions such as seizures in the limbic areas have been particularly associated with extreme spiritual experiences. The limbic system is connected to a structure called the hypothalamus in order to communicate the activity occurring in the brain to the rest of the body. The hypothalamus is a key regulator of the autonomic nervous system and therefore such activity in the brain ultimately activates the arousal (sympathetic) and/or quiescent (parasympathetic) arms of the autonomic nervous system. Part of the result of meditation and other spiritually orientated practices may be to block sensory input to the superior parietal lobes, resulting in a loss of the sense of self and a loss of awareness of discrete objects.

The cognitive state in which there is a unity of all things – including the self, the world, and any objects in the world – is described in the mystical literature of all the world's great religions. When a person is in that state he or she loses all sense of discrete being, and even the difference between self and other is obliterated. There is no sense of the passing of time, and all that remains is a perfect, timeless, undifferentiated consciousness. When such a state is suffused with positive emotion, there is a tendency to describe the experience, after the fact, as personal. Such experiences may be described as a perfect union with God (the *Unio mystica* of the Christian tradition) or else the perfect manifestation of God in the Hindu tradition. When such experiences are accompanied by neutral emotions they tend to be described, after the fact, as impersonal. These states are described in concepts such as the Void or Nirvana of Buddhism or the Absolute of a number of philosophical and mystical traditions. There is no question that, whether the experience is interpreted personally as God or impersonally as the Absolute, it nevertheless possesses a quality of transcendent wholeness without any temporal or spatial division whatsoever.

Neuroscientific assessment of spiritual experiences

Clearly, one of the most important aspects of the study of spiritual experiences is to find careful, rigorous methods for empirically testing hypotheses. One such example of empirical evidence for the neurocognitive basis of the spiritual experiences described above comes from a number of studies that have measured neurophysiological activity during spiritual states and practices. Meditative states comprise perhaps the most fertile testing ground because of the predictable, reproducible, and well-described nature of such experiences, which comply with the basic principles of spiritual experiences. Studies of meditation and prayer practices have evolved over the years to utilize the most advanced technologies for studying neurophysiology. Originally, studies analyzed the relationship between electrical changes in the brain (measured by electroencephalography or EEG) and meditative states. But, EEG is limited in its ability to distinguish particular regions of the brain that may have increased or decreased activity.

For this reason, more recent studies of meditation and spiritual practices have utilized functional brain imaging techniques such as single photon emission computed tomography (SPECT), positron emission tomography (PET), and functional magnetic resonance imaging (fMRI). In the past decade, brain activation studies have utilized neuroimaging techniques to explore cerebral function during various behavioral, motor, and cognitive tasks. There are limitations to each type of technique used for the study of spiritual phenomena. It is important to ensure that the imaging technique is sensitive enough to measure the expected changes. Also, each of these techniques may interfere with the normal environment in which spiritual practices take place. Early data of meditative practices has generally shown increases in brain activity in the region comprising the prefrontal cortex (PFC) , consistent with focusing attention during meditation (Newberg et al., 2001). Studies have also observed decreases of activity in the area of the superior parietal lobe, possibly consistent with inhibition of sensory input into this area. However, more studies, with improved methods, will be necessary to further elucidate the neurocognitive aspects of meditation and spiritual experiences.

In all, these studies can provide a starting point to developing a more detailed neurocognitive model of religious and spiritual experiences. This kind of analysis can also be utilized as the hypothesis for future investigations of such experiences.

Literature

Bucke, R.M. 1961. *Cosmic Consciousness*. Secaucus, NJ: Citadel Press.

d'Aquili, E.G. and Newberg, A.B. 1999. *The Mystical Mind: Probing the Biology of Religious Experience*. Minneapolis, MN: Fortress Press.

Durkheim, E. 1926. *The Elementary Forms of the Religious Life*. New York: Macmillan.

Larson, D.B., Swyers, J.P., and McCullough, M.E. (eds) 1998. *Scientific Research on Spirituality and Health: A Consensus Report*. Washington, DC: National Institute for Healthcare Research.

Newberg, A.B., Alavi, A., Baime, M., Pourdehnad, M., Santanna, J., and d'Aquili, E.G. 2001. "The Measurement of Regional Cerebral Blood Flow During the Complex Cognitive Task of Meditation: A Preliminary SPECT Study," *Psychiatry Research: Neuroimaging*, 106, 113–122.

Newberg, A.B., d'Aquili, E.G., and Rause, V.P. 2001. *Why God Won't Go Away: Brain Science and the Biology of Belief*. New York, NY: Ballantine Publishing Group.

Otto, R. 1970. *The Idea of the Holy*. New York: Oxford University Press.

Smart, N. 1969. *The Religious Experience of Mankind*. London: Macmillan.

Stace, W.T. 1961. *Mysticism and Philosophy*. London: Macmillan.

Streng, F. 1978. "Language and Mystical Awareness." In S. Katz (ed.), *Mysticism and Philosophical Analysis*. New York: Oxford University Press.

Turner, V. 1969. *The Ritual Process: Structure and Anti-Structure*. Ithaca, NY: Cornell University Press.

5
Transpersonal Psychology

John Drew

For over fifty years transpersonal psychology has provided a framework for professionals – including scientists, psychotherapists, and psychologists as well as individuals from different backgrounds – to develop the spiritual aspects of their work and explore matters beyond their everyday personal and material lives. As a concept its strength is confirmed by the increasing number of transpersonal psychotherapists and psychologists, an extensive literature, university posts in transpersonal psychology, and a wide range of associations, seminars, and websites concerned with transpersonal issues. This chapter offers a personal explanation of the transpersonal to a more general public. It indicates associations, websites, and literature for the study of this and related issues in more depth.

The literal meaning of "transpersonal" is "beyond the personal." It describes a philosophy of life that puts less emphasis on individual and material issues and more on wider spiritual considerations. It deals with both inner and outer conduct, with the vertical (the relationship of body, mind, and spirit) and the horizontal (the relationship of the individual to the external world). It is a spiritual approach to living. Religious beliefs are not inconsistent with it. It is neither a religion nor a sect.

The transpersonal approach

Some people develop a transpersonal approach to life because they see the limitations of a material, purely scientific explanation of "consciousness." When matters "beyond the brain" are discussed we need to consider questions such as: Where is consciousness situated if not entirely in our heads? If elsewhere, then where?

Others are attracted to the transpersonal because they no longer fully relate to the religions of their upbringing, which for them may have seemed a top-down canonical framework for living and being told what to do or think in matters spiritual. They seek both wider perspectives and something more than the restricted materialist definition and view of life current in consumer society today.

Tolstoy believed the only questions worth asking are how to live and what to live for. The transpersonal suggests an integrated response to both questions. It affects the material approach by giving lower priority to some aspects of consumer societies and more to the wider issues of living on and with the planet.

You can approach the transpersonal from both a scientific and a spiritual perspective. It seeks to bridge the largely uncharted waters between where science ends and spirituality begins. It can involve the scientific exploration of different levels of consciousness. These might include the ego-level of Western psychology and the mind-level of Eastern psychology. Levels of consciousness can be explained as states developed by meditation or "peak experiences." Many people have peak experiences, a phrase proposed by Abraham Maslow, one of the early fathers of transpersonal psychology and famous for his "hierarchy of human needs." His research initially described peak experiences as states of ecstasy, especially joyous and exciting moments in life involving sudden feelings of intense happiness and well-being, wonder, and awe. They occur rarely, but more often than we realize as our minds can fail to register them. They usually come on suddenly and are often inspired by deep meditation, intense feelings of love, exposure to great art and music or the overwhelming beauty of nature. Some musicians talk of the "tingle effect": a feeling of intense joy experienced through the spine at the back of the head when listening to a particular musical theme or phrase. Toward the end of his life, Maslow felt it was not enough just to note peak experiences and forget them. They somehow needed to be integrated into our daily lives to help provide the driving energy for living them fully. Stan Grof, another early father, pioneered the understanding and development of peak experiences through exercises in holotropic breathing. There are many methods and trainings for learning about and experiencing the transpersonal.

The transpersonal is an aspect of spirituality that can be seen as involving the highest levels of human development in, for example, science, art, philosophy, or sport. It can be pursued through meditation, prayer, ritual, and contemplation. It may just be an attitude toward love, trust, values, and ethics expressed as a way of connecting to wider global issues and considerations. The transpersonal is concerned with what Ken Wilber, another father figure, called ascending and descending issues. Descending issues connect with the work and thinking of scientists like Erwin Laszlo, who developed the theory that all things and thoughts are interconnected at the quantum level. Ascending issues lead to contemplation of spiritual issues and higher consciousness. The transpersonal acknowledges the unity of all life and the value of acting through or seeking higher levels of consciousness.

Definitions of the transpersonal

Definitions are an important and useful exercise, yet a glance at transpersonal websites shows how often definitions of the "transpersonal" lack clarity. Forty or more definitions of "transpersonal" have been identified. Just like "spiritual," "science," or "business," the word is ambiguous and, like them, evades singular definition. The working definition of "spirituality" suggested by the editors of this book is "the multiform search of people for a transcendent meaning of life that connects them to all living beings and brings them in touch with God or 'Ultimate Reality'." The transpersonal, as one aspect of spirituality, relates to this definition.

The purpose here is not to convince or convert but to illustrate the relationship between spiritual and transpersonal awareness, and to suggest that beyond the tangible, visible world of our daily existence there is a higher, nonmaterial dimension waiting to be explored that perhaps contains values and truths relevant to inner development and outward actions.

The transpersonal is a broad concept that brings people together from different races, religions, and political and economic backgrounds who are reflecting on their inner lives and relations with wider global issues. They are doing this in ways that include, rather than exclude, many different traditional approaches to spirituality. One of the definitions of the transpersonal specifically relates it to business:

> Now, as throughout human history, the world is undergoing transformation, and business organizations are caught in the turbulence of a change they are not able to control. The fundamental assumptions of our Western orthodox worldview, on which our business institutions were founded, has proved inadequate to regulate either our society or our business institutions. New business structures – communities – are emerging based on a transpersonal worldview,

one that embraces spirituality, psychology, and science in an integrated perspective on human experience. Transpersonal learning communities combine an emphasis on the development of human consciousness and business performance by adopting triple-loop learning practices. While they do business, transpersonal learning communities will simultaneously transform themselves and society as a competitive advantage (Gozdz, 2000).

Transpersonal psychology

"Transpersonal" has a more specific meaning in therapy and psychology. Transpersonal psychology has developed in the second half of 20th century into the fourth force in modern psychology, following the schools of analytical, behavioral, and humanistic psychology. It came into prominence in the late 1960s in the USA, where leading psychologists such as Abraham Maslow, Anthony Sutich, and Stanislav Grof strove to establish a new approach to the human psyche that focused on the spiritual dimension of existence and liberated the search for meaning from the positivist, reductionist trends of the past. William James first drew attention to the concept over 100 years ago, but in psychology it was an approach identified by Carl Jung, who concluded that many of his patients were concerned about the lack of meaning in their lives. They felt they had outgrown at least some aspects of the religious beliefs of their upbringing and were seeking a suitable spiritual dimension to replace what they no longer found sufficiently fulfilling in traditional top-down religions. Their problems were related less to spirituality than to a lack of meaning. Jung thought these concerns were not being addressed by the conventional therapy and psychology of the time.

Transpersonal psychology has developed through embracing, researching, and incorporating aspects of a multitude of spiritual approaches drawn from Eastern and Western religions; mystical and esoteric beliefs; mythical and ancient stories and rituals; and therapeutic, artistic, and scientific concepts. This influx of philosophies and practices means that transpersonal psychology remains a very flexible framework. Unlike previous schools, it has no unified philosophy or rule book and no central authority, although it is formally recognized as a branch of psychotherapy and psychology in many countries where these professions are regulated. Moreover, its comparatively rapid spread across the world has ensured that the basic aim – the quest for an individual spiritual reality that is part of a greater, universal whole – is colored and enriched by the deep traditions and background of different cultures. While it might seem to be too broad for rigorous study, there are many practitioners who are quite clear what they mean by the term. Granted the felt need for both clients and practitioners to bring into consideration issues dealing with the vertical as well as the horizontal and the inner as well as the outer aspects of being human, the concept of the transpersonal cannot just be dismissed as being too wide. It has to be wide because it concentrates on spiritual issues in a way that previous psychological and psychotherapeutical practices have not.

Transpersonal psychology now represents a framework well developed, well researched, and practiced in its manifold parts and used by therapists and psychologists both for their own development and for helping others contemplate big spiritual and psychological questions: Who am I? Where do I come from? What is the future for humans and our planet? What contribution can I make? Whether approached scientifically or spiritually, it enables everyone who so wishes to reflect and act on these eternal questions as they move from a personal to a wider spiritual perspective. It is a perspective that acknowledges the unity of all life and the need for acting to promote it from a higher level of consciousness – an approach much needed in these troubled times.

The transpersonal in business

The framework of the transpersonal is used and understood in psychology and psychotherapy. It is recognized in business only indirectly and intuitively. Practicing transpersonal therapists and psychologists do not always use the word "transpersonal" with clients in reference to their work. They may refer to holistic values or use words such as personal development, spirituality, inner self, depth psychology, guided imagery, music therapy, breathwork, or consciousness. It may be that transpersonal is subsumed in these descriptions. The reasons for this are in part the difficulty of explaining in simple terms what "transpersonal" means and in part because the transpersonal covers many different specialized or technical terms that cannot readily be explained. Clients, interestingly enough, do not regularly enquire about the schools followed by their therapists.

The word "business" itself raises semantic issues. "The business of America is business" is one of history's famous misquotes, this one attributed to Calvin Coolidge. "After all, the chief business of the American people is business" was what he actually wrote. "[O]f course the accumulation of wealth cannot be justified as the chief end of existence." Nearly all would agree. For Coolidge, business was close to religion, but again it all depends on what we mean by it! There is much disparaging or unthinking talk about "business," especially when referring to its cutting edges such as production, marketing, finance, and particularly activities on the legal fringes of operations.

Most businesses are made up of people, not "business-people." They are perhaps specialists, administrators, receptionists, cooks, telephonists, librarians, researchers, and the like who happen to work in business. They could equally well be working in government, academia, prisons, or social services. The great management writer Peter Drucker once famously suggested that the best managed business in the world was the Salvation Army. Is the checkout person in your supermarket in business? What about the unemployed seller of the *Big Issue* magazine outside? The Body Shop, founded by Anita Roddick, made a decision to employ the unemployable and established a soap factory in Scotland in an area of widespread unemployment. A high proportion of profits were returned to the local community. It "keeps the soul of the company alive," she maintained. She did not specifically mention the transpersonal and yet in talking of the soul of her company, she was not far away from it. The point is that business has become rather a loaded word, often used pejoratively, rather like using "Brussels" to refer respectively to aspects of wealth creation or European legislation in perhaps a too general way. Many of the initiatives described below could just as easily be implemented in a wide range of organizations, not just in businesses.

Groundbreaking initiatives such as the AWARE program of Shell are of interest, although the word "spirituality" is not part of this program. APEX – achieving personal excellence – and the meditation silence service is another initiative; also relevant are Integral Transformational Coaching and the concept of mindfulness. Over 200 US hospitals have introduced mindfulness programs. The Google company allows its people to follow courses in mindfulness, which it supports.

These initiatives address the "softer" functions of management. They seem to be growing rapidly, but again there is little hard analysis of the rate of growth. Are they evidence of spirituality in firms? Perhaps the word "spirituality" will come to be accepted and used by business in the future, just as "meditation" and "mindfulness" have come into common parlance.

Some, but not many, leaders in business talk of their own spiritual convictions, and of course there is widespread development of coaching in companies and concern about work–life balance. Most business coaches avoid talking about "spirituality." Interestingly, companies are not so worried about "ecology" as a word. A growing number of companies see the concept as very tied-in, theoretically and practically, with their business development. Some would claim that ecology has a spiritual dimension, but the "S" word has not yet come into business language and certainly not the "T" word.

Does this mean that the transpersonal and business have nothing in common? The word may not be in common use but the concept may be applied. The growing number of articles and books on spirituality and business reflects an interest in and demand for further information. Many professionals, including psychologists and therapists, are working with companies in their research and programs for personal development of employees. They may indirectly be helping them to develop tentative steps toward new ways of doing business in a society, which needs to take into account individual aspirations in a society fast becoming global.

There are hundreds of small initiatives, many of which have not even been written about, which could indicate there are changes afoot. Following are some examples of known and documented activities:

- Human resources divisions have replaced traditional personnel departments in companies and are headed by senior managers, often professionally trained. As staff rather than line departments they are not always considered as important as marketing and finance, for example, but human resources departments integrate their activities throughout the other functions in ways that would hardly have been understood fifty years ago.
- Coaching has developed considerably to help employees become better members of teams working toward achieving company goals. Many companies train their own staff specifically for this work as well as using external consultants.
- Employees are encouraged to find their own paths for personal and even spiritual development, and some companies will fund internal and external programs. This would not have been considered some decades ago.
- Some companies invite qualified therapists, including transpersonal therapists, to animate training sessions in personal development.
- Individuals in companies feel more free to talk about their inner selves and related personal issues and discuss them with peers and even bosses.
- Programs in yoga, meditation, self-development and alternative therapies are widely available through companies and are advertised

and spoken about in ways that were not possible in Western society until comparatively recently.

- Libraries and bookstores now offer whole sections in spirituality, self-help, and personal development with subsections such as mysticism, death and dying, and near-death experiences.
- Business schools are now more concerned with these personal studies, although courses tend to be optional rather than part of a core curriculum.

Efforts are being made to develop more caring organizations. Many might wish that businesses were more values-based, but suggesting that spirituality is the way ahead is currently too far in advance of the mainstream of companies and their employees in Western countries. Generalizations are difficult. Islamic practice is against the concept of interest, which is based on an historical aversion to usury. Some cultures assume that some form of incentive is necessary to oil the wheels of business, while others see this as bribery. Companies create and distribute wealth according to traditional paradigms, and although new paradigms are emerging, they are not universal. The search continues.

The idea behind the transpersonal is of developing a holistic spiritual journey that embraces both the internal and external aspects of life. It suggests a positive, active approach to the journey and recognizes the relationship of individuals to all other individuals and to the planet. It provides a broad way of reflecting on this, our collective sparrows' flight, from the cradle to the grave.

Literature

Ferrer, J. 2002. *Revisioning Transpersonal Theory: A Participatory Vision of Human Spirituality.* State University of Albamy, NY.

Gozdz, K. 2000. "Toward Transpersonal Learning Communities in Business" *American Behavioral Scientist,* Vol. 43, No. 8, 1262–1285.

Kornfield, J. 2000. *After the Ecstasy the Laundry.* Bantam Books. New York.

Kumar, M. 2008. *Quantum – Einstein, Bohr and the Great Debate about the Nature of* Reality. Icon Books. Cambridge, UK.

Lancaster, B. 2004. *Approaches to Consciousness – The Marriage of Science and Mysticism.* Palgrave Macmillan. New York.

Ray, P.H. and Anderson, S.R. 2000. *The Cultural Creatives.* Random House.

Rowan, J. 1993. *The Transpersonal: Psychotherapy and Counselling.* London: Routledge.

Wilber, K. 1996. *A Brief History of Everything.* Shambhala, Boston and London.

6
Moral Agency and Spiritual Intelligence

Laszlo Zsolnai

The self of decision-makers plays an important role in determining the ethicality of their decisions. Decisions might be understood as self-expressions of the decision-makers. Spiritual experiences have a vital role in developing the self of managers and therefore in improving the ethicality of their decisions. (Zsolnai, 2004)

Ethics and cognition

Modern Western theories of ethics state that ethical decisions can be made either by applying abstract *moral principles* (deontology) or by seeking to produce *good results* in the concrete real-world context (consequentialism). The decision-maker, the agent who makes ethical decisions, usually does not appear explicitly in these theories.

An alternative theory, virtue ethics, which goes back to Aristotle, concentrates on the *character traits* of the decision-maker. Virtue ethicists believe that the essence of ethical behavior is to realize virtues, such as honesty, righteousness, or courage. Virtue ethics considers the decision-maker not as a real individual having a psychological makeup and values, but as an abstract human being who should exercise character traits adequate for the given choice situation.

Since decisions can be interpreted as *self-expressions* of the decision-makers, the chosen alternative (course of action) demonstrates the *ethicality* of the self of the decision-maker in the given situation: "As inside, so outside."

Philosopher Elizabeth Anderson has developed the expressive theory of rational action. She defines rationality as action that adequately expresses our rational attitude toward people and other intrinsically valuable things. The ground of a person's reflectively held values lies in his or her conception of what kind of person he or she ought to be; what kind of character, attitudes, concerns, and commitments he or she should have (Anderson, 1993).

The theory of *moral agency* developed by Stanford University psychologist Albert Bandura gives a more complex picture of how human beings make ethical choices (Bandura, 1986, 1991). In this explanatory framework, personal factors in the form of moral thought and self-evaluative reactions, moral conduct and environmental influences operate as interacting determinants of each other. Within this triadic reciprocal causation, moral agency is exercised through self-regulatory mechanisms.

Transgressive conduct is regulated by two sets of sanctions: social and personal. Social sanctions are rooted in the fear of external punishment; personal (self-) sanctions operate through self-condemning reactions to one's misconduct. After people adopt moral standards, self-sanctions serve as the main guides and deterrents that keep behavior in line with moral standards. The adoption of moral standards does not create a fixed control mechanism within the person. There are many psychosocial mechanisms by which moral control can be selectively engaged or disengaged from detrimental conduct (Bandura, 1990, 1991). The mechanisms of moral disengagement enable otherwise considerate people to commit transgressive acts without experiencing personal distress.

Disengagement mechanisms

Moral justification: People do not ordinarily engage in reprehensible conduct until they have justified to themselves the rightness of their actions. In this process of moral justification, detrimental conduct is made personally and socially acceptable by portraying it in the service of valued social or moral purposes.

Euphemistic labeling: Activities can take on markedly different appearances depending on what they are called. Euphemistic labeling provides a convenient tool for masking reprehensible activities or even conferring a respectable status upon them. Through sanitized and convoluted verbiage, destructive conduct is made benign and those who engage in it are relieved of a sense of personal agency.

Advantageous comparison: Behavior can also assume very different qualities depending on what it is contrasted with. By exploiting advantageous comparison, injurious conduct can be rendered benign or made to appear to be of little consequence. The more flagrant the contrasted activities, the more likely it is that one's own injurious conduct will appear trifling or even benevolent.

Displacement of responsibility: Under displacement of responsibility people view their actions as springing from the social pressures or dictates of others rather than as decisions for which they are personally responsible. Because they are not the actual agents of their actions, they are spared self-censuring reactions. Hence, they are willing to behave in ways they would normally repudiate if a legitimate authority accepts responsibility for the effects of their actions.

Diffusion of responsibility: The exercise of moral control is also weakened when personal agency is obscured by diffusion of responsibility for detrimental conduct. Any harm done by a group can always be attributed largely to the behavior of others. People behave more cruelly under group responsibility than when they hold themselves personally accountable for their actions.

Disregarding or distorting the consequences: Another way of weakening self-deterring reactions is by disregarding or distorting the consequences of action. When people pursue activities harmful to others for personal gain, or because of social inducements, they avoid facing the harm they cause or they minimize it. In addition to selective inattention and cognitive distortion of effects, the misrepresentation may involve active efforts to discredit evidence of the harm that is caused.

Dehumanization: Self-censure for injurious conduct can be disengaged or blunted by dehumanization, which divests people of human qualities or attributes bestial qualities to them. Once dehumanized, they are no longer viewed as persons with feelings, hopes, and concerns but as subhuman objects.

Attribution of blame: Blaming one's adversaries, or compelling circumstances, is still another expedient that can serve self-exoneration purposes. In moral disengagement by attribution of blame, people view themselves as faultless victims driven to injurious conduct by forcible provocation. By fixing the blame on others or on circumstances, not only are one's own injurious actions excusable but one can even feel self-righteous in the process.

Moral disengagement can effect detrimental behavior both directly and indirectly. People have little reason to be troubled by guilt or to feel any need to make amends for harmful conduct if they reconstrue it as serving worthy purposes or if they disown personal agency for it. High moral disengagement is accompanied by low guilt, thus weakening anticipatory self-restraints against engagement in detrimental behavior. Self-exoneration for harmful conduct, and self-protective dehumaniza-tion of others, treating them as blameworthy spawns a low pro-social orientation. Low pro-socialness, in turn, contributes to detrimental conduct in two ways. Having little sympathy for others both removes the restraining influence of empathy and defuses anticipatory guilt over injurious conduct. Under some circumstances, effective moral dis-engagement creates a sense of social rectitude and self-righteousness that breeds ruminative hostility and retaliatory thoughts for perceived grievances.

In many cases the workings of the moral disengagement mechanisms have been demonstrated (Bandura, Caprara, and Zsolna, 2000). What is informative in these cases is that moral collusion can end in justifying actions whose outcomes continue to be disapproved. The belief systems of the decision-makers may remain unaffected for a long time by prac-tices that are detrimental to it as well as to the general public. Selective disengagement mechanisms are deployed to mask such a contradiction and to perpetuate harmful practices.

Research using scales representing each of the eight disengagement mechanisms is adding greatly to an understanding of how disengage-ment of moral self-sanctions fosters involvement in transgressive and antisocial conduct. Some empirical findings suggest that the more people are concerned with self-enhancement goals, the more they are inclined to resort to mechanisms that permit them to disengage from the duties and obligations of civic life and to justify transgressions when their self-interest is at stake (Caprara and Campana, 2007).

The role of the self

If we want to improve the ethicality of management decisions we should enhance the development of the self of decision-makers toward a more inclusive, holistic, and peaceful consciousness. Empirical evi-dence suggests that *spiritual experiences* help people transcend narrow self-conceptions and enable them to exercise genuine empathy with others and assume an all-compassing perspective.

Transpersonal psychologist Stanislav Grof recorded more than thirty thousand spiritual experiences. These included examples from psyche-delic therapy, where nonordinary states of consciousness are induced by chemical means; spiritual emergencies, which develop spontaneously, for unknown reasons, in the midst of everyday life; and holotropic breathwork,which is facilitated by a combination of faster breathing, evocative music, and a specific form of focused body work. These spiritual experiences involve "authentic experimental identification with other people, animals, plants and various other aspects of nature and cosmos. ... We typically undergo profound changes in our understanding of existence and of the nature of reality. We directly experience the divine, sacred, or numinous dimensions of existence in a compelling way" (Grof, 1998, pp. 2–17).

Despite the rich diversity of spiritual experience, the main *ethical message* is always the same: love and compassion, deep reverence for life and empathy with all sentient beings. Grof summarizes the result of spiritual experiences as follows:

> We develop a new system of values that is not based on conventional norms, precepts, commandments, and fear of punishment, but [on] our knowledge and understanding of the universal order. We realize that we are [an] integral part of creation and that by hurting others we would be hurting ourselves. In addition, deep self-exploration leads to ... awareness of the possibility of serious experiential repercussions of harmful behavior, even those that escape societal retribution. (Grof, 1998, p. 129)

Researchers at the *Maharishi University of Management* in the USA proved the development of leadership can be effected through development of transcendental experience. Students using the method of transcendental meditation scored the highest observed in published studies in the so-called Loevinger test, which measures the level of ego-development (Heaton and Schmidt-Wilk, 2008).

Oxford-based management thinker Danah Zohar introduced the term "spiritual intelligence." It is a transformative intelligence that makes us ask basic questions about meaning, purpose, and values. Spiritual intelligence allows us to understand situations and systems deeply, to invent new categories, to be creative, and to go beyond the given paradigms (Zohar, 2002).

In his "Viable Model of Spiritual Intelligence," David B. King defines spiritual intelligence as a set of adaptive mental capacities based on nonmaterial and transcendent aspects of reality, specifically those which are related to the nature of one's existence, personal meaning, transcendence, and expanded states of consciousness. When applied, these processes are adaptive in their ability to facilitate unique means of problem solving, abstract reasoning, and coping (King, 2008).

King suggests four main components of spiritual intelligence:

1. *Critical existential thinking*: the capacity to critically contemplate meaning, purpose, and other existential/metaphysical issues (e.g., existence, reality, death, the universe), and to come to personal existential conclusions or philosophies; also, the capacity to contemplate nonexistential issues in relation to one's existence (i.e., from an existential perspective).
2. *Personal meaning production*: the ability to derive personal meaning and purpose from all physical and mental experiences, including the capacity to create and master (i.e., live according to) a life purpose.
3. *Transcendental awareness*: the capacity to identify transcendent dimensions/patterns of the self (i.e., a transpersonal or transcendent self), of others, and of the physical world (e.g., holism, nonmaterialism) during normal states of consciousness, accompanied by the capacity to identify their relationship to one's self and to the physical world.
4. *Conscious state expansion*: the ability to enter and exit higher/spiritual states of consciousness (e.g., pure consciousness, cosmic consciousness, unity, oneness) at one's own discretion – as in deep contemplation or reflection, meditation, prayer, etc.

Spiritual intelligence is badly needed in management. Management decisions considerably affect the life and fate of human communities, natural ecosystems, and future generations. The well-being of these primordial stakeholders requires *authentic care,* which may develop from experiential oneness with others and with the universal source of creation.

Literature

Anderson, E. 1993. *Value in Ethics and Economics.* Cambridge, MA & London: Harvard University Press.

Bandura, A. 1986. *Social Foundations of Thought and Action: A Social Cognitive Theory.* Englewood Cliffs, NJ: Prentice Hall.

Bandura, A. 1990. "Mechanisms of Moral Disengagement." In W. Reich (ed.), *Origins of Terrorism: Psychology, Ideologies, States of Mind,* pp. 45–103. Cambridge University Press. Cambridge, UK.

Bandura, A. 1991. "Social Cognitive Theory of Moral Thought and Action." In W.M. Kurtines and J.L. Gewirtz (eds), *Handbook of Moral Behavior and Development,* Vol. 1, pp. 45–103. Englewood Cliffs, NJ: Lawrence Erlbaum Associates.

Bandura, A., Caprara, G-V., and Zsolnai, L. 2000. "Corporate Transgressions through Moral Disengagement," *Journal of Human Values,* No. 1. pp. 57–64.

Caprara, G-V. and Campana, C. 2007. "Moral Disengagement in the Exercise of Civic-ness." In Laszlo Zsolnai (ed.), *Interdisciplinary Yearbook of Business Ethics,* pp. 83–94. Oxford: Peter Lang Publishers.

Grof, S. 1998. *The Cosmic Game: Explorations of the Frontiers of Human Consciousness.* Albany, NY: StateUniversity of New York Press.

Heaton, D. and Schmidt-Wilk, J. 2008. "Awakening the Leader Within: Behavior Depends on Consciousness." In Jerry Biberman and Len Tischer (eds), *Spirituality in Business: Theory, Practice, and Future Directions,* pp. 125–140, Palgrave Macmillan. London.

King, D.B. 2008. *The Spiritual Intelligence Project.* http://www.dbking.net/spiritual-intelligence/

Zohar, D. 2002. "Leadership Physicist." In Tom Brown et al. (eds), *Business Minds.* London, New York: Financial Times – Prentice Hall.

Zsolnai, L. 2004. "Spirituality and Management." In Laszlo Zsolnai (ed.), *Spirituality and Ethics in Management,* pp. 3–12, Dordrecht, Boston, London: Kluwer Academic Publishers.

7
Gender and Spirituality

Veerle Draulans

A gender approach to spirituality does more than give a voice to female authors or record data concerning male or female participation; it reflects on the powerful consequences of divisive and dichotomous thinking and pleas for solidarity and for a more prominent and positive place for experiences of corporeality in spiritual life, anchored in the daily life of men and women across the world.

The term "gender: a primary way of signifying relationships of power" (J.W. Scott)

The term "gender" requires a clear definition. Despite the efforts of many, including the UN World Conferences on Women, the concept is not yet well established, even though the basic reference work of Ann Oakley, *Sex, Gender and Society*, dates back to 1972. Oakley opted to use two different terms in order to retain a clear distinction between biological factors and cultural, historical, and social ones. "Sex" refers to being biologically woman or man, "gender" to cultural associations of "masculinity" or "femininity." Historian Joan Wallach Scott (1996, p. 167) assigns two basic dimensions to the gender concept. "Gender is a constitutive element of social relationships based on perceived differences between sexes, and gender is a primary way of signifying relationships of power."

People often reduce gender analysis to: "Here we have the viewpoint of women." It does injustice to what gender analysis actually sets out to do; namely, to analyze the influence of social and discursive constructs concerning masculinity and femininity and their internal power relations. The latter dimension implies resistance to generalization and stereotyping. A clear overview of various general "gender" interpretations and debates can be found in Warne (2000), or, related to world religions, in Jones (2005).

There is no gender analysis without giving attention to the unequal distribution of power. Masculinity and femininity have specific characteristics and associations, which are in turn valued differently. Gender analysis denounces the strongly structuring influence of (Western) divisive thinking. In it, masculinity is associated with transcendence, public life, objectivity, abstract thinking, universality, power, autonomy, rationality, controlled life, activity, etc.. Femininity is associated with immanence, private life, subjectivity, concrete thinking, particularity, heteronomy, emotionality, nature, uncontrolled life, passivity.

Mainstream or marginal, confirmatory or challenging?

Religions and spiritual movements form part of the structuring power distribution within society. They can reinforce or fight existing social relationships while referring to higher, sacred forces. Both the substantive and the institutional/formalistic side of spirituality can be questioned from this dichotomous thinking. Linda Woodhead developed an enlightening typology that delineates potential forms of interaction between gender and religion (Figure 7.1).

Although her analysis focuses more on religion than spirituality, she is nevertheless able to inspire reflections on "spirituality and gender." The vertical axis points to the position of religion within the existing overall power distribution in society. The horizontal axis indicates its strategic relationship to existing gender relationships (Woodhead, 2007, p. 570).

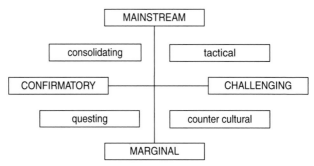

Figure 7.1   Religion and gender
Source: Woodhead, 2007, p. 570.

What does the diagram mean concretely? Let's give some examples. In Chinese religions, the goddess Kuan Yin played an important role, but her presence did not result in improved social status for women; it was the economic policy of the Communist regime that moved to ban practices such as foot binding. Something similar applies to the burning of widows in India, despite the many female gods in Hinduism. Most major world religions glorify motherhood as the ultimate destiny of womanhood (Puttick, King, ,and Campling, 1997, pp. 132, 202–203). Christine Gudorf writes that most world religions tend (or tended) to legitimate forms of violence against women. She refers to: control of female corporeality, with emphasis on reproduction and motherhood as primary tasks for women; in a family unit headed by the man, who is able to implement his own will through physical violence; unequal laws of inheritance and restriction on property law; sexual violence; prohibitions on women becoming engaged in the public realm, or, in the event they do, with the imposition of (dress) restrictions; exclusion from religious leadership; and female spirituality being considered inferior (Gudorf, 2007, pp. 10–11).

Concepts such as "patriarchy" or "kyriarchy" are used as analytical "umbrella concepts" in gender studies, and refer to all these different forms of male-dominated and religiously legitimated practices of oppression. Gender analyses of world religions focus in general on three main fields of investigation: (1) the social and institutional dimensions of religion, including leadership debates; (2) the analysis of language, ideas and ideology, including analysis of holy scriptures and canon formation; and 3) individual and/or collective religious and mystical experiences (King, 2005, pp. 3301–3310). In my further analysis, I will focus mainly on Christianity. My personal religious background is the Roman Catholic tradition, experienced in its Belgian/Flemish modes of institutionalization. Till the late 1960s, the RC Church was absolutely dominant in Flanders' public and private life.

Five decades of "gender and spirituality"

The very beginning of various types of groups in "feminist spirituality" lies in the 1970s, in the USA. The women's movement grew in significance, together with other new social movements. This inspiration from the USA reached Europe. The patriarchate became the ultimate analytical concept of the women's movement's struggle, and the fundamental division between body and spirit was also called into doubt. Catharina Halkes, who was lecturer in "Feminism and Christianity" in

1983–1986 at the University of Nijmegen, the Netherlands, described the then-heterogeneous feminist-spirituality movement as a triad: "the goddess movement, the witch movement, and a current based more on esoteric, psychoanalytic, and therapeutic processes" (Halkes, 1988). In each of these movements, Halkes recognizes various aspects: a religious dimension with an eye for symbolism and the creation of images (about the deity); an ethical component demanding respect for life and for nature; and a political element, in which women use power and force as a route to change.

The founders of the *goddess movement* were familiar with the pre-patriarchal religions from the Near East. Points of criticism of the major monotheist religions included the strong images of male gods and the marginalization of women. With the symbol of the goddess as guidance, women were encouraged to look for the goddess in themselves, in various phases of life. This diversity was recognized in archaeological findings from the Old Near East, in which the mother goddess was depicted in various poses: as a young woman, an adult woman, as mother or an older woman, as a symbol of wisdom. Some theologians saw connections between these archeological sculptures and the Christian images of Mary, Mother of God and the Madonna with Child. A feminist perspective connects this revaluation of female deities with political and social issues, away from a status quo, and strives for just gender relationships.

Halkes called the *witches' movement* "a militant protest movement" that emphasized mutual solidarity through magic and self-created, often profane rituals. Women used these rituals to celebrate important moments in their lives, such as their first menstruation, pregnancy, or menopause. Much attention goes to the healing power of nature and to anything that threatens the life of women. The witches' movement searches for the witch in every woman, which is meant to encourage women to adopt a more positive, confident self-image. Other authors use the broad collective term "paganism," of which Wicca forms a part. These authors define the feminine pagan approach from its contrast with a masculine New Age vision (Puttick, King, and Campling, 1997, p. 210).

Also in Halkes' *third movement*, women are looking, individually or collectively, for their "own, feminine self," generating energy and strength toward change and self-development. Techniques and theories from psychotherapy or psychology, including the anima and animus or yin and yang theories of Jung, have been widely approved. The integration of psychological processes and spirituality led to the concept of "psychospirituality." Key terms include "transformation" or "re-creation." Some women poured scorn on the androgynous thinking, which seemed to be particularly supported by men keen to allow their so-called feminine characteristics to come to the fore, hence distancing themselves from a specific interpretation of masculinity that was dictated by their education, with the emphasis on competition and ambition (Puttick, King, and Campling, 1997, pp. 43 ff, 95 ff).

What about those anchored in Christian tradition?

Various pioneers of these movements had their roots in Christianity, a tradition from which they increasingly dissociated themselves. They took issue with the extreme dualistic thinking in Christian tradition and its negative impact on women's lives. Alternatives developed, making an all-out effort to abolish the rigorous separation between spirituality and corporeality and to approach female sexuality and corporeality in a positive way. However, not all female feminist theologians turned their backs on the Church. Christian feminist theologians motivated others to engage in the many new social movements that had seen the light since the end of the 1960s, including the ecological movement. At the same time, a search was on for a new, liberating interpretation of classical concepts and symbols from Christian liturgy and spirituality, such as the significance of suffering, the Cross and the Resurrection. They developed a line of thought about "liberating spirituality," developing key concepts from the Christian liberation theology. Central themes included liberation, solidarity with people in the margins of society and Church, solidarity among women ("sisterhood"), and an alliance with creation/nature. A great deal of theological research was carried out into the biographies of female saints, teachers, and mystics from the past, based on the principle of giving greater visibility to "forgotten women." One example is the interest in the works and art of Hildegard von Bingen. At the same time, an explicit choice for feminist spirituality nevertheless equally resulted in marginalization in relation to the mainstream options of Church and society: "It creates distance, which is painful but also potent," Halkes wrote in 1988.

"A disproportionate presence of women" (G. Davie)

On analyzing the factual religious involvement, Grace Davie's theory on a "disproportionate presence of women" definitely holds true. (Draulans, 2008). The Kendal Project, "Patterns of the Sacred in

Contemporary Society," carried out in the United Kingdom in 2000–2002 and described by Sointu and Woodhead in 2008, found that 80 percent of participants as well as practitioners and organizers of holistic spirituality initiatives were women. (Sointu & Woodhead, 2008). But it is difficult to determine the precise number of adherents. There is some dispute about whether the content presented and the training programs had the power to change lives. The Internet makes this issue even more complex, as it offers people in search of spirituality forms of experience closely associated to their personal needs, through an individual approach without further social embedding, making notions like center or periphery, mainstream or margin irrelevant. The experience of immediacy and scope for the subjective strongly appeals to women.

Flemish doctoral research by Hildegard van Hove (van Hove, 2000) confirms the strong female presence, particularly of highly educated women, and further confirms the fact that participants did not consider their participation as an expression of religiosity or God worship. They only identified marginally with a potentially larger movement, and considered their participation as an individual step in an individual process. They definitely did not want to identify with a religious group event. Most remarkable is that half of the interviewees had very little involvement with those groups several years later and that they looked back on their participation in those activities as a personal choice that they made at a particular moment in their lives.

The strongly Western-egocentric focus of certain spiritual forms of expression nevertheless attracted growing criticism, and themes such as social justice, commitment to others, and survival of the planet received greater attention. Women from the Two-thirds World take issue with the dominance of white (female) theologians, are developing their own lines of thinking (Korte, 2004), and draw strength and empowerment from Bible passages that are less self-evident to Western white women, such as the story of Hagar in Genesis. In addition, the power factor in spiritual relationships received greater emphasis. Examples are the abuse in charismatic relationships and the sexual ambiguities in the relationship between teacher and pupil (Puttick, King, and Campling, 1997).

Also in the context of institutionalized religion, interest in spirituality is growing, whether or not in response to the large offer of alternative "expressive" forms of spirituality (Heelas, 2007). Conservative Christian churches emphasize the ideal of motherhood and hence provide a mainstay, giving recognition to women who are not professionally active (Woodhead, 2007). Students in Christian theology faculties are currently opposing what they experience as distant, academic theology.

They are explicitly asking for more attention to spirituality anchored in the idiosyncretic religious tradition (Korte, 2004). Academics can obviously answer this in many different ways, but even among researchers there is a renewed interest in spiritual emotions and experiences, also in the context of institutionalized religion, seeking inspiration from sources that provided inspiration in the past.

Gender, spirituality, and leadership

An inspiring example is how Catholic nuns in Amsterdam, the Poor Sisters of the Divine Child, found a striking theological legitimization for their work caring for abandoned children in the nineteenth and twentieth centuries (van Heijst, 2008). As women, they were responsible in sectors compatible with the then-normative image of femininity, but this care-activity offered some of them the possibility to grow into real leadership positions. The central significance of Jesus as a child in the spirituality of the sisters did not only link to the children they looked after "as if it was Jesus himself," but it also made the sisters feel like siblings of the children they cared for, in relationship to the Divine Father. The strong religious belief that they had received more from God than they could ever give, "do quia mihi datum est," was the foundation for their pro-Deo dedication. Religion was an engine for doing good. The principal emphasis was on "seeing the Divine child in the children."

Does an analysis on "gender and spirituality" have a message in relation to leadership today? Certain characteristics such as solidarity, recognition, and acknowledgment are firstly strongly related to "femininity," are secondly central to the "female experience of spirituality," and are thirdly mentioned as potentially strong assets in contemporary leadership. From the great amount of research carried out by social psychologist Alice Eagly, of Northwestern University, it emerges that female leaders are more inclined than their male colleagues toward transformational leadership, with attention given to expressing appreciation, to providing support, and to positively encouraging employees. Male leaders attach slightly more importance to hierarchical relationships. Other authors describe the network of female leaders by using a nonhierarchical metaphor: a "web of relationships." Eagly also argues that a transformational leadership style is preferable nowadays, but that female leaders nevertheless have to face up to conflicting patterns of expectation. Leaders nowadays consider the characteristics in which women excel (such as communication, connection or attention to horizontal relationships) as strong assets for middle management. The top management still holds on to stereotypes of masculinity and the associated characteristics. The question of whether, and if so, how, women in top management positions can be motivated and inspired by specific sources of spirituality definitely deserves further investigation.

I have my reservations about an instrumental use of, or a consumer approach to, spirituality in various training courses and motivational programs. Depending on the context in which they are used, words like "empowerment" or "personal development" can take on an entirely different meaning. In addition, it is debatable whether many people involved in such programs are not losing sight of the transcendent dimension, of the search for God or the "Ultimate Reality," from the definition at the very beginning of this article. The transcendental dimension is and remains a benchmark in *the Search for Spirituality, our global quest for meaning and fulfilment* (King, 2009).

Literature

Draulans, V. 2008. "The Reviving Religion: A New Meaning of Religion for the Ordering of Public Life." Some Critical Remarks, Inspired by European Values Study-data. In H. Goris & M. Heimbach-Steins (Eds.), *Religion in Law and Politics Today/Religion in Recht und Politischer Ordnung Heute*, pp. 31–51. Würzburg: Ergon Verlag.

Eagly, A.H., & Carli, L.L. (2007). *Through the Labyrinth: The Truth About How Women Become Leaders.* Boston: Harvard Business School Press.

Gudorf, C.E. 2007. "Violence against Women in World Religions." In D.C. Maguire and S. Shaikh (eds), *Violence against Women in Contemporary World Religions: Roots and Cures*, pp. 9–29. Cleveland: The Pilgrim Press.

Halkes, C. 1988."Feminism and Spirituality." *Spirituality Today* 40/3, pp. 220–236. http://www.spiritualitytoday.org/spir2day/884033halkes.html, p. 1–10, quotation p. 1(consulted on 08/02/2010).

Heelas, P. 2007. "Expressive Spirituality and Humanistic Expressivism: Sources of Significance Beyond Church and Chapel." In S. Sutcliffe and M. Bowman (eds), *Beyond New Age: Exploring Alternative Spirituality*, pp. 237–254. Edinburgh: Edinburgh University Press.

Jones, L. (ed.) 2005. *Encyclopedia of Religion. Second Edition*, Vol. 15. Detroit: Macmillan Reference.

King, U. 2005. "Gender and Religion: An Overview." In L. Jones (ed.), *Encyclopedia of Religion, Second Edition*, pp. 3296–3310. Detroit: MacMillan Reference.

King, U. 2009. *The Search for Spirituality: Our Global Quest for Meaning and Fulfilment.* London: Canterburry Press.

Korte, A.-M. 2004. "(Feministische) theologie en feministische spiritualiteit: 'in de geest van hetlichaam." In P. De Mey and J. Haers (eds), *Theologie en spiritualiteit: het gesprek heropend*, pp. 175–192. Leuven-Voorburg: Acco.

Oakley, A. (1972). *Sex, Gender and Society.* Temple Smith, London.

Puttick, E., King, U., and Campling, J. 1997. *Women in New Religions. In search of Community, Sexuality and Spiritual Power.* London: MacMillan Press.

Scott, Wallach, J. 1996. "Gender: a Useful Category of Historical Analysis." In Scott, Wallach, J. (ed.), *Feminism and History*, pp.152–180. Oxford, New York: Oxford University Press.

Sointu, E., & Woodhead, L. (2008), Spirituality, Gender and Expressive Selfhood. *Journal for the Scientific Study of Religion* 47 (2): 259–276.

van Heijst, A. 2008. *Models of Charitable Care. Catholic Nuns and Children in Their Care in Amsterdam 1852–2000.* Leiden: Brill.

van Hove, H., 2000. *De weg naar binnen. Spiritualiteit en zelfontplooiing. PhD thesis in Social Sciences no. 43.* Leuven: Katholieke Universiteit Leuven.

Warne, R.R. 2000. "Gender." In W. Braun and R.T. McCutcheon (eds), *Guide to the Study of Religion*, pp. 140–154. London, New York: Cassell.

Woodhead, L. 2007. "Gender Differences in Religious Practice and Significance." In J.A. Beckford and N.J. Demerath III (eds), *The Sage Handbook of the Sociology of Religion,* pp. 566–586. Los Angeles, London: Sage.

Woodhead, L. and Heelas, P. (eds) 2000. *Religion in Modern Times. An Interpretive Anthology.* Oxford, Malden: Blackwell Publishers.

8
Critique as a Notion of Spirituality

Suzan Langenberg

Critique and spirituality are not commonly associated with one another and it is a relationship that is rarely described. Yet the ancient Greek use of critique as an art of life, as an attitude (*ethos*), comes close to the meaning of spirituality as the explicit and deep relationships between thought, emotion, consciousness, and inner experience. Telling the personal truth as a moral act toward the *agora, the other* and *the self,* is based on consulting the spirit, the center of personal spirit, the diaphragm of the body, the moral judgment, the *judgment of taste*. Disclosing (inner) truth by means of speech is a critical process and at the same time a process in which mental motives play a fundamental role.

According to the French philosopher Michel Foucault, the spiritual question in our history is *the price a subject has to pay for telling the truth to others and to himself.* This search for a personal truth is spiritual, critical and is about forming judgments. The expression of critique is the means by which personal truth is disclosed. In this contribution we are not analyzing truth in a religious sense as an already-revealed truth (synonymous with God), nor do we intend to focus on a rational, analytic, and objective truth reached by a scientifically acknowledged method; our focus is on spoken truth, performed in a speech act, close to a spiritual meaning of critique.

The next three paragraphs will elaborate first on the meaning of critique in ancient Greece through the concept of *parrhesia*; second, on the development of the meaning of critique and its relationship to spirituality; third, critique as an exercise in limitation; and fourth, the consequences of this critical approach for spirituality in the organization, and for its leadership.

Critique and parrhesia

The concept of critique originates in ancient Greece, where critique (parrhesia) was practiced as an indispensable part of public politics and private lifestyle. Parrhesia is defined as follows: frankly speaking the truth as a mode of *self-care* (epimeleia heautou – souci de soi) and as a condition to take care of others. In the work of Aristotle parrhesia refers to a personal moral quality and a characteristic of the *sense of honour*. In his view, the generous, liberal (*megalopsuchos*) man possesses this virtue: he is a free person, and at the same time he is committed to his moral consciousness.

Critique as a *parrhesiastic attitude* was a necessity in the political arena. *Attitude* and *ethos* – certainly in the Hellenistic, philosophical schools – were understood as a means for criticizing the polis, the democracy. The use of parrhesia was also conditional: he who used parrhesia had to be a citizen of Athens and must act both courageously and frankly. The parrhesiastès runs the risk of being banned or excluded if his truth turns out to be unacceptable. In order to be able to deal with this risk, the parrhesiastès must have truth and ethos at his disposal. To be able to reach (personal and relational) truth – the essence of life and survival – people practiced dialogue, dispute, and self-criticism.

In *fearlessly speaking the truth* the connection between issue and person is found in the act of speaking itself. This act is a practice of freedom as well as a spiritual way to reach personal truth. In Greek antiquity, in addition to the determination of the truth as an objective and universal entity, truth is understood as a linguistic act driven by a moral impulse, elicited by a critical perception and formed into a personal judgment. The spoken truth opens up space for exchange, negotiation, debate: it is an event that in and of itself constitutes information upon which to take action. In other words parrhesia, as a virtue, a duty and a technique, is a requisite of those who are in the position to shape the consciences of others, and helps them to form their self-relationship. The act initially takes place self-sufficiently and independently. From the moment that the direct connection with the acting agent is interrupted, the coded use of parrhesia and the institutionalized immanent critique takes on a technical-instrumental role up to the point at which critique is expressed from an unexpected source. Then the unbounding and boundary effect will start again.

We can summarize the meaning of parrhesia as follows:

- *necessary condition for democracy*: "Frankly speaking truth" is a necessity and is elicited by the dynamic of the agora;

- *democratic right*: as a citizen of Athens, one had the right to use parrhesia;
- *necessary condition for care*: care for the self as a matter of telling oneself the truth is presupposed in order to be able to take care of others, of the polis;
- *having and displaying courage*: speaking truth in public presupposes the courage to contradict the prevailing discourse, the public, the sovereign. This could mean that the parrhesiastès might risk his life;
- presupposes self-critique as a *moral attitude*.

The use of parrhesia is related to a *method*, a specific *lifestyle* and to the *act*. In order to gain access to truth, the parrhesiastès had to use certain (self-related) techniques such as *self-care, self-criticism, navigation of the self*, asceticism, inner debate, and critical debate with an opponent, to reach the inner sense that opens up a spiritual dimension of living. Individual, philosophical parrhesia is a *praxis*; it is not a concept or a specific matter. This praxis is an embodiment of our own moral subjectivity. The subject gets access to truth through labour, called *techniques of the self*: it is a form of *asceticism*, a work of purification, conversion of the soul by contemplation of the soul itself.

This asceticism includes training, learning, instructing – as practices of freedom – and has been replaced in modern thought by meaning, proof, and the knowledge–power nexus. Since the Enlightenment the relationship to the self no longer has to be an ascetic one as a prerequisite for access to truth. One can be immoral and still know the truth. This is in fact the postmodern problem; the intrinsic connection with the self and thus with the other, as a necessary prerequisite for taking responsibility for the environment, is no longer a given. Speaking the truth as experience, and using personal ethics as the driving force for the determination of the truth, departs from the rational analysis of the truth and has long been banished to the asylum of the *other of reason*. Experiencing inner sense and personal morality is subjugated to a rationalization of the world. Since modernity began and the priority of rationality surfaced, people have forgotten self-care in the meaning of personal truth.

Critique and spirituality

What is the historical evolution of the concept of critique? The etymology starts with the Greek language between 200 BC and 400 AD The Greek word *krinein* means to separate, to distinguish, and to decide. From *krinein* the word *krisis* was derived, which means in ancient Greek:

decision, judgment, research, outcome. Two separate applications of the concept of critique remained:

- the *power of judgment and discernment of the human mind* has been used by the philosophers of the Stoa in text research and the allegorical explanation of text.
- a *dialectical* (as opposed to rhetorical) *doctrine of judgment* or truth.

The specific notion of parrhesia – namely, the individual expressing his or her critique as a courageous act inspired by a moral consciousness of the other, the public, and the environment – disappeared. Also, the inner, moral-driven necessity to speak up, to express critique, especially the political and civic right to use parrhesia in the presence of the agora, vanished. Naturally there are some examples of incidental and personal presentations of parrhesia; for instance, the critical role the jester played at the medieval royal courts, although this ironical presentation of criticism was partly masked through the comic role.

In the late Middle Ages the notion of critique reappeared, thanks to the rise of humanism and its critical position with respect to the domination of Christianity and to the origination of reason, science, discovery of new land, etc. The humanists wrested themselves from the grasp of scholasticism and liberated the human being from traditional boundaries.

In Modernity, beginning with Immanuel Kant and the Enlightenment at the end of the eighteenth century, we see the concept of critique being used as a purifying and unifying effect through distinction of opposites, competing theories and controversy. Furthermore in the revival of critique as of self-critique in the highly developed sense of questioning the reasonableness of reason, the development of the human sciences begins.

The revival of critique happened on a metalevel dominated by an increasingly instrumental use of reason, at the expense of immanent criticism as a personal act of free speech. Ideology (social) critique, aimed toward the analysis of explanatory worldviews (Frankfurter Schule in the nineteenth and twentieth centuries), can be seen as an expression of this revival.

From the Enlightenment on, the evolution of the philosophical meaning of critique in relation to the personal and spiritual search for truth began again after Michel Foucault developed his positive interpretation of critique as a personal act. *It is a rupture with the existing, the prevailing order* that leads to practices of freedom.

The dynamic of critique as *unbounding and boundarying* can be perceived as an attitude. The positive significance of critique leads to practices of freedom, to parrhesia: "Not like this, without principle, without alternative." We will enumerate the different spiritual senses of a positive meaning of critique:

- critique is to reveal, to create spiritual space in the unbounding and boundarying dynamic: *transgression;*
- critique is directed at a *local and specific* praxis – it does not aim for an overall overview;
- giving critique means to discuss oversimplification and is therein *radical and permanent;*
- critique does not exist on its own – it is always involved in something and is as such *parasitic and incomplete;*
- critique makes the certain into something *uncertain and actual;*
- critique is resistance against the existing: not that way, with neither principle nor alternative;
- critique is *spiritual*: in its expression it discloses our spirit and brings us close to the *essence* of being.

Only this positive idea of critique presents the intrinsic relationship with our spirit. The correlations among telling the truth, courage, and critique based on elementary, personal motives describe a spiritual depth that refers to a vital breath, a lifestyle.

Criticism as an exercise in limitation

One of the main questions since the Enlightenment has been, *How should we be governed?* In what way can we rethink our self-organization in relation to the complex environment? In 1784 Kant wrote a small political pamphlet called: *Answering the question: What's Enlightenment?* In this he argues for the people to emancipate themselves from a self-organized voicelessness (*sapere aude*). It is a question of attitude, the critical attitude as a general virtue.

It is this critical attitude that has to be compared with the introduction of ethos, which is understood as an attitude, a certain habitus. What binds us to the Enlightenment is the permanent reactivation of an attitude – a philosophical ethos that can be characterized as a permanent criticism of our historical being. According to Foucault, the *ethos philosophique* (the critique) tries to relaunch the infinite work of freedom as far and as amply as possible. This philosophical elaboration on critique results in the formulation of the *attitude limité*, or critique seen as a nontranscendental and nonmetaphysical examination of boundaries; a discursive practice that articulates what we think, speak, and make; and the *attitude expérimentale*, where the exercise of our boundaries results in the proof of our reality and actuality. In the end, the only way change can be confirmed is through the practice of experimental argumentation that enables us to create other societies, other companies, other cultures, other world-perspectives. From that point of view the theoretical and practical experience we have of our limits and their possible transgression is in itself always limited, determined, and accordingly recommenced. In critique lies the basis for change, and it is absolutely indispensable for any transformation. As soon as one can no longer think things as one formerly thought them, transformation becomes very urgent, very difficult, but quite possible.

Critique as a spiritual exercise in the organization

The perception of what an organization is or should be is changing. We can no longer assume that an organization is the equivalent of its output or that it can be identified with its shareholder value. Environmental, financial, and social pressures on organizations make them permeable and vulnerable. Our recommendation is this:

- The traditional gap between theory and practice should disappear.
- Organizational praxis should happen at, on, and beyond boundaries.
- Organizations should continuously produce critique because of their permanent state of interruption caused by environmental, social, and economic change.
- An organization works as a *third space* between the private and public spheres: it creates power and influences both the private and public sphere. Consequently both the private (profit-driven) and the public organization should become a "polis," a platform where private and public interests continuously interfere.

We thus confront questions such as these: is the room for critique dependent upon the type of organizational design? Within an organization, how is the relationship forged between speaking the truth and freedom, morality, and result? To what extent can a space for critique be organized – or is it merely dependent on chance?

Some examples of the role of critique in the history of organizational paradigms underline that the possibility, quality, and level of critique depends on the organizational design departing from a traditional, modern, or postmodern institutional view. An organization brings together highly divergent and incompatible topics (return on investment versus social responsibility; job security versus job satisfaction; diverse lifestyles, cultures, values of employees, etc.) in a network of partners, competitors, globalizing and changing worldviews. With a static vision of the organization it is impossible to capture and record the organization dynamic. New visions of the organization guarantee that organizational reality constitutes a continuing platform for making existing conflicts visible and their origins arguable and contestable. Apart from the organization as an imperative – a rational and instrumental construct – it also has another immanent existence, manifested in personal and social relations. Both the imperative (rational) and social (relational) realities of an organization interfere with each other constantly, usually at the cost of the latter in the quality of human interdependency.

Critique is self-critique as well as (political–ethical) system critique: we are always situated within a context that is already being controlled by specific culturally and spiritually based views that continually provoke a kind of resistance. The absence of an unambiguous basis in the moment of critique can give cause to raising a communicative platform, revealing a deeper meaning of organizational interaction. The opposition between a discursive and an individual use of reason is characteristic of the tensions in the relationships within and between organizations in which various interests cannot be reconciled, although the organization must unite them by necessity. That is why the dynamic of critique in the sense of *opening up* and *revealing* potential contradictions in current affairs, *without principle and without alternative*, is a necessary prerequisite for business spirituality to be assigned a critical role.

Critical leadership

Critique unbounds and opens up spaces for debate in which not *what* is taking place but *that* it is taking place *at all* becomes the political–economic–ethical point. *That* it takes place, *unmediated,* between agents of critique, is an important characteristic of the organization itself: it facilitates these unmediated spaces. Noticing the *place* and *agent* of critique is a quality of critical leadership. Through the act of taking note of critique it comes into being and is enacted.

The leadership profile in organizations is changing as profoundly as organizations themselves. Instead of placing the emphasis on achieving success targets, the organizations' reality demands that leaders also seek out problem areas, specifically those areas within each organization in which matters can be problematized. A reliable, good, and spirit-driven leader concentrates less on changing and improving people and more on reading the concerns of the employees, how they think, and incorporates this into his decision-making. Organizational changes actually take place where there are constant transactions among people, departments, the organization itself, and units – among various types and genres of discourse and where decisions continually follow one another.

What could this mean for the leadership? Is not every leader a potential business ethicist and for the purposes of our argument, a critic, a parrhesiastès? Just like employees, leaders are part of a system. A leader ought to train himself in self-critique and self-navigation, which would allow him to take the critical distance into consideration, know how to pick up on critique, be open to the unexpected, dare to doubt, and have the courage to call attention to these doubts through deepening the involved spiritual interests. In fact, a leader with these qualities is alert to the mindsets that are actively involved, both within his team and among his superiors, as well as in his network. Beyond his own interests, a leader could increase the reflexive assessment in his organization whereby he both subjugates and de-subjugates himself to existing discourses, opinions, boundaries. A leader who has the courage to dare to think makes his knowledge available to sources of objection, analyses forms of power that distort or block the speech of employees, and points out the obstacles that obstruct their moral imagination rendering them unable or unwilling to dare to speak.

Business examples

It is very hard to come up with concrete business examples that support the spiritual critique praxis: it is an immanent, and primarily individual, bounded, moral speech act. Besides, talking about critique performed as an individual act of free speech is, generally speaking, still perceived as taboo in organizations. Finally, the "working of critique" usually happens underground.

However, several *whistle-blowing* cases show the predominantly negative consequences of the working of critique: fraud in the European Commission (1998 and 2004), the construction fraud case in the Netherlands (2001), and the scandal of Swiss banks destroying Jewish data on their credits (1997). The persons (whistle-blowers) who disclosed the incriminating information were not protected and for some time were banned from their organizations or even from their home-lands. They took these risks in favour of moral conscience in relation to the general interest.

The creation of organizational space for free and critical speech depends on organizational culture. Practicing critique, moral reflection, and receptiveness to otherness challenges business leaders on the most immediate level. They have to exercise these skills, for the sake of the survival of the company, far beyond their self-interest. This is a critical and at the same time a spiritually inspired exercise.

Literature

Aristotle, 1994, *Nicomachean Ethics*, trans. H. Rackham, Loeb classical library®, Suffolk: St. Edmundsburry Press.

Clegg, S. R. (ed.) 2002. *Management and Organization Paradoxes*, Amsterdam, PA: John Benjamins Publishing Company.

Foucault, M. 1978. "Quést-ce que la critique?" *Bulletin de la Société française de la Philosophie*, 84 (1990)2, pp. 35–63.

Foucault, M. 2007. *The Politics of Truth: a History of the Present*. Los Angeles, California: Semiotext(e).

Foucault, M. 2009. *Le courage de la vérité, le gouvernement de soi et des autres II*. Paris: Gallimard.

Goodpaster, K.E. 2007. *Conscience and Corporate Culture*. Oxford: Blackwell Publishing.

Kant, I. 1973. *Kleinere Schriften zur Geschichtsphilosophie Ethik und Politik*. Hamburg: Felix Meiner Verlag.

Habermas, J. 1988. *Nachmetaphysisches Denken*, Frankfurt am Main: Suhrkamp Verlag.

Keulartz, J. 2008. "Boundary-Work, Pluralism and the Environment." In Olsen, K.KB. et al. (eds), *A Companion to the Philosophy of Technology*, pp. 263–270. Denmark: Wiley-Blackwell.

Knudsen, C. and Tsoukas, H. (eds) 2003. *The Oxford Handbook of Organization Theory: Meta-theoretical Perspectives*. Oxford: Oxford University Press.

Lippke, R.L. 1995, *Radical Business Ethics*. Boston : Rowman & Littlefield Publishers.

Lyotard, J-F. 1990. "La mainmise." In Brügger, N. et al., *Lyotard, les déplacements philosophiques*, pp. 125–136. Paris: De Boeck Université.

Painter-Morland, M. 2008. *Business Ethics as Practice*, Cambridge: Cambridge University Press.

Vandekerckhove, W. 2006. *Whistleblowing and Organizational Social Responsibility*. Hampshire: Ashgate.

Part II
Spiritually Inspired Economics

9

Aristotle and Economics

Robert Allinson

It is commonly put forth that Aristotle's ethics is a virtue ethics. This is contrasted with ethics that is orientated toward right actions. For Aristotle, this is a pseudo-distinction. One cannot build one's virtues except through performing right actions. For Aristotle, one performs right actions for their own sake, not for the sake of building virtues or even building character. But the performance of noble deeds, which is the ultimate counsel to life that Aristotle gives, has as its natural consequence the building of virtue and the building of character. This, in turn, brings happiness. Since none of Aristotle's writings is extant, it is not easy to ferret out Aristotle's meaning. However, if one reads the lecture notes of Aristotle's students with some care, it is clear that one should not act for the sake of building character or obtaining happiness. Indeed, the purpose of political society, for Aristotle, is to create a venue for the performance of noble actions. Noble acts, just acts, are the goal for mankind. Nothing else. That happiness flows from this is proof for Aristotle that this is the right path for humankind to take.

Aristotle is different from contemporary philosophers who advocate virtue ethics, that is, an ethics that endorses the building of virtues. This is not quite accurate for Aristotle, for two reasons. First of all, he is interested in building virtues not for their own sake, but for the sake of building character. Second, character building is, for Aristotle, not the end-goal, as it might be for Confucius. What is important to recognize is that Aristotle's notion of character building is intimately tied to his idea of achieving human happiness. *He thinks that building moral character can be identified as the correct pathway to take in life because it is the only way in which the majority of human beings can achieve happiness.* While pursuing pure contemplation may be an even better way to achieve happiness, he rules this out as an unsustainable path for the majority of humankind.

Aristotle's ethics cannot be easily classified in terms of categories utilized today such as deontology or utilitarianism. He did teach that one should do what is right for its own sake (deontology), but at the same time argued that by doing so and only by doing so, one would achieve happiness. He is not an egoist, that is, one who teaches that one should pursue happiness, but, if a label is needed, a naturalist, that is, one should pursue what is appropriate to one's nature. If one pursues what is proper to one's nature, happiness follows, as happiness is a sign that one's nature is fulfilled.

What must be remembered is that for Aristotle, one must pursue what is ethically right for its own sake without any other motive in mind. Then and only then does happiness flow in its wake. The notion that Aristotle's ethics is a self-realization ethics or a self-actualization ethics is not accurate. It is a self-realization ethics if one realizes that the self that one is realizing is the *moral* self. The contentment that follows is not that which one is seeking. It is a natural complement.

Aristotle is classified today by ethicists as an eudaemonist, that is, as standing for an ethics of self-realization or self-actualization. Probably, this classification is derived from the way in which Aristotle constructs his arguments in the *Nicomachean Ethics*. For instance, he starts out by saying that all human beings will agree that the purpose of life is to achieve happiness. He says that we must carefully consider in what happiness consists. Ethics, for Aristotle, is the way in which humans achieve the sort of happiness that properly belongs to human creatures. His argument contains two threads. One thread is the attempt to show that, from the nature of human beings, they cannot achieve happiness by pursuing pleasure, wealth, and honor. Thus, we already have a clue that profit making cannot be the road to happiness for Aristotle, and hence cannot be a course that he recommends.

Another thread is that in determining the end-goal that mankind should strive for, one should choose an end-goal that is not for the sake of something else, but that is pursued for its own sake. Otherwise, one would forever be chasing a less than ultimate goal. Such a goal, if not stable as an end-goal, would not lead to happiness because of its instability. One would not be able to sustain a pursuit of it, and thus would fall into unhappiness.

While a complete discussion of Aristotelian ethics would take us beyond the limits of this chapter, suffice it to say that he makes his case in terms of combining the two threads of his argument. The unique nature of the human animal is rational and thus it is this part of human nature that must be exercised and fulfilled to bring true human happiness. Pleasure taken from eating, for example, is shared with other animals and thus this would be insufficient to produce *human* happiness. We must find the connection with the highest part of human beings, our reason, and thus the unique way in which we can achieve happiness. Otherwise, the happiness we might achieve would not be lasting, and it would not be appropriate.

We can interpret his arguments in this way. Money is a means to an end. It is not an end in itself. It is pursued for what one can buy with it. Aristotle thinks that, for the most part, money would be pursued for the sake of pleasure. Pleasure he takes to be the necessary condition of happiness, but not sufficient for happiness. Human happiness must be something that can last a lifetime. In his famous phrase: "For one swallow does not make a summer, nor does one day" (*Nicomachean Ethics,* 1098s 18–19). Pleasure, or creature comforts – what money can buy – is not suitable as an ultimate goal for human beings, because a state of continuous pleasure would either be ignoble – since it would be shared with the life goal of a mollusc – or it would be meaningless and unsatisfying, since entertainment is pursued as a relaxation so that one can refresh oneself for fulfilling activity, not as an end in itself (*Nicomachean Ethics,* 1176b 29–37). Honor or reputation would depend upon those who bestow it, and thus would not be self-sustaining. In the end, only wisdom does not depend on any outside source and thus can depend upon itself.

The pursuit of wisdom by itself is accomplished through exercising our rational nature, but such a pursuit of pure contemplation is too high a goal to set for most human beings. We must use our rationality to conduce to human happiness in a way that is achievable by all human beings. All can use their reason to make ethical choices. Thus, it is in the area of ethics that all can engage their reason. By exercising our reason in the area of ethics, we can all achieve the kind of happiness that will be satisfying to our human natures.

Happiness

Happiness for Aristotle cannot be a passive state of mind, but must involve action. Noble acts, which are a class of actions in and of themselves, are the only actions that all human beings can sustain throughout the course of their lifetime and are not pursued for any goal outside of themselves. Of course, Aristotle recognizes that some degree of material sufficiency is necessary for lifetime happiness, so he does not exclude this. He just does not see this as forming the main goal of one's lifetime activities.

It may be difficult for us to understand Aristotle's idea of happiness, because it is not confined to a subjective feeling or a state of mind. Virtuous activity is for Aristotle in the end what comprises happiness (*Nicomachean Ethics*, 1098a 16). While this is accompanied by a state of mind, it is the state of mind that only attends the performance of ethical actions. Such a state of happiness is thus defined by the activity that produces it, rather than by the end feeling state. While this choice may be moot – whether to define happiness by the state of mind that accompanies virtuous acts or by the virtuous activity – Aristotle chooses to define happiness by the activity, so as to preclude confusing this state of mind with similar states of mind that might arise from from very different activities. While this choice results in an awkward identification of what we consider to be a mental state with action, Aristotle prefers this definitional disadvantage to the more risky consequence of coming down on the side of defining happiness as a state of mind which could be then possibly be achieved by some other means. He does present arguments on the side of activity – so as not to confuse happiness with a state of sleep for example – but, such arguments, while important, do not entirely do away with the awkwardness of identifying happiness with action.

Aristotle's concept of happiness cannot be separated from his concept of ethical action. The objection to Aristotle could be raised that if you integrate happiness and ethical action, then you run the risk that ethical action would be undertaken for the sake of happiness and thus would lack ethical *intention*. One hears such objections in the form of "You gave that beggar money so that you could ease your own guilt." Of course, such an objection can be countered with the answer, "What difference does it make? What matters is that the beggar received some needed money." For Aristotle, there is another answer available. For Aristotle, there is no separation between feeling happy and performing an ethical act. You *should* feel happiness when you perform an ethical action, because ethics is the only and therefore the proper way in which all human beings gain lasting and complete happiness. Happiness is the sign, for Aristotle, that one has performed an action *appropriate* to the nature of a human being. It is a natural state and hence when nature is fulfilled, happiness must be the result. Happiness is the crown, as he puts it, of an action. In fact, Aristotle goes so far as to say that "the man who does not rejoice in noble acts is not even good" (*Nicomachean Ethics*, 1099a 17–18). Confucius also thought that ethics was natural to human beings, though he did not link it with the achievement of happiness.

Profit making

Another way of analyzing Aristotle's views on profits is as follows: if performing moral acts is the route to human fulfillment and happiness, then making profits is, by definition, immoral. The profiteer becomes unhappy, because the profiteer is seeking money as an end-goal, which is a road to unhappiness.

The argument could be put another way. If performing just actions is the goal that mankind should set its eyes upon, then the achievement of justice must be, for Aristotle, a goal that he valued most highly. Even though Aristotle appears to couch his argument in eudaemonistic terms, which is that it is for the sake of individual happiness that each individual should pursue this goal, the consequences of Aristotle's individualistic goal must be the production of a public justice. This is the logical consequence of following Aristotelian ethics. This consequence could not have escaped such a thinker as Aristotle, a thinker whom for the next thousand years would be simply referred to as "The Philosopher." It follows from this that any action, or set of actions, that produced injustice would not be countenanced by Aristotle. Hence, Aristotle would not endorse profit seeking since profit by its very nature produces injustice, that is, it disadvantages one side of the transaction in order to advantage the other side. According to Sir Ernest Barker, the distinguished translator and editor of *The Politics of Aristotle*, Aristotle speaks out against retail trade for exactly this reason. Barker's interpretation of Aristotle is that the very notion of gaining from another man is for Aristotle, wrong. In his translation of one of Aristotle's comments in the *Politics*, the part in the brackets being his elucidation, it reads, "We can thus see that retail trade (which buys from others to sell at a profit) is not naturally a part of the art of acquisition. If that were the case, it would only be necessary to practice exchange to the extent that sufficed for the needs of both parties (and not to the extent of the making of profit by one of the parties at the expense of the other)" (Barker, 1958, p. 23).

Aristotle's views on profit making bear careful analysis. The word he uses in Greek is "chrematistic" which translates as the "art of acquisition." He regards this as sound when it refers to what he regards as the natural forms of acquisition that are necessary for household and state needs and unsound when practiced for individual purposes that exceed one's needs, that is, profit.

Aristotle puts forth a separate argument against profit making involving the concept of limits. Today's concept of the maximization of profit as the goal of business would not be acceptable to Aristotle. What is natural to Aristotle is what is limited. The acquisition of wealth by the art of household management is limited and "the object of that art is not an unlimited amount of wealth." He is aware that in retail trade, however, "all who are engaged in acquisition increase their fund of currency without any limit or pause." Barker refers to Newman's interpretation here that the problem of profit is a misconception of the purpose of life and the nature of well-being (Barker, 1958, p. 26). All of this points back to the concept that the pursuit of wealth is the road to unhappiness.

Barker's elucidation, that Aristotle's moral condemnation of profit is because profit is made at the expense of other men, is put explicitly in another passage from Aristotle: "There are two sorts of wealth-getting, as I have said; one is a part of household management, the other is retail trade: the former necessary and honourable, while that which consists in exchange is justly censured; for it is unnatural, and a mode by which men gain from one another"(*Politics*, 1258b). It is unnatural for Aristotle, because it takes from other men. In Barker's translation of the same passage, the meaning is equally clear. Aristotle does not condone profit making from retail trade, precisely because it involves injustice to other men: "The natural form, therefore, of the art of acquisition is always, and in all cases, acquisition from fruits and animals. That art, as we have said, has two forms: one which is connected with retail trade, and another which is connected with the management of the household. Of these two forms, the latter is necessary and laudable; the former is a method of exchange which is justly censured, because the gain in which is results is not naturally made [from plants and animals] but is made at the expense of other men" (Barker, 1958, p. 28).

Aristotle proceeds to say that, "The most hated sort, and with the greatest reason, is usury, which makes a gain out of money itself, and not from the natural object of it. ... Wherefore of all modes of getting wealth this is the most unnatural" (*Politics*, 1258b2–1258b15).Barker's translation of this passage conveys the same meaning: "The trade of the petty usurer [the extreme example of that form of the art of acquisition which is connected with retail trade] is hated most. ... Hence we can understand why, of all modes of acquisition, usury is the most unnatural" (Barker, 1958, p. 29). While usury is, as we can see, the form of unnatural acquisition Aristotle regards in the worst light, he does not condone profit made from retail trade.

He justifies his condoning of gain from enemies in war on the grounds of what he considers just wars: "And so, in one point of view, the art of war is a natural art of acquisition, for the act of acquisition includes hunting, an art which we ought to practise against wild beasts, and against men who, though intended by nature to be governed, will not submit; for war of such a kind is naturally just" (*Politics*, 1256b 23–26). While we may disagree with Aristotle on what counts as a just war, he makes an exception to his ethics of not gaining at the expense of other men in the case of just wars.

That slavery was justified by Aristotle is well known. For Barker, Aristotle only justified slavery in the case when the master was superior to the slave in terms of goodness and that slavery was not countenanced in the case of unjust wars (Barker, 1958, p. 13). He owned slaves of his own as did Thomas Jefferson and clearly this involves injustice in our eyes. According to Barker, when Aristotle justified slavery, he did not have in mind factory slaves or plantation slaves (Barker, 1958, p. 11). Aristotle has in mind family slaves. In this sense, human resources as slaves are only part of Aristotle's home-management point of view. For Aristotle, a rational and good household economy without slavery was unrealistic. We may say that Aristotle's acceptance of household slaves made him less than a perfect ethical man, though he did provide for the freedom of his slaves in his will. Near the end of his *Politics,* he even states that all slaves should eventually be emancipated. Aristotle's views on slavery are not the only weak spot in his ethics. His views considering females inferior to males are also well known.

In any case, we must examine Aristotle's stated views on justice, which remain his views, despite the fact that some of them might be contradicted or at least restricted by other views that he held. In other words, one can still consider the validity of the theoretical ground of Aristotle's critique of profit making despite the limitations of the applications of his ethical views when it came to barbarians, slaves, or females.

Ethical action

Given the above restrictions of application, Aristotle is well known for his elevation of ethical action. One sees Aristotle's elevation of ethical action in one particularly telling example. He endorses private ownership, which is the keynote of capitalism. But his reason for the endorsement is that it affords the owner the opportunity for ethical action, that is, to share (*Politics,* 1263 a39–41; 1263b 12–14). If there is no private property, the owner has nothing to share and hence his or her ethical nature is stunted. The acquisition of private property is not advocated because it is the right of an individual to own or to prosper. The acquisition of private property is endorsed because it provides an opportunity to perform ethical actions. By the same token, the possession of money is endorsed when it is used for liberal actions. As Aristotle says, "The liberal man will need money for the doing of his liberal deeds" (*Nicomachean Ethics*, 1178a 28–29).

One may argue that Aristotle's identification of happiness with virtuous activity is not compelling. In order to understand Aristotle properly one would have to take all of his different arguments into account. No one of them by itself is totally convincing. But, taken together, they do make a powerful case. One must take into account his set of arguments, borrowed from his master Plato, that a human being cannot be content by simply pursuing a life of pleasure, for example. One must also take into account his argument, also borrowed from his master Plato, that the pursuit of wealth does not produce happiness but a state of endless desires and hence endless unhappiness. When one puts all of his arguments together, one understands that for Aristotle, the pursuit of the proper definition of happiness is a necessary part of choosing the right path to happiness. Once one understands that in which happiness really consists, one will choose the right sort of life. Economic activity is a subset of ethics. It would be perverse to attempt to define economics on its own, because all action must be defined relative to the role that it plays in the human being achieving happiness.

Some might criticize eudaemonism as not being ethically relevant, because one should act justly whether or not it produces happiness. It is important to keep in mind that for Aristotle, one does not act ethically because it produces happiness. Just acts are to be performed for their own sakes; it is only when they are performed for their own sakes that happiness is the product. Thus, one's life is orientated to acting ethically to relieve the suffering of others.

There is also the possible objection that one should not focus on developing moral character, as this diverts one from bringing about social justice. While this is a fine objection – and every ethical theory should be challenged by alternate models – the advantage of the moral-character approach is that one would naturally perform ethical acts were one to have developed one's moral character – perhaps more efficaciously than if one were simply exhorted to be just regardless of one's inclinations.

In reality, there is no need for a conflict here since, for Aristotle, one builds one's moral character only by performing just actions, and thus the debate between character building and a concern for social justice is a pseudo-conflict. One must bear in mind that one performs just acts only for their own sake, not for the sake of building moral character. The building of moral character is the consequence, not the motivation. Here, there is a slight difference with the thinking of Confucius.

In the end, one must also remember that arguments of philosophers in general (and Aristotle is no exception) when they bear on the subject of ethics, are prescriptive and not simply descriptive. They cannot be totally convincing as logical arguments on their own. The philosopher wishes that such arguments will persuade others to become more ethical in their intentions and actions. But, such persuasion does not carry the force of compulsion. It is still a choice. And such arguments are designed to set a goal for humanity to follow, not to convince by unassailable logic that such a choice must be followed.

Aristotle's idea of morality, in which the Golden Mean prominently figures, advocates a middle path, rather than an extreme. This is true except in the case of goodness, in which case there is no problem in extremes. (One should not choose a middle path between good and evil.) However, Aristotle does say that for total happiness, material welfare must be secured so he does not rule out material well-being. Wealth for Aristotle should be limited to what is necessary to run one's household. An excess of wealth over this is in his mind, unnecessary (*Politics*, 1258a 14–18).*The current notion of maximization of profits as a virtual definition of the goals of business would be anathema to Aristotle.* The late Robert Solomon once wrote, "Aristotle despised the financial community and more generally, all of what we would call profit seeking. He argued that goods should be exchanged for their 'real value', their costs including a 'fair wage' for those who produced them but he then concluded, mistakenly, that any profit (that is, over and above costs) required some sort of theft (for where else could that 'surplus value' come from)…All trade, Aristotle believed was a kind of exploitation" (Solomon, 1999, p. 119).

It is not clear why Solomon interjected the adverb "mistakenly" in his exposition. The real question Aristotle was raising was, where does value come from? While economists today would criticize the concept of "real value," saying that value is simply determined by supply and demand, according to Solomon Aristotle's point is that value should be related to costs and labour, not market forces. The problem of leaving value at the mercy of "market forces" is that it will be determined inequitably (Allinson, 2004, pp. 17–28).

Value-based economics

The only way to accomplish Aristotle's goal in economics would be to introduce a value-based economics which, while not explicitly adopted by Aristotle, is consistent with his general outlook for human motivation. Human motivation, for Aristotle, should be guided by moral acts and just acts. Thus, action that produced goods and services that were for the good of all, and did not create disvalue, would fall within the general category of moral actions. Aristotle's ethics forms the foundation of a value-based economics.

To conclude: while Aristotle argues against the pursuit of wealth – unlike his master Plato who countenances it for the merchant class – wealth, that is, benefit that is enough to take care of one's physical needs, must come from somewhere. For Aristotle, it must come from plants and animals. It follows that the making of money, so long as it is a secondary aim and is limited to taking care of one's life needs, is not irrelevant as a life goal. Aristotle, as distint from Socrates, would not say that one could be happy in a prison. But, money making is perceived by Aristotle as a kind of necessary evil, not as a good in itself. Consider his comment: "The life of money-making is one undertaken under compulsion, and wealth is evidently not the good we are seeking; for it is merely useful and for the sake of something else" (*Nicomachean Ethics*, 1096a 5–7).

The main lesson is for society. A society that is geared toward moral development would be a different sort of society from a society that is geared towards GNP. The proper society is for Aristotle the only way in which ethics can be realized. Aristotle's views cannot be identified with the idea of producing GNH or gross national happiness. That would be to put the cart before the horse. Society is for the sake of providing a venue to perform noble actions. That is its entire point. Happiness is the result of that. If one puts happiness first, one might easily lose the point that happiness is only achieved through the performance of noble actions.

Character building is, for Aristotle, a means to an end. The end is not the development of one's individual character. The end is the performance of that character in society. Creating a moral character is a better way to ensure the production of moral action than simply to counsel humans to perform noble acts. That is why it is difficult to classify Aristotle as simply a deontologist (doing what is right), a utilitarian (doing what produces the consequence of the greatest happiness for society), or a virtue ethicist (building up moral virtues). In his scheme of things, it is only by being a deontologist that one can become a virtue ethicist. One recalls his famous saying, "One becomes just by performing just acts" (*Nicomachean Ethics,* 1105a 16–17). It is only in the performance of these acts that one achieves human happiness. Otherwise, one creates an unethical society of man pitted against man. Such a society, in turn, makes individual ethics difficult to practice.

Literature

Allinson, R.E. 2004. "Circles within a Circle: The Condition for the Possibility of Ethical Business Institutions within a Market System," *Journal of Business Ethics,* 53, pp. 17–28.

Barker, E. 1958. *The Politics of Aristotle.* London, Oxford, New York: Oxford University Press.

Solomon, R.C. 1999. "Historicism, Commutarianism and Commerce." In Peter Koslowski (ed.), *Contemporary Economic Ethics.* Berlin: Springer.

10
Indian Management Philosophy

Sanjoy Mukherjee

The immense diversity and complexity of the 5,000-year-old Indian tradition and culture make it almost impossible to identify one single and unilateral Indian philosophy. Moreover, the concepts developed in the different schools of Indian philosophical systems and the paths outlined often appear conflicting and in contention with each other. This makes the search through this maze of thoughts and ideas difficult and confusing indeed. Hence, in the context of the theme of Spirituality in Business, a few relevant sources of classical Indian literature have been chosen here that may be useful to modern management worldwide as it struggles through a time of turbulence, uncertainty, and crisis for a dawning of wisdom in the minds of business leaders. The texts chosen here include the *Upanishads*, a veritable treasure house of precious wisdom transmitted in the form of conversations between a teacher/master and a learner/disciple. This exploration may throw some light on the framework and the process of holistic learning for leadership development and the art of asking questions. Toward the end of this paper, a few insights will be shared on decision making and conflict resolution in the time of crisis, as offered in the celebrated Indian text *Srimat Bhagavadgita*, which is actually a case study of the applied wisdom of the *Upanishads* in a battlefield on the eve of the unfolding of a drama of death and annihilation. *Darshan*, the classical Indian (Sanskrit) word for philosophy, is all about seeing to start with. Such seeing is not just a matter of visual reception but organic perception. Thus the philosopher is also a "seer" of reality in its totality, a *Rishi*.

Message from an ancient Indian allegory

The *Upanishads*, 108 in number as recorded and available to us today, extol the glory of the perennial flow of human consciousness and its all-pervading nature and scope. Our consciousness has an infinite capacity to traverse the entire cosmic space and time. However, more often than not, it finds limited expression in our engagement with the affairs of our mundane, earthly existence. Even in the microdomain of our life world, while consciousness is more directly involved in the endless flurry of our activities, it also has the inherent capacity to withdraw into a reflective mode and become an observer of our own triumphs and tragedies. However, suffice it to say, both the "witnessing consciousness" and the "involved consciousness" are but two different expressions of the pure and unqualified Self-Consciousness that constitutes the essence of the "I," the core of our being.

The seer of the *Shwetashwatara Upanishad* portrays this dual nature of human consciousness pictorially, displaying a rare mastery of poetic imagination. The following is the simple, yet beautiful, imagery of two birds perched on a branch of the same tree as depicted by a modern Indian seer-poet: "Two winged birds cling about a common tree, comrades, yoke-fellows; and one eats the sweet fruit of the tree, the other eats not, but watches" (Sri Aurobindo, 1972, p. 370).

Like the branch of the tree, our pure Self-Consciousness provides the overarching backdrop for, and the connecting link between, these two apparently conflicting manifestations of our consciousness. But the two birds are in fact comrades who are deeply connected to each other and represent two complementary aspects of our nature that can actually coexist.

Toward shaping a comprehensive life world view

Upanishadic wisdom boldly presents to the world an all-embracing view of spirituality and advocates a harmonious pursuit of both the material and spiritual dimensions of our existence for a richer experience of work and life in fullness. *Ishopanishad*, the oldest available *Upanishad*, deals with this problem upfront, dispelling the myth of a "nonmaterial" notion of spirituality and offering a comprehensive practical resolution in two of its verses in close succession.

The ninth verse of this text (Swami Gambhirananda, 1958, p. 11) clearly pronounces that if we pursue material knowledge to the exclusion of spirit, our life will enter into darkness. The next line of this verse is even more articulate and challenging. It spells out, with no trace of ambiguity, that if we pursue spiritual wisdom to the exclusion of matter, our life will enter into deeper darkness. This may come as a shocking revelation to the uninformed proponents of an "other-worldly" spiritual pursuit. The same *Upanishad* also offers us a comprehensive resolution of this apparent conflict in verse 11. Here, the seer of the *Upanishad* states that if we pursue material knowledge and spiritual wisdom simultaneously, in a balanced manner, then a harmonious blend of these two pursuits will offer us the experience of fulfillment in life – individual as well as collective, personal as well as organizational.

A holistic framework of learning

The *Upanishads* constitute a vast body of literature where knowledge is transmitted in the mode of conversations. They can be compared to our modern classroom situation, where the presence and engagement of the teacher and the student create the context for knowledge dissemination and learning. Here we shall try to explore some of the pertinent leadership lessons embedded in the *Taittiriya Upanishad*, especially in the context of the content and methodology of imparting knowledge to the people within organizations.

From the *Taittiriya Upanishad* (Swami Gambhirananda, 1958, pp. 311–318) one can learn how to unfold a system view of life and the world to oneself and then to others. From the micro to the macro, from the self to the universe, there are five layers of our existence that have been progressively unveiled in this *Upanishad*. These layers have been depicted in the form of spherical sheaths or *koshas*, through which the consciousness of the learner must evolve to reach the all-encompassing experience of fullness of the self and the world.

The five layers or sheaths (*Pancha Kosha*) outlined in this *Upanishad* are as follows, along with their implications for organizations:

1. *Annamaya Kosha* (Sheath of Matter) – constitutes the gross body of the individual and the material universe. The physical layout of the organization comprising land, buildings, plants, and physical structures falls within the ambit of this layer.
2. *Pranamaya Kosha* (Vital Sheath) – constitutes the basic life-giving vital force of the individual, so important for survival and movement, and also the field of energy that flows in the natural universe for its sustenance. In the context of the organization, this refers to the buoyancy and dynamism, abundant flows of information, spirit of aggressive competition for survival, and so on.
3. *Manomaya Kosha* (Mental Sheath) – constitutes the mental world of the individual comprising choices and preferences, vibrations

of desires, thoughts and ideas that also expand to include the universe. A healthy and receptive employee mindset, emotional competence, and an amicable corporate culture are its organizational manifestations.

4. *Vijnanamaya Kosha* (Sheath of Wisdom) – marks the entry from the vast field of worldly knowledge to the pristine Knowledge of the Self and its natural, organic connection with the Universe and its subtle forces. Questions about the purpose of life and sustenance of the planet at large become critically important at this level. Vision, mission, values, self-actualization, and sustainability become organizational priorities at this layer of existence.

5. *Anandamaya Kosha* (Sheath of Bliss) – constitutes the subtlest layer of existence and finds expression in the experience of pure bliss amidst the dualities of joy and sorrow, happiness and misery, success and failure.

A comprehensive framework of inclusive knowledge and system learning covering all possible dimensions of our individual and collective existence have been elegantly portrayed in this *Upanishad.*

Lessons on the learning process

The following pertinent lessons on the process of learning are crystallized for organizational leaders in this ancient text:

1. A graded, incremental, and integral approach is essential for proper assimilation of knowledge. The sage in the *Upanishad* takes the student along all five stages so that the consciousness and knowledge of the recipient can evolve in a progressive manner.

2. There has to be an intrinsic respect for the acquired knowledge at all the five levels – from the grossest to the subtlest. To achieve this, the sage opens his deliberation on each stage by identifying every sheath (*anna, prana,* etc.) with the Highest Principle in the Universe or *Brahman,* the Ultimate Reality. This also safeguards against any feeling of arrogance or disdain toward learners at the preliminary stages by those who have progressed ahead of the others.

3. For a leader, there has to be not only an awareness of the entire spectrum of knowledge but sensitivity to the specific stage of learning of a particular recipient. Otherwise knowledge absorption will not be effective. Often one finds that inspiring messages on vision or values do not create an impact on the people in organizations, as most of

the members of the target audience may be in just the initial stages of the learning path.

4. Each layer has its own significant role to play in our learning path. Often we find the misplaced notion at work in our minds that the stages and experiences we have left behind are no longer important for us. It is as if material knowledge loses its priority amidst our concern for values or sustainability. Wisely enough, the sage, after completing his inputs on all the layers, warns the learner: "Don't despise matter," the first layer (*annam na nindat*).

5. The process of exploration at every stage has been called *tapas* or intense striving for perfection to reach the ultimate goal. What is more profound, at every stage this striving has been identified with Brahman, the Highest Principle. The path is as important as the destination. The following lines from the Nobel-laureate Indian poet Rabindranath Tagore make it succinct:

> My pilgrimage is not
> At the end of the road;
> My temples are all there
> on both sides of my pathway
> (Tagore, 1978, p. 214) [Translation by this author]

Insights from the Bhagavadgita

The celebrated text *Srimat Bhagavadgita* (commonly known as the *Gita*), which treasures the kernel of Upanishadic wisdom, is set in the background of a battlefield, Kurukshetra, where the haunting specter of a holocaust from genocidal action is waiting to unfold. This is the inevitable culmination of the great Indian epic, the *Mahabharata*.

What is the crisis posed in the *Gita*? In our journey through life, personal as well professional, we often face situations that present to us alternative courses of action. This results in ambivalence in our mind-space, whereby we find it difficult to arrive at a decision. The crisis in the *Gita* as described in its first chapter is a crisis of decision making. What is interesting to note is that when the valiant Arjuna makes his glorious entry into the battlefield of Kurukshetra, there is no crisis in the domain of his mind. Upon arriving, he asks his charioteer, the Blessed Lord (Sri Bhagavan), to place the chariot between the two columns of armies so that he can take a good look at the enemy lineup. Arjuna hardly realizes that by making this statement of confidence he is asking for trouble! The Blessed Lord uses his discretion and places the chariot in front of two stalwarts of the enemy camp – Bheeshma, the great-grandfather, and Drona, the revered teacher (of the art of arms and war) for all the brothers in the two opposing camps. Moreover, Arjuna is the dearest to them both among all the others. The fire and vigor of Arjuna begins to dim at the very sight of these venerable and beloved veterans. This leads to his physical as well as psychological collapse, to such an extent that he lays down his arms and declares to his charioteer that he will not fight.

Arjuna's crisis is commonly experienced by most of us in the battlefield of life. It is a conflict of values arising from directions and guidelines from two sets of human faculties – the rational and the emotional. In order to understand and relate to the world, the exercise of both these faculties is necessary. However, under the influence of the dominant emphasis on cognitive methods of learning, we often score rather low on emotional competence in our modern times. To add to this, there is a misconception that emotional problems can be adequately overcome by sharpening our intellectual acumen. Unfortunately this is far from truth! The crisis of the *Gita* serves well to dispel this myth at the very outset. When our emotional disposition is in conflict with the dictates of our reason, neither set of faculties helps us resolve the dilemma. So, where does one look for the answer to this problem?

The *Gita* provides us with a unique and profound principle of resolution in this regard. The root of the problem, according to the *Gita*, is not to be found in the battlefield of Kurukshetra but within the inner world of Arjuna. We are all Arjunas in the arena of life. Here the conflict is actually between "my reason," which directs me to fight, and "my emotion," which dissuades me from taking up arms against those near and dear. The cue to the resolution of this conflict, according to the *Gita*, lies in the common denominator "my," or more specifically and deeply, in the realm of the "I." The "I" or the Real Self of Arjuna, which is trapped and constricted in the spatiotemporal domain of Kurukshetra, must be liberated and experienced in its fullness and glory in order to come to terms with this dilemma. The purpose of this discourse is to bring the consciousness of Arjuna back to the center of his "I," which allows him to experience the full knowledge and potential of the "I" prior to engagement in action.

The *Gita* offers a three-tier, sequential methodology for the resolution of this conflict (Mukherjee, 2008, pp. 111–113). Each stage actually implies a progressive evolution of human consciousness into a superior level of knowledge. The ascent to enlightenment as enunciated in the *Gita* is essentially an adventure of human consciousness from the lower to the higher vistas of knowledge, from the grossest to the subtlest planes of existence. The three steps in this journey are as follows:

1. *Disengagement from the problem* – because with all my existing material and intellectual resources I am unable to cope with the crisis. The first six chapters of the Gita provide us with the necessary insights and details pertaining to this part of the evolution of our consciousness. The dominant theme running through these chapters is *Karma* or action, but action that is centripetal in its denouement, so that the individual can gain inner consolidation and repose.
2. *Engagement in Higher Wisdom* – through loving and emotive communion with a source of enlightened knowledge (Sri Bhagavan in the case of Arjuna) for comprehensive assimilation of this wisdom through intimate personal contact. Chapters 7 through 12 of the *Gita* chart the journey for this part of the ascent of consciousness, where *Bhakti* or devotion is the running theme.
3. *Re-engagement in the problem* – as the *Gita* does not recommend a cessation of this journey at the highest point of attainment of enlightened knowledge. The last six chapters (13 to 18) deal with the descent of human consciousness from the level of highest wisdom to the specific context of the problem in question, in order that the attained wisdom can be translated into the requisite action through a process of re-engagement, but with an enlightened perspective. *Jnana*, or specialized knowledge, which emanates from illumined wisdom but is applied in the immediate context of action, becomes the running theme of this last phase of evolution.

Death as a great learning experience

The pathway to wisdom is usually blocked by our one-dimensional perception of life as a series of desirable outcomes. The limitation of our linear thinking is starkly revealed when we confront the phenomenon of death. Our plans and predictions come to naught when we are faced with the reality of death. The irony of human life is that even though we are aware of the inevitability of death, the uncertainty of the space, time, and context of its advent keeps away from our consciousness the certainty of its presence. One serious lacuna in our present system of imparting knowledge is the almost complete lack of understanding and mastery of the problem of death. Our understanding of the purpose of life can never be complete if we fail to internalize and appreciate the constant and dynamic interplay of life and death in the existential drama. Hence we find the stereotypes of business leadership obsessed with success and profits, along with a skewed notion of progress and development. With the dawning of wisdom one learns to interpret death beyond its physical connotation and expand it to include death of ideas, institutions, models, and relationships. It empowers us with the courage and spirit of adventure to embrace the new and the unknown.

Literature

Mukherjee, S. 2008. "Igniting Spirit in Business: Indian Insights." In Laszlo Zsolnai (ed.), *Europe-Asia Dialogue on Business Spirituality*. Antwerp: Garant Publishers.

Rolland, R. 1975. *The Life of Vivekananda and the Universal Gospel*. Kolkata: Advaita Ashrama.

Tagore, R. 1978. *Rabindra-Rachanabali*, Vol. 7, Kolkata: Viswa Bharati.

Sister Nivedita. 1962. *The Master as I Saw Him*. Kolkata: Udbodhan Office.

Sri Aurobindo. 1972. *The Upanishads*. Pondicherry: Sri Aurobindo Ashram Trust.

Swami Gambhirananda. 1958. *Eight Upanishads with the Commentary of Sri Sankaracharya*, Vol.1, Kolkata: Advaita Ashrama.

11
Buddhist Economics

Laszlo Zsolnai

Buddhist economics is a major alternative to the Western economic mindset. It challenges the basic principles of modern Western economics, namely profit-maximization, cultivating desire, introducing markets, instrumental use of the world, and self-interest-based ethics. Buddhist economics proposes alternative principles such as minimizing suffering, simplifying desire, nonviolence, genuine care, and generosity. Buddhist economics is not a system but a strategy that can be applied in any economic setting.

No-self

Thomas Schelling characterized modern Western economics as an "egonomical framework." Modern Western economics is centered on self-interest, understood as satisfaction of the wishes of one's body-mind ego. Buddhism challenges this view because it has a different conception of the self, which is *anatta*, the "no-self" (Elster, 1985).

Anatta specifies the absence of a supposedly permanent and unchanging self in any of the psychophysical constituents of empirical existence. What is normally thought of as the "self" is an agglomeration of constantly changing physical and mental constituents, which gives rise to unhappiness if clung to as though this temporary assemblage represented permanence. The *anatta* doctrine attempts to encourage Buddhist practitioners to detach themselves from the misplaced clinging to what is mistakenly regarded as self, and from such detachment (aided by moral living and meditation) the way to *Nirvana* can be successfully traversed (Figure 11.1)

Modern neuroscience supports the Buddhist view of the self. What neuroscientists have discovered can be called the self-less (or virtual)

Figure 11.1   Buddhist symbol of no-self

self, "a coherent global pattern, which seems to be centrally located, but is nowhere to be found, and yet is essential as a level of interaction for the behavior." The nonlocalizable, nonsubstantial self acts as if it were present, like a virtual interface (Varela, 1999).

The Buddhist cosmology has the entire universe at its center in contrast to the anthropocentric worldview of Western culture. For Buddhists, human beings are humble in the totality and are essentially just grains of sand in the vast, limitless ocean of space (Welford, 2006).

The Four Noble Truths of the Buddha address the dynamics of human life:

1. Life is suffering. This has to be comprehended. With the increasing secularism and dissociation from nature and the environment, and rising expectations inside and outside work, people are becoming less satisfied with life and lifestyles.
2. The cause of suffering is desire. This has to be abandoned. Heightened dissatisfaction arguably has implications for consumerism. First, there is an erroneous perception that purchasing goods will make us happy; and second, we are increasingly dissatisfied, and thus unhappy or stressed, because we are unable to deal with what is needed to change.
3. The cessation of suffering is the cessation of desire. This has to be realized. By becoming aware that there is a root to the general, societal malaise and avoidance of environmental and social responsibilities,

we can understand that there is a way of stopping such complacency and beginning on a path to sustainability.

4. The path to the cessation of desire requires practice. To cease doing what makes us dissatisfied, we have to realize the result of that dissatisfaction and keep trying to behave in a more sustainable manner. Buddhism shows us that this is difficult and requires ongoing commitment and practice.

Even if one gets what one desires, greater desires always emerge. The ego mindset cannot be fulfilled and its greed for more satisfaction and recognition becomes the source of its own destruction. This is a source of suffering, because the human spirit becomes captured by the avaricious mind. The way through this life of constantly unsatisfied desires is the practice of nonattachment – in other words, developing a distance from all desires (Welford, 2006).

Theory

British economist E.F. Schumacher (1911–1977) was the first to develop a Buddhist economics. He argued that the best pattern of consumption is to reach a high level of satisfaction by a low rate of material consumption. This allows people to fulfill the primary injunction of Buddhism: "Cease to do evil; try to do good." As natural resources are limited everywhere, people living simple lifestyles are less likely to be at each other's throats than those dependent on scarce natural resources.

According to Schumacher's Buddhist economics, production using local resources for local needs is the most rational way of organizing economic life. Economies should be based on renewable resources as much as possible. Nonrenewable resources must be used only if they are indispensable, and then only with the greatest care and concern for conservation. Schumacher states that Buddhist economics represents a *middle way* between modern economic growth and traditional economic stagnation. It seeks an appropriate form of development, the "right livelihood" for people.

Thai Buddhist monk Venerable P.A. Payutto (1939–) developed his own conception of Buddhist economics. He suggests differentiating between two kinds of *desire*. One is "tanha" and the other is "chanda." Tanha is directed toward feeling; it leads to seeking objects that pander to self-interest, and is supported and nourished by ignorance. Chanda is directed toward true well-being; it leads to effort and is founded on intelligent reflection. By training we can live less and less by the directives of ignorance and tanha, and more under the guidance of wisdom and chanda. Economic activity should be a means to a good and noble life.

At the heart of Buddhist economics is the wisdom of moderation. In Western economics unlimited desire is controlled by scarcity, but in Buddhist economics it is controlled by an appreciation of moderation and the aim of well-being. Whenever we use things we can take the time to reflect on their true purpose, rather than using them heedlessly. In this way we can avoid overconsumption and understand the middle way.

Nonconsumption can contribute to well-being. Buddhist monks eat only one meal a day and strive for a kind of well-being that is dependent on little. Buddhist economics recognizes that certain demands can be satisfied through nonconsumption. The path to true contentment involves reducing the artificial desire for sense-pleasure, while encouraging and supporting the desire for *quality of life*. Buddhist economics judges the ethical value of wealth by the way in which it is obtained and the uses to which it is put. Harmful actions associated with wealth can appear in three forms: seeking wealth in dishonest or unethical ways; hoarding wealth for its own sake; and using wealth in ways that are harmful. Buddhist economics aims at the realization of true well-being by activities that neither harm oneself nor others.

Principles

While modern Western economics promotes doing business based on individual, self-interested, profit-maximizing ways, Buddhist economics aims at minimizing suffering of all sentient beings, including nonhuman beings. In Buddhist economics a project is worthy to be undertaken if it can reduce the suffering of all beings who are affected. Also, any change in economic-activity systems that reduces suffering should be welcomed.

Modern Western economics cultivates desire. People are encouraged to develop new desire for things to acquire and for activities to do. The profit motive of companies requires creating more demand. But psychological research shows that *materialistic value orientation* undermines well-being. Psychologists call the mechanism through which people seek to satisfy their desires "auto-projection." It is a *loser strategy*, whether or not people achieve their desired goals. When they fail to reach the goals they envision, they attribute their continuing dissatisfaction to that failure. When they succeed in attaining their goals, this usually does not bring about what they hoped for and their feelings of discomfort are not relieved. So striving to satisfy desires never brings people the fulfillment they expect from it (Grof, 1998).

Buddhist economics aims not to multiply but to *simplify our desires*. Above the minimum material comfort, which includes enough food, clothing, shelter, and medicine, it is wise to try to reduce one's desires. Wanting less can bring substantial benefits for the person, for the community, and for nature. Buddhist economics recommends moderate consumption and is directly aimed at changing one's preferences through meditation, reflection, analysis, autosuggestion and the like (Kolm, 1985).

Modern Western economics aims to introduce markets wherever social problems need solving. Karl Polanyi refers to the process of marketization as "The Great Transformation", by which spheres of society became subordinated to the market mechanism (Polanyi, 1946). In the age of *globalization* we can experience this marketization process on a much larger scale and in a speedier way than ever.

The main guiding principle of Buddhist economics for solving social problems is *nonviolence* ("ahimsa"). It requires that an act does not cause harm to the doer or the receivers. Nonviolence forbids actions that directly cause suffering for oneself or others and urges participative solutions.

In modern Western economics the value of an entity (be it human being, other sentient being, object, or anything else) is determined by its marginal contribution to the production output. A project is considered worthy of undertaking if and only if its discounted cash flow is positive. Buddhist economics proposes abandoning this kind of calculative thinking. It urges taking genuine *care* of all the beings affected by one's actions. Caring organizations are rewarded for the higher costs of their socially responsible behavior by their ability to form commitments among owners, managers, and employees and to establish trust relationships with customers and subcontractors.

The basic problem with the instrumental approach is that it generates the worst response from the beings involved. To get the best from the partners requires taking genuine care in their existence.

Robert Frank developed five distinct types of ways in which socially responsible organizations are rewarded for the higher cost of caring: (1)opportunistic behavior can be avoided between owners and managers; (2) in getting moral satisfaction, employees are ready to work more for lower salaries; (3) high-quality new employees can be recruited; (4) customers' loyalty can be gained; (5) the trust of subcontractors can be established (Frank, 2004).

In modern Western economics there is little room for ethics. The Western economic man is allowed to consider the interest of others only if it serves his or her own interest. This self-interest-based, opportunistic approach often fails. Buddhist economics encourages *generosity* in business and social life. It usually works because people tend to reciprocate what they get and often they give back more in value than what the giver originally gave to them.

Ernst Fehr and Simon Gaechter designed a gift exchange game in which the employer makes a wage offer with a stipulated desired level of effort from the worker. The worker may then choose an effort level, which costs to him or her rising with effort. The employer may fine the worker if his or her effort level is thought to be inadequate. The surplus from the interaction is the employer's profits and the worker's wage minus the cost of effort (and the fine, where applicable). The self-regarding worker would choose the minimum feasible level of effort, and, anticipating this, the self-regarding employer would offer the minimum wage. But experimental subjects did not conform to this expectation. Employers made generous offers and workers' effort levels were strongly conditioned on these offers. High wages were reciprocated by high levels of effort (Bowles, 2004).

Not a system but a strategy

Buddhist economics represents a minimizing framework where suffering, desire, violence, instrumental use, and self-interest have to be minimized. The saying "less is more" nicely expresses the essence of Buddhist economics. Modern Western economics represents a maximizing framework. It wants to maximize profit, desire, markets, instrumental use, and self-interest and tends to build a world where "more is more" (Table 11.1).

Buddhist economics represents a strategy that can be applied in any economic setting. It helps to create *livelihood solutions* that reduce the

Table 11.1   Modern Western economics versus Buddhist economics

Modern Western economics	Buddhist economics
maximize profit	minimize suffering
maximize desire	minimize desire
maximize markets	minimize violence
maximize instrumental use	minimize instrumental use
maximize self-interest	minimize self-interest
"more is more"	"less is more"

suffering of sentient beings through practicing want negation, non-violence, caring, and generosity.

Modern Western economics cultivates narrow self-centeredness. Buddhist economics points out that emphasizing individuality and promoting the greatest fulfillment of the desires of the individual conjointly lead to destruction. Contemporary research on *happiness* shows that not material wealth but the richness of personal relationships determines a happy life. Western economics tries to make people happy by supplying enormous quantities of things and services. But what people need are caring relationships and generous love. Buddhist economics makes these values accessible by direct provision. Wanting less and living in a nonviolent way can substantially contribute to *peace*. Permanence, or *ecological sustainability*, requires a considerable reduction in the present level of consumption and production. This reduction should not be an inconvenient exercise of self-sacrifice. In the noble ethos of reducing suffering it can be a positive development path for humanity.

Literature

Bowles, S. 2004. *Microeconomics. Behavior, Institutions, and Evolution.* New York: Russell Sage Foundation, and Princeton and Oxford: Princeton University Press.

Elster, J. 1985. "Introduction." In Jon Elster (ed.), *The Multiple Self,* pp. 1–34. Cambridge: Cambridge University Press.

Frank, R. 2004. "Can Socially Responsible Firms Survive in Competitive Environments?" In Robert Frank, *What Price the Moral High Ground? Ethical Dilemmas in Competitive Environments.* Princeton and Oxford: Princeton University Press.

Grof, S. 1998. *The Cosmic Game. Explorations of the Frontiers of Human Consciousness.* Albany: State University of New York Press.

Kolm, S-C. 1985. "The Buddhist Theory of 'No-Self'." In Jon Elster (ed.), *The Multiple Self,* pp. 233–265. Cambridge: Cambridge University Press.

Payutto, P.A. 1994. *Buddhist Economics. A Middle Way for the Market Place.* http://www.geocities.com/Athens/Academy/9280/payutto.htm

Polanyi, K. 1946. *The Great Transformation. Origins of Our Time.* London: Victor Gollancz Ltd.

Schumacher, E.F. 1973. *Small is Beautiful. Economics as if People Mattered.* Abacus. London.

Varela, F. J. 1999. *Ethical Know-How. Action, Wisdom, and Cognition.* Stanford: Stanford University Press,

Welford, R. 2006. "Tackling Greed and Achieving Sustainable Development." In Laszlo Zsolnai   and Knut J. Ims (eds), *Business within Limits: Deep Ecology and Buddhist Economics,* pp. 25–52. Oxford: Peter Lang.

12
Confucianism and Taoism

Robert Allinson

Confucius' ideas on economics are few, but through his ethics one may attain an idea of what kind of economics he would have found acceptable. Confucius' ethics are based upon the natural goodness of human nature. In his mind, human beings are naturally kind to one another. One does not really need the Christian concept of benevolence for Confucius, because benevolence implies that one is going a step beyond what one would ordinarily do. The meaning of benevolence is to be greater than oneself, greater than the normal. For Confucius, kindness is intrinsic to human nature. His is the idea of natural kindness.

One way in which Confucius teaches that one can reach one's natural kindness is through the application of his version of the Golden Rule, which is a proscriptive version: "Do not unto others what you would not have them do unto you." From this maxim, which Confucius indicates is his central ethical principle, one can deduce his views on economics. One would not like oneself to be taken advantage of by others; hence, one would not endeavor to disadvantage others. Since profit over someone else implies that that someone else would suffer a loss, Confucius would not be in favor of an economic system that endorsed or encouraged a maximization of profits. While Confucius does not directly say this, he does say that a gentleman, by which he means not so much a member of the gentry as a noble-minded person, is not ashamed of poor food and poor clothes (*Analects* IV, 9). While he does say that there is nothing wrong with wealth achieved by proper means (*Analects* IV, 5), in the same breath he says there is also nothing wrong with poverty that is obtained by proper means. His emphasis is on what is moral, not on what is profitable. This is clear in *Analects* IV, 10. There are many passages that demonstrate that Confucius valued right action and not material gain (*Analects* XIV, 1; XV, 32). There are also passages that indicate that Confucius valued the simple life (*Analects* VII, 16; VII, 36).

Indeed, Confucius states that only small-minded people pursue profit. He also teaches that if there is an option between a moral choice and making profit, one should always take the moral choice (*Analects* IV, 16).

Confucius is also famous for saying that man's nature (which is to be kind), is always right at hand. One need only to think on it and one will be at one with it. From this standpoint, if one's mind is focused on making profits, one would move further and further from one's nature. Since profit means taking advantage of others, one would move one's character further and further away from one's own nature. Confucius' notion of life is that one of its main purposes is moral growth and moral development. If a life is devoted to making profit, it could not be devoted to the achievement of this kind of moral growth.

In certain ways, Confucius resembles Socrates. A famous saying of Confucius' is "In the eating of coarse rice and the drinking of water, the using of one's elbow for a pillow, joy is to be found. Wealth and rank attained through immoral means have as much to do with me as passing clouds" (*Analects* VII, 16). From this statement we may deduce that Confucius would recommend a minimalist approach to making profits. His approach would, like Socrates', be one in which economic activity was geared to making enough money to earn a modest living.

His teaching differs from Socrates' in one regard. Socrates states that it is better to suffer evil than to commit evil. For Confucius, if evil is committed against one, one should not accept it. One should, in his words, return evil with straightness, that is, with appropriate action.

Mencius, whose views also represent Confucianism, is famous for his example of the compassion that all human beings would feel if they were to observe a child about to fall into a well. This idea is that all human beings (who deserve the label of human beings) will feel compassion over someone's suffering. It would follow from this that one would not pursue profits if one were aware that this pursuit caused suffering to others.

While much has been written to explain the economic growth of Chinese countries by referring to Confucianism, it is difficult to find evidence from the texts to justify this inference. One could for example, as Max Weber did, deduce from Calvinism that Protestantism was a boost to capitalism since in its Calvinist version, one took profit to be a sign that one had been favored by the Deity. There is no such parallel in

Confucianism. To argue that Confucianism is responsible for the economic growth of China and the Far East would be equivalent to saying that Christianity, with its point of view that the poor are blessed and the meek shall inherit the earth, is responsible for the economic growth of the West. The economic growth of the East and the Christian West seems, if anything, to demonstrate the lack of influence of classical religion or philosophy on economic behavior. In 1989, when I was asked on public radio in Hong Kong, what the Tianamin Massacre demonstrated about Chinese philosophy, I answered: "It showed the absence of Chinese philosophy." I think that the influence of philosophy on economic behavior has been greatly exaggerated.

Philosophers such as Socrates and Confucius raised critiques of social behavior but were not responsible for mass behavior. Consider Confucius' saying: "Cunning words, an ingratiating countenance...I, too, find them shameful. To be friendly towards someone while concealing a sense of grievance...I, too, find it shameful" (*Analects*, V, 25). Was he not observing contemporary social behavior to make a comment like this?

While it is true that Confucius also spoke about observing certain rites, and was a proponent of filial piety, one must separate these ideas from his central philosophical principles. When he was asked what his central ethical principle was, he did not answer "filial piety." He answered "Do not do onto others what you would not have them do onto you" (Allinson, 1985).

With regard to Taoism, taking into account the philosophies of Laoji and Zhuangzi, the situation is more complex. On the one hand, one can certainly point to statements on the part of both philosophers that embrace the idea of the simple, and hence of the modest, economic life. Laoji's famous portrait of the peaceful village is a case in point. Laoji does not rave about palaces, jade, and pearls. His depiction of a happy community is one in which one looks over in peace at one's neighbor (*Tao de Jing* chapter 80).

Zhuangzi's statements are of like kind. He has praise for the simple life of carpenters. He even extols the useless, which would seem to be the opposite of extolling what is useful, or profitable. Zhuangzi also extols the value of a harmonious society, and it is difficult to create social harmony through the kind of fierce competition and the kinds of resulting inequalities that are characteristic of capitalism (*Zhuangzi* chapter 2).

The concept of harmony is a key concept in Chinese philosophy and extends to the notion of human beings in harmony with nature and with heaven (Allinson, 1998). It would be difficult to imagine a philosophy such as existentialism arising in China, whereby man is perceived as being thrown into a world in which he is an alien intruder (Allinson, 2000). The concept of moral, psychological, aesthetic, and metaphysical harmony is illustrated by Chinese paintings that show human beings in harmony with nature. It would be difficult to find a Chinese painting showing a ship struggling against rough seas as in a painting by Joseph Turner. The concept of harmony, however, can be easily utilized by political rulers to encourage passive obedience or acceptance on the part of citizens.

There is a way in which Taoism can be perceived to be an ally of economic growth, and that is in the case of Japan. Japanese entrepreneurs are famous for their ability to take products made by other countries and improve upon them. Japanese cars are perhaps the most visible evidence of this, but one can find no end of examples: televisions, cameras, electronic goods of all kinds and varieties. It is difficult to find an example of a product that the Japanese have not improved upon. One can also point to the remarkable recovery of the Japanese economy after its severe loss in the Second World War. What does Taoism have to do with the economic success of Japan?

Taoism emphasizes that one should not be burdened by hardened points of view. In the *Zhuangzi*, in the famous chapter about the cackling goose, knowing the point of view of Zhuangzi, who favors silence over speech, when it comes to the case of which goose to cook Zhuangzi favors killing the silent goose. This seems directly opposed to everything that he has been teaching. His answer to this paradox is that silence, in the case of geese, is unnatural. One should always follow what is natural. In Zhuangzi, there is no set of rules to follow. One must be free to innovate; one must be free to adapt to a situation. Flexibility is the key. There is also the famous story in chapter one of the *Zhuangzi* where it is pointed out that the person who could not figure out what to do with large gourds and broke them into pieces is criticized for not being innovative. Why did he not think of using them in their entirety to make a boat, for example?

One can also consider the example of the extolling of nothingness, both in Laoji and Zhuangzi, as possibly influencing the creativity of Japanese design. While the Japanese are primarily known as improvers, in some cases, as in the case of the Sony Walkman, they were the innovators. Could it be that the notion of nothingness, much praised in Laoji in particular, might be conducive to thinking of the idea of making something very small, that is, next to nothing?

But, let us return to idea of harmony, an idea which is embraced by both Laoji and Zhuangzi. In Laoji's case, harmony is depicted in the illustration of the small, peaceful village (*Tao de Jing* chapter 80). In Zhuangzi's case, harmony is depicted as made up of many individual-istic inputs or, if you like, distinct and individualistic voices (*Zhuangzi* chapter 2). Such a depiction is very compatible with capitalism and an element of competition since there is a suggestion in Zhuangzi's illus-tration that distinctive voices can blend together to make a harmony (*Zhuangzi* chapter 2).

The case of Confucianism is clear. It is difficult, if not impossible, to see a linkage between Confucianism and the pursuit of profit. They do appear to be at opposite ends. It was ironic that Confucianism came into ill repute during the Chinese Cultural Revolution. It was thought that Confucianism stood for class division and the primacy of the family.

It was a misunderstanding of Confucianism to connect it to social classes. It is possible that this misunderstanding arose from Confucius' frequent honorific references to the noble-minded person as opposed to his pejorative references to the petty-minded person. The idea of the noble mind, as commended by Confucius, was taken to refer to the social class of gentility or nobility. While there may well have been some overlap here in the mind of Confucius in that education that should teach manners is normally affordable only by those of certain social classes,nonetheless since he also strongly advocated humility it is clear that by a gentle person or a gentleman he did not mean someone of noble birth – he was thinking of the cultivated person.

As for the primacy of the family, while Confucius did strongly advo-cate filial piety and related family values, at the same time if one takes into account works written by his grandson, such as the *Great Learning,* into account family values are plainly described as the forerunners of loyalty to the state. Confucius could have been used to support the Cultural Revolution, though his emphasis on learning and studying the classics would not have been acceptable.

It is interesting that, now that the People's Republic of China has adopted a very robust capitalism (albeit without any accompany-ing democracy), Confucianism is being encouraged. What kind of Confucianism this is, is another story. Most likely, it is a version of Confucianism that values obedience to the state. It is this bowdlerized version of Confucianism that had been so well utilized by Chinese emperors to strengthen their rule throughout Chinese history.

Current Chinese capitalism is carried out with the idea that Western capitalism is that of the robber barons of the nineteenth century. It is this style of capitalism that is emulated. During the Cultural Revolution, capitalism was taught to be a system that nourished itself on the blood of the peasants. Now that the Cultural Revolution has passed and capitalism has been installed, this is the idea of capitalism that is considered as the proper understanding of capitalism.

Taoism, with its emphasis on freedom of mind and its encouragement of creativity, can be linked to the successful entrepreneurship of Japan. Taoism is more influential in Japan than it is in China. On the other hand, it can also be said that Taoism, with its emphasis on a spiritual rather than a materialistic life, would act as a brake against unbridled capitalism. Could it be that some features of the Japanese economy, such as the limitation in large corporations of the salary of the CEO to eight times the maximum of the lowest paid worker, be due to a sense of wanting to retain some sense of social harmony? Taoism might work in both ways in Japan: to support entrepreneurship (that leads to profit making) and to encourage the simple life and to value social harmony (two values that would tend to reduce the tendency to *maximize* profit or to *value* profit above all else).

When one considers Japanese aesthetics, for example, one is struck by the simplicity, even starkness, of Japanese design. The Japanese rock garden at Ryoanji, for example, is a marvelous example of this. While one might argue that this is Zen, one must also at the same time realize that Zen is a child of Taoism.

To be fair, Taoism contributes more to the creative entrepreneurship of Japan than to any motivation toward profit making. Profit making may be a natural result of creative entrepreneurship, but there is no inherent connection between Taoism and profit seeking. If anything, there is a disconnection, since Taoism directs one toward the attainment of spiritual values, not materialistic ones.

Since Confucianism directs one to the attainment of moral values rather than materialistic values, one might wonder why there is no correlative checkpoint on materialistic ambitions and practices in China. One part of the answer is that the spirit of Taoism had altogether a stronger influence in Japan than Confucianism had in China, because the kind of Confucianism taught in China was of the bowdlerized variety. Taoism, with its emphasis on spiritual, artistic, and literary expression, created more avenues to transcend materialistic preoccupations. When one looks at Japanese culture, Japanese architecture, and Japanese poetry, one realizes that one is looking at Tang dynasty China, transplanted to Japan. While China proceeded to go from there to develop according to different influences, Japanese culture was frozen at Tang dynasty.

Another part of the answer is that Japanese culture is also subject to influences from Buddhism and Shinto, both of which temper materialistic ambitions and desires. For China, apart from the Tang dynasty, influenced in the main by a bowdlerized Confucianism and Legalism, it was easier to escape the influence of philosophical restraint.

With respect to Hong Kong, where I lived and worked for over a quarter of a century, one could say that an economic model flourished that possessed both Eastern and Western influences. While difficult to ferret out Confucian and Taoist influences, it is interesting to speculate that the laissez-faire system of capitalism that prompted the late distinguished economist Milton Friedman (in a speech, upon his visit to Hong Kong at The Chinese University of Hong Kong, at which I was present) to assert that Hong Kong represented a model of his economic theory. What Friedman did not recognize was that the government did play an active role in economics, by being a business partner with private enterprise, for example, an investor in the MTR, the mass transit system. But what was true about what he said was that Hong Kong was in a way an excellent example of Laszlo Zsolnai's concept of a Taoist economic system, in that there seemed to be an effort to find a harmony between self-interest and public interest (Zsolnai, 2002). For example, individual and business income tax was kept extremely low, but not graduated (approximately 15–16% for individual income tax and only slightly higher for corporations). This approach advantaged private interests. At the same time, government entered into the private sector and purchased stock at times when such action was necessary. This approach shows concern for the public sector. Concern for the public sector is also shown by the government providing for a complete system of socialized medicine for all people. At the same time, provident funds and social security funds are either nominal or nonexistent, illustrating perhaps the influence of Confucianism wherein the elders of the family will be taken care of by their families. With Confucianism added to the mixture (and a British-inspired legal system thrown in for good measure), Hong Kong represents Laszlo Zsolnai's apt description of the Taoist ideal: "Taoist social policy aims at the elimination of artificial inequalities among people but does not try to eliminate natural inequalities altogether" (Zsolnai, 2002). The minimal taxation system does create the potential for great inequalities and massive acquisition of wealth on the part of some individuals (it is amazing to take note of the number of billionaires cited in a recent issue of Forbes magazine that come from the seven million people in Hong Kong – a percentage way out of proportion to its population). On the other hand, with socialized medicine and a minimal taxation system, the public sector is also taken into account. With all the current furor over health insurance in America and the worries that a government-provided healthcare system will be too draining on the economy, more attention should be paid to Hong Kong where socialized medicine is available free of charge to the public alongside private medical care available to those who can afford it. Of course, the quality of the socialized medical care is also a product of an education system that is of a very high quality and not a mass education system. In addition, since social welfare is nominal, the costs of social security are eliminated. This in turn requires the Confucian value of caring for one's elder parents. In this indirect way, it could be said that Confucianism is a contributor to the economic productivity of Hong Kong. However, its contribution is from its ethical values, not from endorsement of profit seeking.

Literature

Allinson, R.E. 1985. "The Negative Formulation of the Golden Rule in Confucius." *Journal of Chinese Philosophy*, Vol. 12, no. 3, September.

Allinson, R.E. 1998. "Complementarity as a Model for East-West Integrative Philosophy." *Journal of Chinese Philosophy*, Vol. 25, no. 4, pp. 505–517.

Allinson, R.E. 2000. "An Overview of the Chinese Mind." In Robert Elliott Allinson (ed.), *Understanding the Chinese Mind*. Oxford: Oxford University Press.

Zsolnai, L. 2002. "Future of Capitalism." In Laszlo Zsolnai (ed.), *Ethics in the Economy – Handbook of Business Ethics*, pp.295–308. Oxford, Bern and Berlin: Peter Lang..

13
Budo Philosophy

Henk Oosterling

Budo philosophy classifies a coherent set of views that has been developed over a period of approximately 400 years as the discursive matrix of the teachings of Japanese martial arts. As a lifestyle it is known as the way (*do*) of the warrior (*bu*). The exponentially growing power of the Japanese economy in the 1980s raised questions about the specific role of this martial tradition with its psychology of alertness, determination, endurance, and loyalty. It was thought to be one of the keys to the overwhelming success of Japanese corporations. As a result a vast number of books were published trying to explain the relation between so-called *samurai* mentality and business.

Main sources

After the philosophically inspired bestsellers of Robert Pirsig (*Zen and the Art of Motorcycle Maintenance*, 1974) and Fritjof Capra (*The Tao of Physics*, 1975), many books were published using identical openings: "Tao of ..." and "Zen and ...". The first wave focused on being successful in corporative entrepreneurship. In the nineties the emphasis shifted to management. Leadership is the most recent field of interest. On the content level the attention shifts from strategic and tactical matters, such as how to plan and run your business, to mental and even spiritual aspects: what kind of mentality guarantees efficient and decisive leadership and management?

The first perspective mainly refers to *The Art of War*, imputed to the Chinese general Sun Tzu who led the Chinese forces to victory around 500 BC by emphasizing strategy and tactics. The latter perspective, focusing on the lord–retainer relationship and the spiritual aspects of an individual ethos, frequently uses Japanese sources: Miyamoto Musashi's

Go Rin no Sho (The Book of the Five Rings, 1645[1982]) and Yamamoto Tsunetomo's *Hagakure* (Hidden in Leaves, 1709–1716[2001]). Tao and Zen are contextualized as the mindset of budo, mixed with indigenous animistic Shinto – the way (*to*) of the Gods (*shin*) – and bureaucratic Confucianism.

Short history

Next to Shinto and Confucianism, Buddhism became one of the main religious systems that determined the mindset of the Japanese people. Rooted in Mahayana Buddhism, Chan Buddhism gained importance and power in China during the seventh century. After its introduction in Japan, Zen Buddhism's influence grew in the twelfth century. Crucial for Zen is the emphasis on experiential learning through austere meditation in order to attain enlightenment (*satori*).

Budo gained momentum during the Tokugawa reign after 1600, when this clan ended a long warfare period of domestic struggles between competing warlords. The power of the emperor was formally acknowledged, but actual power was bestowed on the commander of the forces, the *Shogun*. The Tokugawa Shogunate was installed and Japan was closed off from the rest of the world. Only a small trading post of the Dutch on the artificial island of Deshima, in the harbor of Nagasaki, was allowed.

It is not in Shinto-based sumo wrestling that budo has its roots, but in sword (*ken*) fighting (*jutsu*). Later, the pacification warrior (*bu*) knights (*shi*) or *samurai* (he who waits upon or accompanies, i.e., an attendant) had to discard their warlike lifestyle in which survival of the clan and unconditional loyalty to their warlord was imperative. Trained to face death equanimously, bushi conceived both life (*sho*) and death (*ji*) as sheer appearance. "In the martial arts there is no time to wait.…One has to live in an instant. It is exactly there that the decision of life and death falls" (Deshimura, 1977). The most radical gesture of this "actuality" is ceremonial suicide – *seppuku* or the cutting (*kiri*) of the stomach (*hara*) – which settles conflicting interests, effacing shame inflicted on one's ancestors and descendants.

Zen in action

In a sense bushido, as "the way of the samurai," is an ideological reconstruction (Faure, 2009, p. 81). This practice flourished from 1600 until 1853, when Japan was forced by the USA to open its markets to Western trade. In 1867 the power of the emperor was reinstalled within a modern nation-state infrastructure. The Japanese martial-arts tradition – bujutsu – was transformed into modern budo. Thereafter Japan modernized exponentially, nourishing its exclusiveness by expanding the idea of a Greater Japan (Dai Nippon) in Asia. As a result budo – like Zen – was identified with the military ruling class that led Japan to war. After the war the practice of budo was forbidden, but actually only for a short period. In the fifties Zen was introduced to a broader audience worldwide (Suzuki, 1970[1959]), while Japanese experts swarmed all over the world to teach their specific martial styles. Budo was reintroduced in school curricula, and Western practitioners of budo (budo ka) started to record and research martial arts (Draeger, 1973–1975; Ratti and Westbrook, 1973).

Next to techniques (*waza*) and basic forms (*kata*), budoka explicitly cultivate a meditative posture, orientated on "killing" the selfish desires of the ego. In this way Zen Buddhism, with its austere determination, intuitive knowledge, selfless action, and contempt of death turned the handling of weapons (*jutsu*) into a new *way* of life, that is, a *do*. In contrast to the contemplative meditation of the sitting (*za*) Zen, budo is called Zen in action.

As well as the sword the handling of other weaponry like bows (*kyu*), spears (*naginata*), and staffs (*bo*) underwent this mental transformation. Okinawa-based schools (*ryu*) handled farm tools, like the short flail to crush rice or soybeans (*nunchaku*), the wooden handle of a millstone (*tonfa*), the sickle (*kama*), and even bare (*kara*) hands (*te*). These esoteric schools were rooted in a farmer-fighter tradition that forged farm tools into lethal weapons to resist the Japanese occupation of the island. In the late nineteenth century this overall transformation process culminated in the creation of composite styles like Jigoro Kano's judo – the "soft" (*ju*) way (*do*) that grew out of jujutsu – and Morihei Ueshiba's aikido – the way (*do*) of harmonizing (*ai*) energy (*ki*). After the Second World War a dissemination of all sorts of karate styles with Chinese, Korean, and Thai elements followed.

Basic concepts

It is hard to formulate a budo doctrine, because as in Zen, theoretical knowledge is considered inferior to the experiential, intuitive grasping of the truth: "Zen has no special doctrine or philosophy, no set of concepts or intellectual formulas, except that it tries to release one from the bondage of birth and death by means of certain intuitive modes of understanding peculiar to itself" (Suzuki, 1970[1959], p. 63). Different disciplines and schools developed their own styles. These were transmitted from master to student, based on the principle of shuhari: obey and protect (shu) the basics of the school, then break free (ha) from these techniques by exploring one's own potential, and finally separate (ri) to found one's own school.

This process of exercise, transfer, and transformation makes it even harder to speak of a systematic corpus of budo philosophy. The way of the sword (*ken*) or kendo stresses aspects other than karate, judo, or aikido. Physical proportions of teachers led to different styles and schools. A modern composite karate style like *wado* aims at harmony (*wa*) using evasive bodily movements, while *kyokushinkai* favors full contact. Nevertheless there are some key "concepts" that overlap coherently without becoming a doctrine. The result is a Zen-inspired, shared corpus of understanding of how men, world, and cosmos are intertwined.

Ki: energy

Basic to budo is the unity of matter and mind. The substance of human agency is *ki* (Chinese *ch'i*). As cosmic energy it embeds and penetrates all beings, transgressing all oppositions. Concentrated energy is localized in the abdomen, called *tanden* (red field). As the center of gravity this is the pivotal point of action, comparable with yoga's locus of breathing: *hara*. *Ki* operates on different levels. While attacking, *ki* is harmonized (*ai*) in a spirited shout (*ki ai*) that stuns the opponent. In kendo skilled performance of an attack unites (*itchi*) this energy (*ki*) with sword technique (*ken*) and body movement (*tai*): *ki ken tai itchi*. Aikido defines its endeavor exclusively as the way (*do*) that is in harmony and harmonizes (*ai*) cosmic energy (*ki*). The basic idea, however, is that everyone and everything is connected.

Ma: time–space interval

Ki centers, both physically and mentally. The center is always contextual. It can be everywhere. Space is not an empty container for objects to be situated. This "nothing" is always already filled with *ki*. Time–space is therefore an interval, called *ma*: "Ma is perceived behind everything as an indefinable musical chord, a sense of the precise interval eliciting the fullest and finest resonance" (Random, 1985, pp. 150–151). In the spatiotemporal interval as a dynamic in-between, persons are defined by being embedded in time–space. Awareness and alertness are both active and passive, being one and the same, yet discernible. Attacking means breaking the opponent's center without losing one's own balanced center. Once this distance (*ma*) is harmonized (*ai*) and this *ma ai* is maintained, apparently nothing (*mu*) happens. This is the highest form of fighting: no-fight, no-sword – empty (*mu*) mind (*shin*).

Kokoro/shin: mind/heart/spirit

The concept of staying energetically centered in an ever-changing situation disrupts the presuppositions of Western metaphysics and ontology, which search for an unshakeable foundation, a *fundamentum inconcussum*. Agency is not the mind as the seat of rationality; neither is the heart an exclusive locus of love, affection, and compassion. Both inhere in *kokoro* or *shin*. In kendo this energized center of intuitive action is articulated in different ways. First, there is *senshin,* an awareness (*shin*) of what comes before and has precedence (*sen*), referring to an enlightened attitude that is motivated by compassion transcending disharmony and opposition. *Zanshin* literally means a remaining (*zan*) mind, referring to awareness as a relaxed, yet open, alertness. *Shoshin* is a beginner's (*sho*) mind, entailing an attitude of openness, eagerness, and lack of preconceptions, as if each situation were new. *Fudoshin*, a state of imperturbability, emphasizes the immovable or unmoving (*fudo*) heart or mind and relates to *heijoshin*: an awareness of always (*jo*) being "flat" (*hei*), that is, being undisturbed. Presence of mind in the here-and-now is what matters. But as *mushin,* a shortened form of *mushin no shin* – mind of no mind – this here-and-now is also a nowhere. Emptiness (*mu*) is an energized state of not being fixed or occupied by thought or emotion, realizing *muga* (no self) as a state of alert and energized egolessness.

Kata: form

Body and mind are one. Reaching *muga* presupposes an unrelenting training in techniques (*waza*) in ever-increasing combinations and contexts. These techniques are prefigured in detailed choreographed patterns of movements. These forms (*kata*) are performed either solo or in pairs. Kata harmonizes the *ki* and empties the mind. The perfection of form enables the budoka to grasp truth intuitively in action. In *kata* training movements are executed without anticipation: "Ma is the way to sense the moment of movement" (Isozaki, 1979). In Japanese society everything is *kata*. Due to the strict hierarchy and the social need to avoid shaming or being shamed, formal behavior is imperative. Drinking tea (*cha do*) and arranging flowers (*ikebana*) have become spiritual art forms. In performing fundamental forms without stopping, skills are perfected, *ki* is harmonized and emptiness is realized.

Shikai: four illnesses

Mushin cannot be achieved as long as the budoka is calculating and anticipating the movements of his opponent, underestimating his skills or overestimating his own technique and posture. He has to cure himself of the four (*shi*) ilnesses (*kai*): surprise (*kyo*), fear (*ku*), doubt (*gi*), and confusion (*waku*). Once discursive thought and judgmental anticipation are literally a-voided – made empty – by flawless skill, knowledge becomes intuitive. Reflections become reflexes. To rephrase it in a Hegelian way, matter minds: "Training in budo involves much more than just technique. Budo provides you with a solid foundation that will help you be successful in any endeavor. Budo is the base that enables you to advance" (Ueshiba, 2007). Skills and spirituality – body and mind – are no longer separate spheres.

Budo and business

Does this provide an understanding of Japan's economic boom in the 1980s? Is this understanding applicable to the West? Does this enable the tackling of deep-rooted problems in capitalist economics such as unemployment, waste, pollution, and credit crunches? The first question is not hard to answer. Although the Japanese are socioeconomically adapting more and more to Western imperatives due to the globalization of socioeconomic transactions, their Shinto affinity with nature and purity, Confucian focus on form and harmony (*wa*), and Buddhist rejection of selfishness still underpin their work ethic. Budo philosophy provides a deeper understanding of specific aspects of this ethic. It explains the curiosity, alertness, determination, and dedication of the workforce.

The second question is harder to answer. Though many a commentator is eager to emphasize the transference of Japanese views to Western business practices, this may be wishful thinking. One has to acknowledge the fact that the modern (hyper) individualism of the West, which presupposes critical autonomy and egalitarian politics, does not mesh with the collective approaches and sacrificial willingness of Japanese employers. Budo ideas can be applied pragmatically in a political and economic context, but they only gain ethical meaning once issues such as responsibility, loyalty, and respect are addressed existentially. Where does the spiritual dimension of compassion, selflessness, and enlightenment methodically unfold in this context?

Uncritical application of budo concepts in order to make the secret source of Japanese success work for the West underestimates these sociocultural differences. Although the transference of Sun Tzu's strategic and tactical views to the corporative sphere is – to a certain extent – plausible, the implicitly Zen Buddhist approach to business ethics contains a fundamental paradox: the quest to break egoism and detach from one's individual desire in order to fit into a cosmic "texture" might work for a company as a whole – the master-retainer loyalty serving the corporative imperatives – but once positioned on the level of CEOs, CFOs, or captains of industry, this paradox entails a concept of leadership that is in itself a paradox: servant leadership.

Beyond scarcity

This paradox hints at the direction of an answer to the third question: redefining the basic assumptions of economics, such as individualism, scarcity, and externalization. Applying budo philosophical insights fruitfully to counter the thrifty economics of global capitalism therefore demands an intercultural move that touches upon the fundamentals of economic thinking and acting. First the primacy of individualism in Western thought is set adrift. Given the Zen inspiration in budo, every individual is first and for all defined contextually by his or her relations. The priority to fit in, and the productive connectivity of relations, can still be rephrased in terms of networks, with individuals becoming nodes in these networks. This, however, demands the replacement of the cult of the individual by a culture of relations, of the in-between, of the "inter-" (Oosterling, 2000). Within this "intercultural" perspective mutual respect and compassion become spiritual components that redefine the very core of economics.

This rephrasing exposes the roots of Western economics. It unmasks the ideology of scarcity in a world that is smothered in its plenty. In Buddhist perspective emptiness "is merely another name for plenitude" (Faure, 2009, p. 23). The Shinto aspects in budo combine a reverence for nature with the idea that all beings are respected in their proper place and time. The "horor vacui" of the West is ontologically countered with a primary plenitude. Applying budo concepts on this profound level changes the focus of the *Homo economicus* and redresses its basic concepts. In a globalized world we are all part of the deal. There is no longer an outside. Externalization of costs and linear production lines that pile waste on top of waste are no longer credible practices. In the final instance the concept of being in-between demands a redefinition of socioeconomic interactions and transactions in socioecological terms.

Literature

Deshimura, Taisen. 1977. *Zen & Arts Martiaux*. Paris: Albin Michel.

Draeger, Donn F. 1973–1975. *The Martial Arts and Ways of Japan: Volumes I, II, III*. New York and Tokyo: Weatherhill.

Faure, Bernard. 2009. *Unmasking Buddhism*. Malden, Oxford, Chichester: Wiley-Blackwell.

Isozaki, Arata. 1979. "Ma: Japanese Time–Space." In *The Japanese Architect*: International Edition of Shinkenchiku, no. 262, p. 69–80.

Musashi, Miyamoto. 1982. *TheBook of the Five Rings: The Real Art of Japanese Management*. New York: Bantam Books.

Oosterling, Henk. 2000. "A Culture of the Inter. Japanese Notions of Ma and Basho." In Heinz Kimmerle & Henk Oosterling (eds), *Sensus Communis in Multi- and Intercultural Perspective: On the Possibility of Common Judgements in Arts and Politics*, pp. 61–84. Würzburg: Königshausen & Neumann.

Random , Michael. 1985. *Japon. La stratégie de l'invisible*. Paris: Éditions du Félin.

Ratti, Oscar and Adele Westbrook. 1973. *Secrets of the Samurai: A Survey of the Martial Arts of Feudal Japan*. Rutland, Tokyo: Charles E, Tuttle Company.

Sun Tzu. 1963. *The Art of War*. Oxford, London, New York: OxfordUniversity Press.

Suzuki, Daisetz, T. 1970 (1959). *Zen and Japanese Culture*. Bollingen Series LXIV, Princeton: Princeton University Press.

Ueshiba, Morihei. 2007. *The Secret Teachings of Aikido*. Tokyo, New York, London: Kodansha International.

Yamamoto, Tsunetomo. 2001. *Bushido: The Way of the Samurai*. Justin F. Stone (ed.), trans. M. Tanaka, New York: Square One Classics.

14
Jewish Ethical Perspective on Income and Wealth Distribution

Moses L. Pava

The goal of a religiously grounded ethics should be to critique, enhance, and strengthen the democratic values and institutions of society. These values include noncoercion, transparency, equal rights, compromise, equality of opportunity, individual and communal responsibility, and many others. To the extent that religious institutions are dedicated to promoting and enlarging democracy, religion can take an open and very active role in the public sphere. By contrast, to the extent that religion exploits the public domain to promote its own particular agenda and parochial needs, it is overreaching and harmful to both society and itself. While this might seem to some too limited a role for religion to play, I disagree. In fact, I think that abiding by the simple rule that religion must support democracy opens up the political debates and allows them to take place in a more honest and forthright way than ever before. Given this framework, this chapter specifically raises the following question: what role can the Jewish tradition play with regard to the contemporary question of income and wealth inequality?

Historical perspective

The Jewish tradition can provide a much-needed historical perspective on the question of wealth distribution. The experiences of the Jewish people throughout the millennia provide a vast reservoir of practical knowledge and know-how. To ignore this history would be a type of willful ignorance.

Poverty is not a new problem. As Deuteronomy states, "the poor shall never cease out of your land." But it is precisely because of this fact of life that Judaism requires us to "open our hands to the poor and needy." Perhaps one of Judaism's most important lessons to us is that *when it comes to economics, if the rules of the game are not fair, we've got to fix them.* We see this principle in operation in many situations. For example, the Mishna (Kritut 8a) relates how Rabbi Shimon ben Gamliel changed the sacrificial laws in order to promote economic equity. When the price of pigeons shot up to a golden dinar because of high demand, Rabbi Shimon ben Gamliel promised, "I will not go to sleep tonight until the price comes down." As head of the Sanhedrin, he stepped in and reduced the number of birds required for sacrifice by women after childbirth. This dramatically lowered the demand and the price of the birds fell almost instantly. Rashi, the preeminent Talmudic commentator, explains that this case provides an example of changing the law for the "sake of God."

Another famous example of creative interpretation in the interest of economic equity is Hillel's innovation of the *prosbol*, a legal document that allowed the lender and borrower to circumvent the cancellation of debt in the sabbatical year. Hillel's creative reading of the biblical text removed a tremendous barrier to the free flow of funds and is correctly seen as a boost to economic development and communal equity and welfare (see Gittin 36a–36b). Jewish thought is deeply conservative in the special sense that it is concerned with conserving the Jewish people over time. Judaism also recognizes the reality of changing circumstances. Its survival has often depended on the appropriate balance between respect for the status quo and respect for appropriate and measured change.

One of the most pernicious effects of income and wealth inequality is its effect on access to education. Simply put, the likelihood of graduating from a four-year college if you are at the bottom of the economic ladder is much less than if you are at the top. About half of all students from the top quartile of the economic hierarchy graduate from college while only seven percent of those from the lowest quartile will graduate. These statistics are particularly disturbing when it is recognized that future economic success is highly dependent on education levels.

Judaism, of course, has much to teach the world on the topic of education. Interestingly, the very same Hillel who invented the *prosbol*, and who contributed so much to Judaism's progressive tendencies, was at one time himself barred from the house of study because of his own abject poverty. As the Talmud tells it at Yoma 35b:

> Everyday Hillel used to work and earn one tropaik, half of which he would give to the guard at the house of learning, the other half being spent on food. One day he found nothing to earn and the guard at

the House of Learning would not permit him to enter. He climbed up and sat upon the window to hear the words of the living God... .They say, that day was the eve of Sabbath in the winter solstice and snow fell down upon him from heaven. When the dawn rose, Shemayah said to Abtalion: "Brother, on every day this house is light and today it is dark, is it perhaps a cloudy day." They looked up and saw the figure of a man in the window. He was covered by three cubits of snow. They removed him, bathed and anointed him, and placed him opposite the fire. They said, "This man deserves that the Sabbath be profaned on his behalf."

To the extent that poverty is a bar to education, think how much poorer society is in the long run. How many contemporary Hillels are out there? We do not know, but even if it is just one, the outcome of barring him or her from obtaining an education could be truly alarming.

This, of course, is just a story, and drawing specific policy prescriptions from it would be irresponsible at best. Nevertheless, it does demonstrate a deep practical wisdom earned through thousands of years by a single community attempting to live out biblical ideals in a real world of scarce resources.

Chesed in the contemporary world

In addition to the important historical perspective that Judaism offers, Judaism's highly refined notion of *chesed* (usually translated as "loving kindness" or "acts of loving kindness") is a useful and usable paradigm for contemporary democratic thought. *Chesed* is active and optimistic. It must go beyond the letter of the law. It requires imagination. *Chesed* is so essential to Judaism that Isadore Twersky writes, in an important paper titled "The Jewish Attitude Toward the Welfare State" that it is the "distinctive function which legitimatizes our worldly existence" (Lamm and Wurzburger, 1967, p. 224).

At its best, *chesed* is about *bringing the outsiders inside*. All of this is emphasized in the following beautiful *midrash* comparing Job and Abraham:

Now when that great calamity came upon Job, he said unto the Holy One, blessed be He: "Master of the Universe, did I not feed the hungry and give the thirsty to drink? And did I not clothe the naked?"

Nevertheless the Holy One, blessed be He, said to Job: "Job, thou has not yet reached half the measure of Abraham. Thou sittest and tarriest within thy house and the wayfarers come in to thee. To him who is accustomed to eat wheat bread, thou givest wheat bread to eat; to him who is accustomed to eat meat, thou givest meat to eat; to him who is accustomed to drink wine, thou givest wine to drink. But Abraham did not act in this way. Instead he would go forth and make the rounds everywhere, and when he found wayfarers *he brought them into his house*. To him who was unaccustomed to eat wheat bread, he gave wheat bread to eat; to him who was unaccustomed to eat meat, he gave them meat to eat; to him who was unaccustomed to drink wine, he gave wine to drink. Moreover he arose and built stately mansions on the highways and left there food and drink, and every passerby ate and drank and blessed Heaven. (Abot de R. Natan, 7 as translated by J. Goldin)

I believe that it is precisely this idea of bringing the wayfarer into the house that makes Judaism's idea of *chesed* most useful to the contemporary debate about wealth and income inequalities. Ethics is ultimately about seeing our own humanity in the other, and seeing the other's humanity in ourselves. On Passover, we invite the poor to join us at our festive meals. This is not just an act of charity; this is an act of self-preservation. Treating everyone with equal human dignity may not be the sole aim of community, but it is certainly a necessary means for every other aim.

The huge and increasing gap between the haves and the have-nots is not compatible with a world in which true *chesed* is even possible. To "bring the wayfarer into the house" does not mean merely providing for subsistence, although surely it must include the basic necessities of life, such as food, shelter, and healthcare.

From an Abrahamic point of view, it also means providing decent education, safe streets, hope for the future, and equal opportunities for every single citizen. To "bring the wayfarer into the house" requires us to open our eyes and see the economic conditions in which such a large fraction of our population is seemingly trapped.

Statistically it has been demonstrated that increases in income and wealth inequality lead to greater unemployment, less spending on education, more babies born with low birth weights, higher rates of incarceration and of homicide. These findings hold even when the researchers controlled for absolute levels of wealth. What this means is that it is the inequality itself and not the amount of wealth or poverty that leads to a deterioration in all of these social indicators.

Chesed is active caring in the context of community. It may very well be true that in the end all of us are merely "strangers and settlers" (see Leviticus 25:23) in God's eyes. But in Jewish thought, it is the preeminent human job to lessen and soften this felt strangeness. This is exactly what we are here for! Maimonides puts it perfectly when he warns that "he who locks the doors to his courtyard and eats and drinks with his wife and family without feeding the poor and bitter of soul – his meal is not a rejoicing in a divine commandment but a rejoicing in his own stomach."

The issue of wealth inequality is not a purely economic question

Bringing the outsider inside is an economic goal. That 37.3 million human beings are living in poverty in the United States today would seem to prove that we have not achieved anything close to economic stability or sustainability. But wealth inequality is not just an economic issue. In Jewish thought, the question of how wealth is allocated is linked to human dignity and self-worth. Unlike other religious systems, from a Torah perspective poverty is not considered to be a "blessed state."

One of the amazing facts about Maimonides' famous "Eight Levels of Charity" is that there is no mention of the amount of *tzedakah* (charity) required. (For a contemporary discussion of Maimonides' formulation see Salamon, 2003.) The focus is solely on the manner in which *tzedakah* is given. This is because Maimonides recognizes how profoundly wealth, power, and dignity are interrelated. This emphasis on providing jobs for the poor is obviously still a timely insight. In addition, his concern for anonymity in the process and his emphasis on a central collection and distribution agency are also still extremely urgent lessons. Furthermore, from a more conservative political perspective, his warning that one should "not put into the box unless he knows that the one responsible for the box is faithful" is pregnant with meaning.

Judaism is a form of practical idealism

Judaism's standards are consistently high but not of another world. Judaism has a realistic view of human nature. It is not naive, for example, about the "cunning rogue" who gives a poor man a single dinar in order to give him just enough money to make him technically ineligible for "the gleanings, forgotten sheaves, the produce of the corner of the field, or the poor tithe." Given Judaism's penchant for practical idealism, from a traditional perspective there are two types of errors we can make when it comes to ethics. On the one hand, we can view Judaism as merely a set of rules and distance ourselves from the very purposes of those rules. On the other hand, we can get so carried away with an imagined prophetic passion that we can forget the facts on the ground.

Aaron Levine states flatly that Judaism "does not subscribe to the notion of income redistribution" (1987, p. 135). I will state just as flatly that he is making the first kind of error. He cannot find a Talmudic passage that says that in the year 2009 the United States shall adopt a program of income redistribution, and he draws his conclusion from the Talmud's silence. In focusing on the rule book, he has lost sight of Judaism's basic ethos. By contrast, Michael Lerner's passionate call for a constitutional amendment to ensure greater income equality becomes so unhinged from reality that he does more harm than good (2002). He is making the second kind of mistake.

Conclusion

So where does this leave the rest of us? In the end Judaism will not magically produce a Solomon-like solution to the problem of income and wealth inequality. Any proposed solution must begin with an examination of the root causes for the increasing disparity between the haves and the have-nots. Further, policy prescriptions must be based on economic data and rigorous empirical analysis.

In the end, though I do not think that a Jewish approach to this question can provide the *one* solution, it certainly can rule out proposals based on ideological ideas like the sanctity of private property or the elimination of private property. And more importantly, it can help us identify and recognize some interesting proposals that are worth looking into. Robert Frank's call for a progressive consumption tax to replace the current income tax is one of the most thoughtful and carefully constructed economic arguments in this area (1999). Similarly, Anne Alstott and Bruce Ackerman's idea of a "stakeholder society" in which every citizen enters adult life with $80,000, although seemingly radical, would satisfy many of Judaism's own aspirations (2000).

From a Jewish perspective, there has always been a communal aspect to *tzedakah* and it is wrong to think of it as a purely individual responsibility. To support this I merely cite the laws of Jubilee and also note Maimonides' useful distinction in his "Guide to the Perplexed" between *tzedek* and *tzedakah*. The former is legally prescribed and regulated and the latter stems from one's own moral conscience.

Is Judaism conservative or liberal in its political philosophy? I do not think that this is the right question. Judaism's contribution to democracy is in helping us frame the debate: in its historical experience, in its getting us to see beyond the economics, and in its practical idealism. In other words, Judaism, among other religious traditions, provides a critical morality to help us all bring the outsiders inside and to thus strengthen and promote democratic societies.

Literature

Alstott, A. and Ackerman, B. 2000. *The Stakeholder Society.* New Haven: Yale University Press.

Frank, R. 1999: *Luxury Fever: Money and Happiness in an Era of Excess.* Princeton: Princeton University Press.

Lerner, M. 2002. *Spirit Matter.* Charlottesville, VA: Hampton Roads Publishing.

Levine, A. 1987. *Economics and Jewish Law.* New York: Yeshiva University Press.

Lamm, N. and Wurzburger, W. (eds) 1967. *A Treasury of Tradition.* New York: Rabbinical Council of America.

Salamon, J. 2003. *Rambam's Ladder: A Meditation on Generosity and Why It Is Necessary to Give.* New York: Workman Publishing Co.

15
Catholic Social Teaching

Domènec Melé

Since the latter part of the nineteenth century the Roman Catholic Church has developed a rich body of teachings, based on Christian spirituality and morality, regarding how a Christian should behave in social life, including in business and other economic activities.[1] This is known as Catholic Social Doctrine and also as Catholic Social Teaching (CST). The aim of this chapter is to present a brief outline of such teaching,[2] with special reference given to business and economic activities and their connection with Christian spirituality and morality.

Christian spirituality is characterized by a progressive identification with Christ, and more specifically with Christ's love. Explicitly, St. Paul affirms that "for those [God] fore-knew He also predestinated to be conformed to the image of His Son" (*Bible, Romans* 8:29). Thus, "Christian spirituality is distinguished by the disciple's commitment to become conformed ever more fully to his Master" (Pope John Paul II, 2002, n. 15). This identification with Christ requires following and imitating Him. Every disciple must follow Jesus, towards whom he is drawn by the Father Himself (*Bible, John* 6:44). Following Christ is "the essential and primordial foundation of Christian morality," and Christ asks His followers "to imitate Him along the path of love, a love which gives itself completely to the brethren out of love for God"(Pope John Paul II, 1993, nn. 19–20).

Love is inseparable from the truth, as St. Paul says: charity (love in its genuine sense) "rejoices in the truth" (*Bible, 1 Corinthians* 13:6). Christ left as his New Commandment: "love one another as I have loved you" (*Bible, John* 15:12). But, at the same time, He is presented as the truth itself (*Bible, John 14:6*) and explains that He came to give witness to the truth (*Bible, John* 18:37). Love without truth may be reduced to a pool

118

of good sentiments or a set of good relations, without any reference to the true love of Christ.

Thus, Christian spirituality and morality are closely related. While Christian spirituality consists in the progressive identification with Christ's love in the truth, Christian morality is based on following a person, Jesus Christ. Some directions to this end can be expressed through values and virtues, along with some principles and norms.

Following Christ has important consequences for each individual and also for promoting sound relationships in society and in the business world, and this is what CST tries to express. To carry out the task received from Christ, the Church considers that she has the duty of scrutinizing the signs of the times and of interpreting them in the light of the Gospel. Accordingly, CST has been developed by reading events as they unfold in the course of history in the light of word revealed by Christ Jesus, and accompanied by rational reflection.

CST includes several documents on ethical aspects of economic and social issues (see a selection in Table 15.1).[3] These writings are authored by the *Magisterium* of the Roman Catholic Church, which is constituted of the Pope, who is the bishop of Rome and head of the Church, and all other bishops in communion with him. Among these texts, particularly relevant are a document of the Second Vatican Council (*Gaudium et spes*) and a set of Papal writings called "Encyclicals" (formally "encyclical letters," the original meaning of which is a widely disseminated letter). They are addressed to Catholics worldwide but also to everyone of "good will," as is frequently stated explicitly in the address of the Encyclicals. In these documents there is a homogeneous evolution in which some permanent values and principles are accompanied by judgments and criteria for specific situations.[4] Episcopal Conferences or Conferences of Catholic Bishops (official assemblies of all the bishops of a given territory, frequently a nation) also issue documents that are more contextualized, considering particular problems of the territory.[5]These documents usually include interesting hermeneutical considerations. Among the Bishops' documents, one of the better known is the Pastoral Letter "Justice for all" published by the US National Conference of Catholic Bishops in 1986,[6] of which "topics were chosen because of their relevance to both the economic 'signs of the times' and the ethical norms of the Catholic tradition" (n.133).

If love and truth are crucial in following Christ, then they are so in CST. As has been pointed out by Pope Benedict XVI, "love in the truth" is the principle around which the Church's social doctrine turns (CV, 6).

Table 15.1 Main documents of Catholic Social Teaching

Author	Document (all available at www. vatican.va)	Year	Abbr.
Pope Leo XIII	Encyclical Letter "Rerum Novarum"	1891	RN
Pope Pius XI	Encyclical Letter "Quadragesimo anno"	1931	QA
Pope John XXIII	Encyclical Letter "Mater et Magistra"	1961	MM
Pope John XXIII	Encyclical Letter "Pacem in terris"	1963	PT
Vatican Council II	Pastoral Constitution "Gaudium et spes"	1965	GS
Pope Paul VI	Encyclical Letter "Populorum Progressio"	1967	PP
Pope John Paul II	Encyclical Letter "Laborem execerns"	1981	LE
Pope John Paul II	Encyclical Letter "Sollicitudo Rei Socialis"	1987	SRS
Pope John Paul II	Encyclical Letter "Centesimus annus"	1991	CA
Catholic Church	Catechism of the Catholic Church (mainly nn. 2401–2436)	2003	CCC
Pontifical Commission for Justice and Pace	Compendium of the Social Doctrine of the Church	2004	CSDC
Pope Benedict XVI	Encyclical Letter "Caritate in veritate"	2009	CV

Christian humanism

In CST there are no technical solutions, nor models, nor specific policies, but instead a continuous defense of human dignity and the right of every human being to pursue his or her integral human development. In "the social doctrine of the Church can be found the principles for reflection, the criteria for judgment and the directives for action which are the starting point for the promotion of an integral and solidary humanism" (CSDC, 7).

CST presents a Christian humanism, in which a universal and unconditional respect for human dignity and a deep view of the person are crucial. In CST, human dignity is not only a finding of human reason as a consequence of human rationality and freedom, but a consequence of being in the image of God. It is a transcendent dignity founded in God. In the words of Pope John Paul II, "all of the Church's social doctrine is a correct view of the human person and of his unique value, inasmuch as 'man [meaning human beings]... is the only creature on earth which God willed for itself' (GS, 24). God has imprinted His own image and likeness on man (cf. *Bible, Genesis* 1:26), conferring upon him an incomparable dignity" (CA, 11).

The human person is seen as a being at once corporeal and spiritual. The spiritual principle of humans, endowed with intellect and free will, commonly called soul, and body form a profound unity, and by virtue of this unity, human dignity includes both soul and body. Although every human being shares the same rational nature, every person is unique and unrepeatable – with a specific biography and interior life – and exists as an "I" capable of self-understanding, self-possession, and self-determination. Through his or her intellect and will, the person is opened to transcendence. That means humans are open to the infinite –God – and to all created beings, searching for a total truth and the absolute good. The human person is essentially a social being, capable of freely giving himself and entering into communion with God and other persons (see CSDC, 108–151).

Human dignity belongs to every human being from conception to death, regardless of race, sex, religion, or social condition, in any phase of life in which a human being can exist. Thus, every person is unique, but all persons are equal in their dignity and possession of innate human rights.

CST considers protecting human rights as the most significant way to respond effectively to the inescapable demands of human dignity (CSDC, nn.152–159). Consequently, the Roman Catholic Church defends and promotes human rights and positively values the UN Universal Declaration of Human Rights. CST, particularly in the Encyclical *Pacem in Terris* and other documents (GS, 26; CA, 47; CV, 43–44 and others), contains abundant references to human rights and their corresponding duties. According to CST, the ultimate sources of human rights are the human being and God, as the Creator. Thus, human rights are neither a mere matter of consensus nor a concession of the state or public powers, nor a result of a human consensus; they are innate. The field of human rights has expanded to include the rights of peoples and nations.

The concept of *authentic* or *integral human development* is also very important in the humanism proposed by CST (and it is particularly emphasized in encyclicals PP and CV). As Pope Paul VI writes, "in God's plan, every man is born to seek self-fulfillment, for every human life is called to some task by God" (PP, 15). Because life itself is a vocation, "integral human development is primarily a vocation and therefore it involves a free assumption of responsibility in solidarity on the part of everyone" (CV, 16). Endowed with intellect and free will, each man is responsible for his self-fulfillment even as he is for his salvation" (PP,

15). In a certain sense, "human self-fulfillment may be said to sum up our obligations" (PP, 16). Authentic human development concerns the whole of the person in every single dimension, including the perspective of eternal life (CV, 11). Thus, humanism promoted by CST is a transcendent humanism, because "there is no true humanism but that which is open to the Absolute, and is conscious of a vocation which gives human life its true meaning" (PP, 42). Transcendent humanism gives to the human being "his greatest possible perfection: this is the highest goal of personal development" (PP, 16).

The obligation of working for an integral human development is not, by any means, an individualistic position. On the contrary, integral human development requires solidarity, that is, concern and care for others. Explicitly it is stated: "Man cannot fully find himself except through a sincere gift of himself" (GS, 24). "Every human being exists 'with' others and 'for' others" (CSDC, 165).

Fundamental values and permanent principles for social life

Apart from love and truth, or more precisely, "love in the truth," there are other closely related values which are fundamental to a proper structuring and ordered leading of life in society, as well as in business organizations (CSCT, nn. 197–208, 193,194) – namely, justice, solidarity and freedom with responsibility. Peace is also highly emphasized in CST, but rather than as a value, peace is a fruit of living these values. Let us review briefly these values in social life.

Social love, sometimes called "civic friendship," is concern for others and working for cooperation and harmony in human and social relations. Social love contributes to the maintenance of cohesion in society beyond any hypothetical social contract, as individualistic ideologies proclaim.

Truth, and more specifically "living in the truth," has special significance in social relationships. In fact, when the coexistence of human beings within a community is founded on truth, it is ordered and fruitful, and it corresponds to their dignity as persons. Otherwise, trust is not established and social cohesion withers. Searching for truth makes a dialogue among people of different backgrounds and cultures possible.

Justice is the primary way of love (charity). It refers to the constant and firm will to give to each what is due. It does not make sense to see justice and charity as being in opposition. Justice is a duty of charity, but, as Pope Benedict XVI explains, "*Charity goes beyond justice*, because to love is to give, to offer what is 'mine' to the other; but it never lacks justice, which prompts us to give the other what is 'his,' what is due to him by reason of his being or his acting. I cannot 'give' what is mine to the other, without first giving him what pertains to him in justice" (CV, 6).

Solidarity is defined by Pope John Paul II as "a firm and persevering determination to commit oneself to the common good; that is to say to the good of all and of each individual, because we are all really responsible for all" (SRS, 38). Solidarity is closely related to justice and social charity. It entails sharing material and spiritual goods with others and a favorable attitude and action toward social justice.

Freedom with responsibility: Freedom is a great Christian value as it is an essential condition for authentic human development. But freedom is not understood as a mere capacity of choice; freedom must be accompanied by responsibility. CST stresses that no structure can guarantee the integral human development without human responsibility (CV, 17). This does not mean denying the importance of economic structures and institutions, but they should be means to human freedom, never instruments of oppression nor a means that dissuades personal involvement in one's own development.

Closely related with these values, and at the very heart of CST, are some *permanent principles* of reflection that help in the evaluation, discernment, and orientation of social action (CSCT, nn. 160–196). These principles are of a general and fundamental character, since they concern the reality of society in its entirety. They are permanent in time and have universality of meaning. The principles of the Church's social doctrine must be appreciated in their unity, interrelatedness, and articulation. Applying only one without respecting the others does not lead to a sound social order.

Paramount among these permanent principles are the principles of human dignity and the common good on the one hand, and the principles of solidarity and subsidiarity on the other. These two pairs of principles consider both the individuality and sociability (or social dimension) of the person. A brief explanation follows:

The principle of the dignity of the human person requires a society organized around respect for and promotion of the transcendent dignity of the human person and his or her integral human development. Thus, "the social order and its development must invariably work to the benefit of the human person, since the order of things is to be subordinate to the order of persons, and not the other way around"(GS, 26).

The principle of the common good refers to the goods shared by those who are within a community or the society (the common good). This allows people to reach their proper fulfillment. It entails respect for and promotion of the person and of human rights, an effective contribution to social well-being and the development of the spiritual and material goods of persons and society, and also promotion of the peace and security of all within a just order. The principle of the common good states that every society, community, social institution – indeed, every aspect of social life – must be related to the common good, and each individual should contribute to it in accordance with his or her own capacities.

The principle of human dignity emphasizes the importance of each person, while the principle of the common good considers each person a part of the whole, and one should live within communities sharing common goods. In this way, CST is far from either individualism or collectivism.

Similarly, the principle of solidarity is balanced with the principle of subsidiarity. The *principle of solidarity* requires concern and support related to the needs of the communities of which one has become part. *The principle of subsidiarity* states that a community of higher order should not assume the task belonging to a community of a lower order and deprive it of its authority. The principle of solidarity highlights the intrinsic social nature of the human person and the common path of individuals and peoples towards an ever-more-committed unity; the principle of subsidiarity stresses the freedom, autonomy and capacity of initiative. The latter also entails *participation* in the society or community to which one belongs, in manners appropriate to each situation.

Related to the principle of the common good is another important principle, known as the *principle of universal destination of goods*. This principle states that the goods of creation are destined for the whole human race. This principle is in harmony with the right of private property, since "the appropriation of property is legitimate for guaranteeing the freedom and dignity of persons and for helping each of them to meet his basic needs and the needs of those in his charge" (CCC, 2402). But inherent in the notion of private property is a social function. This requires finding appropriate ways to make the universal destination of goods effective. One such way is through business enterprises, which provide a livelihood for many people.

Catholic Social Teaching in managing business

CST stresses spirituality in work. The Encyclical *Laborem execerns*, the most relevant CST document on human work, explains that work has been in the plans of God for human persons since the very beginning. Humans are called to prolong the work of creation and somehow be cocreators. Work can also be redemptive, if it is carried out in union with Jesus. In this way, Christians collaborate in a certain fashion with Jesus, the Son of God, in his redemptive work.

There are other values and principles proposed by CST that have direct consequences for business. According to CST, economic life is not meant solely to multiply goods produced and increase profit or power; it is ordered first of all toward the service of persons.

Freedom as a value has its expression in business, first of all in the context of economic initiative, the right to which is supported by CST, although it should be pursued observing regulations issued by the legitimate authority for the sake of the common good (CA, 32, 34; CCC, 2429). Economic initiative is a way to make legitimate use of the talents each has received and to contribute to the abundance that will benefit all. Respect for freedom requires that the state should not absorb what can be done by social initiative (the principle of subsidiarity), including economic matters.

CST emphasizes the economic, social and environmental responsibility of business (CCC, 2432). There is no doubt that management should foster efficiency, but a type of management "determined solely by efficiency, with a view to increasing profits" is not acceptable (CA, 4).

The purpose of the business is not maximizing shareholder value, nor simply making a profit. The firm's purpose "is to be found in its very existence as a community of persons who in various ways are endeavoring to satisfy their basic needs, and who form a particular group at the service of the whole of society" (CA, 35). Profits are necessary, since they make possible the investments that ensure the future of a business and they guarantee employment, but a business bears an obligation to consider the good of persons and not only increase profits (CCE, 2432). Thus, "the reduction of cultures to the technological dimension, even if it favors short-term profits," should be avoided, as "in the long term [it] impedes reciprocal enrichment and the dynamics of cooperation" (CV, 32). CST is in favor of a company's sense of responsibility towards the stakeholders: "business management cannot concern itself only with the interests of the proprietors, but must also assume responsibility for all the other stakeholders who contribute to the life of the business" (CV 40).

Human work, including managerial work, is particularly highlighted in CST both from spiritual and ethical perspectives. Work is not a mere commodity. It proceeds directly from persons created in the image of

God and called to subdue the earth through their work. This has significant ethical requirements for the *organization of work*. One must respect
labor rights as an aspect of human rights, including first of all a just
wage, determined by the needs and contributions of each worker, safe
working conditions, and equal treatment free from discrimination or
alienation (see LE, particularly chap. 4). CST stands for avoiding alienation, understood in its genuine sense, which is quite different from
the Marxist sense of alienation defined by the mere fact of working for
another. Pope John Paul II expresses it as follows:

> Alienation is found also in work, when it is organized so as to ensure
> maximum returns and profits with no concern about whether the
> worker, through his own labour, grows or diminishes as a person,
> either through increased sharing in a genuinely supportive commu-
> nity or through increased isolation in a maze of relationships marked
> by destructive competitiveness and estrangement, in which he is
> considered only a means and not an end (CA, 41).

CST encourages us to pay particular attention to the quality of the
services provided by a business, along with the quality of the environment and of life in general (CA 36). At the same time it warns about consumerism and calls for responsible behavior. Responsible behavior in
consumer matters is that which, in reference to the consumer, "respects
all the dimensions of his being and which subordinates his material
and instinctive dimensions to his interior and spiritual ones...while
ignoring in various ways the reality of the person as intelligent and
free – then consumer attitudes and lifestyles can be created which are
objectively improper and often damaging to his physical and spiritual
health." Avoiding consumerism requires educational and cultural work,
a strong sense of responsibility among producers and among people in
the mass media in particular, as well as the necessary intervention by
public authorities (CA, 36).

Another important point in CST is bearing responsibility for the *natural environment* through a sense of stewardship. In the beginning God
entrusted the earth and its resources to humankind. Humans are called
to subdue the earth, not through a tyrannical domination but with
a strong sense of *stewardship*: taking care of creation, mastering it by
labor, and enjoying its fruits. People should guide their use of the earth
with concern for the quality of life of people, including future generations (sustainability), and with a religious respect for the integrity
of the creation (CA, 37–38; CV, 27, 49–52). Along with *environmental*

ecology, CST defends what is called *human ecology,* understood as a culture that shapes human coexistence and an authentic human development through family life, work organization, housing and urban settings (CA, 38; CV, 51).

Notes

1. Actually, the Church's teachings on social issues are much older. They can be found in the Bible, in early Christian writers, and in outstanding theologians such as St. Thomas Aquinas. However, a major development of such teachings has been taking place since the late 19th century.
2. For a more extended view of these teachings, see Compendium of Social Doctrine of the Church (2004), published by Pontifical Council for Justice and Peace, and also Pope John Paul II (1991) and Pope Benedict XVI (2009).
3. This table includes abbreviations, which we will use henceforth. The number(s) following each abbreviation refer to the number in the corresponding document.
4. Encyclicals and other universal documents of the Catholic Church are available on www.vatican.va
5. There is a comprehensive research catalog containing listings and abstracts of statements issued by the worldwide Episcopal conferences from 1891 to 1991. It was conducted at the Institute of Moral Theology at the University of Fribourg, with the collaboration of the International Jacques Maritain Institute in Rome: Roger Berthouzoz, Roberto Papini, Carlos J. Pinto de Oliveira, and Ramon Sugranyes de Franch (eds), *Economie et developpement: repertoire des documents episcopaux des cinq continents* (1891–1991). Fribourg: Editions Universitaires, Paris: Cerf, 1997.

Literature

Bible, The Holy 1966. *New Revised Standard Version* (Catholic Edition). Princeton, NJ: Scepter.

Catholic Church. 2003. *Catechism of the Catholic Church,* 2nd ed., London: Random House. Also available at: www.vatican.va/archive/ENG0015/_INDEX.HTM (this and the other websites were accessed on September 3, 2009).

Pontifical Council for Justice and Peace. 2004. *Compendium of the Social Doctrine of the Church.* Città del Vaticano: Libreria Editrice Vaticana. Also available at http://www.vatican.va/roman_curia/pontifical_councils/justpeace/documents/rc_pc_justpeace_doc_20060526_compendio-dott-soc_en.html.

Pope Benedict XVI. 2009. *Encyclical Letter "Caritas in veritate"* (June 29). http://www.vatican.va/holy_father/benedict_xvi/encyclicals/documents/hf_ben-xvi_enc_20090629_caritas-in-veritate_en.html.

Pope John Paul II. 1981. *Encyclical Letter "Laborem execerns"* (September 14). http://www.vatican.va/edocs/ENG0217/_INDEX.HTM.

Pope John Paul II. 1987. *Encyclical Letter "Sollicitudo Rei Socialis"* (December 30). http://www.vatican.va/edocs/ENG0223/_INDEX.HTM.

Pope John Paul II. 1991. *Encyclical Letter "Centesimus annus"* (May 1). http://www.vatican.va/edocs/ENG0214/_INDEX.HTM.

Pope John Paul II. 1993. *Encyclical Letter "Veritatis Splendor"* on Christian Ethics (August 6). http://www.vatican.va/edocs/ENG0222/_INDEX.HTM.

Pope John Paul II. 2002. *Apostolic Letter "Rosarium Virginis Mariae"* (October 16). http://www.vatican.va/holy_father/john_paul_ii/apost_letters/documents/hf_jp-ii_apl_20021016_rosarium-virginis-mariae_en.html.

Pope John XXIII. 1961. *Encyclical Letter "Mater et Magistra"* (May 15). http://www.vatican.va/holy_father/john_xxiii/encyclicals/documents/hf_j-xxiii_enc_15051961_mater_en.html.

Pope John XXIII. 1963. *Encyclical Letter "Pacem in terris"* (April 11). h t t p : / / www.vatican.va/holy_father/john_xxiii/encyclicals/documents/hf_j-xxiii_enc_15051961_mater_en.html.

Pope Leo XIII. 1891. *Encyclical Letter "Rerum Novarum"* (May 15). http://www.vatican.va/holy_father/leo_xiii/encyclicals/documents/hf_l-xiii_enc_15051891_rerum-novarum_en.html.

Pope Paul VI. 1967. *Encyclical Letter "Populorum Progressio"* (March 26). http://www.vatican.va/holy_father/paul_vi/encyclicals/documents/hf_p-vi_enc_26031967_populorum_en.html.

Pope Pius XI. 1931. *Encyclical Letter "Quadragesimo anno"* (May 15). http://www.vatican.va/holy_father/pius_xi/encyclicals/documents/hf_p-xi_enc_19310515_quadragesimo-anno_en.html.

Vatican Council II. 1965. *Pastoral Constitution "Gaudium et spes"* (December 7). http://www.vatican.va/archive/hist_councils/ii_vatican_council/documents/vat-ii_const_19651207_gaudium-et-spes_en.html.

16
Protestant Economic Principles and Practices

Jurjen Wiersma

During the sixteenth century the Renaissance had rediscovered the fruitfulness of antiquity, from which humanity's resilience and responsibility were reshaped. Following the Renaissance, the Protestant Reformation began. Protestantism was both a belief system and a strategy for liberation from extortion and oppression, an exodus comparable to that of Moses and the Hebrews who had fled from the fleshpots of Egypt.

Early Protestants were released from the medieval obligation to earn salvation through ecclesial dogma and doctrine, and were convinced that they had received the gift of a new freedom. They felt spiritually emancipated and learned to behave as free persons. Equipped with a newly won set of principles, standards, and values they set to work, stimulated by the leitmotif *ora et labora*, pray and work.

Although Protestantism has become a religion with many branches, the unifying theological theme is freedom through God's grace (*sola gratia*) to share in community-, society-, and even continent-building. Reacting to the gospel and God's claim upon their lives, Lutherans, Calvinists, Mennonites, Puritans, etc experienced this claim as a vocation to build a better world and struggle for human rights and liberty, justice, and peace.

In his formative study, *The Protestant Ethic and the Spirit of Capitalism* (Weber, 1958), the German sociologist Max Weber (1864–1920) highlighted and witnessed the socio-economic-political sense of vocation essential to this authentic religious experience (Villa-Vicencio, 1992, pp. 137–138, 145–148).

Back to the basics

In describing my topic further I would like to point out some important Protestant principles. The first principle is the *Protestant understanding of the human person.* Individual capabilities, needs, and desires are of major importance to the Protestant point of view. Specifically the individual conscience is considered to be extremely valuable. It has the right to choose, decide, and refuse. Ultimately ecclesiastical, moral, political, or secular authorities are not allowed to determine a person's ethical decisions. The only authority to obey, to rely on, and to listen to is God.

He is Sovereign, but not in an absolute, abstract, or detached sense. All sovereignty is limited, both the sovereignty of a state and the sovereignty of a person, including the sovereignty of God. No doubt he is a superior being, but he sides with human beings, especially with human beings deemed inferior. He has incarnational power. That is his *kenosis*, his humbling condescendence, the grace of his merciful yielding toward men and women.

In response, (post)modern men and women are urged to find creative expressions of incarnational strength. As the German theologian Dorothee Sölle would say, God is in need of humans to incarnate and materialize himself and to become flesh. What kind of human does he require? Another German theologian, the anti-Nazi resistance fighter Dietrich Bonhoeffer made it clear that the God who humbles himself and who is there-for-others expects an analogous response among human persons. By responding to God's action one becomes a responsible self, reacting both in a sovereign and a responsible fashion.

Clearly, this divine and human humbling and being-there-for-others is the very opposite of the perception of the human person that seems to be widely accepted as normal in the (post)modern world of the twenty-first century: the human person as the self-maximizer of the economic system and the market conditions (Elshtain, 2008, pp. 227–233).

The greed of this self-maximizer, and the negligence of the regulator, generated a financial crisis throughout the world in the first decade of the third millennium. This was almost unprecedented and reminded some observers of the collapse of the New York Stock Exchange in 1929. However, it is inherent to Protestantism to promote such virtues as humility and modesty and to curb such vices as self-aggrandizement and pride (*hybris*).

This observation leads to another principle for consideration – the *Weberian concept of inner-worldly asceticism.* Max Weber holds in his already mentioned *TheProtestant Ethic and the Spirit of Capitalism* that certain Protestant values have particular consequences that first and foremost can lead to a capitalist ethos. One of their implications is the acquisition of goods and possessions.

Specifically, Protestants believe(d) that before the face of God (*coram Deo*) one should work industriously and exhibit true discipleship (Weber, 1958; Gerth and Wright Mills, 1958). One is God's deputy and one is supposed to exploit and govern his creation prudently and piously by protecting it from harm, chaos, and ruin.

In other words, before the face of God people ought to behave in what Weber calls an "inner-worldly ascetic" manner, which may be equated with a human person's limited sovereignty. Before the face of God one's labor, work, and action, to use Hannah Arendt's well-known triptych, are vital in sustaining life. However, one is not permitted to transgress certain limits and ought to acknowledge restrictions and restraints (Berger,1963, p. 39).

Critics of Protestantism usually argue that its worldview is dull and pessimistic. Luther, for instance, considered a human person *simul justus ac peccator*. He never stopped proclaiming those who are justified are at the same time still sinners. "Once a thief always a thief," a famous nostrum would assert. Life so characterized seems burdensome rather than joyful, which is a reason to move quickly to the third principle, a metaphor.

This metaphor makes clear that from a theological angle the created world has a peculiar status. It is *"the theater of God's glory, honor and splendor"*; it is *mundus theatrum gloriae Dei*, in Latin. A theater is generally speaking a public location frequented by a wide variety of people who are committed spectators of a theatrical performance. When it is over, people go home with uplifted spirits, relieved from day-to-day worries. The theater of God's glory can be seen as a safe haven in which humans can exist in a relaxed and cheerful way. It enables them to play a role as steward in order to honor God.

Augustine was the first representative of church and theology to wholeheartedly shoulder this "light burden." So did John Calvin and Karl Barth and many laypersons in their wake. They saw and dealt with the world as an instrument to glorify God (Kraemer, 1958; Smedema, 2009, pp. 257–258). Barth, for example, maintained that God has left and leaves marks in the created reality. The Swiss theologian expected believers to represent God's presence in the world. In addition, he made them aware of their limited sovereignty, as he himself was aware of humans' imperfectability in relation to the glory of God. In this respect, he underscored the Old Testament text of Psalm 8:

What is man, that thou art mindful of him? And the son of man, that thou visitest him?

For thou hast made him a little lower than the angels, and crowned him with glory and honour.

What then is a human being – this image of God, crowned with glory and honor – invited to do? To put it briefly, one is incited to deliver – in an excited manner, indeed – responsible and just services to society, including economic ones, without indulging desires for self-glorification.

Building efforts

So far, the principles of the Protestant legacy have been brought to the fore. Now the practice is examined, a practice considered a corollary of the three principles proposed: limited sovereignty, a modest asceticism, and joyful commitment to life and work.

What Weber may have actually meant in his *Protestant Ethic* is still subject to debate and criticism, and rightly so. Nonetheless, it is obvious that his argument regarding how people conduct the affairs of the world is still valid, especially economic affairs such as the current credit-system collapse and its impact on the employment sector. These days, economic crashes and financial crises have devastating and alienating effects on men and women, young and old, black and white.

Many, hit and hurt, are desperate because they have lost fundamental human rights and their basic sense of dignity. Therefore, the three principles and their potentially analogous practices should constitute an indispensable element of the contemporary economic and financial agenda to be taken seriously by bankers, captains of industry, managers, and other protagonists in the socioeconomic-political landscape.

In this section on building efforts I will evoke three practices, not in an informal and detached but an engaged way, and adapted to contemporary conditions and contexts. Consecutively, I address the issue of limits to power, the theme of global justice, and the need for a new concept of a just and responsible society.

1. *The issue of the limits to power* leads to Jimmy (James Earl) Carter, Democrat and Baptist. He was the thirty-ninth president of the United States of America and was in office from 1977 till 1981. On July 15, 1979, Carter, about to contend for a second term as president, delivered a pivotal speech in which he wanted to discuss the serious problems of the nation, not least of which were a couple of serious threats.

In American political and public discourse fundamental threats are by definition external. That very year, an Islamic revolution had exploded in Iran and posed another external threat. However, Carter dared to suggest "that the real danger to American democracy lay within" and maintained that the nation as a whole was experiencing "a crisis of confidence." According to him this crisis was an outward manifestation of "an underlying crisis of values." His fellow citizens had a mistaken idea of freedom. It was quantitative and centered on "a never-ending quest for more while exalting narrow self-interest."

Carter lost the presidential campaign and threw away a second presidential term largely due to his "crisis-of-confidence" address, in which he tried to promote moral renewal at home. He was outflanked by Ronald Reagan, his successor, who seemed far better than Carter to understand what made Americans tick: "They wanted self-gratification, not self-denial."

Reagan encouraged his compatriots to carry on and to keep track of national self-interest, presenting as an example his Strategic Defense Initiative, an "impermeable" antimissile shield that his critics labeled "Star Wars." This initiative took place during the frightening historic episode of the cold war and demonstrated that Reagan and his Republican government had decided to wield US power to ensure access to oil and other sources of energy, "hoping thereby to prolong the empire of consumption's lease on life."

Instead, Carter's target was authentic freedom; it was not satisfying immediate needs and other material utilities. He wanted *quality* to increase, whereas Reagan wanted *quantity* to increase. "We must decide that 'less' is not enough," Reagan once declared. On January 20, 1981, Ronald Reagan became the next president of the United States (Bacevich, 2008, pp. 32–43).

In other words, if one examines his policies in retrospect one may conclude that Jimmy Carter, often crushed in his days, had demonstrated remarkable foresight by his political will to rely on soft power. In hindsight Carter can be said to have acted as a wise statesman. He was a conciliatory instead of a conflictive president. He demonstrated peace-seeking rather than war-mongering leadership, which was truly an exceptional personal characteristic in American internal and foreign politics.

As he was a practicing Christian, knew his Bible well, and tried to put into practice its wisdom, it is not too far-fetched to let him associate with a deep insight of the Old Testament book of Proverbs 29,18: "Where there is no vision, the people perish: but he that keepeth the law, happy is he."

2. The theme of global justice. Evidently President Carter was excellent in discerning the signs of the times, acting himself and urging people to act correspondingly. This affirmation constitutes a bridge to passage to the WARC, the World Alliance of Reformed Churches, a fellowship of 75 million Reformed Christians in 214 churches in 107 countries.

Its member churches are Congregational, Presbyterian, Reformed, and United churches with roots in the sixteenth-century Reformation led by John Knox, John Calvin, and others. It has a long-standing commitment to justice, which culminated in the twenty-third General Council in Debrecen, Hungary. There the WARC made the historic decision to admonish member churches and the ecumenical movement into a process of confessing – *processus confessionis* – in the midst of economic injustice and degradation of the earth.

In affirming this decision the WARC, gathering in Accra, Ghana, from July 30 to August 13, 2004, agreed upon a Covenant for Justice in the Economy and the Earth. Those attending the symposium in the Ghanaian capital had read the signs of the times and found they had become very alarming and needed to be profoundly interpreted.

In particular, the current economic and financial crises were diagnosed as being directly linked to neoliberal economic globalization, which is based on a great number of beliefs including:

- unrestrained competition, consumerism and the unlimited economic growth, and accumulation of wealth is the best for the entire world;
- capital speculation, liberalization, and deregulation of the market, privatization of public utilities, and the unrestricted movement of capital will achieve wealth for all;
- social obligations, protection of the poor and the weak, trade unions, and relationships between people are subordinate to the processes of economic growth and capital accumulation.

The WARC rejected this neoliberal ideology and its TINA (There Is No Alternative)-claim:. It took a firm stance, looking for support from liberation theology. This branch of theology advocates the point of view that a true reading of the Bible leads to democracy and socialism, which goes hand-in-hand with democratic intervention in the economy. This is neither dogmatic *laissez-faire* capitalism nor dogmatic scientific socialism (Villa-Vicencio, 1992, pp. 230–233).

The WARC affirms that global economic justice is essential to Christians' integrity of faith. Such Christians believe that their credibility is at stake if they remain silent or refuse to act in the face of the current system of neoliberal economic globalization. Therefore, Accra rejected any church practice and teaching that excludes the poor, ignores care for creation, or gives comfort to those who come to steal, kill, and destroy.

No doubt, the worldview of the WARC was and is inclusive rather than exclusive, constructive rather than destructive. It is used to step into the breach for all creatures and all creation, while it continues to groan, in bondage, waiting for its liberation, as Paul wrote in Romans 8, 22 (WARC papers).

3. *A just and responsible society.*   In this climate Harry de Lange, a Dutch economist (1919–2001), felt very much at ease. De Lange and his colleague Bob Goudzwaard were elucidating and advocating a social-ethical economy, which they outlined in "Beyond Poverty and Affluence: Towards an Economy of Care." De Lange was also an activist and a scientist. In the eighties he became professor in Applied Social Ethics at the Theological Faculty of the UtrechtUniversity.

He earned himself a name for his dissertation, *Shaping a Responsible Society* (1966), an exploration into the ecumenical movement and its impact on macroeconomic matters. It was his conviction that in societal life almost everything involves ethical considerations and he assigned churchpersons the right to interfere in economic, political, and technical evolutions. To him such interference was a given, but in addition he pressed them in advance to do serious homework and analyze any potential problem. Failing this, one is not capable of effectively confronting academics, bankers, top managers, and other specialists.

Justice, support for the poor, responsible society, and world peace were issues de Lange was interested in and always prepared to stand up for. His energy and commitment were astounding. He also became involved in "the making of Europe," taking part in the struggle for the human face of Europe and backing up Jacques Delors, the former chair of the European Commission, when airing his opinion that Europe was lacking a heart and a soul. According to de Lange, in a paper in 1993, Europe was in need of a renewed model for its future evolution (De Lange, 1993). In particular, it should reconsider its insufficient environmental development and implement the support for the poor. It occurred to him that the biblical concept of justice is "the guide for such a model" (de Lange, 1993, pp. 155, 166).

In de Lange's numerous preoccupations, anthropology and theology (he belonged to Dutch Arminianism, a liberal reform church) often merged, which can be illustrated by the following: "God needs man. He looks for him. He invites him to take part in His work of creation. He counts on the cooperation of man." This was his understanding of the human person and this was the way he understood himself (Witte-Rang, 2008, pp. 127–128, 304–311, 587–591).

Conclusion

The three principles and practices, outlined above, reflect a vigorous strategy of liberation from social-political exploitation and economic distress, from which both males and females still suffer throughout the world. Their pain and deprivation must be relieved and must come to an end.

This obligation and the necessity to read the signs of the times may bring about a *kairos*. Kairos is the Greek word used in the Bible (for example in Mark 1;15 and 13;33, Luke 8;13 and 19;44, Romans 13;11–13, 1 Corinthians 7; 29, 2 Corinthians 6; 2, Titus 1;3, Revelation 1;3 and 22;10) to designate a special moment of time when God visits his people to offer them a unique opportunity for repentance and conversion, for change and decisive action. It is a time for judgment, a moment of truth and of crisis, for example, the actual financial and economic crises (The Kairos Document, 1986, p. 33).

Fortunately any crisis is accompanied by chances and changes as well. "Yes, we can," US President Barack Obama would insist. We can, certainly, but only if we are imbued with a robust sense of duty, a lesson taught by Immanuel Kant.

Literature

Bacevich, A.J. 2008. *The Limits of Power: The End of American Exceptionalism.* New York: Henry Holt.

Berger, P.L.1963. *Invitation to Sociology: A Humanistic Perspective.* New York: Doubleday.

De Lange, H.M. 1993. "Struggling for the Human Face of Europe." In Wiersma, J. (ed.), *Discernment and Commitment: On the Making of Europe*, pp. 155–168. Kampen: Kok Pharos Publishing House.

Elshtain, B.J. 2008. *Sovereignty. God, State, and Self* (The Gifford Lectures). New York: Basic Books.

Gerth, H.H. and Wright Mills, C. (eds) 1958. *From Max Weber: Essays in Sociology.* New York: New York University Press.

Kraemer, H. 1958. *Godsdienst, Godsdiensten en het Christelijk Geloof,* pp. 142–144. Nijkerk: Callenbach.

Smedema, I.J. 2009. *Grond onder de Voeten. Karl Barths scheppingsleer in KD III, 1 opnieuw gelezen* (doctoral dissertation, Free University Amsterdam), Zoetermeer, Boekencentrum.

The Kairos Document 1986. *A Theological Comment on the Political Crisis in South Africa,* Braamfontein: Skotaville Publishers and Grand Rapids, MI: Wm. B. Eerdmans.

Villa-Vicencio, C. 1992. *A Theology of Reconstruction: Nation-Building and Human Rights.* Cambrdige: CambridgeUniversity Press.

WARC papers 1983. *Document GC 23-e. World Alliance of Reformed Churches,* Geneva.

Weber, M. 1958. *The Protestant Ethic and the Spirit of Capitalism.* New York: Harper and Row.

Witte-Rang, G. 2008. *Geen Recht de Moed te Verliezen. Leven en werk van dr. H.M. de Lange (1919–2001).* Zoetermeer: Boekencentrum.

17
Islamic Economics

Feisal Khan

Islamic economics is an important alternative to the market-based (often termed "Western") economic model that, in one variant or another, is now found in most formal economic systems worldwide. Islamic economics is, perforce, confined to Muslim-majority countries, but there is no Muslim country whose economy can actually be described as "Islamic." However, Islamic revivalism worldwide, the sheer number (one billion plus) of Muslims, and their predominance among the world's petroleum exporters – Saudi Arabia, Kuwait, Iran, United Arab Emirates, and Libya (plus some key emerging market economies, such as Malaysia and Turkey) – ensures that Islamic economics will continue to be a serious alternative to Western-style market capitalism. For its advocates, Islamic economics is the "third way" between the two main Western extremes of free market capitalism (with its emphasis on the rational individual's self-maximizing behavior) and socialism (with its emphasis on social ownership of the means of production and the sublimation of the individual's needs to those of society's).

Sharia'h context of Islamic economics

To understand what Islamic economics is and how it came about, it is necessary to have some understanding of Islamic history and fiqh (jurisprudence). Islam – specifically the Qur'an, its holy book – was revealed to the Prophet Muhammad[1] (c.570–632 CE) over the last 23 years of his life. By 630 CE Muhammad was the undisputed ruler of Mecca, and the Muslim expansion out of Arabia and into the world beyond had begun.

In a remarkably short period of time, Islamic rule and governance was firmly established in much of the Mediterranean world, the Middle

East, and parts of the Far East. Islamic law, in its major variants, was the legal code in most of these areas and economic life was generally regulated, to a greater or lesser degree and with varying levels of enforcement rigor, according to its tenets.

The advocates of Islamic economics all agree that economic life cannot be considered in isolation from the rest of society. Quite the contrary, Islamic economics forms an integral component of Islamic governance. The principles of Islamic governance are derived from the *Sharia'h* (literally "path," i.e., the Divine Path or Law that all Muslims must follow) as revealed by Allah to his Messenger, the Prophet Muhammad, in the Qur'an, and the *Sunnah* (i.e., the actions and collected sayings, *Hadith*) of the Prophet.

At its most basic, Islam is the submission of the individual to the Will of Allah, and the ideal form of Islamic governance is a nomocracy where the *Sharia'h* reigns supreme (Nasr S.H, 2004/2002). As Islam is a "complete" religion, the *Sharia'h* accordingly governs all aspects of Muslim life, from personal hygiene to marriage to property rights to economic activities to rules of warfare.

Since humans are not capable of altering *Sharia'h*, the Law is unchanging and unchangeable, and the underlying basis of the Law is the Qur'anic commandment (Qur'an 3:104) to all Muslims "to do good and prevent evil" (*al-amr bi al-maruf wa al-nahy an al-munkar*), and the purpose of *Sharia'h* (i.e., *maqasid al Sharia'h*) is improving the overall material and spiritual well-being of the *ummah* (the Muslim community of believers). It is in this context that Islamic economics has to be understood and analyzed.

A necessary distinction should be made between *fiqh* (Islamic jurisprudence) and *Sharia'h*. While the two terms are often used interchangeably, *fiqh* is simply the result of human attempts to interpret *Sharia'h* and should not be viewed as immutable and unchangeable. Where no clear answer is forthcoming from the Qur'an or the *Sunnah*, then *ijma* (consensus of the believers) and *qiyas* (deduction by analogy) may be used to decide if something is or is not permissible in Islam. Only the first two sources are infallible, while the latter two are, in theory, open to reinterpretation. Thus most of what is often called *Sharia'h* should be more properly referred to as *fiqh*, which can be changed by a consensus of the *mujtahiddeen* (Islamic scholars well versed in *hadith*, *fiqh*, *ijma*, and *qiyas*). While in practical terms a great deal of leeway is possible for the *mujtahid*, a de facto conservative consensus has emerged, and established Islamic *fiqh* is now very difficult to change/reinterpret. This is exemplified by the centuries-old (Sunni) Muslim saying that "the gates of *Ijtihad* are closed" (i.e., no further extensive reinterpretation is needed or indeed possible).

Muslims, while not ascribing divinity to Muhammad, hold his life to be the *uswah hasanah* (the beau ideal) of human behavior, and his interpretation of the Qur'an and his resulting decisions are unquestionable and form binding precedents for all observant mainstream Muslims. These form the *Sunnah* of the Prophet (i.e., his actions, including the *Hadith*, his collected sayings), and many of the contemporary interpretations of Islamic economics are derived, implicitly or explicitly, from the *Sunnah* since the Qur'an has relatively little direct economic content.

Therefore some conservative Muslims (usually termed *Salafis*, righteous ancestors) hold that the Qur'an, the *Sunnah* and, where the *Sunnah* is silent, the practices of the first three generations of Muslims, especially the *Sahaba* (Companions) of the Prophet, are the only acceptable sources of guidance for contemporary Muslims. This is based on a *sahih hadith*[2] of the Prophet that the first three generations of Muslims will be the best ones (MSA online searchable *hadith* database: *Sahih Bukhari* vol.3, book 48, nos. 819–820). This view, again, colors much of the current conservative interpretation of Islamic economics, and many contemporary advocates of Islamic economics harken back to the *Sunnah* and the early works of Muslim scholars in an attempt to legitimize or delegitimize contemporary economic practices, since nothing else is "authentically Muslim" and acceptable (Nasr S.V.R., 1996).

Islamic economics

Islamic economics in its current form is a twentieth century construct. While Muslim thinkers had of course written voluminously on economic issues in the millennia-plus before the last century (see Chapra, 2008 for a detailed discussion of early Muslim contributions to economic thought), modern Islamic economics arose in the 1940s as a direct response to the European colonial domination of Muslim societies (Chapra, 2004; Kuran, 2004; Zaman, 2008).

The majority of present-day Islamic economists adhere to a relatively traditional interpretation of *Sharia'h* and so desire what the contemporary Iranian philosopher Abdolkarim Soroush has termed the *maximalist* approach to Islam, where "everything has to be derived from religion" (Fremont, 2000). Thus most definitions of Islamic economics make explicit reference to *Sharia'h* and are unintelligible to those who lack some Islamic knowledge. For example, M. Akram Khan (1984) defines Islamic economics as being the study of human *falah* [well-being/success achieved by follow-ing Islamic injunctions] achieved by organising the resources of the earth on the basis of cooperation and participation.

While for Zaman (1984) Islamic economics is

the knowledge and application of injunctions and rules of *Sharia'h* that prevent injustice in the acquisition and disposal of mater-ial resources in order to provide satisfaction to human beings and enable them to perform their obligations to Allah and the society.

Asad Zaman (2008) and M. Umer Chapra (2008) provide even more complex definitions that are not easily reduced to a few lines.

In a more practical vein, Kuran (2004) characterizes Islamic econom-ics as having the following three basic tenets:

1. the prohibition of *riba* (i.e., interest or usury) in all financial transac-tions;
2. wealth redistribution through the levy of *zakat* (religious alms tax) on all movable wealth; this is usually levied at the rate of 2.5 percent of the value per lunar year for most Muslims, although the exact rate varies according to *madhab* (school of *fiqh*/thought);
3. adherence to Islamic economic norms that "command good" and "forbid evil"; this includes forbearing from products and activities deemed *haram*(forbidden) for Muslims, such as economic activities involving alcohol, pork, gambling, or pornography.

In addition to *zakat*, a separate tax, *ushr*, is levied at the rate of 5–10 percent of output on certain categories of agricultural products. All Islamic taxes are levied only if the minimum taxable amount (*nisab*) is reached. Non-Muslim subjects (*dhimmis*) are not liable for *zakat* or *ushr* but do have to pay the *jizya* (poll) tax; they are also exempt from com-pulsory military service. Some extremely devout Muslims hold that the only forms of taxation permissible are those explicitly mentioned (e.g., *zakat* and *ushr*) in the Qur'an and the *Sunnah* and so modern innova-tions, such as a progressive income tax, are strictly un-Islamic. This is a minority view that, for obvious reasons, has not found much favor among Muslim governments.

All five main schools (*madhab*) of Islamic jurisprudence (*fiqh*) – four Sunni (*Hanafi, Maliki, Shafi'i,* and *Hanbali*) and one Shia (*Ja'afri*) – are in substantial agreement on the broad principles discussed here, although there can be significant differences on specific issues (e.g., Shias calculate *zakat* on a different basis than do Sunnis).

There is general agreement among advocates of Islamic economics that it, like *Sharia'h* itself, is essentially transformative. Unlike Western economics, which prides itself on positive analysis, Islamic economics goes beyond even normative policy prescriptions into the transformative realm. That is, rather than being simple normative economic analysis that advocates a desired economic outcome, Islamic economics, being a part of the *Sharia'h*, is aimed at achieving a "transformation of human beings from followers of base desires to people concerned with achieving higher goals" (Zaman, 2008; see also Chapra, 2008 and Khan, M. and Bhatti, 2008). For its advocates, the transformation of "base" (i.e., self-centered if not outright selfish) desires into "higher goals" of peace, human-welfare improvement and spirituality is a key difference between Islamic and Western/capitalist economics. Its advocates deny that Islamic economics is utopian wishful thinking since this would mean that *Sharia'h* is neither practical nor implementable.

In their pursuit of human transformation, Islamic economists have, among other issues, advocated for greater wealth and income equality (citing Quranic verses that encourage believers to donate generously to the poor and forgive debts owed by them, in exchange for a manifold return in the afterlife); the communal/public ownership of some key physical resources such as forests, mineral deposits, grazing lands; the immorality and illegality of business transactions where the gains are disproportionately one-sided; profit sharing in good times and loss/belt-tightening in bad times among all the workers of a firm, and so on. However, unlike medieval Roman Catholicism, for example, Islam explicitly rejects monasticism or St Thomas Aquinas' condemnation of all trade as "unjustly acquired" gains. On the contrary, trading and making a profit is not only entirely legal but highly encouraged, provided that it is done "justly" (i.e., with commensurate risk-sharing and without exploitation). However, many of Aquinas' other teachings regarding "just prices" (understood as nonexploitative pricing) and condemnation of usury/interest would resonate among contemporary Islamic economists.

Islamic economics in practice: Islamic Banking and Finance

The most advanced and developed part of Islamic economics is Islamic Banking and Finance (IBF). While commonly synonymous with "interest-free banking" for most observers, IBF is actually more complex than that. In addition to the prohibition on *riba* (interest/usury), *gharar* (speculation), and *haram* (forbidden products), El Hawary et al. (2004) include the following three additional requirements within IBF:

1. *risk-sharing:* the terms of financial transactions need to reflect a symmetrical risk/return distribution that each participant to the transaction may face;
2. *materiality*: all financial transaction must have "material finality," that is, be directly linked to a real underlying economic transaction; thus options and most other financial derivatives are banned;
3. *no exploitation*: neither party to the transaction should be exploited.

Despite these restrictions placed on it, IBF has been growing extremely rapidly in much of the Islamic world and beyond. *The Economist* (2008) estimates the value of IBF assets at approximately US $700 billion worldwide, with Islamic banks being found in over 70 countries.

The preferred form of financing in Islam is Profit and Loss Sharing (PLS), where the financier takes a direct equity stake in the venture, rather than a fully collateralized, interest-based loan (non-PLS, as is the norm in conventional banking). This grows out of the emphasis on risk-sharing as promoting greater societal equity and leads directly to the belief among many Muslims that "in Islam, one does not lend to make money, and one does not borrow to finance business" (El-Gamal, 2000). However, despite the ostensible emphasis on risk-sharing, IBF in practice is overwhelmingly dominated by non-PLS modes of financing (sometimes referred to as "trade-based" modes), with *murabaha* (deferred-payment purchase at a marked-up price or, often, explicitly stated "markup rate"), and *ijara* (leasing) transactions dominating all financing.

An example of a *murabaha* transaction might be where the clients approach the financier and request that, say, machinery costing US $1,000,000 be purchased on their behalf. They then concomitantly agree to purchase the equipment from the financier for, say, US $1,100,000, with payments being made on a regular schedule. Obviously, if the repayment time period is known, calculating the implicit interest rate is a trivial matter. *Ijara* is the functional equivalent of a conventional lease. Mansoor Khan and Ishaq Bhatti (2008) determined that, in 2006, PLS-financing modes constituted only 6.34 percent of all Islamic bank financing, while these two non-PLS (i.e., trade-based) modes constituted most of the rest (*murabaha* 54.42% and *ijara* 16.31%).

That IBF closely mimics conventional banking is not surprising. In 1993 Timur Kuran (2004) argued that Islamic banking would have to replicate the standard, collateralized debt-financing model of conventional banking if it were to operate in a highly information-asymmetric economic environment (i.e., one where the lender cannot accurately discern the borrower's intentions or true measure of credit risk, and where the borrower may have an incentive to take excessive risks with the lender's money). Many of the more conservative *ulema* (Islamic scholars) concur in the assessment of much of current IBF being simply "disguised interest" and so condemn virtually all non-PLS modes of financing as being, at best, only weakly Islamic. It was on these grounds that Pakistan's highest court, the Supreme Court's Shariat Appellate Bench, ruled against all non-PLS forms of financing in 1999 and mandated PLS as the sole permissible form of financing in an Islamic society; this ruling was overturned on final appeal in 2002 and the case remanded to the lower court for further deliberation (see Khan, F., 2008 for more details).

A more liberal interpretation of IBF?

There is a dissenting view among some *ulema* that holds that *riba*, which has a literal meaning of "increase," is best understood as extreme usury or gross exploitation and not as interest. Thus conventional banking is permissible. For example, the late Professor Fazlur Rahman (Harold H. Swift Distinguished Service Professor of Islamic Thought at the University of Chicago) argued that the Qur'an banned a particularly loathsome pre-Islamic lending norm where a creditor would ask a debtor, upon his debt coming due, "Will you pay up or will you *riba* (increase)?" (Rahman, 1964, quoting Imam Malik, *c.*715–796 CE, founder of the Maliki school of *fiqh*). If he could not repay the normal accrued interest and principal, his debt would be doubled. If the borrower still could not repay the doubled debt when it came due again, he would be granted another extension but at the cost of his debt being doubled again (Rahman, 1964). This, then, is the context of one of the Qur'anic verses that prohibits *riba*:

> O you who believe! do not devour usury, making it double and redouble, and be careful of (your duty to) Allah, that you may be successful. (Qur'an 3:130; Yusufali translation)

A defaulting debtor would then be auctioned off into slavery and his goods seized to satisfy his creditors. Thus Rahman concludes that the

Qur'an bans extreme usury and not interest since the original loan and interest was lawful. Furthermore, the prohibition applies really only to personal-consumption loans. El-Gamal (2000) has a more recent exposition of this argument from Muhammad Sayyid Tantawy, the Grand Sheikh of Al-Azhar University, a leading Sunni Muslim *madrassah* (center of Islamic learning). However, this view is now in a definite minority among the *ulema*.

This interpretation of the Koranic ban on *riba* is consistent with Posner's (1980) view of the economics of "primitive economies" and Glaeser and Scheinkman's (1998) economic analysis of interest-rate restrictions. The basic argument here is that a ban on interest or usury is a risk-reduction mechanism that arises when there is a missing insurance market and when the majority of the population lives near the subsistence level. Thus, in the case of economic setbacks incurred by borrowers who lack adequate resources to absorb the setback, they would owe less to their creditors than they would if it were a fixed-interest-rate loan.

Conclusion

For its advocates, Islam is a complete way of life, one regulated by the *Sharia'h*; and Islamic economics is an integral part of this and cannot be understood or applied without a full understanding and application of *Sharia'h*. By submitting themselves to the Will of Allah in all respects (i.e., by following the *Sharia'h*), observant Muslims are able to fulfill Allah's wishes and ensure themselves a reward in the afterlife. Islamic religious practices, in the meantime, help transform humanity by guiding it away from its baser (self-aggrandizing and self-seeking) instincts towards those that benefit all of society, and especially its weakest members.

Notes

1. It is customary for Muslims to utter the phrase *sallallahu alayhi wasallam* (may Allah bless and grant peace to him) after saying the name of the Prophet Muhammad. The omission of this salutation here is not intended to convey any disrespect but rather to keep to Western academic conventions.
2. Over the centuries both Sunni and Shia Muslim *fiqh* have developed an extremely detailed and elaborate *ulm al hadith* (science/knowledge of *hadith*) to differentiate "authentic" from "fabricated" *hadith*, and all observant Muslims accept the *sahih hadith* (authentic sayings) as binding guidelines.

Literature

Chapra, M.U. 2008. "Islamic Economics: What It Is and How It Developed." *EH.Net Encyclopedia*, edited by R. Whaples. [Online]. Available at: http://eh.net/encyclopedia/article/chapra.islamic.

Chapra, M.U. 2004. "Mawlana Mawdudi's Contribution to Islamic Economics." *The Muslim World*, 94, pp. 163–180.

The Economist 2008. "Savings and Souls; Islamic Finance." [Online]. Available at: www.economist.com. 2008, September 6.

El-Gamal, M.A. 2000. *A Basic Guide to Contemporary Islamic Banking and Finance*, Plainfied, in Islamic Society of North America. [Online]. Available at: http://www.ruf.rice.edu/~elgamal/files/primer.pdf.

El Hawary, Dahlia, Wafik Grais, and Zamir Iqbal. 2004. "Regulating Islamic Financial Institutions: The Nature of the Regulated." World Bank Policy Research Working Paper No. 3227.

Fremont, R. 2000: "Islamic Democracy and Islamic Governance." Seminar at *The Middle East Institute*, [Online]. Available at: http://www.drsoroush.com/English/By_DrSoroush/E- CMB-20001121-Islamic_Democracy_and_Islamic_Governance.html.

Glaeser, Edward L. and Scheinkman, Jose 1998. "Neither a Borrower nor a Lender Be: An Economic Analysis of Interest Restrictions and Usury Laws." *Journal of Law & Economics*, 41(1), pp. 1–36.

Hadith. Translation of Sahih Muslim, Book 10: *Kitab Al-Buyu'* (The Book of Transactions). USC-MSA Compendium of Muslim Texts. Available at: http://www.usc.edu/dept/MSA/fundamentals/hadithsunnah/muslim/010.smt.html#010.3613.

Khan, F. 2008. "Islamic Banking by Judiciary: The 'backdoor' for Islamism in Pakistan?" *South Asia: Journal of South Asian Studies*, 31, pp.535–555.

Khan, M.M. and Bhatti, M.I. 2008. *Developments in Islamic Banking: The Case of Pakistan*. Basingstoke and New York: Palgrave Macmillan.

Khan, M.A. 1984. "Islamic Economics: Nature and Need." *Journal of Research in Islamic Economics*, 1, pp. 55–61.

Kuran, T. 2004. *Islam and Mammon: The Economic Predicaments of Islamism*. Princeton, NJ: Princeton University Press.

Nasr, S. H. 2004/2002. *The Heart of Islam: Enduring Values for Humanity*. Reprint edition. San Francisco: Harper San Francisco.

Nasr, S.V.R. 1996. *Mawdudi and the Making of Islamic Revivalism*. Oxford and New York: Oxford University Press.

Posner, R.A. 1980: "A Theory of Primitive Society, with Special Reference to Law," *Journal of Law and Economics*, 23, pp. 1–53.

Qur'an. Online database, with three separate translations, available at: http://www.usc.edu/schools/college/crcc/engagement/resources/texts/muslim/quran/.

Rahman, F. 1964. "Riba and Interest." *Islamic Studies*, 3, pp. 1–43. English translation by Mazheruddin Siddiqi of the 1963 original "Tahaqiq-i-Riba," *Fikr-o-Nazar*.

Zaman, A. 2008. *Islamic Economics: A Survey of the Literature*. Religion and Development Working Programme, Working Paper 22, International Development Department, University of Birmingham.

18
Quaker Spirituality and the Economy

Laurie Michaelis

Quaker spirituality centers on listening inwardly and to others. It is a collective spirituality, as Quaker meetings seek a "gathered stillness." And it is an engaged spirituality practiced through ways of living, speaking and acting in the world. Quaker social values including integrity, equality and community have shaped their approach to business and trade and led them to engage in campaigning and taking action for economic reform.

An experiential spirituality

The Religious Society of Friends (Quakers) originated in mid-seventeenth-century England. There are now Quakers on every continent, with some of their largest congregations in Africa and Central America. Their approaches to religion and spirituality vary considerably. The majority of the world's 340,000 Quakers have "programmed" meetings led by pastors, with a strong Christian and scriptural focus. This chapter will focus on British Quakerism, where the author has most experience. The Society of Friends in Britain has about 24,000 members and regular attenders at its meetings for worship.

In Britain, Quaker worship largely dispenses with outward form so that participants, sitting together in silence, can focus on listening for "the inner promptings of the Spirit." Quaker meeting houses are usually simply furnished without the use of imagery. There is no altar during meetings for worship, but there is normally a table in the middle of the room bearing copies of the Bible, *Quaker Faith and Practice* (BYM, 1995), and flowers.

Quaker spiritual method is analogous to scientific method, which was approaching its modern form at about the time Quakerism emerged in Britain. Early Friends spoke of "knowing the truth experimentally" – from personal experience or the "inner light."

> You will say, Christ saith this, and the apostles say this, but what canst thou say? Art thou a child of Light and hast walked in the Light, and what thou speakest is it inwardly from God? (Margaret Fell in 1692, quoting George Fox speaking in 1652: BYM, 1995, 19.07)

At the same time, as in scientific method, the truth found through experience is shared and tested with reference to others. There are no ministers. Scripture is valued for its poetry and insight but is not taken as the prime authority. Quakers are committed to shared processes and values, but not to theology or religious belief, which vary widely among them. Some Friends describe themselves as atheists and very few hold to a belief system along the lines of a conventional Christian creed.

A listening spirituality

Quaker practice centers on the "meeting for worship" and some describe what they do in the meeting as "praying" – although most Friends understand both "worship" and "praying" in unconventional terms. The spiritual method centers on listening, both inwardly and to others, as shown below, respectively:

> Take heed, dear Friends, to the promptings of love and truth in your hearts. Trust them as the leadings of God whose Light shows us our darkness and brings us to new life. (BYM, 1995, 1.02.1)

> Receive the vocal ministry of others in a tender and creative spirit. Reach for the meaning deep within it, recognising that even if it is not God's word for you, it may be so for others. (BYM, 1995, 1.02.12)

Quakers say that they are not meditating in their meetings, although many follow meditative processes such as watching the breath, stilling the mind, or focusing on mantras.

Answering "that of God in everyone" is a core commitment that informs much Quaker practice. Friends interpret this in different ways. Those who do not believe in or experience a personal god may understand it as simply meaning that we should seek to recognize the good in everyone, or to acknowledge our common humanity. Quakers acknowledge the validity of different religious and spiritual paths and usually welcome "dual membership," with Friends playing active roles in other faith groups.

A collective spirituality

Quaker spiritual practice is fundamentally collective, through the emphasis on mutual listening. Although Quaker meetings are mostly silent, Friends may speak when "moved by the spirit" to share some experience, reflection, or insight. They are encouraged to take care that their contribution is for the meeting rather than just their own need to speak. They do not (or should not) reply directly to each other's contributions, or enter into debate. This practice of occasional spoken contributions out of silence can help the meeting to become "gathered," with a sense of shared consciousness or a kind of collective inwardness.

This collective spiritual experience is made most explicit in Quaker decision-making practice, known as "Quaker business method." It involves a meeting for worship in which agenda items are put before the group and Friends speak out of the silence, seeking to let go of personal positions and refraining from debate, as during a normal meeting for worship. Normally the meeting can unite around a position or a way forward, and the "clerk" of the meeting is responsible for preparing a minute which expresses that "sense of the meeting" (Morley, 1993). If the meeting cannot find unity, that is recorded in the minute. Quaker business method is practiced in a range of settings, from small local meetings and committees to the annual gathering or "Yearly Meeting," which can include over 1,000 Friends.

For much of the history of the Society of Friends, it formed a small, intimate, tightly bound and largely closed community. Corporate decisions – including those on personal and corporate ethics – were essentially binding on members at pain of disownment. This ethos changed considerably from the mid-nineteenth century and the Society of Friends is now an open, inclusive community with a culture of individual freedom. Britain Yearly Meeting still admits "advices and queries," which provide guidance and encourage Friends to reflect on all aspects of spiritual, social, and practical life (BYM, 1995, 1.02).

An engaged spirituality

Friends seek to make the whole of life spiritually centered and so have traditionally avoided distinctions such as holy days and places. Although meetings for worship are normally held on Sundays, Friends used to call this simply "first day" rather than the Sabbath. Friends' speech, lifestyles, and action in the world are seen as integral parts of their spiritual life, and a commitment to social and political reform is a central part of Quakerism.

Spoken contributions in meeting often relate to concerns about peace, social justice, or the environment. British Friends have been particularly engaged in issues including antiwar campaigning, the abolition of the slave trade, prison reform, and restorative justice. They have helped create well-known organizations for international aid and human rights. Recently they have been closely involved in the movements for nonviolent social change related to globalization and climate change.

Quakers speak of expressing their own values and ethics, in contrast with the values of the world, through "testimonies." A Quaker testimony is not just a policy statement or cluster of words but is embodied in a way of living, speaking, and acting in the world:

> It seems to us that a testimony should spring from a place of love rather than fear, have a corporate dimension, be about witness as well as coming from the divine, and, like an act of worship, lead us back to the divine. But the ultimate test of testimony is whether Friends live it, (QPSW, 2007)

So testimony is at the same time:

- a way of being and a form of communication;
- an expression in and to the world of spiritual insight and experience; and
- a spiritual practice in itself.

The area of testimony for which Quakers are most widely known is peace. This is not simple pacifism, or seeking a world without conflict, but it does mean working to address conflict through listening for the voice of God in the other, seeking to understand, rather than using force or even trying to persuade others that they are wrong.

The peace testimony has had direct implications for Quaker involvement in the economy. In the eighteenth and nineteenth centuries Quaker industrialists were expected to avoid involvement in weapons manufacture. Friends have also repeatedly challenged the levying of taxes for fighting wars, and some have withheld a proportion of their taxes in protest.

Testimonies in other areas – in particular simplicity, sustainability, equality, justice, truth, integrity, and community – have also been essential to Quakerism since its earliest days. The testimonies shape the way Quakers approach money, trade, business, and the economy.

Truth and integrity: Quakers as producers

Quaker testimony on truth and integrity has implications for the way Friends engage in business:

> Are you honest and truthful in all you say and do? Do you maintain strict integrity in business transactions and in your dealings with individuals and organisations? Do you use money and information entrusted to you with discretion and responsibility? Taking oaths implies a double standard of truth; in choosing to affirm instead, be aware of the claim to integrity that you are making. (BYM, 1995, 1.02:37)

Many early Friends were merchants and artisans. They insisted on absolute truth and refused to swear oaths, based on the biblical injunction to "not swear at all ... but let your word be 'yes, yes' or 'no, no'" (Matthew, 5:34, 37). They were committed to publishing prices rather than haggling over transactions.

Despite their anticonsumption stance, Quakers were closely involved in the development of the capitalist system in Britain in the eighteenth and nineteenth centuries. The Society of Friends now relies heavily on buildings and charitable funds left by manufacturers such as the Rowntrees and Cadburys. Earlier Quaker capitalists included the Lloyds, a family of iron and steel makers who turned bankers; the Barclays, whose bank emerged from a goldsmith's business; and Edward Pease and other Friends who financed and built the world's first public railway (Walvin, 1997).

Quakers thrived in the capitalist system. Hard work and simple living meant that they reinvested the money they made. Their strong national community brought mutual support, scrutiny of each other's business practices, exchange of skills, and an ability to innovate. Their reputation for truth and integrity made Quakers a trusted brand, in modern terms.

Some Quakers, along with many other industrialists, used their wealth and power to improve their employees' quality of life. They built "model villages" for their workers – such as Bournville in Birmingham around the site of the Cadbury chocolate factory – and organized education, social support systems, and leisure opportunities. They also had an eye to the religious and moral development of their employees – the sale of alcohol is still prohibited in Bournville.

Quakers have been much less involved in business throughout the past century. This is partly the result of an increasing number of people joining the Society of Friends from non-Quaker families. There has been a shift in the income and class mix of Quakers, and the industrialists have been largely replaced by teachers and social workers (Dale, 1996).

Simplicity and sustainability: Quakers as consumers

Until the mid-nineteenth century, Friends were recognizable by their simple, plain clothes. They avoided jewelry, ornate furniture, and popular entertainment. Their distaste for conspicuous consumption was not unusual for an egalitarian religious community. It related partly to a concern for wider social equality, and partly to a commitment to the spiritual life (Michaelis, 2008).

Simplicity became less important and less visible for twentieth-century Friends. However, Quakers still have frugal tendencies. Britain Yearly Meeting calls on Friends through the Advices and Queries to be discerning in their consumption:

> Consider which of the ways to happiness offered by society are truly fulfilling and which are potentially corrupting and destructive. Be discriminating when choosing means of entertainment and information. Resist the desire to acquire possessions or income through unethical investment, speculation or games of chance.

> In view of the harm done by the use of alcohol, tobacco and other habit-forming drugs, consider whether you should limit your use of them or refrain from using them altogether. Remember that any use of alcohol or drugs may impair judgement and put both the user and others in danger.

> Try to live simply. A simple lifestyle freely chosen is a source of strength. Do not be persuaded into buying what you do not need or cannot afford. Do you keep yourself informed about the effects your style of living is having on the global economy and environment? (BYM, 1995, 1.02:39–41)

Since 2000 British Friends have increasingly seen their lifestyle choices as related to sustainability, and this has renewed their tendency to question consumerism.

Friends have maintained a concern for the way the world of business operates. This has taken perhaps its most concrete form recently in Quaker approaches to investment. Friends Provident, originally a Quaker-owned and -run company, developed the first socially responsible British investment product in 1984, in the shape of its Stewardship Fund.

Equality, justice and community: standing for economic reform

Quakerism emerged during the English Revolution and was closely related to the political movement to abolish the system of hierarchical power. Early Friends refused to remove their hats in the presence of those in power and used the informal "thou" instead of the formal "you." However, despite advocating radical economic reform (e.g., Penn, 1668), in practice Quakers were financially very successful and by the mid-nineteenth century had considerable economic power. Quakers developed strong support mechanisms within their own community, and established funds for the relief of poverty more generally, but became lukewarm about true reform.

In the twentieth century many Friends were active socialist campaigners and connected this to their faith. Quakers have also included economists who took radical positions on the need for reform, notably the American Friend Kenneth Boulding, whose paper on "the coming spaceship Earth" (Boulding, 1966) predates the better-known writings of Herman Daly and the Club of Rome on the ecological imperative to move to a steady-state economy. In a Quaker lecture (Boulding, 1964) he contrasts love as a basis for organizing society with the world's principles of threat and exchange.

Recently, as the threat of climate change becomes increasingly real, Friends have seen economic reform as an essential part of the changes needed in society. Brown and Garver (2009) set out an agenda to develop a "moral economy," largely using the principles delineated by Kenneth Boulding. British Friends have held a series of conferences on the "Zero Growth Economy." However, there is as yet no clear Quaker position on the direction required. Some Friends believe that the economy will need to shrink considerably to avoid dangerous climate change and have acted accordingly, by downshifting in their work, income, and consumption and devoting time to voluntary work in their communities. Others are less ready for change and cite concerns about unemployment and reduced income for producers in low-income countries as reasons for maintaining an affluent lifestyle.

Literature

Boulding, K. 1964. *The Evolutionary Potential of Quakerism.* Wallingford, PA: Pendle Hill Publications.

Boulding, K. 1966. "The Economics of the Coming Spaceship Earth." In *Environmental Quality in a Growing Society.* Baltimore, MD: Johns Hopkins University Press.

Brown, P. and Garver, G. 2009. *Right Relationship: Building a Whole Earth Economy.* San Francisco, CA: Berrett-Koehler.

BYM [Britain Yearly Meeting of the Religious Society of Friends] 1995. *Quaker Faith and Practice,* London: BYM.

Dale, J. 1996. *Beyond the Spirit of the Age.* London: Quaker Home Service.

Jonathan D. 1996. "Beyond the Spirit of the Age" (Swarthmore Lecture) *QHS* 1996.

McIntosh, A. 2004. *Soil and Soul: People versus Corporate Power.* London: Aurum Press.

Michaelis, L. 2008. "Quaker Simplicity." In L. Bouckaert, H. Opdebeeck, and L. Zsolnai (eds), *Frugality: Rebalancing Material and Spiritual Values in Economic Life,* Oxford: Peter Lang.

Morley, B. 1993. *Beyond Consensus: Salvaging the Sense of the Meeting.* Pendle Hill Pamphlet 307, Wallingford, PA: Pendle Hill Publications.

Penn, W. 1668. *No Cross, No Crown.* Shippenburg, PA: Destiny Image Publishers.

QPSW [Quaker Peace and Social Witness] 2007. *Engaging with the Quaker Testimonies: A Toolkit.* London: Quaker Books.

Walvin, J. 1997. *The Quakers: Money & Morals.* London: John Murray.

19
Personalism

Luk Bouckaert

"Personalism" emerged as a modern philosophical and ethical stance in academic and public debate in the beginning of the twentieth century. Independently from each other, three books were published: in France, *Le Personnalisme* (1903) by Charles Renouvier; in Germany, *Person und Sache* (1906) by William Stern; and in the USA, *Personalism* (1908) by Border Parker Bowne. In each of these philosophical works, there is a strong focus on the uniqueness of the human person and a defense of the person against the mechanisms of depersonalization in society. Personalism stands for a spiritual humanism characterized by a belief that human self-realization has its roots in the deeper sources of the self and not primarily in the ideological, religious, political, or economic systems manipulating and socializing the individual. Only free and responsible persons can engage in joint ventures to make freer and more responsible institutions.

But behind the shared focus there is a lot of difference. The American stream of personalism centered on *The Personalist,* a journal founded by Ralph Tyler Flewelling in 1920, is rooted in the idealism of Hegel and Kant, while the European movement with Emmanuel Mounier and the journal *Esprit,* set up in 1932, was a response to the voices of existentialism (Nietzsche, Kierkegaard, Heidegger) and to the political debates on Fascism and Marxism. Although personalism is deeply inspired by Christian humanism, the argument and style of personalism is philosophical and therefore open to religious and nonreligious people.

If we look at the economic ideas of personalism, there is again a gap between the American and European traditions. For example, the Acton Institute promoting "economic personalism" in its *Journal of Markets & Morality* presents a much stronger belief in free markets than do the European personalists defending the *Rijnland* model of economic governance and its "social market" philosophy. But despite how different some practical positions may be, the argument involved is always based on a concept of the human person as a free and responsible being and proceeds to an analysis of the arrogance of systems, bureaucracies, and ideologies. Because of this author's familiarity with European personalism, the following contribution presents the guiding ideas of the European movement with its strong social drive,(for which reason it is sometimes called social or communitarian personalism). The next section is a brief sketch of the historical setting giving birth to European personalism in and after the 1930s. The following section (The primacy of the spiritual) deals with its spiritual commitment, and the final section (Personalist economics) with some of its economic ideas.

The historical context

European personalism, as an intellectual and political voice, came through during the crisis of the 1930s with its mix of a deep economic depression, a failing democracy, and a cultural climate of existential uncertainty. Personalism never did constitute a unified system of thought. It was rather a collection of "personalisms." For most of the personalists, reading the work of Henri Bergson (1859–1941) was the crucial eye-opener. Bergson introduced a completely new metaphysics of time, *élan vital*, which stimulated an awareness of the creative sources in people and history. However, readers of Bergson followed their own ways of creativity. Jacques and Raïssa Maritain, initially great admirers and later critics of Bergson, remain a familiar reference when speaking of personalism. *Humanisme intégral (True Humanism)* was a visionary book disclosing a new model of civilization (Maritain, 1936). But there were many other groups, too. An article by the historian Christian Roy sheds an interesting light on the forgotten ecological personalism of Bernard Charbonneau and Jacques Ellul in Bordeaux (Roy, 1999). Another group was formed around Alexandre Marc who, along with Raymond Aron and other friends, kept the journal *Ordre Nouveau* alive for five years (1931–36). They elaborated the idea of federalism as a way out of liberalism and totalitarianism. The most important and durable group, however, was formed around the journal *Esprit*, which was launched in 1932 by Emmanuel Mounier and George Izard. The name of *Esprit(Spirit)* underlined the spiritual commitment of the group, though Mounier always made a clear distinction between spirituality embedded in social engagement and evasive spiritualism. Mounier's *Manifeste au service du personnalisme* contained a passionate critique of liberal bourgeois individualism and all systems of collectivism as forms of depersonalization (Mounier, 1936). In many countries after the Second World War, we find a lot of new circles mostly gathered around some inspiring figures. (Postwar personalist inspirators in Germany were D. Von Hildebrand, R. Guardini, Max Sheler, P. Landsberg; in France, Louis-Joseph Lebret, P. Blondel, P. Ricoeur; in Italy, the founders of The Maritain Institute; in Belgium, A. Dondeyne, L. Janssens, J. Leclercq; in the Netherlands, P. Kohnstamm, H. Brugmans, W. Banning; in Switzerland, Denis De Rougemont; in Czechoslovakia, J. Patocka, V. Havel; in Poland, T. Mazowiecki, K. Wojtila. The list is far from exhaustive.)

Personalists were not seeking in the first instance a new academic theory about the person, but rather a practical philosophy of engagement. In the 1930s, quite a few personalists finished their university studies and chose not to pursue academic careers, but instead chose nonconformist, demanding, and vulnerable commitments with limited financial means. They were motivated by a sense of urgency, inspired by the belief that the time they were living in was a turning point, which was mostly ignored by the academic world. They interpreted the diverse economic, political, and cultural crises as symptoms of a more global crisis of civilization that demanded a response through radical change. Hence they often used the rhetoric of a "new order," "spiritual revolution," "radical reform," and "rebirth." But the rhetoric was supported by innovative ideas regarding political federalism, basic income, economic democracy, and a "third way" economics between individualistic capitalism and statist socialism.

The primacy of the spiritual

La primauté du spiritual (translated: *The Things That Are Not Cæsar's*) was the title of one of J. Maritain's books (Maritain, 1927). As a personalist manisfesto, it expressed a critique of the anthropocentric humanism and rationalism of modernity. Maritain thought that modern humanism's shortcomings would lead to a renewed interest in spirituality, not as a return to the sacred spirituality of medieval society but as a quest for a *profane spirituality* that does not segregate the spiritual to a separate sphere but integrates it as a component of our political, social, economic, and scientific activities. He pleaded for a new Christianity in Europe to promote the emergence of this spiritual humanism. However, the much younger Emmanuel Mounier believed in a more pluralistic approach. In his view *Esprit* should have been a journal for Christians and non-Christians alike. He looked for an inclusive approach to spirituality, leaving it open to the person to discover his/her own experience and definition of self-transcendence. The aim of *Esprit* was to set up a platform where people could freely share and discuss their spiritual commitment but, most of all, could translate it into a contextual, social engagement.

The personalist "primacy of the spiritual" is deeply related to a concept of the human person, distinguishing the person from the individual. This distinction is a basic one for personalism. Individuality is a characteristic of all beings belonging to the material world where things are separated and differentiated from each other. Personality is the capacity of human beings to move out from the individual self to others in freedom and love. It relates the self to all beings and to Life as a transcendent Being. Only a spiritual being, gifted with self-consciousness and autonomy, is able to give of him/herself in relations of mutual responsibility and respect. The difference between individual and person finds its echo in the more recent discourse about the ego and the self (See Chapter 3, Spirituality and Rationality).

Personalist economics

One cannot speak of a school of personalist economists. The term "personalist economics" refers rather to a style of doing economics that does not simply reconstruct the problem of efficient allocation as an individual or collective problem of utility, but initially as a problem of human dignity and social justice. To reduce the problem of rational choice to a problem of maximizing subjective utility is in itself a far-reaching normative standpoint. As soon as one realizes this, there is no reason to exclude other *normative* assumptions, such as personalist or Buddhist or Islamic ones.

We believe that the following four assumptions are characteristic of a personalist approach to economics (Bouckaert, 1999). They defend the human person against all unreasonable forms of instrumentalization. They can be found in an implicit or explicit way in the works of economists and sociologists such as François Perroux, Joseph Lebret, Kenneth Boulding, Ernst Schumacher, Serge Christophe Kolm, Amitai Etzioni, Amartya Sen, Martha Nussbaum, Stefano Zamagni, and many others. Although these "personalist assumptions" can be formulated as descriptive generalizations for theory construction, they are first of all meant as a set of normative principles expressing the priority of the spiritual and relational over the instrumental and rational aspects of economics. Let me briefly comment on these four principles:

1. *The priority of basic needs over subjective preferences.* Preferences are individual and social constructions that express, intensify, and transform basic needs, and in certain cases suppress and obstruct them. Basic needs, on the other hand, are the *necessary* preconditions for humane functioning in a historically and culturally determined community. From a political point of view, one can translate basic needs into *rights* that one can claim on the basis of one's human dignity. As A. Sen has noted, rights can be considered as goals of economic activity (Sen, 1985). Such an economy of human rights differs from a neoclassical welfare economy in that it considers the criterion of Pareto efficiency to be necessary but insufficient as a welfare norm.

   The classical objection to the basic needs approach is that there is no consensus about the content of basic needs. What people experience as a basic need, according to this argument, depends precisely on their individual preferences. This is partially true. One cannot separate basic needs from an individual's subjective aspirations, but that does not mean that basic needs should be reduced to those aspirations. They are embedded in human nature and human history and go beyond individual preferences similar to the way that human rights transcend particular interests. Amartya Sen has attempted, with his concept of "capabilities," to find a middle way between subjective utility and objective necessity. Capabilities express a person's *capacity* to fulfill his or her basic needs. Well known is the humanistic psychologist Abraham Maslow's pyramid depicting a hierarchy of various needs, with material needs at the bottom of the scale (food, clothing, and shelter). The highest level is reached when one is able to discover the intrinsic value of things and people, so that values such as beauty, truth, and goodness are sought for their own sake and no longer because of utilitarian considerations. Although a lot of criticism has been formulated on Maslow's pyramid, the interesting point for a personalist is that the pyramid reveals the duality between lower needs (striving for instrumental values) and higher needs (striving for intrinsic values), which is consistent with the distinction between the individual and the person or between the ego and the relational self.

2. *The priority of commitment over self-interest.* It is sufficiently well known that extrapolations and predictions made by economists are often contradicted by the facts. One of the reasons for this failure is that most economic models narrowly start from the self-interest hypothesis. During the last decade experimental economics and

economic psychology have proved that social motivations based on inequity aversion, reciprocal fairness, and pure altruism are substantial parts of economic behavior (for an overview, see Fehr and Fishbacher, 2002). This research gives some empirical support to the ethical claim that social commitment has a moral priority over selfish behavior. Genuine commitment has its own logic. One who selflessly devotes one's life to justice is aiming at something other than the pleasure of satisfying his/her own altruistic preference. He or she does it for the sake of justice itself, not (at least not primarily) as a means to an extrinsic end such as personal happiness or prestige. A true artist does not use art as a way of fulfilling his own artistic preferences. Rather, the reverse is usually the case: artistic preferences are the result of a more original fascination with what manifests itself in art. Commitment arises through a noninstrumental attachment to something that appears intrinsically meaningful. This original attachment introduces a new order and weight to our preferences. An artist orders his preferences differently than a nonartist. A mystic will be attached to or detached from different preferences than a person who has no religious feelings. Various economists have focused attention on these metaprocesses, speaking in this regard about the distinction between preferences and metapreferences. Metapreference suggests, however, that it is only a matter of a higher-order preference, whereas "commitment" makes clear that there is an essential difference between the instrumental structure of a preference and the noninstrumental structure of a commitment. Another way of expressing this is to say that commitment is directed at bringing about an identity, a way of being, while preference satisfaction aims at bringing about an advantage or a pleasure.

3. *The priority of mutual trust over mutual advantage in the market.* An efficient market requires cooperation and mutual trust. In the words of the renowned welfare economist K. Arrow, "one of the characteristics of a well-functioning economic system is that relations of confidence among the parties must be sufficiently strong so that one cannot deceive the other, even if that might constitute 'economically rational behavior'" (quoted in Gui, 1987). The market does not, by definition, entail a rejection of the "higher values" that make social, moral, and spiritual life possible. One can sell and buy aesthetically and socially qualified products. One can distribute valuable books and ideas in the market. Moreover, the free play of supply and demand can prevent any single instance from acquiring a monopoly on the higher

values. The market guarantees freedom. Yet it is equally true that the market instrumentalizes and individualizes all values in order to maximize an individual's subjective welfare. When everyone determines his values himself, a lack of moral cohesion can open the way to far-reaching opportunistic behavior, which is in the long term a threat to a good functioning of the market. Hence there is the growing awareness that moral self-regulation and "social capital" in the form of mutual trust are constitutive of a good, functioning market.

4. *The priority of economic democracy over shareholder capitalism.* Personalists, inspired by the utopian socialists and by Christian social ethics, see economic democracy as an alternative to bourgeois capitalism and to Marxist collectivism. The search for economic democracy has always been more than an intellectual debate. A lot of democratic experiments have been set up, mostly in the form of cooperative associations. Some could survive and are flourishing, such as the Mondragon complex in Spain, but some of them were less successful. The idea of economic cooperation is gaining ground again in management theory and business ethics. Stakeholder management and co-creative entrepreneurship are highly valued in today's capitalism. Business ethics criticizes shareholder capitalism and promotes the stakeholder theory of the firm. However, it is important to make a distinction between weak and strong versions of the stakeholder theory of the firm. The weak version incorporates stakeholder management within a capitalist theory of the firm. This incorporation leads to a broadened concept of corporate governance where stakeholder interests are taken into account by the board of directors but without a democratic representation of the stakeholders. The strong version of stakeholder theory empowers the stakeholders and makes them full partners of the firm. They get the rights and claims of partners and form a community of co-responsible persons. In principle, economic democracy is broader than workers' democracy, while it aims at a balanced participation of all stakeholders. But the juridical mould of the capitalist firm does not fit this democratic concept of partnership. Hence, there is a challenge for institutional creativity. But whatever the future practices and institutional arrangements of economic democracy will be, the core idea for a personalist is the principle, formulated by John Paul II in his encyclical *Laborem Exercens,* that there is a priority of labor over capital, whereby labor is not reduced to the class of workers but to every person investing his labor, loyalty, and creativity in a company.

Conclusion

Personalism is an engaged philosophy defending the person as a free and spiritual self against the manipulation of systems that try to control and manipulate people. After the Second World War, social personalism, bringing into the fore the role of civil society, "third way" economics and federalism, has deeply inspired the political agenda of Christian Democrats in Europe. Today personalism is reactivating its spiritual potential in the field of economics. The European SPES forum, promoting "Spirituality in Economics and Society," is one of its heirs.

Literature

Bergson, H 1932. *Les deux sources de la morale et de la religion.* Paris, 1941: P.U.F.

Bouckaert, L. and Bouckaert, G. (eds) 1992: Metafysiek en engagement. Een personalistische visie op gemeenschap en economie. Leuven: Acco.

Bouckaert, L. (ed.) 1999. Is Personalism Still Alive in Europe? *Ethical Perspectives,* vol.6, no.1.

Bouckaert, L. 1999. "The Project of a Personalistic Economics." In *Ethical Perspectives,* vol.6, no.1, pp.10–20.

Bouckaert, L. 2004: "Spirituality and Economic Democracy." In L. Zsolnai (ed.), *Spirituality and Ethics in Management,* Dordrecht: Kluwer.

Bruni, L. and Zamagni, S. 2007. *Civil Economy: Efficiency, Equity, Public Happiness.* Oxford: Peter Lang.

Etzioni, A. 1988: *The Moral Dimension: Toward a New Economics.* New York: Free Press.

Fehr, E. and Fishbacher, U. 2002. "Why Social Preferences Matter." *The Economic Journal,* 112, March, pp. 1–33.

Gui, B. 1987. "Eléments pour une définition d'économie communautaire." *Notes et Documents,* 12, pp. 32–42.

Kolm, S.C. 1986. *L'homme pluridimensionnel. Pour une économie de l'esprit.* Paris: Albin Michel.

Maritain, J. 1927. *Primauté du spirituel.* Paris: Plon.

Maritain, J. 1936. *Humanisme Intégral.* Paris: Aubier.

Maslow, H. A. 1954. *Motivation and Personality.* New York: Harper.

Mounier, E. 1936. *Manifeste au service du personnalisme.* Paris : Montaigne.

Roy, C. 1999. "Ecological Personalism. The Bourdeaux School of Bernard Charbonneau and Jacques Ellul." *Ethical Perspectives,* vol.6, no.1, pp. 33–45.

Sen, A. 1985. *Resources, Values and Development.* Oxford: Clarendon Press.

Sen, A. 1987. *On Ethics and Economics.* Oxford: Blackwell.

20
Liberation Theology

Eelco van den Dool

Liberation theology indicates the struggle for a just world as the way to meet God. In working and fighting for socioeconomic justice we can experience grace, fulfillment, and joy along with the hardships of struggle. German theologian Dorothee Sölle has explicitly addressed the relevance of liberation theology for people in Western societies. Her theology may help us to deepen the understanding of the processes of socioeconomic and business reform we are involved in and raise our awareness of the spiritual aspects of these transitions.

The rise of liberation theology

In the early 1960s a change in the Christian theological climate occurred. The second Vatican Council, which adopted a more society-oriented, modern course, stimulated new theologies. The World Council of Churches reconsidered the relationship between church and society and a new generation of theologians emerged that emphasized the practical, public, and critical nature of the Christian faith (Fierro, 1977). German theologian Jürgen Moltmann presented his "Theology of Hope" in 1964. According to Moltmann eschatological hope encourages a positive, critical commitment to the present in which we live and work. In 1965 American theologian Harvey Cox published "The Secular City," in which he develops the idea that God manifests Himself in society and in social change. The Medellin conference of bishops in 1968 can be considered as the official "start" of liberation theology in Latin America.

Liberation theology is critical of the dogmatic perspective on faith: faith as a system of ideas and concepts. It wants to move from orthodoxy to orthopraxis: social action aimed at bringing justice to oppressed groups. It considers faith to be a truth that has to be lived and practiced. Therefore it stresses the relationship between faith and social praxis, often from a more or less (Marxist) dialectical point of view.

Liberation theology has become influential, especially in Latin America in the form of bottom-up movements in which base ecclesial communities appear and poor farmers and workers organize themselves in cooperatives and unions. Some well-known Latin American liberation theologians are Gustavo Gutiérrez, Jon Sobrino, and Leonardo Boff. Liberation theology has met resistance from the Roman Catholic Church.

Liberation theology in Latin America

In the 1950s Latin America had high expectations for development aid (*desarrollismo*). In the following decades it was becoming clear that the ideal of planned development could not live up to its expectations. Desarrollismo was criticized for being directed from rich, Western, industrialized countries who wanted to mold the developing countries to the model, needs, and vested interests of the Western world. Critics from Latin America insisted on analyzing the cultural, social, economic, and political causes of poverty and injustice instead of fighting the superficial symptoms of underdevelopment. These emerging analyses gave way to a more radical view of development and bringing justice to Latin America. The concept of "development" was being replaced by "liberation": a (revolutionary) rupture with structures that disadvantage groups, classes, and persons.

From a dialectical point of view "liberation" coincides with a growing critical awareness of man and an increasing competence for initiating change that is aimed at winning freedom for mankind. History is seen as the process of man's liberation: a never-ending, permanent, cultural revolution.

With the failure of traditional development programs in mind, this perspective was an appealing alternative for many Latin Americans, including Latin American Christians. Many Latin American theologians, however, felt that the views of the Roman Catholic Church on development and the abolition of injustice were too moderate. They started to stress that the Christian view on liberation and breaking with sin has both a personal dimension and a collective or structural dimension. A Latin American school of liberation theology began to develop.

Gustavo Gutiérrez's book *Theology of Revolution* (Gutiérrez, 1978) highlights the main aspects of the spirituality of liberation theology.

Gutiérrez argues out that history is the place where God reveals Himself. God is actively present on earth, among us and in us, engaged in working on justice as opposed to being an otherwordly, abstract deity. The incarnation of God in Christ demonstrates that people are the necessary way through which we can find God. Therefore "the ultimate horizon of faith takes on flesh and blood in the penultimate horizon of the political" (Fiero, 1977). In line with the biblical prophetic tradition Gutiérrez stresses that especially in loving and helping the poor and oppressed we meet God: this is called the option for the poor. The spirituality of liberation theology is rooted in situations where oppression is challenged by protest and liberation. To convert means to "consciously, realistically and concretely engage oneself in the process of liberating the poor and oppressed" (Gutiérrez, 1978). According to Gutiérrez the spirituality of liberation is characterized by the experience of grace and joy. As we become increasingly aware of our involvement in structures of injustice or of being a victim of injustice, getting involved in the struggle for liberation is by no means natural or obvious. Despite the hardships and the inevitable disappointments of struggle, Gutiérrez also points at the joy being an agent of the liberation movement brings.

As liberation theology thinks of liberation in terms of protest, revolutionary change, and struggle, some liberation theologians are not in principle opposed to the use of violence. It considers principled nonviolence an unrealistic attitude, as society is permeated with violence. Violence may very well be necessary and justified to bring about the desired change and to eliminate unjust structures.

Liberation theology for the Western world

Although liberation theology has been less influential in the Western world, in this part of the chapter I want to focus on the German liberation theologian Dorothee Sölle. Her liberation theology has a number of features that make it interesting for our reinvention of economic and business models.

Sölle's liberation theology aims at making the world (including the business community) more democratic, more just, and more sustainable. These worldly issues and worldly relations are the key to spirituality. By "sanctifying the world" (Sölle, 1998) the traditional boundaries between the sacred and the profane disappear, and within the profane the sacred is discovered, "but particularly in engagement with and commitment to 'here' and 'now,' where God comes to us in unforeseeable ways, we meet the God of mysticism, whose ways we do not know"

(Sölle, 1998). This is what she calls the democratization of mysticism: "I mean to say that the mystical sensitivity, which resides in all of us, is being allowed to return, is being dug out of the rubble and wreck of triviality" (Sölle,1998). Luk Bouckaert describes this as a "fundamental transformation of our commitment to people and things" (Bouckaert, 2004). The spirituality of Sölle Liberation Theology is best understood as three interconnected processes or movements:

1. development of a critical, moral understanding of the world and of oneself;
2. initial resistance and action on a public issue;
3. development of a collective praxis of resistance, action, and liberation.

What constitutes the spiritual nature of these three movements is Sölle's recognition that divine–human encounter and transformation can be experienced in each of them. From the early 1960s to the first decade of the twenty-first century Sölle develops a critique of Western society that is built upon a basic scheme of center–periphery. The center stands for the Western, capitalist society, the world of the "haves"; whereas the world of the "have-nots," the Third World, and the outcasts of Western society, are represented by the periphery. According to Sölle the periphery is being exploited and oppressed by the center. In fact, Sölle states, the West is waging an economic war against the periphery in which thousands die of starvation every day. Sölle describes the center in utterly negative terms: extremely violent, alienated, addicted, and dependent. The spiritual atmosphere in the center is one of repressed violence, relational, and mental emptiness and at the same time a hard-to-ignore awareness of future an onward doom and a yearning for change.

Against all odds resistance and liberation movements are beginning to manifest themselves in the periphery. The oppressed and the poor are beginning to stand up for themselves, raise their voices and bring forward their oppression and misery, and initiate change. The agents of change can be poor farmers organizing themselves in a cooperative union, workers fighting for political freedom, or ethnic groups trying to preserve their culture. They uncover injustice, inculpate the center and try to restore justice in their lives or society. The call from the periphery has hit and shocked many people in the center. Listening to these voices opens their eyes to the structures of injustice their lives are built upon: political and economic power blocks, race and gender divides, ecological destruction, access to or blockage from technology and knowledge. They begin to realize that these deeply rooted structures that give wealth to the center also destroy the chances of prosperity and justice in the periphery.

Listening to the voices from the periphery makes some people in the center realize that life, spirit, vitality, soul, transformation, and meaning are much more to be found in the periphery than in the center. Whether it is a cry from the poor or the marginalized in the West stepping forward, "they affirm life in the midst of death" (Murray, 1998). In them we hear a silent cry from God or see a sudden blossoming of life.

A critical understanding of the world, our society, and our lives gains a spiritual quality, which distinguishes it from mere intellectual understanding and knowing if it makes us transcend ourselves. For Sölle this transcendence does not simply mean some form of enlightenment, happiness, or superior wisdom. Rather it is characterized by sadness, shame, or embarrassment.

Developing a critical, moral understanding of the world is, according to Sölle, realizing that one is in a state of powerless (near-) death and that the only way to overcome this life-threatening force is to confront it. Power and vitality can only be regained by resurrection and resurgence from incapacity and numbness. Sölle points out that many people who resist realize that the meaning and value of their lives are at stake. They are aware that refraining from resistance equals self-betrayal and a choice against life and self-realization. In that sense resistance is a life-saving act.

Resistance against structural injustice and oppression can take on many forms, ranging from a small "no" with possible big consequences to wilfully pursuing new ideas and sharing arguments and analysis with the "cheated and betrayed" (Sölle, 1998). It starts with a creative, one-sided initiative. It is creative in the sense that we do not continue to reproduce regular patterns but do something unexpected and new that we hope will last. In this attempt we can discover our own power, knowledge, and courage. If our act of resistance is a joint effort we may well experience that a community of fellow resisters carries the resistance. As an individual resister we may sense being part of a larger whole that has more potential than we ever imagined.

Those who resist are often small and powerless relative to the adversaries that represent the cause they resist. From that perspective the efforts of the resisters seem useless and futile. That is why resistance has the nature of struggle and of surrender. Exactly in surrendering to something or someone who is powerless resides the spiritual core of resistance, according to Sölle. In surrendering to the powerless we experience that the cause we care for is dependent on our efforts. At the same time we experience that our life and our spiritual development are only possible through bonding with the vulnerable and the powerless. Experiencing this mutual dependence and growth equates to experiencing the mutual dependence and union between God and man. In this relationship the weak and dependent represent God to us and at the same time we represent God to the weak and dependent. "This experience makes us more free, it lifts my boundaries and makes me grow to that which is different" (Sölle, 1998). If we are sensitive, as Sölle suggests, to the representational character of the interdependence between ourselves and the weak cause we have begun to commit ourselves to, resistance can be considered a form of co-creation between God and ourselves. This awareness may lift our experience from an "ordinary" protest to a manifestation of divine self-realization. That is not to say that our actions become instant-success miracles. It only means that we experience our actions as part of the "living, active, breathing divine dynamic of love we experience in relation to one another" (Heyward, 2003).

As resistance assumes the form of a struggle, initial resistance by itself will probably not do the job. Some form of follow-up action is necessary. The resisters need to develop a collective praxis of resistance that is durable and will enable them to relive, re-experience, practice, and develop the experience of both an indestructible, empowering bonding with people and through each other with God and a mutual, vulnerable, and wide-open interdependency.

Sölle stresses the integral aspect of salvation. Salvation is aimed at all sins of the whole person, at all people, and at the whole creation, as "the whole creation has been groaning as in the pains of childbirth right up to the present time" (Romans 8: 22) (Sölle, 1983). Salvation is only credible if it engages us in the liberation, conversion, and salvation of others and the world. The universal character of salvation points at another feature of the spirituality of Sölle's liberation theology. Liberation tends to spread like an oil spill on water. Being aimed at the whole person, all people, and ultimately all of creation, liberation may start in one domain or level in life but may well extend to other domains, ranging from economic liberation to political, cultural, or worldview liberation.

Sölle warns us that we should not be overly optimistic about the results of active, critical resistance. One is more likely to meet ridicule, misunderstanding, and contempt than praise and change. Resistance resembles hopping between defeats and hopes (Sölle, 1998). The nature of the cause that resistance has committed itself to asks for dependence and surrender instead of power and force. We can only serve this cause, and in the process help ourselves, if we learn to put aside our tendency to rule, to determine, to plan, to control, and to execute. Success or results are not the ultimate spiritual categories. Sölle points at being united and one with others, with nature, with life, and with God in an active, engaged, practical way as the foundation of life – and not letting results and effectiveness legitimize our spirituality.

Liberation theology and business reform

A study by the author of this chapter suggests there is a close association between the three processes of the spirituality of liberation theology as described by Sölle and actual processes of business reform (Dool, 2009). Five successful innovators participated in this qualitative study: two entrepreneurs who have radically democratized their construction companies, a cofounder of the first "green" bank in the Netherlands, the initiator of one of the first commercially viable fair trade initiatives, and a cofounder of the first feminist magazine in the Netherlands. A significant correlation between the actions and the experiences of the five socially innovative pioneers and Sölle's liberation theology was found:

- The pioneers have a critical view of one or more issues. The issues involved range from our basic assumptions on business and economy to gender issues. This criticism, of course, is an important motivator for developing and implementing an innovation;
- The element of a feeling of fear and guilt for one's own involvement in injustice can also be traced in the experiences of the pioneers; for example, fear of causing family conflicts through business and fear of becoming caught in negative, conflict-loaded organizational patterns;
- For the pioneers, starting the implementation of the business reform was not merely an exciting experiment. According to some of them, doing nothing equates to losing their credibility. Committing themselves to a cause meant, at one stage or another in the process, putting everything (in their professional careers) at risk;
- Another remarkable similarity between Sölle's liberation theology and actual business reform is the tendency to diffuse. In the five cases of business reform the innovation has been transferred to other

companies, other sectors, other countries, and other or new products. This suggests that business reform tends to spread like an oil spill on water, just as liberation does. Liberation theology may help us understand why it does so.

Given the correlation between Sölle's liberation theology and actual processes of business reform, identifying the relevant mystagogic themes involved may provide opportunities to enhance these reforms by means of spiritual counseling. These counseling techniques have yet to be developed.

Literature

Bouckaert, L. 2004. "Democratisering van de mystiek – Sölles visie op maatschappelijk verze," *Ethische perspectieven*, nr. 14, pp.190–198.
Dool, van den, E.C. 2009. "Spiritual Dynamics in Social Innovation: Empirical Research into a 'via Transformativa' for Organizations." Paper presented at the 6th International Critical Management Studies Conference, 2009. Warwick, UK.
Fierro, A. 1977. *The Militant Gospel: A Critical Introduction to Political Theologies*, New York: Orbis.
Gutiérrez, G. 1978. *Theologie van de bevrijding*. Baarn: Uitgeverij Ten Have.
Heyward, C. 2003. "Crossing over, Dorothee Solle and the Transcendence of God." In Pinnock, S. (ed.), *The Theology of Dorothee Soelle*. Trinity Press International.
Murray, C.S.J. 1998. "Liberation for Communion in the Soteriology of Gustavo Gutierrez." *Theological Studies*, 59, pp. 51–59.
Sölle, D. 1983. *Politieke theologie*. Baarn: Ten Have.
Sölle, D. 1998. *Mystiek en verzet*. Kampen: Ten Have.

21
Schumacher's People-Centered Economics

Hendrik Opdebeeck

The environmental and economic crisis of our era, in which profit counts above people or the planet, is put into question by John Elkington (Elkington, 2004). Elkington elaborates on the triple bottom line (also known as "people, planet, profit") to capture a broad spectrum of factors for measuring the economic, ecological, and social impacts of the globalization process. Economist and philosopher Ernst Friedrich Schumacher (1911–1977) was already writing about the phenomenon described by Elkington 40 years ago in his theories on a more planet- and people-centered economics. Indeed, looking at the environmental degradation alone makes the faith in progress seem untenable in reality and appears to offer no guarantee for smooth economic progress. In a special edition of *Time* (April/May 2000) on *How to Save the Earth*, Schumacher was described as one of the heroes of the planet.

This contribution on Schumacher and planet- and people-centered economics rediscovering spirituality begins with a biographical summary and then considers Schumacher's view on the consequences of the supremacy of science-for-use over science-for-insight. In our globalized economy this leads to what Schumacher calls the neglect of man's important *diverging* problems. Schumacher's view on the importance of frugality in economics then becomes crucial. This philosophical–ethical exploration brings him to the forgotten dimension of spirituality in economics.

Schumacher's life

Ernst Friedrich Schumacher was born in Bonn on August 16, 1911. He emigrated to England in January 1937. Being an economist, he found employment as a financial adviser in the City of London. He grappled with the problem of what form of international monetary system should come into being after the war. In a correspondence with J.M. Keynes, Schumacher was deeply convinced of the necessity of providing monetary safeguards if world peace was to be guaranteed. From 1943 to 1945 Schumacher was employed by the Oxford Institute of Statistics. With N. Kaldor and J. Robinson, Schumacher was one of Lord Beveridge's most important collaborators on the latter's well-known Full Employment in a Free Society, in which the concept of "full employment" was elaborated for the first time. Beveridge went on to become even better known for the Beveridge Report that was to become the basis for the growth of social security in Britain after the Second World War.

In the 1950s Schumacher achieved a crucial breakthrough in terms of his view of the world. Before the war Schumacher had obviously been a humanist who chose not to become involved in any kind of religion. His humanist stance was further developed in the work on full employment he did for Beveridge. The ruined Germany of 1945 convinced him even more of the dire consequences of a political and economic system that is not primarily concerned with the value of human beings.

Yet little by little Schumacher's fundamental concern with man in the system of economics was to find a place in another worldview. In the beginning of the fifties the author distanced himself from his secular stance and he began to study Buddhism by reading the work of experts like G. Gurdjieff and E. Conze. His fascination with Buddhism was so great that it made him decide to accept an economic mission to Burma. Via Buddhism Schumacher came to Christianity, following Gandhi's well-known dictum that no matter how strongly people may be attracted to a particular religion, they will eventually find the same profound experience in their own culture and in the religion of their own environment. In 1953 Schumacher had already read the work of M. Nicoll, in which the Buddhist thinking is related to Christianity. After his travels to Burma, Schumacher embarked on an intensive study of the work of Thomas Aquinas and that of other Christian philosophers like R. Guénon and Jacques Maritain.

In 1965 Schumacher founded the Intermediate Technology Development Group (ITDG) in London, together with the group's chairman, G. McRobie. Schumacher had introduced the concept of "intermediate technology" in 1963, in a report written for the Planning Commission of the Republic of India. In this report Schumacher stresses the necessity of developing a type of intermediate technology that would function on a smaller scale, would be simpler to use, less capital intensive, and more nonviolent. The Club of Rome's second report contains a forceful plea for the type of technology advocated by Schumacher. In 1970 he became president of the Soil Association, an organization that had been advocating the use of organic methods in agriculture since the 1940s. The organization trained interested farmers, guaranteed the sale of their produce, and grouped the producers into a cooperative.

In 1973 Schumacher's bestseller, *Small is Beautiful: Economics as if People Mattered*, was published (Schumacher, 1973). This book contains the core of Schumacher's views on the problems of contemporary economics. In the seventies Schumacher also wrote contributions to the philosophy of science from the point of view of economics. An example of these contributions can be found in the collection of essays *After Keynes*, edited by the well-known economist J. Robinson. Schumacher elaborated the philosophical foundation of his economic theories in his *A Guide for the Perplexed*, among other writings (Schumacher, 1977). It is obvious from his correspondence that this book represents an essential link in his multifaceted life and work. This *Guide* is a clear expression of the breakthrough described above in Schumacher's view of the world. In *Good Work*, published only after his death, Schumacher treated an important theme from *Small is Beautiful* in more detail by asking how methods of labor and production that attach more value to man function both on the theoretical and the practical level (Schumacher, 1979). Schumacher died on September 4, 1977.

Science-for-use versus science-for-insight

Schumacher's view on man is fundamentally different from the Western scientific paradigm, which considers man as nothing but the result of the natural processes and forces described in the theory of evolution. By not acknowledging the different levels of being – with the distinctions among the elements of lifeless matter, life, consciousness, and self-consciousness – a modern science like economics (usually) only gains its knowledge through the perception of the five classic senses. This contradicts what the author calls the "intellectual senses," which are required to recognize life,consciousness, and self-consciousness, in addition to lifeless matter such as can be found in minerals. One neglects the fact that by limiting oneself to the five senses, one exclusively works with the specific faculties used to perceive the lowest level of being: the level of lifeless nature.Even though man is very capable by this means of acquiring knowledge of this one level of being, the other levels are actually kept out of the scientific spotlight. This form of science comes down to a maximum objectification and reduction of the whole of reality to merely nonliving nature. In line with the theory of evolution, one believes that the phenomena of life, consciousness, and self-consciousness are nothing but extremely complex composites of lifeless particles.By taking this stand, observers are deprived of the capacity to perceive higher levels of being, let alone know them.

Schumacher therefore distinguishes between classical science "for the sake of insight" – which he calls wisdom, in line with the Greeks – and modern science "for the sake of usefulness" or "for the sake of power" – which is simply called science. In the context of the contemporary dialogue between East and West, one could say that in the West it is becoming more and more accepted that one can also learn a lot from the vision of science for the sake of insight, which normally is associated with the East. Think about the central idea of wisdom in Buddhism.

The distinction between *wisdom* and *science* is to be made on the basis of their respective aims. Classicalscience was mainly focused on gaining insight into what was felt to be "the highest good": Truth, Goodness, and Beauty. Given the fact that, according to this science, knowledge leads to the greatest possible kind of happiness, this science was called "wisdom." In line with theories of Francis Bacon ("Knowledge is Power"), for example, modern science only serves an underlying thirst for (material) power. It is a phenomenon that has manifested itself in the justification of the publications of scientific work, quite often expressed as adding to political and economic power. Contrary to wisdom, modern scientific knowledge should be verifiable or refutable by everybody. Otherwise knowledge is called "subjective" or "unscientific." More and more, modern science has focused on its function in the domain of usefulness in gaining power over the environment and man.

According to Schumacher, the supremacy of science-for-use over science-for-insight has three important consequences. In the first place one constantly neglects answers to questions people really are interested in, for instance the meaning and the goal of human existence. Second, more and more people who would normally be captivated by science-for-insight are almost hypnotically fascinated by the "objectivity" to which modern science leads. Third, the typically human capacities that lead to people's knowledge of science-for-insight are applied less and less, which makes these capacities grow weak and subsequently reduces the chance for an at least balanced coexistence of science-for-use and science-for-insight (Schumacher, 1977, pp. 64–67).

The neglect of people's diverging problems

Let us now compare Schumacher's philosophical foundation "as if people mattered" with the foundation of the prevailing economic paradigm. Here Schumacher's commitment to the Aristotelian–Thomistic tradition comes to the fore, along with the way he links that connection with Buddhism. His view of man takes into account the different levels of being: mineral, plant, animal, and human.These are given the respective corresponding elements of lifeless matter, life, consciousness, and self-consciousness, characterized by a gradual transition from passivity to activity: from a given determined order to freedom. If one sticks to lifeless nature such as minerals, one only deals with converging problems.Tackling these problems leads to unambiguous solutions. But if we want to try to solve problems at the higher levels of being suggested in people-centered economics, then we no longer exclusively deal with the given order. More and more, freedom comes into play. This means that to solve such problems we need to build in both order and freedom. Therefore we speak of diverging problems. These diverging problems exist not only in pedagogy, law, sociology, and politics but also in the economic sciences.

The fact that a problem such as the advantages versus disadvantages of economic progress in a globalized context divides people, both among each other and individually, is a consequence of the lack of due respect for the typical character of these diverging problems.Economic progress is indeed rooted in both the strong craving for order and the motif of freedom. Economic progress inducing too much environmental degradation, for instance, is a typical example of disorder. And a crucial element of the philosophical basis of the free market-economy is of course freedom. When we stand up for or against globalization, diverging problems, which require a solution in the form of a synthesis of order and freedom, are tackled as typical converging problems.

A converging problem does not require a synthesis of two poles and leads to a specific, unambiguous solution. In order to come to a so-called converging solution, a Western approach alternately opts for the autonomous pole (pro-globalization) and the heteronomous pole (anti-globalization).Even though we of course never really come up with the desired (converging) solution, we still continue the process, blind to the diverging character of the (globalization) problem.In the very same way in which we are either for or against more technology in our daily life, we are either for or against globalization. Schumacher, however, develops an alternative, economic system based on intermediate technology. For, as he states, people are in need of simple technology as well as high technology, of stability as well as change, of traditions as well as reforms, of the protection of public as well as private interest, of growth as well as decay, and to summarize: of order as well as freedom.That is to say, it is not either/or thinking but and/and thinking – not pro or contra globalization but globalization in a more human way, as if people mattered.

The importance of peace and frugality

In contrast with the philosophical foundations of the prevailing economic paradigm, Schumacher's people-centered economics also reacts against the proposition that the foundations for peace can be laid just by bringing about prosperity.This happens because he considers this prosperity to be essentially based on an ethics that stimulates tendencies such as greed and envy that provoke violence instead of peace. History provides scarce evidence that rich people pursue peace more than poor people do. The aggression of the prosperous has stemmed more from fear and longing for power than from scarcity. What peace requires is our stepping away from an economic ethics that, to put it sharply, holds that mean is useful and honest is not (Schumacher, 1973, pp. 19, 28, and 34).The ethics of an economy that really guarantees peace insists on the value of "enough," or frugality, so that the forms of discontentment or violence with respect to planet and people can be avoided.

The Religion of Economics

Long before people became aware of possible globalization problems, Schumacher had already criticized what he called the Religion of Economics. In this Religion of Economics, economic becomes synonymous with good and useful, and uneconomic is increasingly associated with bad and useless. So-called uneconomic activities are having an ever-harder time justifying their right to existence (Schumacher, 1973, pp. 36–38). The absence of frugal limits to the applicability of the economic realm increasingly gives rise to the same erroneous thought processes used by medieval theologians who quoted the Bible to answer problems of physics (Schumacher, 1973, p. 42). Schumacher cites J.M.Keynes, who warned not to overestimate the importance of the economic problem, or sacrifice to its supposed necessities other matters of greater significance. Still, economics became a science with a universal impact in nearly all human domains, not only in the domains where the principle of private profit comes into play, but also in those domains where the interest of the people should prevail. Instead of limiting the utilitarian economic view to short-term visions, which could be sufficient on a micro level, it was also carried through in domains that needed to consider matters that span several generations – for instance, the environment.

The philosophical foundations of economy also cut away the vertical dimension from its arsenal of concepts (Schumacher, 1973, pp. 83, 90). The deeper questions of life remained only to be sustained in a utilitarian fashion. In this way, Schumacher once again stands up for the possibility of a broader-orientated philosophical foundation for the economic sciences. He does not so much react against the (economic) sciences, but rather questions the direction they are taking and their development. The direction in which technique was developed was mainly determined by the underlying philosophical foundations.This indeed led to the kind of thinking in which anything that is technologically possible becomes obligatory as soon as the economic means allow it.

The main reason Schumacher looks for an alternative to the philosophical foundations of economics is that they are never clear about what people really want, what makes them really happy, or what their goals are (Schumacher, 1979, pp.123–124). Both classical Western philosophy, such as the Scholastic school, and Buddhism are a lot clearer about this and state that people acquire happiness by "aspiring upwards," by trying to develop their higher faculties and to acquire knowledge of the higher (Schumacher, 1977, p. 149–150). This presupposes the aforementioned hierarchy in the levels of being (mineral, plant, animal, human) as well as in the human capacities and draws a link to a frugality-based ethics and spirituality.

Literature

Colander, D. 2005. "Economics as an Ideologically Challenged Science." *Revue de Philosophie économique,* no. 1, pp. 9–30.

Daniels, P. 2005. "Economic Systems and the Buddhist Worldview." *Journal of Socio- Economics*, no 2, pp. 245–268.

Ekins, P. and Max-Neef, M. 1992. *Real Life Economics*. London: Routledge.

Elkington, J. 2004. "Enter the Triple Bottom Line." In A. Henriques, and J. Richardson (eds),*The Triple Bottom Line: Does It All Add Up.* London: EarthScan.

Fullbrook, E. 2003. *The Crisis in Economics*. London: Routledge.

Lutz, M. and Lux, K. 1979. *The Challenge of Humanistic Economics*. London, Menlo, CA: The Benjamin Cummings Publishing Company.

Opdebeeck, H. 2002. *Building Towers, Perspectives on Globalisation*. Leuven: Peeters.

Opdebeeck, H. 1986. *Schumacher Is Beautiful.* Kapellen: DNB.

Opdebeeck, H. 2000. *The Foundation and Application of Moral Philosophy.* Leuven: Peeters.

Schumacher, E. 1973. *Small Is Beautiful.* London: Blond and Briggs.

Schumacher, E. 1977. *A Guide for the Perplexed.* London: Jonathan Cape.

Schumacher, E. 1979. *Good Work.* London: Jonathan Cape.

Stern, P. 2000. "New Environmental Theories: Toward a Coherent Theory of Environmentally Significant Behavior." *Journal of Social Issues,* Fall 2000, vol. 56, no. 3, pp. 407–424.

Tawney R. (1921) 1962. *The Acquisitive Society.* London: Collins.

Varma, R. 2003. "E.F. Schumacher: Changing the Paradigm of Bigger is Better." *Bulletin of Science, Technology & Society,* 2003 no 2. pp. 114–124.

Zsolnai, L. and Ims, K. (ed.) 2006. *Business within Limits: Deep Ecology and Buddhist Economics.* Oxford: Peter Lang.

22

Bahá'í Perspective on Business and Organization

Marjolein Lips-Wiersma

In this chapter I set out to clarify what it means to be human and the implications of this for business from a Bahá'í perspective. I aim at holding the Bahá'i worldview up to be examined so that it can be compared with others and contribute to alternative ways of theorizing about management and the ends it pursues.

The Bahá'í Faith

Founded more than 150 years ago, the Bahá'í Faith has spread around the globe. Members of the Bahá'í Faith live in more than 100,000 localities and come from nearly every nation, ethnic group, culture, profession, and social or economic background. Bahá'ís believe that Bahá'u'lláh, the latest of the Messengers, brought new spiritual and social teachings for our time. His essential message is one of unity. He taught the oneness of God, the oneness of the human family, and the oneness of religion. Bahá'u'lláh said, "The earth is but one country and mankind its citizens," and that, as foretold in all the sacred scriptures of the past, now is the time for humanity to live in unity (The Bahá'í Faith 2011).

> The Bahá'í Faith recognizes the unity of God and of His Prophets, upholds the principle of an unfettered search after truth, condemns all forms of superstition and prejudice, teaches that the fundamental purpose of religion is to promote concord and harmony, that it must go hand-in-hand with science, and that it constitutes the sole and ultimate basis of a peaceful, an ordered and progressive society. It inculcates the principle of equal opportunity, rights and privileges for both sexes, advocates compulsory education, abolishes extremes of poverty and wealth, exalts work performed in the spirit of service

to the rank of worship, recommends the adoption of an auxiliary international language, and provides the necessary agencies for the establishment and safeguarding of a permanent and universal peace. (The Bahá'í Faith 2011).

The Bahá'í Faith assumes that reality is fundamentally spiritual in nature. It not only sees the individual as a spiritual being, but also insists that the entire enterprise we call civilization is itself a spiritual and evolutionary process; one in which the human mind and heart create progressively more complex and efficient means to express their inherent moral and intellectual capacities (BIC, 1999). I explore this worldview in relation to three assumptions about human nature and purpose and outline their implications for business and organizations: (1) any form of organizing needs to enable individuals to take personal responsibility for their spiritual growth; (2) any form of organizing needs to contribute to the prosperity of humanity as a whole; and (3) any form of organizing needs to support the unity of mankind.

Enabling individuals to take personal responsibility for their spiritual growth

Ultimately individual spiritual development is between the person and God, and such growth will emerge from participation in, and reflection on, a range of important life roles such as that of parent or volunteer in the community. However, the structures and practices of the workplace also have an important role to play in supporting such growth.

From a Bahá'í perspective the physical journey on earth is about discerning the truth with one's own eyes, making choices on the basis of free will, and collectively discerning what is important by making worldviews (assumptions, spiritual principles) part of the decision-making process. Such a worldview, it is suggested, needs to be at the foundation of how participation in organizations is structured. Questions such as "What kind of persons do we become as a result of working here?" and "What are we here for?" and "How do we do the most good?" are therefore in the domain of *every* worker and not just the manager or leader. This does not mean that Bahá'ís aspire to a power-free state. Their view of human nature is that we live, as Simone Weil puts it, between grace and gravity: "Human beings do have a lower nature and a capacity to be deceitful and self-serving, exercising power for their own ends" (Lample, 2009, p.208).

At the same time Bahá'ís believe that (1) all human beings aspire to a higher purpose (it is therefore not just the role of the leader to set a vision or take ownership of the purpose of the organization) and (2) all people are drawn to both grace and gravity (leaders are therefore not assumed to occupy the moral high ground). While recently we have seen the rise of empowerment programs and flatter organizational hierarchies, concern has also been expressed that we do not fundamentally move beyond control and demand forms of organizing (Ciulla, 2000) and that this impacts significantly on the extent to which individuals can experience meaningful work.

The precise nature of such a purpose needs to be arrived at through consultation, as it needs to be valued by the individual and enhance her/his ability to be in charge of her/his spiritual growth:

> When the individual values the corporation's purpose, work becomes more a "free act", moving closer to the ideals of creative expression and fulfillment of one's potential. When such purpose is not valued by the individual, behavior needs to be manipulated by other means such as management systems. (Ellsworth, 2002, p. 79)

The way that the Bahá'í Faith is structured suggests the possibility for fundamentally different organizational structures that enable the individual to take responsibility for her/his spiritual growth.

Bahá'ís are governed by two parallel bodies that work closely together, "the arm of the learned" and "the arm of the rulers." The arm of the learned consists of wise individuals who are appointed to a particular geographical area, usually for a period of five years. They provide guidance but have no control over resources. The arm of the rulers consists of elective bodies, called Assemblies. They consist of nine individuals and operate at local, national, and global levels. Outside these Assembly meetings "individuals have no power of jurisdiction or executive authority at all" (Schaefer, 1983, p. 245). This has a humbling effect on the individual but also prevents misuse of power for those (and that is at times all of us) who lean towards gravity. Every Bahá'í is eligible to be elected to such bodies, which are usually richly diverse with regard to demographic and ethnic criteria. Unless there are special circumstances, no elected member can refuse to sit on an Assembly. In other words, only others can decide whether the individual is a suitable candidate, as candidates cannot put themselves forward, nor can they put up a campaign. Once elected, one does not have to be concerned about why one is there and whether one will still be there the next time, but can simply get on with doing the best job one can possibly do. Every individual in the community can participate in the elections, and such elections are viewed as a sacred duty (as without such wide participation the system does not work and hence humanity cannot take charge of its own affairs). "In the Bahá'í Faith, neither the elected bodies nor their individual members are responsible to their electors. They have no imperative mandate, nor are they constantly supervised by electors" (Schaefer, 1983). However it is the duty of Assemblies to consult amongst themselves on every decision and to consult with the community when appropriate. Thus the duty of the Assembly members is to discern what is right rather than what is the popular decision. At the same time the Assembly seeks input from the community to obtain different viewpoints and discern possible causes of action. This guidance is designed to procure wide participation while at the same time enhancing personal spiritual growth, as participating in this process aids in taking responsibility and in getting the ego out of the way.

Next to a structure that supports taking personal responsibility, the Bahá'í writings contain a clear process for participative decision-making, which is called "consultation." Bahá'ís consult on all matters and need to rise to the requirements that good consultation demands. These requirements consist of personal qualities such as purity of motive, radiance of spirit, humility, patience, and detachment. They also establish the collective conditions for good outcomes of consultation, such as establishing harmony before making decisions. Finally, the members of Assemblies are asked to turn their faces to the Kingdom of God and ask for assistance. A simple pattern of decision-making is also laid out. It consists of understanding the situation (including the spiritual principles relating to it); searching out the right avenue of action (without insisting on personal opinion and with all freedom to add one's ideas). Finally the Assembly must decide what to do. Once it has decided, all members of the Assembly as well as the community must obey this decision until such a time that it is found to be wanting. This would be discerned through ongoing consultation and reflection. This obedience is not based on blind allegiance but rather on the belief that it is better to take a united action than be right and divided. (This is in fact an efficient process, as flaws in decision-making quickly become apparent when the action is taken in unity and adequate reflection processes on such action are in place.) Participants in these processes, by and large, have a sense that they can (and should) make a difference (instead of feeling alienated and powerless).

This structure and processes go further than empowerment programs within existing structures and encourage the individual to take responsibility, lead to clear ownership of decisions, and a high level of trust and unity.

Contributing to the prosperity of mankind as a whole[1]

The spiritual purpose of business, from a Bahá'í perspective, is to "serve the real needs of humanity." The precise nature of such a purpose, as seen in the previous section needs to be arrived at through consultation so that each individual feels responsible to meet the higher aspirations of being human. This is also increasingly recognized in secular management literature:

> When the individual values the corporation's purpose, work becomes more a "free act", moving closer to the ideals of creative expression and fulfillment of one's potential. When such purpose is not valued by the individual, behavior needs to be manipulated by other means such as management systems. (Ellsworth, 2002, p. 79)

From a Bahá'í perspective, purpose is not just another set of negotiable values, but is the raison d'être for the company itself. It is the foundation upon which the company is built, the future it is striving towards and the ultimate standard by which the organization measures its success:

> Adopting service to society as an overriding business goal goes well beyond existing notions of corporate philanthropy, for it implies establishing an objective as important as the viability of the firm itself. In some sense, the firm, regardless of financial success, would not be viewed as viable without a true service orientation. (EBBF, 2009)

Such a purpose serves as the moral foundation of an organization and demands that the company make choices that transcend organizational self-interest. As such it transcends vision: "The power of vision rests in its ability to define a future that connects individuals within the organization with the service of noble ends beyond themselves. The vision defines something worth contributing to, something that brings meaning to the individual life. This aspiration is founded on the firm's purpose" (Ellsworth, 2002, p. 97). A purpose of "serving the real needs of humanity" is inspirational and aspirational and guides companies, and the societies within which they operate, in healthy and sustainable directions.

On the surface it could be argued that all businesses are serving the real needs of humanity. After all, businesses only exist while customers buy their products and services, and in order to do so consumers must have identified a need for the product or service. However, a spiritual purpose, while supporting human well-being which can include pleasure, is not orientated towards creating unsustainable consumer demands or creating excessive consumerism, as is often the practice in the Western world. Rather it focuses on the real needs of humanity and produces those products and services that enhance the well-being of all people. Such purpose asks the organization not only to consider reducing its environmental footprint or contributing to the well-being of the community which it affects, but also to consider how the purpose of the company is embodied in its core products or services. While this might sound somewhat utopian there are increasing numbers of corporations that have purposes beyond profit, that align a range of strategies such as advertising and choice of product lines with those purposes, or that are set up with the very purpose of providing life-enhancing products and services, such as social enterprises. At the same time corporations that promote products that are harmful to humankind are finding themselves under increasing scrutiny.

For Bahá'í managers and workers, the ultimate spiritual end is to help build a better world through business. This does not mean that profit is to be ignored, as it is the lifeblood of the organization. It is therefore anticipated that, at the present time, there will be a range of tensions between "doing well" and "doing good" (Lips-Wiersma and Nilakant, 2008). The Bahá'í Faith does, however, affirm that altruistic action is possible and stands for the possibility that once a collective organizational commitment to such altruistic purposes is made, they can drive every part of decision-making and evaluation.

Supporting the unity of mankind

Bahá'ís believe that the golden age of civilization is yet to come and that currently a twin process is taking place. On the one hand we see a process of disintegration. For example we have seen the rise of extreme secular and religious ideologies that suffocate the spiritual life of entire nations, damage to the physical environment of the planet that will take a long time to heal, and economic systems that have not been able to curtail greed and seem unable to contribute to the bridging of extremes of poverty and wealth. On the other hand we see a process of integration. We have made tremendous scientific progress, developed technologies that enhance fast worldwide communication, increased access to education, and many life-threatening diseases have been all but eliminated. The challenge for this day and age, as the Bahá'ís see it, is to unify humanity. This is not to be understood in terms of homogenizing individual differences; Unity in Diversity is an integral part of the writings of Baha'u'llah. It relates instead to what is seen to be an inevitable stage of human evolution:

> The unification of the earth's inhabitants is neither a remote utopian vision nor, ultimately, a matter of choice. It constitutes the next, inescapable stage in the process of social evolution, a stage toward which all the experience of past and present is impelling us. Until this issue is acknowledged and addressed, none of the ills afflicting our planet will find solutions, because all the essential challenges of the age we have entered are global and universal, not particular or regional. (BIC, 1999)

Business currently plays a role in both uniting and dividing humanity. To play its role in uniting mankind it requires a world-embracing vision. Clearly involvement of all stakeholders in decision-making is a prerequisite to unity. Such involvement goes beyond "managing" to consultation and involves being transparent and being open to the viewpoints of stakeholders influencing strategic direction. Practices that serve the wants of a few but do nothing to meet the needs of many (such as an unfair distribution of patents, and corruption) or that undermine democracy (such as covert lobbying, and the exploitation of loopholes by creative tax practices) need to be weeded out, as unity cannot take place without justice. Increasing cooperation is envisioned (EBBF, 2009). Such cooperation can already increasingly be seen where corporations work together with government and civil society to, for example, alleviate poverty. Clearly such forms of cooperation will not occur at the required scale overnight and are often hindered by divergent interests. However, Bahá'ís are hopeful that humankind can find ways to unite and it is likely that with the aid of business this process will expedite.

Conclusion

The Bahá'í Faith, and other religions, have contributions to make to our understanding of the spiritual nature and purpose of humanity. Such understanding can aid management theorizing so as to take the spiritual nature of humanity into account. Bahá'ís believe such theorizing to be very important, as spirituality is at the foundation of our existence and our future choices:

> The profound and far-reaching changes, the unity and unprecedented cooperation required to reorient the world toward an environmentally sustainable and just future, will only be possible by touching the human spirit, by appealing to those universal values which alone can empower individuals and communities to act in accordance with the long-term interests of the planet and humanity as a whole. (BIC, 1992, p. 34)

Note

1. Parts of this section of the chapter were previously published in the author's paper "Purpose beyond Profit" at the European Bahá'i Business Forum (EBBF). These parts are reprinted with permission.

Literature

The Bahá'í Faith 2011. The International Website of the Bahá'ís of the World. http://www.bahai.org/ Accessed on May 31, 2011.

BIC 1999. "Who is Writing the Future? Reflections on the 21st Century." In Bahai-International-Community (ed.) New York.

BIC 1992. Sustainable Development and the Human Spirit. doi: http://statements.bahai.org/92–0604.htm

EBBF 2009. An Ethical Perspective on Today's Economic Crisis: European Bahai Business Forum. Retrieved September 20, 2009.

Ciulla, J. B. 2000. *The working life; The promise and betrayal of modern work*. New York: Three Rivers Press.

Ellsworth, R. 2002. *Leading with Purpose; The New Corporate Realities*. Stanford, CA: Stanford University Press.

Lample, P. 2009. *Revelation & Social Reality; Learning to Translate What is Written in to Reality*. West Palm Beach, FL: Palabra Publications.

Lips-Wiersma, M. and Nilakant, V. 2008. "Practical Compassion: Toward a Critical Spiritual Foundation for Corporate Responsibility." In J. Biberman and L. Tischler (eds), *Spirituality in Business: Theory, Practice, and Future Directions* (pp. 51–72). New York: Palgrave Macmillan.

Schaefer, U. 1983. *The Imperishable Dominion; The Bahá'í Faith and the Future of Mankind*. Oxford: George Ronald.

23
Teaching of the Elders

Michael Bell

In aboriginal cultures, elders are teachers. Their teachings are inevitably lessons in proper behavior and "right living" based upon an earth-based cosmology – a deep understanding of the land (the physical universe) and the behavior of its creatures.

Though the teachings may vary – depending upon the particular aboriginal culture – they all seem to share a common set of fundamental principles. Here is my understanding of these principles, based upon what I have heard at meetings and from reading some of the writings of elders.

1. Each person born into this life is a unique individual with his or her own Spirit or energy force (sometimes referred to as "medicine power") that manifests itself in one's personality and lifestyle. This Spirit confers upon the individual a role or purpose. Each one of us is called to recognize this Spirit in ourselves and in others. Certain duties and responsibilities come with this recognition.
2. Our primary relationship as spiritual beings is with the land. The land is living. It was created by "the one who provides for all, and we came from this land." It is our father and our mother, our guide and our teacher, our healer, and the source of our energy and vitality. If we destroy the land, we destroy ourselves. We don't own the land. It owns us. It is our relationship with the land that renews Spirit and keeps it alive.
3. We are called to live in community – first of all with the land and its creatures, then with our natural and extended families, our communities, and with people in other communities with whom we share the land. The call to community links us to our ancestors, to our traditions, and to our culture and contains within it clearly defined

responsibilities to future generations. A traditional aboriginal definition of community is: *an intimate relationship with all living things both animate and inanimate.*

4. If the land is living, and we are living, and our families and communities are living, then our organizations must be living. They have unique Spirits that are linked to our culture. Our organizations can only be as healthy as our culture; and our culture can only be as healthy as our organizations. As members of organizations we are called to represent and serve our people – and to care for and nurture the Spirit of our organizations.

5. If we are to succeed in our calling we must find a way of realigning our primary relationships and maintaining a balance of Spirit. Our primary relationships are our relationships with

- the Spirit of the land;
- our own inner Spirit;
- the Spirit of our families, relatives, and the people who are closest to us; and
- the Spirit within our organizations and in our relationships with other peoples and organizations.

The need for systems thinking

As we look closely at the teaching of the elders and try to apply them to organizations, we see that their teachings are very close to what the New Science calls systems thinking. Though the elders do not use the words "systems," "networks," or "ecology," they present us with a worldview that links everything – including our organizations – to a living universe. To apply their teachings we have to move away from the highly analytical and reductionist thinking of Descartes and adopt a systems-thinking approach. Fritjof Capra has described the characteristics of this way of thinking:

> The ideas set forth by organismic biologists during the first half of the century helped give birth to a new way of thinking – systems thinking – in terms of connectedness, relationships, context. According to the systems view, the essential properties of an organism, or living system, are properties of the whole which none of the parts have. They arise from the interactions and relationships among the parts. These properties are destroyed when the system is dissected, either

physically or theoretically, into isolated elements. Although we can discern individual parts in a system, these parts are not isolated, and the nature of the whole system is always different from the mere sum of its parts. (Capra, 1982)

Applying the teachings of the elders to organizations

We can gain some insights by focusing on the essential elements of the teachings of the elders. These elements are the concepts of interconnectedness, Spirit, purpose, and a fourth element that I will call vocation.

All things are interconnected

The elders teach us that all things are interconnected. All things are linked to one another, relate to one another, and share the same wholeness. Our organizations are inseparably linked to a larger outside world that helps define the nature of our organization. The environment does not determine the nature of our organization – that comes from within. But the outside world – the things the organization is linked to – helps define the nature of the organization. These linkages give the organization its reason for existence. Thus, an organization is not simply an entity in itself; it is an entity in relationship.

In practical terms we cannot understand the nature of any organization unless we understand its relationships to its customers, its clients, the other organizations that are part of its existence, the environment that surrounds it, and the universe of which it is a part. Every organization is part of a greater whole.

In like manner, it is the relationships within the organization – how the people within the organization relate to one another and to people outside of the organization – that determine the nature of the organization. For those of us accustomed to identifying an organization as a stand-alone entity with its own programs, products, services, facilities, assets, stock prices, mission statements, and legal structure – this idea will come as somewhat of a shock. But the elders teach us that organizations are part of a greater whole – and it is an organization's relationship to this greater whole which gives it its meaning.

Organizations are living organisms with a Life-Spirit

According to the elders, organizations share – to varying degrees – the Life-Spirit that links the organization to its environment and to the universe as a whole. This life force manifests itself in different forms: as animal life, human life, the life within community, the life of the universe itself. But here is the important part – this is always the same life force or Spirit. It is the same unifying element that brings things into relationship with one another.

Because they are part of living systems, organizations enjoy a fundamental characteristic of living systems: consciousness. And here we are talking not only about the ability of people within organizations to reflect upon their existence as members of those organizations. We are also talking about the ability of the organization as a whole to function as a conscious entity. This ability of an organization to function as a conscious entity relates to its capacity to deal with information. Getting our mind around this concept has something to do with getting beyond our tendency always to identify consciousness with human consciousness. As Margaret Wheatley notes,

> If the capacity to deal with information, to communicate, defines a system as conscious, then the world is rich in consciousness extending to include even those things we have classified as inanimate. Consciousness occurs in systems that do not even have a human brain. Organizations, then, are conscious entities with the capacity for generating and absorbing information, for feedback, for self-regulation. (Wheatley, 1992)

The concept that an organization or even a community can have a consciousness that is greater than the individual consciousness of its members is not a new concept. For centuries the Jewish people have thought of themselves as "God's Chosen People," and many Christians have thought of themselves as part of the "Mystical Body of Christ." What's new is the awareness that organizational consciousness is not simply a religious phenomenon. It extends to all living organizations that deal with information.

Organizations have a built-in sense of purpose and order

The elders are quite clear that things are created for a purpose – to fulfill a certain predetermined destiny. Closely tied to this concept of purpose is the recognition of a certain inherent order manifested most directly in the mysteries of nature: the seasonal changes, the migrations, the cycles of birth and death. Even natural catastrophes – floods, forest fires, and earthquakes – are seen as part of the plan, part of the inevitable chaos that gives rise to order and harmony.

The New Science identifies this phenomenon of purpose and order with the concept of self-organization – a characteristic of all living systems. Chaos and complexity theories have helped us understand that living systems – including organizations – must go through periods of upheaval and change. And yet, they tend to be conscious of certain boundaries that allow them to grow while maintaining their identities (and/or to merge into a higher identity as the case may be).

When it comes to applying the teachings of purpose and order to organizations, nothing seems more difficult. For generations our business schools have been teaching that organizations are static entities. They have no life in themselves, other than that which exists within the people in them. Because managers do not recognize organizations as living entities, they do not recognize any inherent order within organizations. On the contrary, they recognize the inherent tendency of organizations to "get out of control." And so, because they do not recognize organizations as living entities, they confuse the organization's need for order with control. Rather than opening themselves up to the living Spirit within organizations, they confuse the map with the territory. They spend most of their time tinkering with the systems and processes – many of them atomic flyswatters – which they themselves have imposed.

The vocation of being in organizations

In a world where many of us are accustomed to changing jobs almost as we change our clothing, the concept of "a call to being within an organization" in a way where we recognize and nurture its Spirit seems strange indeed. Yet that seems to be the teaching of the elders. For them the organization is a reflection of the people – serving their needs and sharing their Spirit. Our organizations will be strong if our culture is strong; and our culture will be strong if our organizations are strong.

The call to be within an organization and care for its Spirit does not mean a life of total, unquestioning commitment to an organization. We are not talking "burn-out city" here. On the contrary, the teaching of the elders always speaks of the need to maintain a balance. While living the life of our organizations we must reconcile and harmonize the call of the Spirit of the organization with our other primary relationships: with our own inner Spirit and with the Spirit of our human community – our own family, relatives, and friends. We cannot keep entering the rat race temporarily fortified with stress-reduction workshops; we cannot have healthy organizations populated with sick people.

In a special way, we must reconcile the demands of the Spirit of our organizations with the demands of the Spirit of the land and the universe. For many of us who work with large corporations or government departments in large cities, our exposure to nature might mean raking leaves on the weekend, the occasional walk in a park, or a summer vacation off the beaten path. But is this enough to nourish our Spirit? Our relationship with the living universe is not only a primary relationship; it is the primordial relationship – the relationship of the "first order." It is the foundation for all other relationships. Our Spirit has come from the Spirit of the land, and our Spirit will return to the Spirit of the land.

Rediscovering and realigning our organizational relationships with our relationships to the land does not mean that we must move out of the cities, abandon our companies, and adopt some kind of aboriginal lifestyle. The teaching of the elders is not about lifestyles; it is about relationships. Renewing the Spirit of our organizations means finding ways of "going deeper": finding our way beneath our organizational coding, our personal and family coding, and our cultural coding to discover our genetic coding. Our individual Spirit and the Spirit of our organizations come from the Spirit of the universe.

Discerning the Spirit of organizations

How do we recognize or "discern" Spirit in our organizations? Though the discerning of Spirit is not an exact science (it seems to rely as much upon intuition as logic), I think we can make headway by knowing what to look for and how to look.

What to look for

We know that Spirit is something more than a temporary outburst of emotional enthusiasm (team spirit), and we know that it is not some kind of superimposed expression of religious fervor. We also know that it is not something that manifests itself primarily in structures, systems, procedures, services, and products.

I think we recognize Spirit in all of those things that our management science has chosen to label "soft" or "touchy-feely" or – dare we say it?– "feminine." Spirit is a life principle that manifests itself primarily in relationships and processes. The way people relate to one another in the workplace, and the way they relate to people outside the organization, tells us a great deal about Spirit in an organization. The processes – the way they make decisions, communicate with one another, share information, carry out work, create a work environment – these things give us a clue about the true identity of the organization. Also important are the rituals: the stories people tell, the events they celebrate, the values they hold in common, the myths and symbols they share.

Of special significance are those four abilities that are touchstones for Spirit within organizations. They flow from the principles of consciousness and self-organization. They are the ability to envision, to pursue the vision through leadership, to heal the organization's members and its relationships with others, and to learn so that it can continually remain in relationship with its environment.

How to discern Spirit

I think there are two indispensable tools needed to discern Spirit: reflection and dialogue.

It continually occurs to me in my practice as an organizational consultant that people hire me to do their thinking for them – because they do not have time to think for themselves. I suspect that there is very little I do that people couldn't do for themselves if they just took the time to do it.

Most people working within organizations find very little time for reflection – or meditation, or envisioning, or thinking, or whatever you want to call it. They are run off their feet and live their lives in meetings. They are drowning in information but starved for knowledge. Any reflecting they do usually occurs on their way home from work at night, tossing and turning in their beds in the wee hours, or on their way back to work in the morning. In the workplace we are not at ease with silence. The person who sits in silence and thinks is, well, odd – and costing the company money.

I suspect that our ability to discern Spirit within our organization begins with an ability to discern our own Spirit – to go deep within ourselves to discover the essence of our being and its essential relationships. And I think the practice of doing this on a regular, even daily basis – whether we call it meditation, or prayer, or envisioning, or just plain thinking – is the indispensable key that opens the door to the discovery of Spirit within our organization.

Dialogue is not just talk. As David Bohm notes, it is the ability to engage in meaningful discourse with others in an effort to discover the deeper issues. It is the willingness to explore our assumptions; it is the courage to reframe. It is the twin – the indispensable partner – of reflection because silence is an indispensable dimension of dialogue.

Reflection and dialogue are essential tools for anyone seeking to discover the Spirit of organizations and to find a new way of being within organizations. But they are especially important for those in leadership positions. As Harrison Owen points out, leadership is the capacity to focus Spirit. Empowering Spirit is what leadership is all about.

The challenge of Spirit

Schopenhauer once said, "Thus the task is not so much to see what no one yet has seen, but to think what nobody yet has thought about that which everybody sees." The challenge of Spirit is, first and foremost, an epistemological challenge. Learning from the wisdom of the elders requires a metanoia – a complete shift in our way of thinking about our organizations and about the nature of Spirit within us. We have to reframe on both an organizational and personal level.

On an organizational level, to use a common aboriginal expression, "We must make the path by walking it." As I've tried to do this over the years, I often find myself guided by those words of Margaret Wheatley that echo the teachings of the elders: "How would we organize human endeavours if we developed a different understanding of how life organizes itself?" (Wheatley and Kellner-Rogers, 1996)

On the level of a personal spirituality, I continually reflect on these words of Teilhard de Chardin that I write on the first page of my Daytimer at the beginning each new year. *"We are not human beings on a spiritual journey; we are spiritual beings on a human journey."*

Literature

Berry, T. 1998. *The Dream of the Earth*. San Francisco: Sierra Club.
Capra, F. 1982. *The Turning Point*. New York: Bantam Books.
Wheatley, M. 1992. *Leadership and the New Science: Learning about Organizations from an Orderly Universe,* San Francisco: Berrett-Koehler.
Wheatley, M. and Kellner-Rogers, M. 1996. *A Simpler Way*. San Francisco: Berrett-Koehler.

Part III

Socioeconomic Problems in Spiritual Perspective

24
Spiritual Meaning of the Economic Crisis

Carlos Hoevel

Over the past several months we have been listening to and reading many explanations about the technical, political, juridical, ethical, cultural, and even psychological causes of the financial and economic world crisis. However, not very much has been said about its spiritual dimension. The reason for this could be that we seldom use the terms "spirit" or "spiritual" in relation to economic issues. Besides, we also tend to identify or subsume under the terms "ethical" or "psychological" other specifically different human phenomena that cannot really be so simply identified with the former. In this chapter I will argue that the crisis shows us, apart from these other dimensions, a specific spiritual dimension. I will also assume a meaning of spirituality understood as our deepest –or highest – activity as human beings, through which we can communicate at some point with the ultimate roots of ourselves that constitute us as beings and with our ultimate ends that orientate and give a final meaning and purpose to our lives.

Many behavioral economists have argued that borrowers, loan origi-nators, investment banks, rating agencies, regulators, and end inves-tors involved in the financial crisis have not shown the kind of rational behavior expected by mainstream economists. On the contrary, they believe that such a serious and extended crisis was necessarily caused by a series of psychological irrationalities in all these players. It seems to me that behavioral analysis describes accurately the psychological dimension of the crisis. However, in my opinion, these psychological or behavioral factors presuppose a deeper and broader existential or spiritual transformation on which to grow. In other words, such fac-tors in the levels of cognition, emotion, and behavior need a series of specific conditions in the level of *being*. Thus, departing from this psy-chological perspective of behavioral economists, I will try to show how the crisis has its roots in a *much deeper internal or spiritual transformation* of human beings.

Self-collectivization

According to Nicholas Barberis from the Yale School of Management conformity, groupthink, obedience, and diffusion of responsibility were some of the most important psychological factors that facilitated the financial crisis. Barberis argues that on some level banks were aware that there were problems with their business and economic models, but as a result of these psychological forces they deluded themselves into thinking that everything was all right. Conformity means that there is a strong tendency to adapt to what the group one belongs to is doing, even if one does not think it makes sense. Therefore even if some bankers or traders saw problems, they remained silent for the sake of this conformity. Experiments also show that conformity and blind obedience increase with the strength and immediacy of the group, especially when the group is isolated from other opinions, has a strong leader, or is under a stressful situation (Barberis, 2009). As the behavioral economist Robert Shiller puts it – contrary to conventional mainstream arguments, which blame asymmetric information as the primary problem in the crisis – the main issue was really an "information cascade" characterized by the submission of individuals to collective "thinking" and the abandonment of personal critical examination of this information (Shiller, 2008).

What behavioral economists like Barberis and Shiller say about the micro-climate of group thinking and conformist opinions matches very well with the vivid description of trading rooms given by the financial researchers Donald MacKenzie and Iain Hardie. What mostly impressed these researchers was that even the physical disposition of elements in these trading rooms augmented the suspension of personal thinking and the reinforcement of self-collectivization, potentiated by the use of new communications technologies. Rather than being distributed for privacy, desks generally formed a single rectangle in the middle of a room and their occupants would normally face one another to induce mutual control and visibility. There were also more computer screens than occupants of the rooms, and the screens usually interfered with lines of sight when people were seated. Moreover, this self-collectivization that began *inside* the rooms was prolonged and intensified *outside* them. In fact, the capacity of many of these small groups to act depended on people and technical systems not physically present in the trading rooms, which led to the formation – via teleconferences, "webinars," and group e-mails – of an enlarged "body" of collectivized thinking (MacKenzie, 2009).

As has been clearly shown by authors like Robert Reich, Marc Augé, Cristopher Lasch, and Zygmunt Bauman, the new global financial elites have much more in common with their almost anonymous partners plugged into the network of global communication than with their own concrete national, regional, or local neighbors. In fact, whether they are in the middle of an African desert, in the foggy mornings of northern Europe, or on the super-humid coasts of Brazil is a matter of indifference for the de-corporatized people circulating in Dubai's, Amsterdam's, or Sao Paulo's workplaces. The smooth and homogeneous climate (made possible by universal air conditioning), globalized language (a sort of washed English), and standardized thinking found in offices, conference rooms, airports, and international hotels teaches people that they are not supposed to conceive themselves as idiosyncratic and truly diverse subjects, but only as tiny pieces of a vast and overwhelming totality. Based on this assumption, it seems much more natural to adapt oneself to a preformed and comfortable collectivized thinking than to face the effort of confrontation and risk that personal thinking always implies.

The phenomenon of self-collectivization that characterized the crisis was not, however, only an elite phenomenon. It would have been a surprise if this relatively small group of financial agents, analysts, and policymakers could have imposed an impersonal way of thinking on millions of "personalized" people from cities, communities, and regions of the United States and from all over the world. But the truth is that uprootedness – to use one of Simone Weil's preferred expressions – that is, a disconnection from one's own feelings, inner memories, desires, and critical thinking, has not been the exclusive patrimony of financial and political elites but of millions of borrowers, consumers, and common financial investors around the globe. A truly globalized "herd" formed by millions of common people, largely influenced by media and "public opinion," proved to have insufficient instincts, intuition, and personal character to limit the excesses of the bubble during the years preceding the crisis.

Reification and loss of references

Another typical behavior that made the crisis possible was, according to behavioral economists, what they call "cognitive dissonance" and "ambiguity aversion." Cognitive dissonance means people feeling uncomfortable when taking an action that conflicts with their pre-conceived positive images. In order to reduce the feeling of discom-fort towards new and sometimes problematic realities, people often manipulate and reinforce their unexamined beliefs and convince them-selves that everything is all right. Thus, even if they think something is wrong – or if they doubt or feel ambiguous about it – instead of deliberat-ing, they will enclose the problem inside a comfortable conventional or abstract formula, cliché, or prejudice and just go on (Barberis, 2009).

But what permits people to behave in that way is a deep transfor-mation of their cognitive capabilities in relation to reality. Using the terminology of the twentieth century's neo-Marxist thinkers, we could call this phenomenon "reification," meaning the perception of our own selves, people, and reality in general as simplified, stereotyped, and dead things (res) or objects that we can manipulate at will (Honneth, 2007). In fact, in order to trade bonds, currencies, and derivatives origi-nating in every continent, financial agents have to turn the infinite complexity of the world into patterns that are simple enough to grasp, and then take appropriate action (MacKenzie, 2009). The same could be said about many economists, global managers, policymakers, and "sym-bolic analysts" of every species who tend to perceive people, places, and events as abstract points to be ranged in their busy academic, political, business, or travel agendas. Although the economist Jeffrey Sachs knew that Bolivia was landlocked and mountainous, only after many years spent applying drastic monetary and economic reform in that country did he realize that these conditions were the key factors in Bolivia's chronic poverty. However, he excused himself for this ignorance by say-ing that almost all the international commentary and academic eco-nomic writing about Bolivia he had previously read had neglected this very basic point (MacKenzie, Muniesa, and Siu, 2007).

Models, computerized calculus, and abstract predictions played a crucial role in building reified thinking in the crisis. Think only – as proposed by the Italian economist Stefano Zamagni – of mechanisms such as the computerized trading program, which is something anal-ogous to a particle accelerator that amplifies in a procyclical trend, upwards and downwards, market stock values. Think also of the famous Scholes–Merton model, supposedly designed to reduce financial risk almost to zero (Zamagni, 2009). In both cases the assumption was the possibility of replacing a living mind open to living realities by what Donald MacKenzie calls a "mechanized proof." In fact, after having investigated the interrelations of computing, risk and mathematical proof over the last half century in most aspects of our private and social lives, MacKenzie argues that in mechanizing proof, and in pursuing dependable computer systems, we cannot obviate the need for trust in our human judgment (MacKenzie, 2004). Taking into account the consequences of an exaggerated trust in modeling before this crisis, what MacKenzie wrote in 2004 seems to have been clearly on the right track.

Finally, as B. Maurer argued also before the crisis, stock options assigned to managers and financial derivatives in general have stressed up to an unbelievable tension some of the oldest metaphysical and spiritual problems of humanity. From the instantiation of time through particular modalities of risk to the destabilization of all referentiality, the indiscriminate use of financial instruments created the illusion of overcoming the limits of time and reality. According to Maurer, while the "scandal" of imaginary money in the nineteenth century was that it could be increased without backing by gold or silver – creating itself out of nothing – the "scandal" of money created by derivative instruments of the late twentieth and early twenty-first century was the fact that it was a sign which created itself out of the future. In fact, any particular future state of money, when it arrives, will not be something "objective," a referent waiting out there and determined by "real" trade forces, but will have been brought into being by the very money-market activity designed to predict its value (Maurer, 2002). In a word, opening up the black box of the mathematical and accounting techniques of derivatives and options, we can find another founding trauma animating the crisis: the reification of the spirit through its separation from reality, historical time, and a providential rule of the world.

Compulsion and fallen freedom

Finally, a third behavior pattern considered by behavioral economists relevant to the genesis of the crisis was overconfidence and exaggerated optimism. According to these economists, overconfidence made financial agents overestimate the precision of their forecasts and assume their predictions of future house-price movements were more accurate than they actually were. An optimistic attitude, on the other hand, makes people think that setbacks are more likely to happen to other people than to themselves. But what are the sources of this behavior? After the crisis, we read that the Bank for International Settlements (BIS) had announced that financial products should undergo registration, like drugs, to curb investor access until safety is proven. In a scheme analogous to the hierarchy controlling the availability of pharmaceuticals, the BIS, which acts as a forum for the world's central banks, said in its annual report that the safest securities would, like nonprescription medicines, be available for purchase by everyone. Next would be financial instruments available only to those with an authorization, like prescription drugs. Another level down would be securities available only in limited amounts to prescreened individuals and institutions, like drugs in experimental trials. Finally, at the lowest level would be securities that are deemed illegal. A new instrument would be rated or an existing one moved to a higher safety category only after successful tests. This will mean –according to the BIS report – that issuers bear increased responsibility for the risk assessment of their products (BIS, 2009).

This report is particularly clarifying not because of the supposedly extraordinary qualities of derivatives, which it compares with highly dangerous chemical substances, but especially because it reveals the dimension of compulsion and addiction experienced by financial agents and common people during the crisis. When properly used, derivatives and loans – much like new, approved medications – were helpful in augmenting returns, managing risk, and even helping the poor. Financial agents made a lot of money based on these "medications," but many people on the lowest part of the pyramid also benefited and started to climb. However, not unlike "designer drugs," the abuse of these financial instruments can be deadly. Through them many people started to think that they were no longer subjected to the limits given to us by nature, but that they were powerful enough to overcome them all in an indefinite way.

Carl Jung argues that "when an inner situation is not made conscious, it happens outside, as fate." In fact, once critical personal thinking, cognitive resonance, and a living connection with time and reality are lost, there is no room for free and responsible action. On the contrary, the inevitable consequence is the rule of primary impulses, compulsion, and an irresponsible praxis without light. In other words, seen from a spiritual perspective, the infinite Faustian race to overcome every limit and obtain more and more money that we saw during the last big bubble preceding the great crisis seems to have been the result of an addictive and compulsory multiplication of illusions, which, in its turn, can be conceived as a deformed and perverse imitation of our call for a responsible, intelligent, and free itinerary towards an Ultimate and Infinite Reality.

Literature

Augé, M. 1995. *Non-places: Introduction to an Anthropology of Supermodernity.* London: Verso.

Barberis, N. 2009. *The Psychology of the Financial Crisis.* Lecture delivered at the Association of Yale Alumni Reunion Weekend.

Bauman, Z. 2002. *Society under Siege.* Malden, MA: Wiley-Blackwell.

BIS 79th Annual Report 2009: *Report presented at the Bank's Annual Meeting* in Basel, Switzerland.

Honneth, A. 2007. *Reificación. Un estudio en la teoría del reconocimiento.* Buenos Aires: Katz.

Janis, I. L. 1983. Groupthink: *Psychological Studies of Policy Decisions and Fiascoes.* Boston: Houghton Mifflin.

Lasch, C. 1996. *The Revolt of the Elites and the Betrayal of Democracy.* New York: W.W. Norton.

MacKenzie, D. 2004. *Mechanizing Proof: Computing, Risk, and Trust.* Cambridge, MA: MIT Press.

MacKenzie, D. 2006. *An Engine, Not a Camera: How Financial Models Shape Markets.* Cambridge, MA: MIT Press.

MacKenzie, D. 2009: *Material Markets: How Economic Agents Are Constructed.* Oxford: Oxford University Press.

MacKenzie, D., Muniesa, F., and Siu, L. (eds) 2007. *Do Economists Make Markets? On the Performativity of Economics.* Princeton, NJ: Princeton University Press.

Maurer, B. 2002. "Repressed Futures: Financial Derivatives' Theological Unconscious." *Economy and Society,* Volume 31, no. 1, pp. 15–36.

Reich, R. B. 1992. *The Work of Nations: Preparing Ourselves for 21st Century Capitalism.* New York: Vintage Books.

Shefrin, H. 2002: *Beyond Greed and Fear: Understanding Behavioral Finance and the Psychology of Investing.* Oxford: Oxford University Press.

Shiller, R.J. 2008. *The Subprime Solution: How Today's Global Financial Crisis Happened, and What to Do about It.* Princeton, NJ: Princeton University Press.

Wärneryd, K.E. 2001. *Stock-market Psychology: How People Value and Trade Stocks.* Northampton: Edward Elgar.

Zamagni, S. 2009. *La lezione e il monito di una crisi annunciata.* Paper presented at the University of Bologna in 2009.

25
Materialistic Value Orientation

Tim Kasser

Materialistic values reflect the priority that individuals give to goals such as money, possessions, image, and status. Confirming the concerns of many spiritual traditions, empirical research supports the idea that materialistic and spiritual values are relatively incompatible aims in life. For instance, research shows that the more that people focus on materialistic goals, the less they tend to care about spiritual goals. Further, while most spiritual traditions aim to reduce personal suffering and to encourage compassionate behaviors, numerous studies document that the more people prioritize materialistic goals, the lower their personal well-being and the more likely they are to engage in manipulative, competitive, and ecologically degrading behaviors.

Conflicts between spiritual and material goals

In order for any spiritual tradition to maintain itself and survive over the long term, it is necessary that people take on the particular set of beliefs or *ideologies* supportive of that religion. To take a concrete example, consider Christianity, a spiritual tradition characterized by the particular ideology of monotheism, the divinity of Christ, and the possibility of reaching heaven. Through this ideology, people are encouraged to engage in behaviors that are consistent with and supportive of Christianity, including praying, going to church, tithing, and following the Ten Commandments. Through these beliefs and behaviors, the spiritual tradition of Christianity continues.

Spiritual traditions of course exist in a broader world alongside other, sometimes competing, ideologies that might be at odds with spirituality. One ideology that many people have historically considered to be a threat to spirituality is the set of beliefs involved in a *materialistic value orientation.* Materialistic values involve placing a high priority on "attaining financial success, having nice possessions, having the right image (produced, in large part, through consumer goods), and having a high status (defined mostly by the size of one's pocketbook and the scope of one's possessions)" (Kasser, Ryan, Couchman, and Sheldon, 2004, p. 13). Just as with spiritual ideologies, a materialistic value orientation has "high priests" (e.g., CEOs, marketers, economic advisers), places of worship (e.g., the malls and Internet sales sites), behaviors it encourages (e.g., shopping, investing, working long hours), and a conception of the ideal (e.g., the attainment of wealth in order to buy the goods and services available in the marketplace).

Although some spiritual leaders have embraced materialism and incorporated it into their spiritual teachings (e.g., the prosperity gospel, which preaches that God blesses believers with material wealth), most spiritual traditions warn their followers not to orientate their lives around materialistic strivings. For example, Taoism contains aphorisms such as "Chase after money and security, and your heart will never unclench" and "He who knows he has enough is rich." The Bhagavad Gita of Hinduism poetically warns that "Pondering on objects of the senses gives rise to attraction; from attraction grows desire, desire flames to passion, passion breeds recklessness; and then betrayed memory lets noble purpose go, and saps the mind, till purpose, mind and man are all undone." Christianity also expresses concerns about materialism, with its seven deadly sins (materialism being involved in four of them: greed, pride, gluttony, and envy; Belk, 1983), and Jesus' preaching: "Do not store up for yourselves treasure on earth, where it grows rusty and moth-eaten and thieves break in to steal it. Store up treasure in heaven…. For wherever your treasure is, there will your heart be also" (Matthew 6: 19–21).

These spiritual traditions seem mostly to be concerned that if people focus their lives and minds on materialistic values, they may become distracted from the higher virtues and truths that spiritual traditions propound. Three recent scientific studies support this belief that spiritual and materialistic aims stand in opposition to one another. In the first study, US subjects' recollections of their experience of Christmas revealed that the more their holiday was characterized by spending money, shopping, and receiving gifts, the less it was characterized by spiritual activities (Kasser and Sheldon, 2002). Another study, which asked 373 US adults how much they cared about 16 different types of values, found that materialistic and religious values were in direct opposition to each other (Burroughs and Rindfleisch, 2002). This finding was corroborated in a cross-cultural study of 1,800 college students from 15 cultures (Grouzet et al., 2005). Here, students rated the importance of 11 different types of life aspirations, including financial success and spirituality. Using a statistical procedure called circular stochastic modeling, the researchers modeled the extent to which different types of aspirations were psychologically compatible or in conflict. Those aspirations that subjects' ratings suggested were psychologically consistent were located nearby each other on the circumference of a circle (i.e., less than 90 degrees apart), whereas aspirations that were experienced by the subjects as being in psychological conflict were on opposite sides of the circle (and thus closer to 180 degrees apart). Figure 25.1 reproduces the results of these analyses.

As can be seen in Figure 25.1, the goal of spirituality is most strongly opposed by the goal of *hedonism*, or the concern with sensual pleasure; this is a sensible result, given that most spiritual traditions also

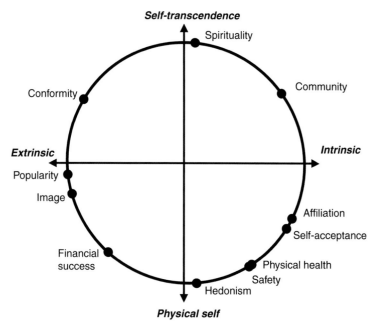

Figure 25.1   Circumplex structure of life aspirations based on 1,800 college students from 15 cultures
Source: Grouzet et al., 2005.

advocate ignoring the pleasures of the flesh. But the goal of financial success was also found to be in psychological opposition to spirituality goals. Interestingly, this opposition was stronger in poorer cultures (e.g.,India, Egypt), than in wealthier cultures (e.g., the US, France).

Materialism's relationship to personal happiness and compassionate behavior

The results of these three studies support the long-standing spiritual intuition that it is difficult for humans to pursue spiritual and materialistic goals simultaneously, for they seem to be aims that stand in psychological conflict with each other. But research shows that a strong materialistic value orientation also interferes with at least two other outcomes of importance to most spiritual traditions: the reduction of suffering and the promotion of compassion.

Suffering. A growing body of research documents that people experience lower psychological well-being to the extent they believe in the messages of consumer society and organize their lives and goals around becoming wealthy, obtaining possessions, looking good, and enhancing their status (see Kasser, 2002). These studies show, for example, that to the extent people rate materialistic goals as important in life, they report higher levels of depression and anxiety, two of the most common psychological disorders around the world. Headaches, stomachaches, and backaches are also higher in people with strong materialistic values. When scientists ask study participants to keep diaries of the emotions they experience every day, people who strongly endorse materialistic values report stronger, more frequent experiences of unpleasant emotions such as anger, frustration, sadness, anxiety, and worry. Materialistic values are also associated with using more alcohol, tobacco, and other mind-altering substances; perhaps people take these drugs to distract themselves from their suffering.

Materialistic values are not only associated with higher levels of suffering, but also with lower levels of happiness. For example, people report feeling less vital and alive when they endorse such beliefs. They are also less satisfied with their lives and, when asked to complete diaries of their emotional experience, report fewer pleasant emotions such as being happy, pleased, joyous, or content.

It is important to note that these findings regarding the negative associations between materialistic values and personal well-being have been replicated in a variety of settings using a variety of types of subjects. For example, similar results have been reported in samples from North America, Europe, and Asia. Studies with children as young as 10 and with adults in their 70s have also found that materialistic values correlate with unhappiness. And among business students and entrepreneurs, whose professions might lead them to care more about wealth and possessions, those who are especially focused on materialistic goals still report lower levels of well-being than do those who pursue business with a less materialistic mindset.

Two studies have also suggested that the negative associations between materialism and some aspects of well-being may be particularly pronounced for religious individuals. La Barbera and Gurhan (1997) compared how three different measures of materialism related to the general affect and stress levels of born-again American Christians and non-born-again Americans. Of the six statistical tests the researchers conducted, two were significant, showing that a non-generous attitude was especially negative for born-again Christians' general affect and that strong feelings of envy were particularly negative for born-again Christians' stress levels; these negative associations were not present, and were perhaps reversed, for the non-born-again sample. Burroughs and Rindfleisch (2002) followed up on these results in a sample of US adults by measuring both people's materialistic values and their sense of religious values and identity. Results showed that while materialistic values were associated with more anxiety, regardless of people's religious values, those individuals who expressed strong religious and strong materialistic values reported especially high levels of stress. Burroughs and Rindfleisch argue that this stress resulted from the conflict these subjects experienced between their spiritual and materialistic values, and went on to show that this stress predicted higher levels of depression and lower levels of life satisfaction for participants high in both religious and materialistic values.

In sum, the beliefs central to the materialistic ideology seem to increase, rather than to reduce, personal suffering, and this may be especially true for more religious individuals.

Compassion. Empirical research also suggests that materialistic values may not be compatible with the kinds of pro-social, compassionate behaviors encouraged by most spiritual traditions, as to the extent people take on materialistic values and beliefs, they are less likely to behave in ways that promote the well-being of other people, and they may actually behave in ways that hurt others. For example, cross-cultural research on values and goals consistently demonstrates that materialistic aims not only stand in opposition to spiritual goals, but also to other values that promote good interpersonal behavior. For example, Figure 25.1 shows that materialistic values tend to oppose community-feeling aspirations which involve attempts to try to make the world a better place. Shalom Schwartz's (1992) cross-cultural research similarly shows that values for money, power, achievement, and status stand in opposition to values such as being "helpful" and "loyal," obtaining "true friendship" and "mature love," and working for "social justice" and "equality."

A strong focus on money and possessions also seems to increase the likelihood of "objectifying" other people (see Kasser, Vansteenkiste, and Deckop, 2006). That is, materialistic values apparently increase the likelihood that other people are treated as objects to be manipulated in the pursuit of one's goals, rather than as unique, subjective individuals with their own desires, experiences, and needs. This tendency towards objectification can be seen in some of the attitudes empirically associated with strong endorsement of materialistic values, including lower empathy, more manipulative tendencies, and a stronger likelihood of being socially dominant and prejudicial. Materialistic individuals also report engaging in fewer pro-social activities (like sharing and helping) and more anti-social activities (like cheating and vandalism), including ethically questionable activities in business settings. Finally, a few studies suggest that when placed in resource-dilemma games, materialistic values are associated with being less generous and with acting in more competitive and less cooperative ways.

Some experiments in the US even suggest that activating materialistic values by making people think about money and possessions may *cause* them to be less likely to engage in friendly, helpful, cooperative acts. For example, in one series of studies (by Vohs, Mead, and Goode 2006), US college students were randomly assigned to create meaningful phrases out of money-related words or out of neutral words. Later, they were presented with opportunities to behave in a generous or a selfish manner. The findings showed that those students who had thoughts of money activated in their minds (by unscrambling money-related phrases) spent less time helping an experimenter pick up pencils that had been dropped and less time helping a confused person who asked for help. When rewarded for being in the study with a small bit of money, they also donated less of it to charity.

Many spiritual traditions suggest that compassion should not be limited to one's families and friends, or even to one's own species, but should be extended to all living beings and to nature as a whole. Once again, however, the empirical research suggests that materialist values and beliefs interfere with such a compassionate stance and instead drive humans to consume and pollute in ways that are fundamentally damaging earth's ecosystem and pushing many species to the brink of extinction (see Crompton and Kasser, 2009, for a review).

For example, cross-cultural research reveals that to the extent people value aims such as wealth and status, they tend to care less about values such as "protecting the environment," "attaining unity with nature," and having "a world of beauty." A study in Australia also documented that a strong consumer orientation is associated with less love for and feelings of connection with all living things. What's more, the values of wealth and status were also associated with worse environmental attitudes in a recent study of almost 1,000 undergraduates from Brazil, the Czech Republic, Germany, India, New Zealand, and Russia.

These values and beliefs of consumer society are also associated with behaving in less ecologically sustainable ways. Studies of American adults find that people are less likely to engage in ecologically friendly behaviors such as riding one's bike, reusing paper, buying secondhand items, and recycling when they strongly value materialistic goals; these findings have also been replicated in samples of US and UK adolescents. What's more, results from a sample of 400 American adults showed that those who cared more about materialistic values used significantly more of the earth's resources in order to support their lifestyle choices around transportation, housing, and food. That is, caring about materialistic aims was associated with driving and flying more (and using public transportation or bicycles less), living in bigger (rather than smaller) homes, and eating a good deal of meat and exotic foods (rather than practicing vegetarianism and eating locally grown foods).

In sum, this body of research suggests that materialistic values are associated with lower levels of interpersonal (and interspecies) compassion. Such findings provide further evidence that a materialistic value orientation is at odds with the aims of most spiritual traditions.

Literature

Belk, R.W. 1983. "Worldly Possessions: Issues and Criticisms." *Advances in Consumer Research, 10,* pp. 514–519.

Burroughs, J.E., and Rindfleisch, A. 2002. "Materialism and Well-being: A Conflicting Values Perspective." *Journal of Consumer Research, 29,* pp. 348–370.

Crompton, T., and Kasser, T. 2009. *Meeting Environmental Challenges: The Role of Human Identity.* Godalming, UK: WWF-UK.

Grouzet, F.M.E., Kasser, T., Ahuvia, A., Fernandez-Dols, J.M., Kim, Y., Lau, S., Ryan, R. M., Saunders, S., Schmuck, P., and Sheldon, K.M. 2005. "The Structure of Goal Contents across Fifteen Cultures." *Journal of Personality and Social Psychology, 89*, pp. 800–816.

Kasser, T. 2002. *The High Price of Materialism*. Cambridge, MA: MIT Press.

Kasser, T., Ryan, R.M., Couchman, C.E., and Sheldon, K.M. 2004. "Materialistic Values: Their Causes and Consequences." In T. Kasser and A. D. Kanner (eds), *Psychology and Consumer Culture: The Struggle for a Good Life in a Materialistic World*, pp. 11–28. Washington DC: American Psychological Association.

Kasser, T. and Sheldon, K.M. 2002. "What makes for a merry Christmas?" *Journal of Happiness Studies, 3*, pp. 313–329.

Kasser, T., Vansteenkiste, M., and Deckop, J.R. 2006. "The Ethical Problems of a Materialistic Value Orientation for Businesses (and Some Ssuggestions for Alternatives)." In J.R. Deckop (ed.), *Human Resource Management Ethics*, pp. 283–306. Greenwich, CT: Information Age Publishing.

La Barbera, P.A., and Gurhan, Z. 1997. "The Role of Materialism, Religiosity and Demographics in Subjective Well-Being." *Psychology & Marketing, 14*, pp. 71–97.

Schwartz, S.H. 1992. "Universals in the Content and Structure of Values: Theoretical Advances and Empirical tests in 20 Countries." In M. Zanna (ed.), *Advances in Experimental Social Psychology, Vol. 25*, pp. 1–65. Orlando: Academic Press.

Vohs, K.D., Mead, N.L., and Goode, M.R. 2006. "The Psychological Consequences of Money." *Science, 314*, pp. 1154–1156.

26
Avarice
Stefano Zamagni

The nature of avarice

Avarice, or greed, is a capital sin that rarely emerges as such. Rather, from case to case it is dressed up as avidity, cupidity, covetousness, usury, lust for wealth, love of money, stinginess, meanness. From the annoyance that other people's avarice triggers, the miser may infer how the others feel about him. Out of *amour propre*, the greedy man is induced to act as if he were not greedy. The capacity of avarice for camouflage is such that in some circumstances it may even resemble virtue, as Juvenal intuited. Prudentius, in his celebrated *Psychomachia* (405AD) – an allegorical poem narrating seven fierce battles for the conquest of souls, each pitting a deadly sin against the matching virtue – says of greed that when this sin fails to capture the souls of the faithful (including priests) by force, it does so by stealth. By feigning a certain nobility of the spirit, avarice conceals its true attributes, so that greed and stinginess are attributed to the laudable aim of providing for the needs of one's children. Laying down its arms, avarice thus disguises itself as parsimony, becoming – Prudentius writes – "that virtue which is called economy" (in the end, however, *operatio* definitively defeats *avaritia*). There are many terms for avarice or greed, and if we want to understand its specific nature we must look into its many styles and consider its semantics as they have developed and have been articulated over time.

Among economists especially, the idea is quite common that, all in all, greed is a minor vice and one that is readily corrected by adequate incentives. It is not by accident that texts in economics, from the most sophisticated to the most popularizing, never speak of avaricious behavior. These works, in fact, consider that the very question of whether the preferences of *homo oeconomicus* are avaricious is meaningless.

"Economic man" must only act rationally, maximizing under proper conditions his own self-interest, whatever it is. Yet greed or avarice – the most "economic" of the deadly sins – is one of the most common "failures of reason" in economics. Because he lacks a well-rounded sense of reason, the greedy man does not know how to direct the passion for possession that is part of every human being. In particular, he fails to turn that passion –natural, in itself – towards the goods that it is reasonable to desire. The miser accumulates, hoards wealth, takes it out of circulation. He does not fuel production but impedes it, even dissipates output. It is a fact that lacking a theory of the motivation to act rationally – what motives we have to do what we recognize that we should do – economics is unable to comprehend the phenomenon of greed in its multiple manifestations (in fact, economics simply does not treat this issue). Why does the miser continue insatiably accumulating money despite his knowledge that the power that wealth gives can never be realized? Economics does have a theory of the *reasons* to do what *homo oeconomicus* judges he should do; but it has no theory of the *motives* for doing what he recognizes he should do.

The sin of avarice is also characterized by a second element: since late antiquity, the notion has undergone a series of semantic shifts, alternations unparalleled by any of the other "deadly sins." How can we account for a phenomenon so peculiar as to seem a real *curiosum*? In late ancient times it was branded as the source of evil in the world ("For the love of money is the root of all evil" wrote St. Paul in I Timothy 6:10; *"Radix Omnium Malorum Avaritia,"* whence came the acronym R.O.M.A., used commonly in the fourth and fifth centuries during the decline and fall of the Roman Empire). But in the early Middle Ages, with the imprint of monasticism, the title of *"initium omnium malorum"*(the beginning of all evils) was assigned to pride. Pride is the inception of evil because it is the desire to *be* like God. Avarice is the root, because it is the desire to *have* like God. As Aristotle had observed, vices are a serious impediment to perfection that is, to the flowering of the human being. With respect to the monastic ideal of perfection, the worst impediment is *inobedientia*, which prevents you from taking *contemptus mundi* (contempt for the world) as the rule of life, which St Peter Damian and Innocent III exalted.

With the advent of the commercial revolution of the eleventh century and its attendant theological and pastoral renovation – just think of the Gregorian reforms – avarice regained its place at the top of the ranking of sins. At the dawn of the new millennium, "cities" were born, and with them trade, markets, the medieval communes. But the radical change in the socioeconomic order was not accompanied by a corresponding improvement in morals. The sins of pride and envy typical of the rural, feudal world were now flanked, in a new form, by the typical urban sins of greed and lust. But the most insidious and perilous of the deadly sins was greed, because this is the sin of merchants, the most powerful representatives of the "new economy" that threatened the power of the clergy.

There was a sudden change of perspective with the advent of civic humanism, when such influential thinkers as Poggio Bracciolini, Coluccio Salutati, Leonardo Bruni, Matteo Palmieri, Lorenzo Valla, and Marsilius of Padua began, not without risk, to contend that greed or avarice was indeed a sin when it consisted in the unbridled urge for money, but not when it was merely the desire for the superfluous – unlike the economic doctrine of the Church, which held that the only "good and true economy" was the subsistence economy – the "stationary state" so highly praised by John Stuart Mill in the nineteenth century. In his celebrated *De Avaritia* (1428), Poggio Bracciolini not only asserted that "avarice is not unnatural," but went so far as to call the avaricious "strong, prudent, industrious, severe, temperate, great-souled and of great wisdom[sic!]". Avarice not only teaches men to provide for themselves but also favors the accumulation of capital, and so hastens the growth of the entire community.

The seeds sown by these "secular humanists" and by Thomas Hobbes – under whose contractualistic doctrine it is the social contract, not theology, that determines what is virtue and what vice – would bear fruit in the Enlightenment. In the wake of Bernard de Mandeville and then of Jeremy Bentham, greed was promoted from vice to quasi-virtue. The man who seeks money – the merchant, say, but not only he – might not be happy, but his action nevertheless has positive social effects. As noted above, the term greed or avarice then virtually disappeared from the lexicon of economics that began to circulate in Europe and America with Adam Smith's *Wealth of Nations* (1776). With the Enlightenment, whether Scottish or French, there was a growing belief that thanks to the heterogeneity of ends the most effective way to help the poor was to favor the actions of the greedy.

The last quarter of the twentieth century, in approximate concomitance with the new globalization and the third industrial revolution (information and communications technology), saw an unexpected resurgence of interest in the problem of greed. Now accused of being a main source of secondary scarcity, in that it keeps us from distinguishing between needs and desires, this vice is the one that expanded its domain more than any other, and in spectacular manner, in the last century. But the limitless lust for things today seems once again to be perceived as a serious impediment to our civil and moral progress. If the prideful are possessed of themselves, the greedy are possessed of things. Their conduct is unmistakable: the miser accumulates but does not invest; he hoards but does not use; and this is precisely the problem for social progress. Machiavelli's age-old warning seems topical again: "Peoples are more harmed by the avarice of their own citizens than by the rapaciousness of their enemies."

Avarice between vice and virtue

What explanation can be given for this pendulum of doctrinal positions and moral stances not found in judgments on any of the other "deadly sins"? The answer lies in social change, and in particular in the transformation, over time, of the forms of wealth and the ways it is generated. It is now well established that there is close interdependence between the evolution of social and ethical norms on the one hand and changes in economic and financial structure on the other. Usury is perhaps the best example to illustrate how a radical change in moral teachings about economic life can originate in the transformation of the economy itself. But it is not the underlying principle – the rule that you should not take advantage of another's state of need – but its application in practice that changes.

Religion, as an essential component of a society's institutional infrastructure, obviously sets formal and informal constraints on human action, but on the other hand it also unleashes opportunities. This may be especially true in the economic field, where action is typically subject to constraints. In fact, the basic structure of economic action always involves some end to attain under the condition of specific constraints. There are two types of constraint: natural–technical (e.g., knowing the production technology required to obtain a given good); and moral (e.g., the norm that you cannot betray the trust of others for your own gain).

The first type of constraint is the province of the natural sciences. It is to the system of religious beliefs, or more generally cultural norms, that we assign the role of setting moral constraints. Clearly, different ethical systems – the Hobbesian social contract, Kantian ethics, Benthamite utilitarianism, the Aristotelian–Thomist ethics of virtue, and others still – generate different moral constraints, which will produce highly divergent economic behavior and outcomes. But there is a fundamental difference between the two types of constraints. Where technical or natural constraints, even when they arise in different institutional frameworks, tend towards uniformity, that is, to converge among themselves – which explains the relative ease with which technical–scientific knowledge is transferred from one context to another – moral constraints are more specifically conditioned by the particular religious or philosophical tradition that prevails in a given environment or historical period. In turn, however, moral constraints are not indifferent to the results of economic activity, so that there are complex feedback effects between the two. The economic mechanism has an impact on social and ethical norms and vice versa.

Greed offers a prime case study of this interdependence, which gives us plausible explanations for the historical swings in judgment on this sin. What is the essential nature of greed? There is in every human being a sentiment urging passionate effort to satisfy his needs – this we call "desire." Human desire, when it is not deviated, seeks things out as goods to satisfy it. But it may be misdirected. This is because some of the goods to which it is directed are only apparent goods, but are in fact evils: goods that seem to satisfy desire but actually turn it towards disorder and drive it towards unhappiness. Desire as such is the life force, but we may desire some things that cause us to flower or others that cause us to shrivel. Greed, avarice, is one of those desires that shrivel us up. It is the derailing of desire that grows upon itself. And we know why. Goods become "good" when they are put in common. Goods that are not shared always lead to unhappiness, even in an affluent world. Money tightly held, jealously hoarded, actually impoverishes its holder, by depriving him/her of the capacity of giving. Misers, by definition, cannot give and therefore cannot be happy. They can, of course, make donations – engage in philanthropy – if this is instrumental to increasing their possessions.

We thus grasp the profound sense of Heraclitus' dictum: "It is hard to contend against one's heart's desire; for whatever it wishes to have it buys at the cost of soul." This fits the existential condition of misers perfectly: they "sell" their souls to "buy" limitless accumulation – because misers are persons who accumulate objects repetitively, obsessively, regardless of their real worth. Yet without extensive practices of giving in a society, the conditions for a happy life can never be realized. There may be an efficient market and an authoritative (and possibly even just) state, but there will never be a solution to the "discontents" of civilization cited in Freud's famous essay. There are in fact two categories of goods whose necessity is perceived by all: the goods of justice and the goods of gratuitousness. The former – for instance, the goods dispensed by the welfare state – place a specific *duty* upon one agent (typically a public body) to ensure that citizens' rights to these goods are realized. The goods of gratuitousness – relational goods, for instance – place an *obligation* that stems from the connections that link us together. In fact, it is the recognition of a mutual *ligatio* (bond) between persons that underlies the *ob-ligatio*. So where in order to defend your right you can and must resort to law, one complies with an obligation by means of reciprocity. No law can ever impose the practice of reciprocity upon citizens, and no economic incentive can ever foster the gratuitous behavior of gift-giving. Yet there is no one who fails to see how important the goods of gratuitousness are to serving the inherent need of happiness within each and every one of us.

Even the miser knows this, but he cannot obtain these goods, because by refusing all bonds with others he fails to practice the golden rule, "Love thy neighbor as thyself." The fact is that the miser does not love himself but only the possessions he accumulates. All the less can he love others, in whose respect the most he can do is practice the "copper rule": "Do unto others as others do unto you." How do other people treat the miser? They treat him as a miser, and so the circle closes, ever more tightly. In Kierkegaard's famous saying, the door to happiness opens only outward, so it can be opened only by going "outside oneself." This is precisely what the miser – the greedy person – cannot do.

Today, perhaps, we are in a position to go beyond Voltaire's cynical interpretation according to which "[m]en hate the individual whom they call avaricious only because nothing can be gained from him" (*Philosophical Dictionary*, 1764) and see greed as the deadly sin which, if not counterbalanced by authentic, widespread practices of gratuitousness, will threaten the very sustainability of our civilization. Charles Dickens understood this perfectly. In *A Christmas Carol* (1843), his archetypical, unfeeling miser, Ebenezer Scrooge, makes the unforgettable gesture. The old city financier, who had never spent a penny on gifts and considered Christmas a lot of "humbug" and a waste of time and money, in the end discovers the truth about himself, and learns something of the life that he has never savored. Amidst general incredulity, he begins to dispense not just the money obsessively hoarded in the course of a lifetime dominated by the passion of having, but also sympathy and tenderness. And he takes leave of every recipient saying, "Thank you. I am much obliged to you." At long last, as an old man, Ebenezer Scrooge the miser had found what reciprocity is, and with it he tasted happiness.

Literature

Barrera, A. 2005. *God and the Evil of Scarcity: Moral Foundations of Economic Giving.* Notre Dame: University of Notre Dame Press.

Bloomfield, M.W. 1952. *The Seven Deadly Sins.* East Lansing: Michigan State College Press.

Little, L. K. 1971. "Pride Goes before Avarice: Social Change and the Vices in Latin Christendom." *American Historical Review,* no. 1.

Noonan, J. 1957. *The Scholastic Analysis of Usury.* Cambridge, MA: Harvard University Press.

Schimmel, S. 1997. *The Seven Deadly Sins.* Oxford: Oxford University Press.

27
Globalization

Jean-Jacques Rosé and François Lépineux

Following the sunlight, we left the old world.
(Christopher Columbus, 1493)

Globalization is a widely used term that is the subject of various definitions and interpretations. It can be described both as an ongoing transformation process and as an outcome, but it is not a new phenomenon; its historical origins themselves are debated – should they be situated in the modern era, or much before, for instance in the Hellenistic age? Globalization refers to the integration of economies, societies, and cultures around the globe, through the development of trade, communication, and technological advances; at the political level, it entails the weakening of the power of states and the rise of transnational actors. The business community, whose internationalization has played a major role in fueling the globalization movement, has been heaved into the turmoil of accusations and appeals to its sense of responsibility. The aim of this article is to synthesize the historical debate so as to try to elaborate a conception of the globalization process that, on a theoretical level, gives it meaning and, on a practical level, indicates ways to transcend new, planetary risks.

A problematic history

Historians are divided concerning globalization: is it a new concept or is it old wine in new bottles? Most historians agree on the ancient origins of globalization or its representation. Bearing this in mind, its historical process is closely linked to the development of civilizations and has engendered an autonomous school of research called world/global history, which came to fruition in the United States in the early sixties. This school was well organized in the United States before expanding to the rest of the Anglo-Saxon world, with the creation of academic associations, such as the World History Association in 1982; with several research centers and periodicals, such as the *Journal of World History* (Hawaii University), the *Journal of Global History* (Cambridge University), and *Globality Studies Journal: Global History, Society, Civilization* (Stony Brook University); with websites and online newsletters. In 2009 the theme of the 123rd annual meeting of the American Historical Association was: "Doing Transnational History." Despite all appearances, the world/global history area is far from being monolithic; several diverging currents coexist within it.

- For numerous contemporary authors, studying the history of globalization is not a new ambition; they lay claim to a classical heritage, as did previously M. Weber, N. Elias, K. Jaspers, K. Polanyi, and "l'Ecole des Annales" (especially M. Bloch, F. Braudel); others are also inspired by the history of civilizations (following A. Toynbee).
- All forms of universal or global history boil down to two models: history whose ends are constituted in the course of centuries (Aristotle), in contrast to history whose ends (aim and achievement) can be anticipated and pre-conceived through human reasoning (Hegel).
- Another opposition imposes itself, namely whether one evaluates positively or negatively the idea of this final step in human history. In this sense, the successive universal historical narratives have always been either apologetic (Bossuet) or critical (Marx).

A minimum consensus

These different approaches determine a myriad of perceptions and contradictory evaluations of the current stage of globalization. However, a relative consensus exists concerning the three phenomena that define the modern state of the world:

- A brutal acceleration of long-term demographic indicators: several millennia were necessary for the human species to reach a population of one billion, at the beginning of the nineteenth century, whereas two more centuries were necessary to reach six billion today – and the same trend holds true for life expectancy;
- The continuation of cyclical figures concerning the evolution of economic indicators;

- Important geographical divisions that separate countries that participate in the planetary development and those which are excluded from it.

These dynamics have led to contemporary globalization through two stages:

- Nineteenth-century globalization, which brought about three catastrophes in the first half of the twentieth century – the Great Depression and the First and Second World Wars;
- The second, current globalization, which was inaugurated by the international agreements of Bretton-Woods and the era of economic expansion known as the "trenteglorieuses," and which is now characterized by economic instability and the multiplication of risks and threats of all kinds at the planetary level.

A systemic phenomenon

The consensus concerning these conclusions is the basis of globalism stereotypes and provokes numerous questions on the causes, nature, and consequences of this state of the world. Scholte (2000) sums it up in this way: *"What is global about globalization?"* In answer to this simplified question, the most commonly cited responses would be these:

- The development of scientific rationality has induced its application to technologies aimed at mastering nature (the planet Earth and life) – recent advances include biotechnologies, nanotechnologies, etc.
- Modernization is a Westernizing of the world, dominated in the nineteenth century by European colonial empires and then in the twentieth century by the spreading of the American way of life (typically McDonald's, Hollywood, and CNN), coupled with a generalization of consumer society as a universal claim of many peoples.
- Transformations that occur in cycles affect continents in different and unequal ways – hence the emergence of a multipolar world which puts an end to the "great divergence" (why did the Industrial Revolution take place in the West and not in China?).
- Internationalization (a substantive to describe cross-border relations between countries) has been followed by the extension of transnational activities based on a principle of de-territorialization in the domains of transportation, communication, production, and finance.

- The relationship between time and space changes: with the compression of the world (Robertson, 1992), time is accelerated and space shrinks (Bauman, 2007).
- Liberalization or political decisions have abolished barriers and obstacles concerning trade or foreign investments, and have led to the generalization of market economy.
- The birth of a planetary conscience generates the moving up to the universal level and the structuring of a global civil society (notably through the net of NGOs).
- The institutionalization of supra-state sovereignty is illustrated by the European Union or the UN agencies (Held and McGrew, 1999).
- New, global subjects of study have emerged, which are at the same time threats and challenges for mankind; for example, the earth's climate, access to water resources, pandemic diseases, cross-border regulations on the planetary scale.

These phenomena are described by many scholars from different disciplines. For some, globalization can be defined by only one of them. Yet, globalization cannot be reduced to one single factor: it consists of interdependent processes and domains, which partially overlap and inter-react one upon the others like feedback effects; this justifies nomenclature such as "world-system" (Braudel, 1985). These transformations of societies, human action, and knowledge can only be understood by transdisciplinary approaches, which call for a shift in perspectives (Latour, 1991) and for the introduction of critical approaches coming from outside and from above. Thus, history must redefine not only itself but, gradually, the whole of human and social sciences: Ulrich Beck (2000) demonstrates this with an acute perception, while such authors as Cohen and Kennedy (2007) or Braithwaite and Drahos (2000) have applied this idea in their respective works.

The globalization conflict

These approaches to the phenomena mentioned above create conflicting evaluations with either beneficial or prejudicial consequences, provoking a radical division of attitudes and movements (zealous apostles against resolute, even violent, opponents). This division backlashes and accentuates the divergent academic definitions. The theoretical impossibility of establishing a consensus concerning the definition expresses the practical divergence concerning the meaning one gives to globalization: the *scientific* difficulty conceals an *ethical* aporia in the understanding of a global and multifaceted process. Ricœur (1967) describes this irreducible aporia by defining globalization through two diverging but imperious necessities: the progress of rationality and the loss of meaning in the dissolution of purpose. He brings to light the two major conflicts, which define the theoretical and practical divisions in the governance of globalization:

- The issue of the nature of progress and the conflicting exchanges between global standardization of cultures and the dynamism of traditional cultures (D'Iribarne, 2002);
- The question of the legitimate demarcation lines among the economic, political, and ethical spheres.

Business at the heart of the conflict

This is where globalization intervenes in the domains well-known to the fields of business ethics and corporate social responsibility, which are themselves affected by the aporia diagnosed by Ricœur.

1. The neoliberal economists claim that global (and multinational) corporations, being the driving forces of globalization, should only take into consideration profit-orientated criteria, the market being the guarantee for the accomplishment of the common good of global society. Almost 30 years ago, T. Levitt described in a striking manner the "globalization of markets":

   The global corporation operates with resolute constancy, as if the entire world (or major regions of it) were a single entity; it sells the same things in the same way everywhere ... The world's needs and desires have been irrevocably homogenized. This makes the multinational corporation obsolete and the global corporation absolute. (Levitt, 1983)

2. This claim is rejected by (almost) all the authors working in the fields of corporate social responsibility and business ethics, represented on the five continents today. In 1989 the creation of ISBEE (the International Society of Business, Economics and Ethics) flowed from the collective will of American and European business ethicists to foster the evolution of their respective fields in the direction of international multicultural ethics.

The opposition between these two standpoints cannot be resolved by means of instrumental reasoning alone, since the loss of meaning is dependent on the ethics order. Hans Küng (1997) expresses this truth in its simplest form: a global question calls for a global answer. He demonstrates how such global answers are now formulated by intercultural circles such as the International Commission on Global Governance, the Parliament of the World's Religions, and the World Commission on Culture and Development – which collaborate with the United Nations.

The cave myth – a means, for the present time, to understand and react to globalization

Globalization has become, in the literal sense, "the human condition," according to H. Arendt's book title (Arendt, 1998). She experienced living under a totalitarian regime during the Second World War, and for her the loss of meaning leads to the existential alternative of skepticism or despair. The way out is an assumed contradiction, that is to say, a mind that controls an inversion of perspective. This capacity to control such a reversal has predominated in Western historical thinking since Plato's cave myth, which overturned the Homeric world order.

> Whoever reads the cave allegory in Plato's Republic in the light of Greek history will soon be aware that the *periagoge*, the turning-about that Plato demands of the philosopher, actually amounts to a reversal of the Homeric world order. Not life after death, as in the Homeric Hades, but ordinary life on earth, is located in a "cave," in an underworld; the soul is not the shadow of the body, but the body the shadow of the soul; and the senseless, ghostlike motion ascribed by Homer to the lifeless existence of the soul after death in Hades is now ascribed to the senseless doings of men who do not leave the cave of human existence to behold the eternal ideas visible in the sky. (Arendt, 1998, p. 292)

Mankind's praxis at the beginning of the twenty-first century reproduces, on the planetary scale, quarrels, wars, and ruses of the Mediterranean microcosm, as told by Homer in the *Iliad* and the *Odyssey*: the Platonic inversion evoked by H. Arendt as she faced the twentieth-century's tragedies remains peculiarly true today. This capacity of reversibility expressed in the Platonic myth is a human spiritual dimension; a contemporary rereading may interpret it in two different ways.

A cosmogonic reading

The cave is the whole world. The central force that governs the universe is the sun (*The Republic*, 2006, 516b), which is the source of all things: it gives light and warmth to the visible world (light and energy, *The Republic*, 517c).

- Industrial civilization has relied on the transformation of fossilized solar energy in order to replace or multiply human workforce (increasing its productivity).
- The outlook of the green economy rests on the use of alternative energy, that is, energy which is not stored in the soil, but converted from solar energy – either directly (photovoltaic) or indirectly (tides, biomass).

A philosophical and spiritual reading

The visible world is a prison (*The Republic*, 2006, 517b): reversal and conversion (518b) imply leaving this prison and going to the furthest limits of the intelligible world to perceive, with effort, the idea of the Good (517c). The ending of this myth is tragic. He, who has apprehended the intelligible world, goes back to the cave to try and free his companions, who react with sarcasm and mockery, before condemning him to death (517a). This outcome ends the narrative and clearly indicates the historical, practical, and spiritual significance of the myth: to consider the world as a whole makes it possible for us to understand the signification of Socrates' death, to define political tasks, and to show how none of this is possible if one refuses to act in the light of good, whatever the price he must pay.

Globalization is the fulfillment (as defined by Hegel) of Western thought and spirituality. But this fulfillment reaches its limits, which need to be surpassed through an alternative, now clearly perceived by the international community: sustainable development or chaos. Making the right choice presumes that mankind as a whole rises above the values of the society of (economic) development, through the structuring of the ethical and spiritual framework of global society. Faced with this inevitable ambition, and as the Asian continent is now entering the modern world, will humankind be able to assimilate the major contributions that the Kyosei and No-self paradigms represent?

Literature

Arendt, H. 1998..*The Human Condition*. Chicago: The University of Chicago Press.

Bauman, Z. 2007. *Liquid Times: Living in an Age of Uncertainty*. Cambridge: Polity Press.

Beck, U. 2000. *What is Globalization?* Cambridge, UK and Malden, MA: Polity Press and Blackwell Publishing Company.

Braithwaite, J. and Drahos, P. 2000. *Global Business Regulation*. Cambridge: Cambridge University Press.

Braudel, F. 1985. *Dynamique du capitalisme,* Paris: Arthaud.

Cohen, R. and Kennedy, P. 2007. *Global Sociology*. New York: New York University Press.

D'Iribarne, P. (ed.) 2002. *Cultures et mondialisation. Gérer par-delà les frontières*. Paris: Seuil.

Held, D. and McGrew, A. 1999. *Global Transformations: Politics, Economics and Culture*. Cambridge: Polity Press.

Küng, H. 1997. "A Global Ethic in an Age of Globalization." *Business Ethics Quarterly*, Vol.1, no. 3, pp. 17–31.

Latour, B. 1991. *Nous n'avons jamais été modernes*. Paris: La Découverte.

Levitt, T. 1983. "The Globalization of Markets." *Harvard Business Review*, Vol. 61, No. 3, pp. 92–102.

Plato 2006. *The Republic*. New Haven: Yale University Press.

Ricoeur, P. 1967. *Histoire et Vérité*. Paris: Seuil.

Robertson, R. 1992. *Globalization: Social Theory and Global Culture*. London: Sage.

Scherer, A.G. and Palazzo, G. (eds) 2008. *Handbook of Research on Global Corporate Citizenship*. Cheltenham, UK and Northampton, MA: Edward Elgar.

Scholte, J.A. 2000: *Globalization: A Critical Introduction*. New York: Palgrave.

28
Deep Ecology
Knut Johannessen Ims

Deep ecology is an alternative philosophy also called ecophilosophy as well as a campaign platform. As ecophilosophy, deep ecology is a fundamental approach to environmental problems and focuses on underlying causes, the roots of problems. It assumes a relational, total-field perspective that fits into a holistic, nonreductionist, nonanthropocentric worldview. It is in contrast to shallow ecology, which represents the technocratic attitude to pollution and resource depletion. Shallow ecology uses rules such as "the polluter pays" and assumes that treating the symptoms through technological quick fixes will reduce the ecological footprint. According to deep ecology, we have to change the basic ideological structure, which ultimately means changing ourselves.

Deep ecology is highly relevant because global reports (WWF International, 2008: Millennium Ecosystem Assessment, 2005) describe a serious bio(logical) diversity crisis. Annual loss due to extinction might be in the range of 10,000–100,000 different species. Human activities are almost wholly responsible for this loss, and the loss of species and habitats is occurring at an ever-increasing rate. According to deep ecology, humans are an integral part of nature, and thus the human fate is tightly linked with biodiversity, whose loss will weaken the ability of the living systems – the web of life on which we depend – to survive. The United Nations had proclaimed the year 2010 as the International Year of Biodiversity.

A much more debated problem of our planet is climate change, which in large part can be explained by a continuous rise in greenhouse gas emissions (in particular CO_2). Since 1961 the ecological footprint has more than doubled. In 2005 the ecological footprint exceeded biocapacity by 30 percent, which means that the world's resources are being used faster than they can be renewed.

Inspirational sources – The deep ecological tree

There are many supporters of deep ecology. The Norwegian philosopher Arne Næss (1912–2009) is acknowledged as a pioneer who formulated some of the core concepts. A metaphor used by Næss to suggest the inspirational sources behind deep ecology is "the deep ecological tree" (see Hegdal and Strand Olsen, 2001), a tree with long and strong roots, and different branches representing ideas from Hinduism, Confucianism, and Buddhism on the one hand and Aristotle, Spinoza and Heidegger on the other. Thus the ideas of deep ecology are not new, but ancient. One of the inspirational sources is Mahatma Gandhi's concept of oneness, which means that everything is interrelated. Gandhi postulates a holistic worldview that naturally leads to nonviolence.

In his book on Baruch de Spinoza, Næss (1999b) writes that many of his intellectual friends have great respect for Spinoza but wonder how it is possible for anybody to take Spinoza's metaphysics seriously today. Spinoza is an ontologist – not an ethicist. One of Spinoza's core concepts is the substance, and this substance is causasui: its own cause. If there is a God, God has to be in the substance, and God is the substance, and the substance cannot be separated from nature. This teaching represents monism and a kind of panpsychism, which involves the notion that all living entities are internally related to one another. It supports the fundamental idea of the oneness of all life in spite of diversity. People and all sentient beings are related because every species and every being is part of the same substance, and they have an equal right to life-unfolding. Any increase in the level of perfection involves a deep joy *a la hilaritas*. And a perfection cannot develop far without sharing joys and sorrows with others, which follows from our ability to identify with others and thereby become close to all kinds of life (Næss, 1999b).

Spinoza is also a key inspirational source for the importance given to spontaneous experiences in deep ecology. Gestalt psychology – which values the perception of gestalts or a network of relationships – also supports the belief that human beings are able to feel a strong sense of wide identification and a deep sense of empathy with other sentient beings and nature in general. Those identification processes lead to a natural inclination to protect nonhuman life.

Self-realization as the hypernorm

Self-realization is an essential norm in deep ecology, and it must be interpreted as self-realization for all beings (Næss and Rothenberg,

1989; Næss, 1999a). The meaning of self-realization within deep ecology extends the usual concept of realizing oneself in Western society, where self-realization is typically regarded as an ego trip, an individual's effort to satisfy his or her own wishes. Deep ecological thinking involves a redefinition of the human concept of self, and opens up the possibility that all sentient beings are ecological selves or eco-Selves. And as Gregory Bateson (1972) argues, the unit of survival is not the organism alone, but "organism plus environment."

Self-realization in the wide sense assumes that human beings have the ability to identify with other sentient beings and to develop a transpersonal Self. There are empirical as well as intuitive forms of knowledge that support the possibility of a transpersonal Self. The thesis has as a logical consequence that if we damage nature, we hurt our Selves. Næss does not "difficultivate" the concepts of the Self – focusing instead on the human ability of identification with other beings.

Live a rich life with simple means

One central motto of deep ecology is "to live a rich life with simple means," or "simple in means, but rich in ends." The required change in the ideological structure is that life quality is more important than economic welfare, which is typically measured by Gross National Product (GNP). Although GNP is by far the most common measure to compare economic development between countries, it is not appropriate from an environmental perspective, because a high GNP often involves a high degree of pollution. So ironically GNP may be called Gross National Pollution. A central theme in deep ecology is to produce and consume less – treading lighter and wiser on earth, celebrating the virtues of slowness and smallness in an age of speed and scale.

The four-level framework

It may be useful to distinguish between four levels of deep ecological thinking (see Drengson and Inoue, 1995). The most profound level is the metaphysical level, which refers to the ultimate principles a person holds. The next level is the platform level, which might be seen as the core level and which unites different kinds of groups – radical eco-centrists, groups from the peace movement, eco-feminists, direct action groups as well as religious groups. Level three is the policy level and level four is the practical action level, where different activities might range from "ecotage" to the support of politically oppressed people.

This framework admits a great diversity at level one, the level of ultimate philosophies. Thus deep ecologists do not have to subscribe to the same ultimate ecological philosophy to work cooperatively. As Næss claims, the front is very long – and each person may contribute on his own premises. To indicate this long front of level one we can compare the premises of Gandhi and Næss. Metaphorically Gandhi looked upon everybody as drops of water and writes, "This ocean is composed of drops of water; each drop is an entity and yet it is a part of the whole; the one and the many. In this ocean we are little drops." For Næss this is not the appropriate image and he states, "I would rather look upon myself as a little tree in a large forest."

One idea behind the four-level framework is to stimulate continuous back and forth processes between the levels and thereby ensure that our fundamental premises and practice are in harmony. The framework challenges us to pose deep questions in exploring the ultimate premises and norms. When a more or less articulated position on the first level appears, we can move to the other levels.

The core level – the platform

The platform level is summed up in eight points:

1. The well-being and flourishing of human and nonhuman life on earth have value in themselves – independent of their usefulness for human purposes.
2. Richness and diversity of life forms are values in themselves.
3. Humans have no right to reduce this richness and diversity except to satisfy vital human needs.
4. We need a substantial decrease of human population.
5. The present interference with the nonhuman world is excessive.
6. Polices which affect basic economic, technological, and ideological structures must be changed.
7. The ideological change needed is mainly that of appreciating life quality (dwelling in situations of inherent value) rather than adhering to an increasingly higher standard of living. There is a profound difference between big and great.
8. Those who support these points have an obligation to directly or indirectly attempt to implement the necessary changes in a non-violent way.

Personal ecosophy and personal responsibility

Næss invites all people to work out their own subjective ecosophy, by which he means a philosophy of ecological harmony. This kind of *sophia* or wisdom is openly normative and contains norms, value priorities, and hypotheses. Wisdom is policy-wisdom, prescription, and hypothesis, not only scientific description and prediction.

Næss walked his talk and participated directly in society's value struggles. His behavior is in accordance with point 8 at the platform level, and as a good philosopher Næss always argued for his practical position. He admits to having learned much from ecology as a science. But there are limits to science. Even if deep ecology relies on the science of ecology (in particular through acknowledging the value of unity, symbiosis, and diversity), ecologism, the view that takes ecology as the ultimate science and final authority, involves over-generalizing and universalizing ecological concepts. Ecology cannot be a substitute for philosophical analysis. Any change has political implications, and in Næss' own words "we need to fight against depolitization." The science of ecology, concerned as it is with facts and logic, cannot answer the questions on how we should live a good life.

From point 8 at the platform level, it follows that supporters of the movement have the responsibility to act in harmony with all the guiding points in the platform. There are many ways to work for a change toward basic deep ecological values. Næss' life gives many concrete examples of how to act in a responsible way, and he was deeply influenced by Gandhi's nonviolent strategies. Gandhi's lifelong practice of nonviolence against rulers with powerful means was remarkably effective. One primary example is the Salt March in 1930 – a campaign that started with only a few people. The concept behind the campaign was Satyagraha (truth-force) – a nonviolent protest that openly violated the British law. The campaign ended in large-scale acts of civil disobedience in which millions of Indians participated. Gandhi was arrested and put in jail, but the event received extensive news coverage worldwide. More than 80,000 Indians were jailed, but the campaign had a decisive effect on changing world attitudes – and even the British attitudes – toward Indian independence. The Salt March demonstrated the impact of the wise and courageous use of civil disobedience.

Gandhi's practice taught that nonviolent actions require more courage than violent actions, and if nonviolence is to have the intended power, it needs creativity as well as personal suffering. Leaders need extensive training as well as education. The formula for Gandhi consisted of three factors: fearlessness, not fear; self-sustainabilty, not dependency; and identity, not emptiness and alienation. The protesters have to conquer their own fear of suffering and even death; they should not depend upon the suppressor in any way; and finally, they should have a core they believe in, within themselves – an inner flame, a Truth. One has to strengthen oneself, since the power over oneself is a prerequisite for power over another. Any serious conflict should be transformed into a higher level, involving transforming the opponents into partners. The strategy entails breaking cooperation with the other as a suppressor while at the same time developing a good relationship with the other as a human being. The action should not be posed as a threat against the suppressor as a person, only against the system. Nonviolence as *ahimsa* (Hindu) means doing positive acts of love toward the suppressor. The ethics behind this is that the means are essential, and can never be compromised, for a noble purpose. Gandhi's soft law involved always acting in a way that realizes the Good, the nonviolent in everybody including you yourself. Your actions should mirror the society you want to obtain, not the eternal spiral of violence (see Gandhi, 1999, in particular the "Introductory Essay" written by Johan Galtung).

Those thoughts had a major influence on Næss' philosophy and participation in nonviolent actions to protect important wilderness values. When Næss acted against the regulation of a beautiful waterfall Bardøla in 1970, he tied himself with 300 other demonstrators in protest against the building of a dam and the subsequent destruction of the waterfall. The actions were not popular in Norway because the government enjoyed a high level of legitimacy in the postwar era. But the protestors had a major political significance in Norwegian society because they had increased the level of awareness about environmental issues and had contributed to undermining the high position the experts enjoyed. In an action in 1980 to preserve the River Alta in the northern part of Norway, which passed alongside the land of the Sami population, we witnessed five young Sami men who participated in a starvation strike clearly inspired by Gandhi's ideas.

Eco-topia? Real places or romantic nonsense for urban dreamers?

Abu Dhabi is a city-state in the United Arabic Emirates, where there is a plan to construct a modern eco-city – Masdar City. Is it a real eco-topia? The purpose is to develop a genuinely green city with zero carbon emissions and with no garbage. The hypermodern technology used in

United Arabic Emirates is almost the opposite of deep ecological thinking, because it requires a massive use of resources and is based upon the belief that high-tech strategies necessarily represent sustainable solutions to environmental problems. However, high-tech, high-cost, complex hardware and infrastructure lead to a high degree of specialization, elitist expertise, complexity, and vulnerability, and is aligned with a shallow technocentric paradigm. In contrast to Abu Dhabi, close to the city of Bergen in Norway we find "Bergen Ecological Village" using permaculture as one of the key concepts. "Perma" is the first part of the word permanence, and the permaculture philosophy holds that activities should typically have a sustainable character – an indefinite horizon. Other interesting examples of practices that accord with deep ecology are movements like Cittaslow, Slow food, Slow travel, Slowdown, etc. A common denominator of such movements is the mindset that "less is more" and downshifting means an increase in life quality.

Is it possible to create a political and economic system with a green-responsible policy? Since trees and plants absorb and store carbon, forest planting and protection of the rain forest will be part of the solution. However, the possibility of green practice is negated by the centralistic, technical–industrial way of production. We need a movement away from the economic-growth paradigm, and a culture dominated by competition, toward one focused on quality of life, where self-realization for all livings is at the core (Ims and Jakobsen, 2008). We will need to explore which system will work best, but we already know that the role of the economy will be reduced as compared with the prevalent market thinking in the Western world. We know that the economy will have to adapt to local conditions and local cultures and be based upon economic needs – not demands orchestrated by huge marketing departments. We may develop a model that transcends the differences between socialism and capitalism and hints at a deep ecological community using two simple dimensions: vertical/horizontal and collective/individualistic (Galtung, 1999). The first dimension concerns the degree of egalitarian order, and the second dimension concerns the degree of individual freedom and the ability to attain self-fulfillment. This model results in four types of societies (Table 28.1).

To satisfy the criteria for deep ecology we need a combination of the "Horizontal and Individual dimensions," or what amounts to a postrevolutionary society. Such a society is still unrealized in practice. However, within such a society we may seek maximal self-realization for all beings, in combination with minimal differences along the vertical axes, thus eliminating big bureaucratic institutions. It might be

Table 28.1   Four types of society

	Vertical	**Horizontal**
Collective	Conservative	Revolutionary
Individual	Liberal	Postrevolutionary

worthwhile to research Eastern traditions and cultures to study relevant concepts for a new economy. Many interesting concepts do exist; for example, "Sufficiency Economy" (Chaisumritchoke, 2007), "Mindful Economy" (Magnuson, 2007), and Buddhist economics, where simplicity and nonviolence, want negation and purification of human character are central values, and where the main task of economizing is to provide peace and permanence (Zsolnai, 2007; Zsolnai and Ims, 2006).

We may look upon deep ecology as a kind of strategy toward creating a sustainable future. Such a strategy will place an emphasis on culturally appropriate soft and intermediate technologies and make it essential that human beings and all other living creatures can realize their potential within a healthy ecosystem. The eight points from the platform level may inspire the formulation of some of the essential ideological issues in our time: how we can care for future generations, determine what the human's place in nature is, and arrive at technology and consumption patterns that are sustainable.

Literature

Bateson, G. 1972. *Steps to an Ecology of Mind.* New York: Ballantine Books.

Chaisumritchoke, S. T. 2007. "Sufficiency Economy, the King's Philosophy: An Application of Buddhist Economics to Develop Thai Local Pharmaceutical Industries for Sustainable Well-Being," *Society and Economy,* Vol. 29, no. 2, August.

Drengson, A. & Inoue, Y. 1995. *The Deep Ecology Movement: An Introductory Anthology.* Berkeley, CA: North Atlantic Publishers.

Galtung, J. 1999. *"Pluralism and the Future of Human Society,"* and *"Two Ways of Being Western: Some Similarities between Liberalism and Marxism."* (The two papers can be ordered from the Peace Research Institute in Oslo).

Gandhi, M. 1999. *Vierallesøsken.* Med etinnledende essay av Johan Galtung, Oslo, Bokklubben Dagens Bøker, (We Are All Brothers, with an introductory essay by Johan   Galtung in the Norwegian translation).

Hegdal, O.A. and Strand Olsen, T. 2001. *Jeg, Arne Næss. Et tegnet liv,* Oslo: Kaggeforlag (I, Arne Naess. A Drawn Life).

Ims, K.J. and Jakobsen, O. 2008. "Quality of Life – The Golden Mean between Materialistic Consumerism and Spiritual Asceticism." In L. Zsolnai (ed.), *Europe-Asia Dialogue on Business Spirituality.* Antwerp: Garant.

Magnuson, J.C. 2007. "Pathways to a mindful economy." *Society and Economy,* Vol. 29, no. 2, August.

Millennium Ecosystem Assessment 2005. *Ecosystems and Human Well-being: Synthesis.* Washington DC: Island Press. Available at: http://www.millenniumassessment.org/documents/document.356.aspx.pdf.

Naess, A. and Rothenberg, D. 1989. *Ecology, Community and Lifestyle.* Cambridge: Cambridge University Press.

Næss, A. 1999a. *Økologi, samfunnoglivsstil. Utkasttil en økosofi.*Oslo: Bokklubben DagensBøker. (Ecology, Society and Lifestyle: A Draft to an Ecosophia).

Næss, A. 1999b. *Detfriemenneske. En innføring i Spinozasfilosofi,* Oslo: Kaggeforlag. (The Liberated Human Being. An Introduction into the Philosophy of Spinoza.)

WWF International 2008. *Living Planet Report 2008.* Available at: http://www.panda.org/about_our_earth/all_publications/living_planet_report/.

Zsolnai, L., and Ims, K.J. (eds) 2006. *Business within Limits: Deep Ecology and Buddhist Economics.* Oxford: Peter Lang.

Zsolnai, L. 2007. "Western Economics versus Buddhist Economics." *Society and Economy,* Vol.29, no 2, August.

29
Climate Change and Spirituality
Laurie Michaelis

There are signs that the global climate may be close to a tipping point for transition to a warmer world. Amid calls for transition to a zero-carbon economy, politicians and much of the public are in denial. Their preferred technological and market solutions will be insufficient; a transformation is needed in our way of life. The spiritual dimension of the challenge has been neglected. It demands that we question the nature of self, our relationships with each other, the Earth and the beyond, our ways of life, and our sources of meaning.

Climate science

In 2007, the Intergovernmental Panel on Climate Change (IPCC) released its Fourth Assessment Report (AR4), an encyclopaedic review of the science of climate change (IPCC, 2007). It included some clear messages. It is now almost certain that greenhouse-gas (GHG) emissions from human activity are causing climate change. The oceans and atmosphere are warming; glaciers and permafrost are melting; sea levels are rising. Changes in weather patterns are consistent with those anticipated as a result of climate change.

A small number of vociferous scientists and others have claimed either that climate change is not happening or that it is natural, perhaps caused by solar variation. AR4 quantifies this contribution at around 5 percent of total global warming. The vast majority of warming is clearly due to human activity.

AR4 included scenarios in which the world avoids a global temperature rise exceeding 2°C, a benchmark for dangerous climate change widely adopted by governments. Global emissions need to be reduced by at least 50 percent in 2050 relative to 2000 (Meinshausen et al., 2009).

However, recent research suggests that this will be politically impossible (Anderson and Bows, 2009), especially since emissions growth has accelerated since 2000 (Raupach et al., 2007).

Meanwhile signs are growing of feedback effects that amplify climate change, including the melting of arctic sea ice and reduced CO_2 uptake in the Southern Ocean. Perhaps most worrying, columns of methane have been observed rising in the Arctic Ocean, thought to be from the thawing of vast reserves of frozen methane hydrates (Westbrook et al., 2009). Some scientists and a growing part of the environmental movement fear that the atmospheric concentration of GHG may already have passed the tipping point: natural processes may be taking over from anthropogenic emissions to bring a transition to a warmer world. They are calling for more rapid emission cuts and a shift to net sequestration of CO_2 to reduce the atmospheric concentration close to preindustrial levels (PIRC, 2008).

Impacts and implications

Climate change impacts on ecosystems and species have been documented in thousands of instances (IPCC, 2007). The viable ranges of animal and plant species are shifting toward the poles. Isolated species (e.g., on islands and mountains) are threatened because there is no appropriate habitat to which they can move. Over the next 20 years the IPCC anticipates substantial declines in crop and forest productivity and in fresh water availability in some parts of the world, especially Africa and South Asia. In the medium term, crop and forest productivity may increase in temperate zones but in the longer term, as temperatures continue to rise, productivity here, too, is likely to fall (IPCC, 2007).

While the worst impacts are predicted to fall on the world's poorest people, the wealthy are not immune. Price rises in world food markets in 2007 and 2008 demonstrated their sensitivity to fluctuations in production. Low-lying cities such as London and New York will be seriously affected by a sea-level rise. Increased rainfall is already resulting in more frequent flooding. Animal, plant, and human disease ranges are also shifting, with implications for crops, livestock, infestations in homes, and human health.

Relatively little attention has been paid to the social and political implications of climate change. This is difficult territory for the IPCC as a UN body whose reports have to be accepted by member governments. Famine, water shortages, desertification, and inundation are likely to lead to mass displacement of people and eruptions of conflict. There may be a considerable change in the role of the state in many countries, with implications for border controls and policing as well as disaster response (Abbott, 2008).

Greenhouse-gas emissions

Global anthropogenic emissions of CO_2 in 2004 from fossil-fuel use, land-use change, deforestation, and other sources amounted to 38 billion tons (Gt) (IPCC, 2007). This was 80 percent above the 1970 level. Other GHG, including methane and nitrous oxide, contributed the equivalent of a further 11 Gt of CO_2.

There is an ongoing tension between industrialized and developing countries over the responsibility for reducing emissions and over the relative contributions of material consumption in the global "north" and population growth in the "south." The industrialized countries, which have the initial responsibility for controlling their GHG emissions under the UN Framework Convention on Climate Change, account for 20 percent of the world's population and 46 percent of emissions (IPCC, 2007). Developing countries, forming 80 percent of the world's population, accounted for 73 percent of global emissions growth in 2004 but only 23 percent of global cumulative emissions since the mid-eighteenth century (Raupach et al., 2007).

A large part of the growth in emissions in developing countries is associated with producing goods for the industrialized world. In Britain, GHG emissions embodied in trade (those emissions associated with production of imports minus those associated with production of exports) grew from 5 percent of national emissions in 1994 to 20 percent in 2004 (Wiedmann et al., 2008).

The vast majority of emissions – including those from industry – are caused by the supply and consumption of goods and services by households, businesses, governments, and other organizations. Studies in North America and Europe trace around 70–80 percent of emissions to the consumption of food, household energy, and personal transport (Tukker, 2006). The three most significant contributors are car use, the consumption of meat and dairy products, and home heating.

Other aspects of ecological decline

Climate change compounds other impacts of human activities on ecosystems and natural cycles, especially the following:

- Degradation and destruction of habitats through the use of land for agriculture, managed forestry, buildings, and roads;
- The diversion of fresh water for agriculture, industry, and household consumption;
- Extraction of minerals including coal, oil, and other fossil fuels;
- Toxic pollution of air, water, and soil with the waste products of the industrial/consumer society.

The impacts of climate change on biodiversity are exacerbated, for example, by the human domination of the land, which means that plant and animal species in pockets of wilderness are unable to migrate.

These impacts are also profoundly interconnected. For example deforestation and intensive agriculture have negative impacts on the water cycle, accelerating surface runoff, increasing flooding and causing more soil erosion. This leads to the oxidation of soil carbon, which is a major contributor to climate change.

Avoiding the worst?

Governments – and much of the public – would prefer to address climate change at no financial cost, and no reduction in economic output. Policy analysts often see the challenge in terms of reducing the carbon or the GHG intensity of the economy (CO_2 or GHG emissions per unit of economic output). Some portray the imperative of developing climate policies as an opportunity to stimulate technological innovation and economic growth.

AR4 and the Stern Review (Stern, 2007) emphasize the role of policies that place a price on carbon – taxes or emission trading. Their analysis, based on economic models, suggests that quite moderate carbon prices could lead to a halving of CO_2 emissions by 2050. Impacts on the global economy would be small, with GDP in 2050 reduced by no more than 5 percent (IPCC, 2007). In the IPCC's reference scenarios, the world economy grows by a factor of three to five between 2010 and 2050 (Nakicenovic and Swart, 2000). The implied GHG-intensity reduction is therefore 85–90 percent, with an annual rate of reduction of 4.5–5.5 percent per year. Taking account of recent science suggests that much faster reductions are needed to avoid dangerous climate change (PIRC, 2008; Mallon et al., 2009).

Technology does indeed exist that could achieve most of the emission reductions needed, albeit at a cost. However, the carbon intensity of the world economy has fallen by only 1.2 percent per year over the last 50 years, and since 2000 it has increased by 0.3 percent per year (Canadell et al., 2007).

In fact, background analysis carried out in developing the IPCC reference scenarios suggested that GHG intensity would be unlikely to fall globally and economy-wide by more than 2–3 percent per year (Michaelis, 1998). Achieving even this would require maximum efforts in the form of government policies, and in process and product innovation by firms.

It is increasingly clear that governments' preferred strategies are not going to be sufficient. Technological and economic solutions can deliver at most half of the emission reductions needed. Avoiding the risk of triggering a climate tipping point will require rapid and radical changes in both technology and lifestyle in societies dependent on fossil-fuel energy.

Climate change as spiritual challenge

Even if climate change is addressed primarily through outward, technological, and economic means, it will demand change inwardly. It can be understood as a symptom of spiritual malaise or unawareness, or of a need for development in consciousness:

- Greenhouse-gas emissions result mostly from people's efforts to increase their material consumption, comfort, and convenience. However, success in these areas does not lead to lasting happiness, once basic needs are met. True sources of happiness are mostly nonmaterial, related to health, human relationships, and having a sense of meaning in life (see Kasser, Chapter 25, in this volume).
- People in urbanized societies have lost touch with the natural world, spending most of their time in human-constructed environments and rarely if ever experiencing wilderness. They are not aware of, or do not care about, the impacts of their choices on the life around them (see Ims, Chapter 28, in this volume).
- Responding to climate change requires a development of human relationships at all scales from local to global. Climate change is caused mainly by the affluent (in the global north and south), while the worst impacts are falling on people who are already poor and vulnerable. Recognition of God in the other, or of the other as Self, can lead to more equitable behavior and may be the basis for a collective will and the ability to act for change.

Although spiritual and religious traditions have a great deal to say about all of these, they have only recently begun to engage with climate change, as popular awareness has grown (e.g., Spencer and White, 2007). During 2008 and 2009, however, the Alliance of Religions and Conservation organized faith groups to develop plans for environmental action (ARC, 2009) including statements to contribute to the climate negotiations in Copenhagen.

Simplicity or frugality is often an element of the discipline encouraged in spiritual work (Bouckaert et al., 2008). This is partly a matter of reducing the amount of attention paid to the material world and the time spent earning money and spending it, to allow for a greater focus on the spiritual life. It is partly a way of observing and letting go of habits and desires, increasing self-consciousness and moving toward selflessness.

Simplicity may also be a consequence of spiritual development, as self-awareness leads to the realization that material consumption does not satisfy, and to a shift in emphasis to true sources of well-being.

Spiritual understandings of simplicity are not necessarily the same as those needed to address climate change. For example, a lifestyle that is simple in terms of avoiding fossil-fuel use and material consumption can be quite complicated in social and practical terms, partly because it is countercultural. It may require particular effort to find or produce food with low environmental impacts, to maintain relationships without motorized travel, and to manage energy and water use in the home. Low-impact ways of life do emerge, however, when a concern for simplicity is combined with a concern for the natural world and for other people worldwide.

Valuing nature

While deep ecology offers one spiritual response to our relationship with the natural world (Ims, Chapter 28, in this volume), there are several spiritual bases for valuing nature:

- belief in or experience of a creator God, seeing nature as cocreated with humanity;
- an encounter with God immanent in nature; and
- an experience of unity with nature – a sense of self that includes nature.

Each faith tradition has something to say about this – and in many instances what it has to say is complex or contradictory. The Judaeo–

Christian scriptures have sometimes been blamed for the environmental destructiveness of Western civilization, through values stemming from the creation story in which God sets humanity in "dominion" over other creatures. Several religious traditions include narratives about an end time, when the Earth will be destroyed and the faithful will be gathered to a new life. This leads some religious groups to welcome climate change as part of the apocalypse. Similarly, Buddhist teachings about the illusory nature of the world can contribute to an indifference to environmental degradation and a focus on the inward spiritual life.

However, most traditions also include a great deal of thought and practice that can contribute to a positive response to climate change. The Hebrew Bible contains passages emphasizing that the land belongs to God and must be respected and allowed to rest. Several writers have developed strands in Christianity that have much in common with deep ecology (Fox, 1996; Berry, 1999). Joanna Macy has developed a movement based in Buddhism seeking to enable people to engage with the despair engendered by climate change, and to develop a spiritual relationship with nature that can form the basis for action (Macy and Brown, 1998).

Community and agency

Mainstream climate-policy analysis treats people as autonomous individuals and largely neglects the role of the collective in responding to climate change. Community is fundamentally important because it

- involves human relationships, a major source of personal well-being;
- enables collective action;
- provides social support or peer-group solidarity;
- is where ethics are developed, spread, and consolidated;
- provides a dynamic tension between people with different ideas and worldviews.

However, the individualism of modern society is in part a reaction against the conformity and hierarchy of traditional communities. Many people's experience of community is largely negative.

Spiritual approaches to community can be different in that they are founded on recognition of the self, or that of God, in the other. This recognition is key to enabling communities to work positively with diversity rather than seeking conformity. Spiritually based community can also be a bridge enabling members to develop a sense of unity with people outside it, even to develop a universal concern for humanity and for future generations. This is particularly important for a response to climate change, which requires global, long-term caring and action.

Climate change challenges people's belief in themselves as individual agents, and in the self-determination of society. Most people do not believe that they are able to make a difference. In fact, they do not believe that they are able to make the simple changes that would be needed in their own behavior to prevent climate change. Nor do they believe that governments and other institutions are ready or able to take the action required.

Perhaps the most important part of the spiritual work related to climate change is to develop the personal and collective will and capability to change. For the first movers, this calls for deep self-questioning, self-understanding, and a willingness and ability to act against social norms. These are capacities that are developed through spiritual practice and can be supported by involvement in a strong spiritual community.

Literature

Abbott, C. 2008. *An Uncertain Future: Law Enforcement, National Security and Climate Change*. London: Oxford Research Group.

American Psychological Association 2009. *Psychology and Global Climate Change*.

Anderson, K. and Bows, A. 2009. "Reframing the Climate Change Challenge in Light of Post-2000 Emission Trends." *Philosophical Transactions of the Royal Society. A*. doi:10.1098/rsta.2008.0138

ARC [Alliance of Religions and Conservation] 2009. "Faith Group Commitments And Reports on Environmental Activities." Available at http://www.arcworld.org/downloads.asp. Last accessed November 1, 2009.

Berry, T. 1999. *The Great Work: Our Way into the Future*. New York: Bell Tower.

Bouckaert, L., H. Opdebeeck, and L. Zsolnai (eds) 2008. *Frugality: Rebalancing Material and Spiritual Values in Economic Life*. Oxford: Peter Lang.

Canadell, Josep et al. 2007. "Contributions to Accelerating Atmospheric CO_2 Growth from Economic activity, Carbon intensity, and Efficiency of Natural Sinks." *Proceedings of the National Academy of Sciences of the USA*, 10.1073, Washington (2007).

Fox, M., 1996. *Original Blessing: A Primer in Creation Spirituality*, Revised edition. Rochester, VT: Bear &Company.

IPCC [Intergovernmental Panel on Climate Change] 2007. *Climate Change 2007: Synthesis Report*. Available at www.ipcc.ch. Last accessed April 28, 2009.

Macy, J. and Young-Brown, M. 1998. *Coming Back to Life: Practices to Reconnect Our Lives, Our World*. Gabriola Island, BC, Canada: New Society Publishers.

Mallon, K., M. Hughes, and S. Kidney, 2009. *Climate Solutions 2: Low-Carbon Re-Industrialisation. A report to WWF International based on the Climate Risk*

Industry Sector Technology Allocation (CRISTAL) Model Climate Risk. Sydney, Australia: Climate Risk.

Meinshausen, M., Meinshausen, N., Hare, W., Raper, S., Frieler, K., Knutti, R., Frame, D. and Allen, M. 2009. "Greenhouse-Gas Emission Targets for Limiting Global Warming to 2°C." *Nature*, Vol. 458, pp. 1158–1162.

Michaelis, L. 2006. "Consumption Behaviour and Narratives about the Good Life." In S. Moser and L. Dilling (eds), *Beyond Message: Communicating Climate Change – Facilitating Social Change.* Cambridge: Cambridge University Press.

Michaelis, L. 1998. "Economic and Technological Development in Climate Scenarios." *Mitigation and Adaptation Strategies for Global Change*, 3(2–4), pp. 231–261.

Nakicenovic, Nebojsa and Swart, Rob (eds) 2000. *Intergovernmental Panel on Climate Change Special Report on Emission Scenarios.* Cambridge: Cambridge University Press.

PIRC [Public Interest Research Centre] 2008. *Climate Safety.* Available at www.climatesafety.org. Last accessed April 28, 2009.

Raupach, M.R., Marland, G., Ciais, P., Le Quéré, C., Canadell, J.P., Klepper, G., and Field, C.B. 2007. "Global and Regional Drivers of Accelerating CO_2 Emissions." *Proceedings of the National Academy of Sciences of the USA*, vol. 104 no. 24, pp. 10288–10293, Washington.

Spencer, N. and R. White, 2007: *Christianity, Climate Change and Sustainable Living.* London: Society for Promoting Christian Knowledge.

Stern, N. 2007. *The Economics of Climate Change: The Stern Review.* Cambridge: Cambridge University Press.

Tukker, A. 2006. *Environmental Impact of Products: Analysis of the Life Cycle Environmental Impacts Related to the Final Consumption of the EU-25.* European Commission Joint Research Centre report EUR 22284 EN. EU Publications Office. Availabla at: http://publications.europa.eu/.

Westbrook, G. K. et al. 2009. "Escape of Methane Gas from the Seabed along the West Spitsbergen Continental Margin." *Geophysical Research Letters*, 36, L15608, doi:10.1029/2009GL039191.

Wiedmann, Thomas et al. 2008. *Development of an Embedded Carbon Emissions Indicator – Producing a Time Series of Input-Output Tables and Embedded Carbon Dioxide Emissions for the UK by Using a MRIO Data Optimisation System*, Report to the UK Department for Environment, Food and Rural Affairs by Stockholm Environment Institute at the University of York and Centre for Integrated Sustainability Analysis at the University of Sydney. London: DEFRA.

Wilber, K. 2000. *Integral Psychology: Consciousness, Spirit, Psychology, Therapy.* Boston and London: Shambala.

Wink, W. 1998. *Engaging the Powers: Discernment and Resistance in a World of Domination.* Minneapolis: Fortress Press.

WWF 2008. *Weathercocks & Signposts: The Environment Movement at a Crossroads.* Godalming, England. Available at www.wwf.org.uk

30
Ecological Sustainability and Organizational Functioning

John Adams

There are many definitions of ecological sustainability. I consider that ecological sustainability, in the context of organizational functioning, involves learning to operate all of our enterprises today in such a way that there are nondeclining resources and abundant, high-quality choices available to future generations. Much has been written and talked about in the realm of ecological sustainability and the role of organizations in promoting a sustainable and high-quality presence on the planet for future generations, and many organizations have taken significant steps in the direction of ecological sustainability. However, the overall picture at present is bleak, as we realize how much is still needed to secure a sustainable future.

Let us be clear about what ecological sustainability entails from a scientific perspective. First, we must consider the biosphere. The ecological system in which we are interested is that area from a yard or so below the soil or sea bottom to a few dozen miles above the earth – the area where all life as we know it exists. One could think of a basketball with a coat of paint on it. Since life has developed over the millennia in this narrow territory, in general things that exist in the biosphere have a benign or positive effect on life. Things dispersed in the biosphere that are from outside the biosphere, such as minerals and fuels from the crust of the earth and complex manufactured chemicals, are frequently toxic to life forms in the biosphere.

The Natural Step

With this understanding, sustainability that allows for nondeclining resources and value-rich options for future generations must adhere to certain principles. Karl-Henrik Robèrt, a cancer scientist whose medical research led him to have serious concerns about the environment, embarked on a several-years project that eventually led to his articulation of some nonnegotiable sustainability principles, collectively called "The Natural Step," that are now widely applied in the process of working toward ecologically sustainable organizational practices (Natross, and Altomare, 1999; Robèrt, 2002). Robèrt's project involved sending his thoughts, in the form of an essay, to a large number of senior scientists, with the request that they provide feedback on the accuracy of his logic. After 21 cycles of writing and feedback, The Natural Step was born.

Essentially, the principles articulated by Robèrt are reflections of two uncontested laws of physics – the *law of conservation of matter and energy* and the *second law of thermodynamics*.

The law of conservation of matter and energy teaches us that, in the absence of nuclear fission, matter cannot be entirely destroyed, and the molecules always remain in the environment. Thus, when one wears out a set of tyres, all of the rubber molecules are still present on the earth – most of them having eventually been washed into the watershed or absorbed into the soil. When fossil fuels are burned, all of the exhaust-pipe molecules remain in the biosphere, contributing significantly to climate change according to most contemporary, serious scientists. As Robèrt often states in his presentations, "the earth is neither gaining nor losing appreciable weight!" In other words, "stuff does not go away."

The second law of thermodynamics suggests that matter (e.g., molecules from the aforementioned tyres) and energy always have a tendency to disperse, increasing entropy. In other words, "stuff spreads out."

Not being aware of these laws on a day-to-day basis as we operate our enterprises, often with the primary emphasis on short-term profitability, does not mean that these laws are suspended. Nor should we assume that all the essential laws that govern our ecological system have already been "discovered" and articulated.

For centuries before it was possible, mankind wanted to fly. There were probably thousands of failures, costing thousands of lives, before the nineteenth-century successes with hot air balloons and early twentieth-century successes with heavier-than-air flying machines. The laws of aerodynamics are now relatively well understood – we think. But they did not spring into existence in order to be discovered in the last hundred or so years – they were operating all along, regardless of our level of understanding of them!

It is safe to assume that there are still undiscovered ecological "laws" operating in the absence of human understanding. And even the ones we do understand, we often violate for the sake of short-term human self-interest (e.g., profits this quarter). My question regarding the biosphere is this: "Will it *ever* be appropriate for human activity to take a more preventive stance toward the health of the environment?" If the answer is "yes," then my second question becomes, "When is the last moment that we can do this and still maintain a reasonable quality of existence?"

The Natural Step expands the two undisputed laws of physics into four nonnegotiable principles that must be adhered to for true ecological sustainability. Dr. Robèrt crystallized the following system conditions in his consensus-building process. Any violation of these four system conditions necessarily leads to an eventually unsustainable condition.

System condition 1: We must not base our economies on extracting mineral and petroleum deposits from the crust of the earth at a faster rate than the natural cycles are able to reconcentrate them. Since atoms are never lost, everything that is withdrawn from the earth's reserves has to end up somewhere in the biosphere. Therefore, extracted minerals will accumulate as waste, either solid or molecular, for as long as the extraction rate is greater than the earth's ability to reconcentrate them as new ores, coal, or petroleum.

This, of course, means extremely severe restrictions on oil, coal, and mineral extraction – which is not a popular idea among mining, manufacturing, and petroleum companies. For example, our entire global society is addicted to fuels from the earth's crust. Nevertheless, there are by definition finite limits on these materials and we can expect the population to add a few more billions of people over the next several decades, leading to radically increased demands. The faster we consume and create trash, the "healthier" we are told we are economically. It is likely that we will experience the toxic side effects of this process, with outcomes such as cadmium concentrating in our livers, overwhelming costs arising from the destruction of natural resources, and rapidly escalating costs of extraction as the earth's supply of valued resources dwindles.

System condition 2: We must cease the release of persistent unnatural (i.e., synthetic) compounds into the environment. A high percentage of manufacturing processes today involve the production or utilization of man-made materials that are chemically complex and do not occur naturally in nature. Following the two undisputed laws of physics ("stuff doesn't go away" and "stuff disperses"), the gradual dispersal of these materials is like placing drops of ink in a bathtub full of water. For a long time, we aren't aware of them, but eventually, the water turns blue (e.g., we discover toxic chemicals in the breast milk of indigenous mothers in the remote Arctic).

Many of the thousands of synthetics in use around the globe today are not biodegradable; that is, breaking them down into their original components is either impossible or takes a very long time. While scientists and politicians continue to squabble over safe thresholds for this dispersed junk (e.g., plastics, nuclear waste), it continues to accumulate far more rapidly than most of us realize.

System condition 3: We must not reduce the natural biological cycle in its production of "life" through the process of photosynthesis. Ecologists refer to the excess production of green cells, beyond what the plants need for themselves, as the Net Product of Photosynthesis (NPP). They estimate that human activity today is consuming over 40 percent of the NPP in any given year, and that our rate of consumption, especially through agriculture – paving over green space, clear-cutting forests for lumber and paper, and burning rain forests to expand agricultural land – is growing rapidly.

Here again, as scientists and politicians quibble about where, when, and how much impact there will be, the NPP is being inexorably reduced by human activity. The symptoms we are already experiencing include expanding deserts, loss of topsoil, species loss, and soil salinity of lower-elevation farmlands.

System condition 4: The "metabolism" of human activities must not exceed the capacity of nature to maintain balance with respect to the first three conditions, and our economies must be efficient and fair with regard to the amount of resources needed to meet human needs uniformly. We must improve our efficiencies with respect to the use of extracted minerals and fuels from the earth's crust (system condition 1); become more natural and efficient in our manufacturing processes, in order to not produce synthetics and other wastes faster than the earth can process them (system condition 2); and be less destructive of and more efficient in our utilization of renewable natural resources – and all in a way that is fair and equitable for all people everywhere.

Many manufacturing and service companies, and many communities, have adopted these four Natural Step conditions as their ideals as they work toward ecological sustainability (Natross and Altomare, 1999; James and Lahti, 2004). These four nonnegotiable conditions, of course, are impossible or nearly impossible, actually to achieve, so the march toward ecological sustainability is necessarily an ongoing process rather than a "quick-fix." Usually, systems that are working toward sustainability using The Natural Step create challenging goals under each of the principles and then work toward achieving these goals. If and when any is achieved, more challenging goals are created to keep the process going. One of the major reasons such programs often fall apart and are dropped is that people don't realize that they need to shift how they are thinking.

Sustainable consciousness

In my ongoing research (Adams, 2000, 2004, 2006, 2009) into the kind of consciousness that will be needed to establish and maintain sustainability, I have now identified seven essential dimensions of thinking. (Table 30.1) The data I have been able to collect to date indicates that most people, in most places around the world, most of the time, operate mentally from nearer the left pole on each dimension than the right pole. Further, the expressed "range of comfort" is usually fairly narrow. The ways we think greatly influence our actions, which in turn influence the results we can attain.

Shared thinking patterns that are usually focused on aspects that are *short-term, reactive, local, separating, accountability-exacting, doing, and having* are likely to reinforce separation and the present linear "Take-Make-Waste" mode of operating, and are highly unlikely to support deeply initiatives leaning toward ecological sustainability. As Zsolnai (2002) has rightly concluded, when such thinking dominates, immediate profitability takes priority and both tangible and intangible costs are

Table 30.1   Some dimensions of a sustainable consciousness

Most frequent thinking mode	Least frequent thinking mode
Short Term	Long Term
Reactive	Envisioning
Local	Big Picture
Separation	Connections
Accountability	Learning
Doing	Being
Having	Sharing

pushed out to some future date whenever possible. In order to approach ecological sustainability, more versatile thinking styles will be required. I define versatility of thinking as "appropriate flexibility." In order to approach ecological sustainability, cognition that focuses on aspects that are *long-term, envisioning, big-picture, connecting, learning, being, and sharing* styles of thinking will *also* be required.

While a detailed exposition of how to bring about increased cognitive versatility is beyond the scope of this chapter, the reader may benefit from a few brief suggestions. First, versatility can be increased by establishing the habit of asking questions that require thinking from the other end of each spectrum. The following questions require thinking from the right side pole of each dimension – the side that usually gets the least attention in our fast-paced, consumer-driven global economy:

"What will happen if this trend continues for ten years?"
"What would you bring about if you had a magic wand?"
"What would happen if everyone acted this way?"
"Are you remembering to connect all the dots?"
"What can we learn from this experience?"
"What does your inner guidance ask for in this case?"
"What is the greatest good for all?"

Contemplation on, and dialogue about, questions related to ecological sustainability can also foster increased versatility.

The spiritual connection

It is essential that efforts toward ecological sustainability be grounded in solid science, and that there be detailed metrics developed to measure progress. However, it is my contention that in order actually to follow through on good intentions toward sustainability, one must also be comfortably able to think in highly versatile ways. Two of the seven dimensions of a sustainable consciousness posited here clearly have spiritual roots: Doing-Being and Having-Sharing.

Recall the biblical story of Jacob. As the Book of Genesis relates, Jacob was born clutching the heel of his seconds-older twin, Esau. During his early years, Jacob convinced his brother to give up his birthright as the firstborn, and also deceived their dying father into thinking that Jacob was Esau in order to receive the father's final blessing.

After this, Jacob left home for another land, where he eventually married Leah and Rachel, the two daughters of his host, Laban. Jacob was also reputed to have cheated Laban out of his best livestock, and to have swindled Laban and some others in the community out of many material possessions. Clearly, Jacob was DOING anything he felt necessary, in order to HAVE more possessions than anyone else.

When Jacob was returning to his homeland, he had his famous dream of angels on a ladder (spiritual progression) and also had a wrestling match with an angel over his way of life. These turned out to be consciousness-transforming events for Jacob. To mark this transformation, Jacob took the name "Israel."

Esau learned of Jacob's impending return and went out to meet him. While Jacob was fearful for his life, he needn't have been, as Esau was able to perceive the change in his brother and welcomed him back. Jacob immediately gave Esau a large portion of his flocks and other material possessions, stating: *"I have enough."* Jacob then became the loving patriarch of his family, and his 12 sons went on to create the twelve tribes of Israel.

Jacob had moved in his consciousness from Doing to Being and from Having to Sharing. Surely we could not establish ecological sustainability in any organization in which the prevailing modes of shared thinking were reflections of the young Jacob.

I want to close this chapter with "The Prayer of Healing" from the United Nations Environmental Sabbath Program (United Nations, 1990):

> **We join with the earth and with each other.**
> To bring new life to the land
> To restore the waters
> To refresh the air
>
> We join with the earth and with each other.
> To renew the forests
> To care for the plants
> To protect the creatures
>
> We join with the earth and with each other.
> To celebrate the seas
> To rejoice the sunlight
> To sing the song of the stars
>
> We join with the earth and with each other.
> To recall our destiny
> To renew our spirits

To reinvigorate our bodies

We join with the earth and with each other.
To create the human community
To promote justice and peace
To remember our children

We join together as many and diverse expressions of
one loving mystery:
for the healing of the earth and the renewal of all life.

Box 30.1   Questions for contemplation and dialogue

- What do we mean by "Nature's Plan," and do we think that we are separate from it?
- What is the present environmental perspective of most people in my field or line of work?
- How could we bring the values of those in my line of work into alignment with global ecological realities?
- What would it take for my place of work to make the environment a key priority in its strategic planning?
- Will it be possible to motivate enough people to do what really needs to be done?
- What can I do to remember the physical environment in every decision I make?

Literature

Adams, J. 2000. *Thinking Today as if Tomorrow Mattered: The Rise of a Sustainable Consciousness.* San Francisco: Eartheart Enterprises.

Adams, J. 2004. "Mental Models @ Work: Implications for Teaching Sustainability." In C.Galea (ed.), *Teaching Business Sustainability.* Sheffield, UK: Greenleaf Publishing Limited. pp. 20–33.

Adams, J. 2006. "Building a Sustainable World: A Challenging OD Opportunity." In B.B Jones and M. Brazzel (eds), *The NTL Handbook of Organization Development and Change: Principles, Practices, and Perspectives.* pp. 335–352. San Francisco: Pfeiffer.

Adams, J. 2009: "Mental Models for Sustainability – Six Dimensions of Mental Models." In J. Wirtenberg (ed.), *The Sustainable Enterprise Fieldbook: When It All Comes Together.* pp. 60–69. New York: AMACOM.

James, S. and Lahti, T. 2004: *The Natural Step for Communities: How Cities and Towns Can Change to Sustainable Practices.* Gabriola Island, BC, Canada: New Society Publishers.

Natross, B. and Altomare, M. 1999. *The Natural Step for Business: Wealth, Ecology, and the Evolutionary Corporation.* Gabriola Island, BC, Canada: New Society Publishers.

Robèrt, K-H. 2002. *The Natural Step Story: Seeding a Quiet Revolution.* Gabriola Island, BC, Canada: New Society Publishers.

United Nations 1990. Healing Prayer. "Only One Earth." UN Environment Programme, DC2–803, New York.

Zsolnai, L. 2002. "Green Business or Community Economy?" *International Journal of Social Economics*, vol. 29, no. 8.

31
Responsibility for Future Generations

Laszlo Zsolnai

Future generations are not-yet-born human beings. In practice we can envisage future generations as people living in the next 150–200 years. Activities of present generations affect the fate of future generations, for better or worse. What we do with our natural and cultural heritage mainly determines the way future generations can live their own life.

Ethics of responsibility

Hans Jonas has argued that an ethics of responsibility involves not only the existence of future human beings but also the way they exist. The conditions of the existence of future generations should not cause their capacity for freedom and humanness to disappear. "Thus moral responsibility demands that we take into consideration the welfare of those who, without being consulted, will later be affected by what we are doing now. Without our choosing it, responsibility becomes our lot due to the sheer extent of the power we exercise daily" (Jonas, 1996).

In his opus magnum "The Imperative of Responsibility: In Search of an Ethics for the Technological Age" Jonas' basic preoccupation is with the *impact of modern technology* on the human condition (Jonas, 1984)

The major theses on which Jonas' theory of responsibility is based are as follows:

1. "The altered, always enlarged nature of human action, with the magnitude and novelty of its works and their impact on man's global future."
2. "Responsibility is a correlate of power and must be commensurate with the latter's scope and that of its exercise."

3. "An imaginative 'heuristics of fear', replacing the former projections of hope, must tell us what is possibly at stake and what we must beware of."
4. "Metaphysics must underpin ethics. Hence, a speculative attempt is made at such an underpinning of man's duties toward himself, his distant posterity, and the plenitude of life under his dominion."
5. "Objective imperatives for man in the scheme of things enable us to discriminate between legitimate and illegitimate goal-settings to our Promethean power" (Jonas, 1984, p. x).

Jonas argues that the nature of human action has changed so dramatically in our times that it calls for a radical change in ethics as well. He emphasizes that in previous ethics, all dealing with the nonhuman world, that is, the whole realm of *techno* was ethically neutral. "Ethical significance belonged to the direct dealing of man with man, including man dealing with himself: all traditional ethics is *anthropocentric*. The entity of "man" and his basic condition was considered constant in essence and not itself an object of reshaping techno. The effective range of action was small, the time span of foresight, goal-setting, and accountability was short, control of circumstances limited" (Jonas, 1984, pp. 4–5).

According to Jonas, new dimensions of responsibility emerged because *nature* became a subject of human responsibility. This is underlined by the fact of the irreversibility and cumulative character of man's impact on the living world. *Knowledge*, under these circumstances, is a prime duty of man and must be commensurate with the causal scale of human action. Man should seek "not only the human good but also the good of things extra human, that is, to extend the recognition of 'ends in themselves' beyond the sphere of man and make the human good include the care of them" (Jonas, 1984, pp. 7–8).

For Jonas an imperative in responding to this new type of human action might run like this: "Act so that the effects of your action are compatible with the permanence of genuine human life",or expressed negatively, "Act so that the effects of your action are not destructive of the future possibility of such life" (Jonas, 1984, p. 11).

Jonas states that the necessary conditions of moral responsibility are as follows: "The first and most general condition of responsibility is causal power, that is, that acting makes an impact on the world; the second, that such acting is under the agent's control; and the third, that he can foresee its consequences to some extent" (Jonas, 1984, p. 90).

Jonas underlines the fact that prospective responsibility is never formal but always substantive. We feel responsible, not in the first place for our conduct and its consequences but for the matter that has or will have a claim on our acting. The well-being, the interest, the fate of others has, by circumstance or by agreement, come to our care, which means that our control over it involves at the same time an obligation for it (Jonas, 1984, pp. 92, 93).

Jonas differentiates between *natural* responsibility on the one hand and *contractual responsibility* on the other: "It is the distinction between natural responsibility, where the immanent 'ought-to-be' of the object claims its agent a priori and quite unilaterally, and contracted or appointed responsibility, which is conditional a posteriori upon the fact and the terms of the relationship actually entered into" (Jonas, 1984, p. 95).

The parent and the statesman are presented as ideal types of natural responsibility and contractual responsibility, respectively. Concerning their responsibility, the roles of parent and statesman have much in common. These common features are totality, continuity, and future-orientation : responsibilities encompass the total being of their object. The pure being as such, and then the best being of the child, is what parental care is about. The statesman's responsibility, for the duration of his office or his power, is for the total life of the community, the "public weal." Neither parental nor governmental care can allow itself a vacation or pause, for the life of the object continues without intermission, making its demands anew, time after time. More important still is the continuity of the cared-for existence itself as a concern. It is the future with which responsibility for a life, be it individual or communal, is concerned beyond its immediate present. An agent's concrete moral responsibility at the time of action extends further than to its proximate effects (Jonas, 1984, pp. 102, 105.107).

Jonas summarizes the imperative of responsibility as follows: "The concept of responsibility implies that of an ought – first of an ought-to-be of something, then of an ought-to-do of someone in response to the first." This is most evident in the case of a *newborn baby* "whose mere breathing uncontradictably addresses an ought to the world around, namely, to take care of him." Not only does the newborn call us in this way, but so does "the unconditional end-in-itself of everything alive and the still-have-to-come of the faculties for securing this end" (Jonas, 1984, pp. 130, 134).

Our obligations to future generations

We have natural responsibility toward future generations. We should consider every generation as equal and should not presuppose anything about the preferences of future generations.

Edith Brown Weiss developed three principles that underline our obligations to future generations (Brown-Weis, 1989).

1. Each generation should be required to conserve the diversity of the natural and cultural resource base, so that it does not unduly restrict the options available to future generations in solving their problems.
2. Each generation should be required to maintain the quality of the planet so that it is passed on in no worse condition than the present generation received it.
3. Each generation should provide access to the legacy from past generations to future generations.

Accounting for future generations

The Stiglitz, Sen, and Fitoussi Report on *The Measurement of Economic Performance and Social Progress* presents an advanced view on *sustainability*, that is, the possibility of permanence of present activities (Stiglitz, Sen, and Fitussi, 2009, pp. 61–62).

The report says that sustainability poses the challenge of determining whether we can hope to see the current level of well-being at least maintained for future periods or future generations, or whether the most likely scenario is that it will decline. The idea is the following: the well-being of future generations compared to ours will depend on what resources we pass on to them. Many different forms of resource are involved here. Future well-being will depend upon the magnitude of the stocks of exhaustible resources that we leave to the next generations. It will depend also on how well we maintain the quantity and quality of all the other renewable natural resources that are necessary for life. From a more economic point of view, it will also depend upon how much physical capital – machines and buildings – we pass on, and how much we devote to the constitution of the human capital of future generations, essentially through expenditure on education and research. And it also depends upon the quality of the institutions that we transmit to them, which is still another form of "capital" that is crucial for maintaining a properly functioning human society.

The question is how can we measure whether enough of these assets will be left or accumulated for future generations? In other words, when can we say that we are currently living above our means?

The report suggests that in order to measure sustainability we need indicators that inform us about the change in the quantities of the different factors that matter for future well-being. Put differently, sustainability requires the simultaneous preservation or increase in several "stocks": quantities and qualities of natural resources, and of human, social, and physical capital. (Stiglitz, Sen, and Fitussi, 2009, p.17).

We agree with the view that what really count for the well-being of future generations is the quantities and qualities of different stocks or capitals. However, we think we should define *"sustainability thresholds"* for these stocks or capitals against which we can evaluate the current state of affairs (Zsolnai, 2009).

If the state of a certain stock or capital is below its defined sustainability threshold then it indicates that the present generation poses burdens on future generations in this field. Similarly, if the state of a certain stock or capital is above its defined sustainability threshold then it indicates that the present generation gives gifts to future generations in this field. Being identical with the defined sustainability threshold means that the impacts of the present generation are neither negative nor positive for future generations in the given field.

In our model the state of ecological capital, financial capital, human capital, and intellectual capital together determine the fate of future generations. The better the state of these capitals, the better the prospects of future generations, and vice versa.

We developed key indicators for measuring the performance of present generations for future generations (Table 31.1).

Values of the above indicators for selected European countries are shown in Table 31.2.

Table 31.2 figures show the performance of the given countries measured against the required value for future generations in percentage terms. Minus values indicate that present generations are indebted to

Table 31.1   Future generations indicators

Capital	Indicator	Value range	Required value
Ecological	ecological footprint	0.1–12 ha per capita	< 1.6 ha per capita
Financial	debt service per capital formation	0–1.2	< 0.5
Human	share of youths per inactive adults	0.1–1.1	> 0.5
Intellectual	investment in research and development	0–0.04 of GDP	>0.02 of GDP

Table 31.2 The performance of European countries for future generations in 2005

	Ecological capital (%)	Financial capital (%)	Human capital (%)	Intellectual capital (%)
Austria	−335	n/a	−187	+86
Belgium	−346	n/a	−155	−105
Bulgaria	−183	−155	−183	−392
Cyprus	−428	n/a	−154	−541
Czech Republic	−361	+36	−201	−156
Denmark	−541	n/a	−174	+76
Estonia	−430	+92	−195	−220
Finland	−353	n/a	−175	+58
France	−332	n/a	−152	+93
Germany	−284	n/a	−202	+80
Great-Britain	−359	n/a	−173	−106
Greece	−394	n/a	−187	−345
Holland	−295	n/a	−171	−127
Hungary	−239	−181	−161	−227
Italy	−320	n/a	−174	−175
Ireland	−287	n/a	−148	−165
Poland	−267	−118	−168	−345
Latvia	−235	−115	−204	−476
Lithuania	−215	+81	−168	−263
Luxemburg	−810	n/a	−149	−110
Malta	−322	n/a	−142	−690
Portugal	−299	n/a	−198	−256
Romania	−193	+62	−172	−500
Spain	−386	n/a	−197	−180
Sweden	−343	n/a	−186	+53
Slovakia	−221	+88	−177	−377

future generations while plus values indicate that present generations produced surplus for future generations.

From the data several observations can be derived. There is no country in Europe which would not present some burden for future generations in one or more domains. There are some countries (Bulgaria, Hungary, Poland, Latvia) which present burdens in all domains for future generations. There are other countries (Austria, Finland, France, Germany, Sweden, the Czech Republic, Estonia, Romania, Slovakia, Lithuania) which present gifts for future generations in financial or intellectual domains but at the same time present serious ecological and/or human burden for them. The sad fact is that the *fate* of *future generations* is *not assured* in Europe at all.

Caring for future generations is not an altruistic concern only. Improving the position of future generations enhances the future of the present generations too.

Literature

Brown-Weis, E. 1989. I*n Fairness to Future Generations: International Law, Common Patrimony, and Intergeneration Equity.* Tokyo: The United Nations University and Dobbs Ferry, NY: Transnational Publishers.

Jonas, H. 1984. *The Imperative of Responsibility: In Search of an Ethics for the Technological Age.* Chicago and London: The University of Chicago Press.

Jonas, H. 1996. "Toward an Ontological Grounding of an Ethics for the Future." In Hans Jonas, *Mortality and Morality. A Search for the Good after Auschwitz.* pp. 99–112. Evanston, IL: Northwestern University Press.

Stiglitz, J., A. Sen, and J-P. Fitussi. 2009. *Report by the Commission on the Measurement of Economic Performance and Social Progress.* Available at: www.stiglitz-sen-fitoussi.fr

Zsolnai, L. et al. 2009. *The Fate of Future Generations in Hungary.* Business Ethics Center, Corvinus University of Budapest.

32
Authenticity
David Boyle

I used to explain my decision, sometime around 2001, to write a book about the growing demand for authenticity, by telling the story of a dinner party (Boyle, 2001). A friend of mine had told us why he had bought a flat in Paris. It was, he said, "because they have real shops there." Thinking about it afterwards, I realized that this was not "real" in any of its conventional definitions, yet everyone knew immediately what he meant. He meant tiny, colorful, family-owned stores, full of evocative smells and baking on the premises, in neighborhoods where the customers might be known by name to the shopkeeper.

This was more evidence for me that something peculiar was happening to the word "real," not for everybody but among enough of us to matter. Although most people I talked to about this seemed to be unable to define exactly what they meant by "authentic," they knew what it was when we saw it, whether it was real food, real culture, real politics, real schools, real community, real medicine, or real stories. There was something, apparently indefinable, which held these things together.

This was bound to be anecdotal research. But it was clear to me that, whatever people meant by "authentic," they did not mean it in the sense that Freud or Marx might have meant it, or even as Coca-Cola or Ralph Lauren might have meant it either. The business of Coca-Cola's Dasani bottled water, which actually came from the main water supply, underlined the fact that there was some tension going on here. The tension was all the clearer when you realized that brand name shirts were being made in the same Far Eastern factories that were also churning out the fakes.

Paul Ray suggested that the "cultural creatives" phenomenon in the USA included about a quarter of the American population (Ray and Anderson, 2000). This seems to be a parallel but related idea. Ray said that cultural creatives believed themselves to be almost alone in the definitions and tastes, shared just by themselves and a few friends railing against the world, when it was actually a much more widely shared understanding. This is likely to apply also to the new definition of "real." There is actually a sizeable minority who use the word "authentic" in this new way, as part of a growing revolt against what is fake, spun, mass-produced, and manipulated (Yeoman, 2007). Very quietly, and below the radar of the cultural commentators – except perhaps for a few – this is what had been driving the rise of farmers' markets, slow food, real ale, reading groups, organic vegetables, poetry recitals, complementary medicine, unbranded fashions, and much else besides.

The demand for what is real is obvious from the packaging in shops, and in the world of advertising, where there are constant appeals to authenticity, often to obscure the fact that the product is deeply inauthentic in some way. When looking at food packets it becomes clear that "real" is now also a slightly atavistic reaction against some aspects of technological hope. Despite all those predictions by technocrats and globalizers, we are not taking our food in pill form as we were told we would. We haven't had the genius machines, able to think for themselves (predicted in 1970); or human embryo packets in shops (1966); or robots to look after the elderly (1983); or the disappearance of kitchens (1970); or artificial moons instead of streetlighting (1968). We haven't handed over our futures to virtual teachers or doctors, though clearly that remains a possibility (Roszak, 1994).

The combination of all these factors represents a demand for food that tastes of something, does not involve the genes of fish for temperature control or human hair to make the dough stretchy, and comes from a real place somewhere on the map. Far from losing our regional identities in a global world, half of the UK population now lives within a thirty-minute journey of where they were born. To describe the contemporary world as "globalized" clearly is not entirely accurate.

An estimated twelve million Europeans are now downshifting by cutting salary or hours in search of more "authentic" living. Another two million have given up the rat race entirely. And we are seeing the slow decline of the big brands like McDonald's and Coca-Cola as they desperately portray themselves as "local." When I was writing the book, HSBC and Interbrew – two global giants without local roots or culture – were battling over the legal right to call themselves "The world's local …" (Boyle, 2003).

There is another strand behind the new meaning of the word "real", and that is where business theory and New Age self-improvement meet.

One element of this is the emergence of a broad argument about our working lives, that we are likely to be more effective and fulfilled if we are in some sense true to our own natures (Crofts, 2003). There is also an emerging debate about "authentic leadership" in the corporate world, notably following the survey of leaders by Bill George, CEO of Medtronic, which found that authentic leadership related more to self-reflection and honesty than to any inborn gift (George et al., 2007). These are different, but related, meanings. They are also a clue about the central argument of authenticity.

It has become increasingly clear to me since in some ways launching this debate that – when it comes to authenticity in marketing and business – there are essentially two views about all this, and they are broadly about whether authenticity itself is real.

There is a prevailing view among some commentators that takes the opposite view, and you can see why. Authenticity is impossible, they say, because everything is constructed. That means any appeal to authenticity by companies and advertisers must be manipulative. By definition, it is fake. As the social commentator Seth Godin put it: "Authenticity – if you can fake that, the rest will take care of itself" (Godin, 2001).

It is true that advertising and marketing regularly appeals to our insatiable demand for what is real, especially – perhaps inevitably – when the offering is particularly fake. There are now so many overlapping meanings to the word that almost anybody can claim it for anything – ethical, original, natural, pure. We navigate these claims every day, and actually do so quite easily. Despite the predictions that somehow real and fake would become hopelessly interlinked, we actually distinguish the two without difficulty (Boyle, 2001). We do so particularly on television, where "reality" – heavily manipulated by producers – is almost all that is on offer. When we feel particularly manipulated, either by the media or politicians, there is a public outcry. The BBC and ITV ended up paying large fines for the way they had manipulated the people answering their premium phone line quiz programs.

But the marketing of real has moved on as well. Two American business consultants, James Gilmore and Joseph Pine, published a book, also called *Authenticity*, which was designed as a manual for businesses (Gilmore and Pine, 2007). It was full of fascinating insights into the way the culture of real is developing. But they share the opinion of many of my original reviewers. "It's all fake, fake, fake," they said. To prove this, they compared Euro Disneyland with the Netherlands and concluded that both were equally constructed landscapes. All businesses can do successfully is to give the impression of authenticity, "so that people may perceive them as real, real, real."

They advised, helpfully, that "it is easier to be authentic if you don't say you're authentic," and "if you say you're authentic, then you'd better be authentic."

This is a similar point of view to the arguments posed against the idea of "authentic tourism" (Hall, 2007). If authentic means somehow unpackaged, or unreplicable, they argue that this is a meaningless concept.

That is quite right, but there is a contradiction here. If everything is "fake, fake, fake," how can any business possibly *be* authentic? The problem is that using postmodern tools to deconstruct the idea – and discovering, of course, that nothing is real – rather misses the key point. The demand for authenticity is itself a critique of the prevailing postmodern culture. It is a demand for authenticity in the face of this hopeless relativism, accepting it but moving on beyond it. It is an ongoing search for what holds people together despite their atomization by postmodern culture, endlessly deconstructed into their own distant silos. "In an unreal world, people long for reality even more," wrote the American philosopher Robert Nozick, and that is what is happening here (Nozick, 1989).

My sense is that the most enthusiastic doyens of authenticity are not expecting some kind of Platonic ideal. They know that the ground shifts in terms of what is possible all the time. What they are looking for is evidence of effort, of ideals, of truth, of passion – anything which shows that the business they are dealing with is a collection of human beings, rooted in human tradition, and not a shiny one-dimensional construct. In short, what holds people together in a post-postmodern world is our common humanity. This is a flawed possibility. It is hopeful and decaying and weather-beaten, and it is all this that makes it real. Real means human.

We have moved beyond the definition of authentic set out by the sociologist Lionel Trilling in terms of what it is not – not from mankind, not mechanical, and not monetary (Trilling, 1972). Of course, real can still mean natural and unadulterated, but the new meaning primarily signifies something to do with human connection – it is, in some ways, the reverse. That is the clue provided by the literature about authentic work and authentic leadership. It would be incoherent to suggest that business leaders should fake their authentic leadership.

The other evidence that *real* is real is that, despite the huge difficulties of providing authenticity to a mass market, mainstream business is responding. Linux, the open source software, is the product of a virtual community of debuggers, and has been increasingly eating into Microsoft's market share, partly because it has a community of committed human beings at its heart. Other successful corporations in the age of authenticity try to stand back and let people use them in whatever way they want, whether it is eBay or Starbucks. "Mass advertising can help build brands, but authenticity is what makes them last," said Starbucks CEO Howard Schultz (Schultz and Yang, 1997). eBay simply provides a system whereby people can interact. Like Google and Starbucks, it is the customers themselves who are creating the experience.

But there is no doubt it is tough for the big corporate world, which inevitably longs to cut the costs of dealing with ordinary human beings, to provide a human service of any kind. They are up against a plethora of tiny, but authentic, competitors eating away at their market share. The micro-breweries and micro-publishers, the niche food producers and the local services, which provide products from somewhere in particular, often with the name of the person – for example, who fried the crisps – printed on the packet. Café Direct has pictures of some of their growers. Lush packaging even has a picture of the employee who made the box (Boyle, 2005).

It is hardly surprising that the micro-breweries are being snapped up by the big brands, and the big publishers are launching new imprints that look and feel like self-publishing. Kelloggs are even lampooning the whole idea by printing on their Shreddies packets a picture of the old lady who they pretend knitted the Shreddies in the pack. These human stories are the very stuff of authenticity: the real people and the real places that made them. Companies that can't tell stories, because the people who made their products are semi-slaves in dingy sweatshops, are at an increasing disadvantage.

People recognize authentic products immediately, because they can smell them – and because they

- reject glitz and rationalized delivery systems, and garner trust partly by telling simple stories, partly by their resolute ability to wander off-message;
- connect with what is human – either because the brand is an expression of a single personality, or because it reveals the personalities of the range of people behind it, or because the service is genuinely personal;
- have genuine roots to a specific place, or provide a portal to ordinary producers or sellers in specific places; and

- allow customers and employees to feel better connected to their own ideals and values.

Authenticity is not quite the same as ethics. It is possible to be an ethical company without seeming in the least authentic. You can be ethical and still deliver everything virtually. But ethics are a signal that a company or organization is more than its image. It is a sign that it has human depth.

In some ways, its very failures are a sign that a company is somehow real. Real companies have imperfection at their heart. That is why people tend to trust those with the humanity to risk being off-message. "Imperfection carries a story in a way that perfection can only dream about," said a Glasgow-based consultancy called Erasmus in their manifesto. I think they are absolutely right, and imperfection is particularly hard to fake.

On the other hand, there clearly is an ethical dimension to authenticity too. It represents a critique of the way mainstream business operates, as in distancing customers from human reality, replacing human interaction with software or compulsory script. Despite their protestations of humanity, so many companies still plunge callers into call center hell. These are particularly sharp issues for organizations, public and private, that are delivering public services and believing they can do so increasingly virtually. It is also an issue for organizations that try to control every decision, reaction, and detailed interreaction of their staff, which is the other side of the same coin (Head, 2005).

People feel, without even perhaps articulating it, that there is something sinister about this combination. Not perhaps when you try to communicate with a call center or website that omits your particular request on its software. That is merely irritating. But when you need those services, or when they dominate your lives – like immigration authorities – then fakeness can be terrifying. Of course, it would be frightening if you were in a long-term care ward of a hospital that is only interested in Whitehall targets, and would sacrifice you and your fellow patients to achieve them. Or if you had applied for citizenship, and handed over your passport some years before to the immigration authorities, and you were trapped in the country without paperwork, without being able to visit your parents abroad, and with no answer from the bureaucracy as the years went by.

When we go through the great portals of a modern corporation, whether it is public or private, past the disapproving eyes of those with the power to let you in the gate, we know deep down that we are entering – not just a fake world – but an almost Soviet one (Whyte, 1994). It is a world of empire and obscure politics, where hierarchy, control, and bizarre distorted information have a huge effect on the lives of the people who work there or depend on it. That kind of hierarchical system eventually collapsed under its own internal contradictions in Eastern Europe.

We are victims when we work for these systems, and when the pointlessness of another questionnaire on another obscure government target suddenly hits us in the morning as we go to work. But there are bigger victims too, from those whose medical treatment is constrained because of obscure rules based on the cost effectiveness of the treatment to other people, to the eleven-year-olds drilled into dullness on summer afternoons to pass the multiple-choice questions on the SATS.

The symbol of this problem was the poor repairman from the American cable giant Comcast, who fell asleep during a routine home call at the home of a man called Brian Finkelstein in 2006. Finkelstein filmed him snoring and stuck it online, together with the sound track of a song called "I need some sleep." The repairman was fired. But it transpired that he had actually fallen asleep after waiting over an hour on the phone to get through to the useless call center at his own ineffective office.

This is an extension of the whole question of authenticity, which has so far concentrated mainly on products – whether they are food or politicians. There is a parallel problem about services and public institutions, which have become progressively hollowed out by a combination of inappropriate IT, command-and-control call centers and "rationalized" systems that exclude the human element.

The result is that our institutions are often now empty shells, shorn of human emotions and connection, echoing spaces where human values and intricacy ought to be, and prey to the fantasy of efficiency that has corroded them. Actually, organizations that exclude human relationships are probably less effective, more inefficient, more expensive, and more prone to huge mistakes than those that encourage them. That is the side-effect of fake.

Authenticity is bound to be a slippery concept. It is particularly slippery if we leave it to the marketing departments and business academics. The point is that behind it is a real demand, a real need, and a series of real fears, that are important – and especially important now in the next phase of the development of effective organizations, from schools to hospitals, from police stations to justice systems.

Authenticity is not just a vague marketing whim. It is a tool by which we can begin to analyze the failures and successes of our institutions.

Literature

Boyle, D. 2001. *The Tyranny of Numbers: Why Counting Won't Make Us Happy.* London: HarperCollins.

Boyle, D. 2003. "Brands Are no Substitute for the Real Thing." *Financial Times,* August 8, 2003

Boyle, D. 2005. "Is There Such A Thing as a Community Brand." *Viewpoint* 2005. No. 17 (The Future Laboratory).

Crofts, N. 2003. Authentic*: How to Make a Living by Being Yourself.* London: Capstone.

George, W.W. et al., 2007. "Discovering Your Authentic Leadership." *Harvard Business Review,* 1 February 2007.

Gilmore, J.H. and Pine, J. 2007. *Authenticity: What Consumers Really Want.* Cambridge, MA: Harvard Business School Press.

Godin, S. 2001. "Change Agent." *Fast Company,* June 30, 2001.

Hall, M.C. 2007. "Response to Yeoman et al.: The Fakery of 'The Authentic Tourist'." *Tourism Management,* Vol. 28, No. 4.

Head, S. 2005. *The New Ruthless Economy.* New York: Oxford University Press.

Nozick, R. 1989. *Examined Life.* New York: Touchstone.

Ray, P.H. and Anderson, S. 2000. *The Cultural Creatives: How 50 Million People Are Changing the World.* New York: Harmony Books.

Roszak, T. 1994. *The Cult of Information.* University of California Press.

Schultz, H. and Yang, D.J. 1997. "Pour Your Heart Into It: How Starbucks Built a Company One Cup at a Time." *Hyperion,* pp.248–249.

Trilling, L. 1972. *Sincerity and Authenticity.* Cambridge: Harvard University Press.

Whyte, D. 1994. *The Heart Aroused: Poetry and the Preservation of the Soul in Corporate America.* New York: Doubleday.

Yeoman, I. 2007. "Current Issues in Travel: The Authentic Tourist." *Tourism Management,* August.

33
Frugality

Luk Bouckaert, Hendrik Opdebeeck and Laszlo Zsolnai

We can define frugality as *art de vivre*, which implies low material consumption and a simple lifestyle to open the mind for spiritual goods such as inner freedom, social peace, justice, or the quest for "ultimate reality." Frugality as a conception of the good life has deep philosophical and religious roots in the East and the West. Monks and religious people all over the world practice it in different forms of asceticism, self-restriction, or freely chosen poverty ("voluntary simplicity"). But even secular philosophers in the tradition of Epicurean ethics or Stoicism emphasize that frugal tastes and lasting enjoyment go hand in hand. Whereas for religious ethics frugality is a spiritual virtue, for secular ethics it is a rational virtue to enhance happiness. Although both of these approaches, the rational as well as the spiritual, do promote similar practices of self-restriction, their deeper motivational structure is very different. We will explore rational theories of frugality, the economics of frugality, and a spiritual concept and practice of frugality.[1]

Rational theories of frugality

The Greek philosopher Epicurus (Samos 342/341 BC–Athens 271/270 BC) is among the first thinkers to develop a *rational* theory and ethics of frugality. His ethics of sustainable enjoyment provides us with two principles. The first principle states that frugality is the result of a rational assessment of pains and pleasures. We may not know clearly what pleasure is, but we do know pain, anxiety, and confusion, so we can continue to seek pleasure by banishing all forms of pain, anxiety, and confusion. The highest form of pleasure is *ataraxia*– or imperturbability – a state in which the soul is as the sea when the wind has calmed. Frugality is a necessary condition to reach that state of *ataraxia*. The second principle of Epicurus is the simplification of our needs. The more desires one has, the greater the chance that they will not be satisfied, thus leading to suffering. So a person ought to restrict and simplify his or her needs.

Frugality, as Epicurus taught us, is a rational virtue. Activities and needs should be ordered in such a way as to lead to maximal pleasure in the long term and a proper balance between the various sorts of needs. For Epicurus, the cause of our inability to enjoy lies in the short-sightedness of reason: people seek short-term gain rather than durable and lasting satisfaction; they chase after all manner of imagined or inculcated needs at the expense of basic human needs. Sustainability in today's business world has a similar logic. Business sustainability seeks a proper balance between financial, social, and ecological objectives and, in the name of future generations, puts limits on our material welfare. But short-term pressures of the market may lead to quite the opposite of long-term social and ecological value creation.

Modern expressions of the Epicurean idea of giving priority to our natural and necessary needs can be found in Thomas Princen's *The Logic of Sufficiency* (Princen, 2005) or Manfred Max-Neef's *Human Scale Development* (1991). The theory of human development proposed by the Chilean economist Max-Neef is an interesting example of a modern theory integrating frugality not only on the level of personal happiness but also on the macro level of the socioeconomic system (see Esteban, 2008). He aims at rethinking the modern Western notions of poverty and wealth with a systemic understanding of human nature. For him, human nature is defined by a system of human needs that have to be satisfied throughout life to result in human growth. Material (bodily) needs are but a small part of the system of basic needs. There are nine human needs altogether: subsistence, protection, affection, understanding, participation, creation, recreation, identity, and freedom. These human needs have to be satisfied at the four existential modes as follows: being, having, doing, and interacting. When the nine needs are combined with the four existential modes, this produces a matrix of 36 cells, which can be filled with a complex system of satisfiers.

Max-Neef's distinction between "needs" and "satisfiers" and the shift in reflection from material poverty exclusively to a plurality of "poverties" have proven to be first-class tools for assessing the "health" of individuals and groups (families, communities, organizations, cultures). In Max-Neef's perspective, societies and individuals can be dysfunctional not only through deprivation of economic goods but also through the excess consumption of those same goods. The world is not divided between the "haves" and the "have-nots" but between a majority that do not have enough and a minority that has too much. And the real trouble is that the deprived majority does not aspire to have "enough" for a decent human living but instead aspires to participate in the unlimited race to growth of the "consumer society," deepening the unsustainability of their claims to happiness and the good life.

Strategies for real human development have to be based, not on increased production and consumption of economic goods, but on the creation and nurturing of "synergistic satisfiers" supported by a minimum of economic goods. *Frugality* enters the picture here as the ability to find what is the minimum use of material resources and economic goods needed to achieve the satisfaction of all basic needs in a given situation. This puts economic goods in their right place at the service of "healthy (holy) living" and interacting.

The rational, Epicurean argument of self-restriction is also very apparent to the critics of consumerism. According to Geldof, the only way to frame sufficiency and frugality as viable social practices is to underpin them with positive arguments (Geldof, 2008). *Sufficiency* can be approached in different ways. First, sufficiency is a crucial element in strategies for sustainability, in addition to efficiency and consistency. Second, sufficiency and downshifting are alternatives to the rat race resulting from the cycle of work-and-spend. Third, sufficiency and downshifting will give us more time to enjoy our lives, rather than exacerbating tension between our endless desires and the lack of means.

Sufficiency should not be about saying goodbye to material wealth and repressing all our desires. We should focus on how to deal with our wealth, how to satisfy our desires more meaningfully, and how to enjoy a better life by consuming less. The *Slow Food Movement* is a fantastic example. It is a way toward using more qualitative foods and meals, in a more convivial society, while recognizing the ecological limits of the earth. It is a way toward greater and more intense pleasure through accepting limits.

The political economics of frugality

Ecological economist Herman Daly argues that frugality should precede efficiency in achieving sustainability. He suggests understanding *sustainability* in the terms of *throughput*. According to Daly physical throughput should be sustained; that is, the entropic physical flow from nature's sources through the economy and back to nature's sink should be nondeclining (Daly, 2002).

Daly states that the problem with "efficiency first" is what comes second. An improvement in efficiency alone is equivalent to having a larger supply of the factor whose efficiency increased. The price of that factor declines and more uses for the cheaper factor are found. The net result is that there is greater consumption of the resource than before, even if it is produced more efficiently. So scale continues to grow. Frugality, however, is about lowering our consumption and limiting the use of nonrenewable resources. A policy of "frugality first" induces efficiency as a secondary effect while "efficiency first" does not induce frugality. The main task of our age is to *limit* the *scale* of the *economy* relative to the ecosystem by restraining uneconomic growth that increases costs by more than it increases benefits, thus making us poorer instead of richer.

Cornel University economist Robert Frank asks whether consuming more goods makes people happier. The large and growing scientific literature on the determinants of life-satisfaction and psychosocial well-being suggests that, for a broad spectrum of goods, beyond some point the answer is essentially no. Evidence from this literature also suggests, however, that there are ways of spending time and money that do have the potential to increase people's satisfaction with their lives, and herein lies a message of considerable importance for policymaking (Frank, 1997).

In *Luxury Fever* (1999) Frank demonstrates how the demand for luxury goods in the United States went through an enormous acceleration in the past two decades, how people went into debt to pay for them, how personal savings shrank and people began working longer, and how the productive capacity of the American economy began to aim at making all sorts of goods and services more luxurious. The consequences of this shift were significant: relatively less money and time was invested in basic needs such as care for the family, the eradication of poverty, ecological maintenance, etc. Moreover, the relative poverty of some groups became worse: compared with the rich, they are in decline and feel themselves more and more excluded.

In order to counter this trend, Frank proposed a *progressive consumption tax,* which is a tax on our total income minus what we have saved and invested. He argues that if our problem is that some forms of private consumption seem more attractive to individuals than to society as a whole, the simplest solution is to make those forms less attractive by taxing them. Without raising our tax bill at all, a *progressive consumption tax* would change our incentives in precisely the desired way.

Frank's proposal of progressive consumption tax is different from consumption taxes such as the value-added tax. Those types of taxes are levied at the same rate no matter how much a family consumes. They are regressive because wealthy families usually save much higher proportions of their income than poor families. But the consumption tax proposed by Frank is not regressive at all. Its escalating marginal tax rates on consumption, coupled with its large standard deduction, insure that total tax as a proportion of income rises steadily with income, even though the assumed savings rate is sharply higher for high-income families. If consumption were taxed at a progressive rate, we would save more, buy less expensive houses and cars, and feel less pressure to work excessively long hours. And this, on the best available evidence, would *improve* the *quality* of *our lives*.

Frugality as a spiritual concept

In economics, the frugal and industrious man has been praised by Adam Smith and promoted by Max Weber as the embodiment of worldly asceticism, the protestant driver of early capitalism. But by focusing on the instrumental value of frugality as a means to increasing material welfare, they initiated a shift in the meaning of frugality. Frugality became related to savings and to investments for enhancing future welfare. This instrumentalization of frugality ended, paradoxically, in its elimination on the economic scene. Consumerism and material greed, just the opposite of frugality, became the basic drivers for increasing wealth and led to an erosion of the intrinsic and spiritual meaning of frugality.

The danger of rationalizing frugality as a means to an end, be it welfare or happiness or another valuable good, always implies the danger of crowding out its intrinsic meaning. Does frugality have an intrinsic or spiritual meaning, and how can we experience its intrinsic meaning in daily life?

As long as we consider frugality in relation to objects and situations outside ourselves, we will perceive the latter as means to satisfying our needs and desires. In this case our ego or our group remains the center of reference. Even if we have a long-term perspective, our enlightened self-interest will remain the horizon of our sense making. As a rational concept, frugality is an enlightened but ego-centered relation to our environment. In the spiritual traditions frugality gets another meaning. Its first meaning is about self-detachment: a release from the active, self-seeking ego. Living a frugal life means living a life of self-detachment or, in a more positive way, a life of other-directedness. Frugality signifies a release from egocentrism, opening the mind to the inner voice of things in contrast to the instrumental meaning they get from being means to satisfying my/our needs. Things are perceived as unique expressions of Life itself.

The spiritual practice of frugality does not necessarily imply a severe form of asceticism. Many spiritual authors draw our attention to the fact that ascetic exercises as such are no guarantee of self-detachment. Sometimes they are hidden forms of enhancing the ego. A more authentic criterion of self-detachment is inner joy and harmony. The famous painting "St John the Baptist in the Wilderness" (1490–95) by *Geertgen tot Sint Jans* represents an illuminating example of *spiritual frugality*. Although St John the Baptist is well known for his ascetic life and his sermons on penance, his painted face and his clothes do express a nonascetic, very kind, and mild form of frugality. People therefore felt uncertain about the figure and sometimes called him "St John meditating," referring to the mystic evangelist St John instead of the ascetic St John the Baptist. The painting incites us to a joyful self-detachment and other-centeredness.

This interpretation of frugality has an intentional and motivational structure other than the Epicurean *ataraxia* or the ascetic self-control of some religious traditions. The self-detached joy of life originates from the capability of seeing the invisible or hearing the inner voice of things.

Frugality in spiritual traditions is also deeply related to the practice of compassion and solidarity with the poor. The Christian *misericordia*, the Buddhist idea of compassion and many other committed expressions of universal love imply self-detachment and redistribution of welfare. They are expressions of other-centeredness. Frugality as a form of self-chosen simplicity or poverty may express our solidarity with the have-nots and the poor in society. Marta Nussbaum stresses the importance of compassion and advocates for a *compassionate citizenship* (Nussbaum, 2001). As citizens we should develop practices of compassionate frugality on the individual level as well as on the institutional level by developing institutions of redistributive justice, social security, and general education.

A spiritually driven practice of entrepreneurship

The contemporary practice of dealing prudently and frugally with the environment uses arguments that are based mostly on a standpoint of well-considered self-interest and long-term benefit. However, the rational case for frugality is a limited one. By rational choice we can develop a more frugal and sufficient way of life, but material temptations can always overwrite our ecological, social, and ethical considerations. The practice of frugality and sustainability will gain in strength if it is supported by a sense of ecological interconnectedness beyond rational calculation. Although the spiritual *Homo economicus* does not exist in textbooks of mainstream economics, he or she can be found among entrepreneurs and business leaders, whether they are for-profit or social-profit organizations. His or her profile comprises market orientation, efficiency and a genuine drive toward social and ecological spirituality.

The *Trappist Brewery of Westmalle*, in Belgium, provides an inspiring example of how a spiritual concept of frugality can be combined with good entrepreneurship. At present the brewery is a private limited company that belongs to the monks of the Trappist Abbey of Westmalle. Under the monks' supervision the modern brewery is managed by a team of competent laypeople, and their beer is consistently ranked among the best in the world. Although the company is highly modernized and successful in its commercial activities, the balance between spiritual and material needs is part of the production and distribution process. The spirit of frugality is implemented in concrete choices about the quality of the product, the scale of the production, the relations with the personnel, the advertising, and the use of profit. It is clear that the business decisions are not commanded by the logic of maximizing income and financial profit for the Abbey. There is a spiritual bottom line expressed in the charter of the brewery. The key elements of this charter are (1) limits to growth; (2) deep ecological respect; (3) work as a spiritual value; (4) honest and sober advertising; and (5) profit sharing (Bouckaert, 2008).

Many other examples of spiritually based enterprises do exist. These companies are very different in size, type of production, and spiritual background. But we find the same ingredients of frugality praxis in them as in the Trappist Abbey of Westmalle. Of course most entrepreneurs will not make a clear distinction between the ethical/rational and the spiritual approach. The spiritual motivation often is hidden behind a rational discourse. But the opposite is also the case. Behind a spiritual discourse, a rational self-interested calculation can be the main driver. It needs some discernment to see what is really going on. Moreover, it is important to realize that a genuine spirituality of frugality as self-detachment and other-centeredness does not exclude instrumental economic rationality. To be implemented, a spiritually driven praxis of frugality needs always a rationally conceived business plan. And from a macro point of view, spiritually based frugal practices may lead to rational outcomes such as reducing ecological destruction, social disintegration, and the exploitation of future generations.

Notes

1. This chapter is largely indebted to our book *Frugality. Rebalancing Material and Spiritual Values in Economic Life* (edited by Luk Bouckaert, Hendrik Opdebeeck and Laszlo Zsolnai). Oxford, 2008, Peter Lang Academic Publishers.

Literature

Bouckaert, L. 2008. "Rational versus Spiritual Concepts of Frugality." In L. Bouckaert, H. Opdebeeck, and L. Zsolnai (eds), *Frugality: Rebalancing Material and Spiritual Values in Economic Life*. pp. 27–43. Oxford: Peter Lang.

Daly, H. 2002. *Sustainable Development: Definitions, Principles, Policies.* Invited Address at the World Bank on April 30, 2002, Washington, DC.

Esteban, R. 2008. "Frugality and the Body." In L. Bouckaert, H. Opdebeeck, and L. Zsolnai (eds), *Frugality: Rebalancing Material and Spiritual Values in Economic Life*. pp. 45–69. Oxford: Peter Lang.

Frank, R. 1999. *Luxury Fever.* New York: The Free Press.

Frank, R. 1997. "The Frame of Reference as a Public Good." *Economic Journal*, 107, November, pp.1832–1847.

Geldof, D. 2008. "Overconsumption." In L. Bouckaert, H. Opdebeeck, and L. Zsolnai (eds), *Frugality: Rebalancing Material and Spiritual Values in Economic Life*. pp. 125–140. Oxford: Peter Lang.

Max-Neef, M. 1991. *Human Scale Development: Conception, Application and Further Reflections.* New York: Apex Press.

Nussbaum, M. 2001. *Upheavals of Thought: The Intelligence of Emotions.* Cambridge: Cambridge University Press.

Princen, T. 2005. *The Logic of Sufficiency.* Cambridge, MA: MIT Press..

34
Civil Economy
Stefano Zamagni

The necessity of a relational paradigm in economics

The expression "civil economy" is now recurrent in academic discussion as in the media, but it carries multiple, sometimes conflicting meanings. Some confuse it with the expression "social economy," while others maintain that "civil economy" is just a different, older name for "political economy." There are those who identify the term with the variegated world of nonprofit organizations, and others who go so far as to see civil economy as an intellectual project opposed to the economy of solidarity. Misunderstandings and incomprehension of this sort not only complicate dialogue between thinkers who legitimately espouse different worldviews; what is worse is that ignorance of what civil economy is, instead of inducing intellectual humility, often feeds ideological prejudices and is used to justify sectarian closed-mindedness.

What is needed, then, is to clarify, to explain terms, and elucidate concepts that were part of the lexicon of economics until a couple of centuries ago but have now literally vanished. Above all, we need to explain why interpersonal relations cannot be kept outside the main body of economic research any longer. That is, we need to make the case for a different hermeneutic paradigm from those used today: namely, the relational paradigm. Interpersonal relations are one of the central themes in the civil-economy tradition, the Italian school of thought that dominated the scene until the mid-eighteenth century. Our thesis is that in continuing to ignore interpersonal relations as explanations for economic phenomena, social scientists are doing a disservice to themselves and, even more, to society. This is paradoxical indeed for a discipline such as economics, which from its very origins has been intimately concerned with relations between men in society (crucial to such key concepts as the production of goods and services, consumption choices, market exchange, institutional arrangements, and so on). The economist's agenda certainly does include the study of relations between man and nature, but it could never be held that this is the key to economic studies – not, that is, unless we want to reduce economics to a sort of social engineering, to remove it from the realm of the "moral sciences."

To avoid misunderstanding, one specification is in order. We must distinguish between social interaction and interpersonal relations. Whereas in the latter case the personal identities of the persons involved are a constituent of the relation itself, social interactions – as they are studied in the literature on social capital – can perfectly well be anonymous, impersonal. An example drawn from the work of Robert Putnam illustrates this difference: an increase in the number of members of social organizations will not necessarily be accompanied by greater, more intense participation in the activity and the decision-making of those organizations. The statistician will note that the stock of social capital has increased, but it certainly cannot be maintained that quality of interpersonal relations has improved.

The point is important, well worth underscoring. That man is a social animal is a proposition that no one has ever questioned. But the sociability of human nature, defined as a positive attitude toward other human beings, is something quite different. Adam Smith was one of the first to see that social interaction does not necessarily postulate or generate sociability, so that if all we are interested in is the study of market mechanisms there is no need to assume that agents have socially oriented motivations. To explain *how* the market works, it is sufficient to postulate a single attitude on the part of economic agents, namely – in Smith's famous phrase – the "human propensity to truck, barter and exchange things." And this, with rare exceptions, has been the course of economic science for over two centuries. The theories of contracts, of business organization, of prices, of market forms, etc., have no need to bother with the category of "person": an informed, rational individual is sufficient.

Today, however, we have come to the point where even the most "detached" of economists cannot but admit that if we want to attack the new problems of our society – such as the endemic aggravation of inequalities, the scandal of human hunger, recurrent and vast financial crises, the rise of conflicts of identity in addition to the traditional clash between interests, the paradoxes of happiness, unsustainable development, and so on – research simply can no longer confine itself to a sort of anthropological limbo. One must take a position on the matter, selecting a standpoint from which to scrutinize reality. Otherwise, economics will continue to spread, to enrich its technical and analytical apparatus, but if it does not escape self-referentiality it will be less and less capable of actually grasping reality, and thus of suggesting effective lines of action. There is no denying that this is the true risk that our discipline runs today.

For fear of publicly endorsing a precise anthropological option, a good many economists have taken shelter in formal analysis alone, dedicating ever-greater intellectual resources to the deployment of more and more sophisticated logical–mathematical instruments. But there can never be a trade-off between the formal rigor of economic discourse – which is essential, of course – and its capacity to explain, to interpret economic events. We must never forget the reality of the "hermeneutic circle," that is, the fact that the production of economic knowledge, while shaping or modifying the cognitive maps of economic agents, also acts on their propensities and their motivations – or, as Alfred Marshall preferred to say at the end of the nineteenth century, their character.

This is as much as to say that economic theories of human behavior do – sooner or later, to a greater or a lesser extent – influence behavior itself and thus do not leave their field of study unaffected. Ultimately, this is the aim of civil economy: to help economics overcome the acute reductionism from which it suffers, which is the main obstacle to the entry of new ideas in economics and also a dangerous sort of protectionism against the critique implicit in facts and events as well as against innovations deriving from the other social sciences.

It is inconceivable, in fact, that in an "open society," as Karl Popper uses the term, just one theoretical approach – the "mainstream" – should monopolize virtually all research opportunities and cultural attention. And this despite the broad recognition that applying the logic of *Homo economicus* to actual human behavior engenders a deep sense of incongruity. It clashes, first of all, with the very reality that the logic itself intends to explain. Economic processes are fundamentally interactions between men. So it is not true that commodities are produced only by means of commodities – as Piero Sraffa's famous book would have it – but also by interpersonal relations among people, each with a specific identity and not merely interests. Now while the contract is a useful tool for settling conflicts of interest, it is totally inadequate for conflicts of identity, which are increasingly common today.

But there is also a second, deeper level of incongruity. Apart from the fact that contracts are often not complete (owing to imperfect information and informational asymmetries), the *Homo economicus* paradigm considers only what is objectively observable. Hence emotions, beliefs, values, symbolic representations and so forth have only indirect relevance, insofar as they affect behavior. For mainstream economics, the only thing of interest is the results deriving from those actions. This position is commonly justified with the argument that since in the market economy the economic agent is sovereign and free to express whatever preferences he wishes, there is no need to worry about the motivations or propensities underlying his/her choices. (Therein lies the justification, in economics, of consequentialism as an ethical doctrine.) But that is not at all how matters stand. In fact, mainstream economics is founded upon a theoretical construct relating not to the practical dimension – Aristotle's "secondary philosophy" – but to the ontological dimension, that is, to the "primary philosophy." This construction refers to a definite worldview, namely that of axiological individualism. This is the true philosophical infrastructure on which the postulate of *Homo economicus* rests.

This is why reducing human experience to the simple "accounting" dimension of instrumental rationality (the rational-choice model) is more than an act of intellectual arrogance but, worse, a grave methodological error. It is not intellectually fair to assert that the choice of *Homo economicus* is dictated by empirical reasons or considerations of analytical convenience. For one thing, both experimental economics and the empirical evidence show that this is untrue. But above all, the assumption of individualism is in the nature of an ontological assertion that, as such, must be justified on the ontological plane. The real challenge, therefore, is that of extending some acceptable definition of the notion of rationality to the intelligence of a social sense of behavior, which requires the specification of the spatial, temporal, and cultural context where people operate. The fundamental reason for the present unsatisfactory state of affairs, I believe, is that conventional economics hinges on a description of human behavior consisting almost entirely of *acquisitive* aims. From the economic standpoint, human behavior is relevant insofar as it enables individuals to get "things" (goods or services) that they do not yet have and that can significantly increase their welfare. Therefore, the rational man is the man who knows how to "get what he needs." That the notion of rationality can also embrace an *existential* dimension, and that this can conflict, perhaps radically, with the acquisitive dimension is an aspect that the mainstream is unable to elaborate on, meaningfully, within the framework of economic discourse.

The necessity, then, is to go beyond *Homo economicus* to *civil animal* and make a place for the principle of gift within (not outside) economic theory. The power of the gift does not lie in the thing given or the amount donated – as in philanthropy or pure altruism – but in the special human quality that the gift represents as an interpersonal relation. What constitutes the essence of gift-giving, then, is the specific interest in forging a relationship between donor and recipient. Gift-giving can certainly cultivate an interest, but this must always be an interest *for*, never *in*, the other person. This is *relational value*, the third type of value after use value and exchange value. To broaden the horizons of economic research to include relational value is the most urgent intellectual challenge before us today.

The ingredients of a civil economy

What, then, is civil economy? Within economics, civil economy represents a tradition of economic and philosophical thought rooted proximately in fifteenth-century civic humanism and more remotely in Aristotle, Cicero, Aquinas, and the Franciscan school. Its golden age, when it was at the height of its influence as a school of economic thought, came in the Italian and specifically the Neapolitan Enlightenment. While Adam Smith and David Hume in Scotland were developing the principles of political economy, in those same years in Naples Antonio Genovesi, Gaetano Filangieri, Ferdinando Galiani, Giacinto Dragonetti, and others were developing civil economy. The Scottish and Italo-Neapolitan schools had any number of features in common: the polemic against feudalism (the market seen above all as the way out of feudal society); the praise of luxury as a force for social change, with little concern for the "vices" of the consumers of luxury goods and much more for the benefits for all of society; a great ability to comprehend the cultural revolution that the growth of trade was bringing about; the recognition of the essential role of trust in a market economy and for cultural progress; the "modernity" of their views of society and of the world.

Yet there is also a crucial difference between the Scottish school of political economy and that of civil economy. Smith, even while acknowledging that men have a natural tendency toward sociability ("sympathy" and "correspondence of sentiments"), does not consider genuine, noninstrumental sociability or relationality to be relevant to the working of markets. In *The Theory of Moral Sentiments* he says that "civil society can exist between different persons ... on the basis of the consideration of individual utility, *without any form of reciprocal love or affection*" (II,3.2, emphasis added). And in some passages both of the *Theory* and of *The Wealth of Nations* he writes explicitly that sentiments and benevolent actions complicate the operation of the market, which functions proportionately better as the relations within it become more instrumental. For Smith, and for the tradition that, following him, would become the official economics, the market is the means for building relations that are genuinely social (no civil society exists without the market) because it is free of vertical bonds and unchosen status; but the market is not, per se, the locus of all-round relationality. That mercantile relations are impersonal, with mutual indifference, is not a negative but a positive, civilizing characteristic, in Smith's eyes. This is the only way the market can produce the common good.

In other words, friendship and market relations belong to two distinct, separate spheres. The existence of market relations in the public sphere (and there only) ensures that in the private sphere friendship is genuine, freely chosen, and unconnected with status. If a beggar asks a butcher for alms, he cannot have an authentic friendship with him outside the market. But if one day a former beggar comes into the butcher's shop or the brewer's shop to buy goods at the going price, that same evening the ex-mendicant can meet his shopkeepers at the pub on a plane of equal dignity and possibly be friends with them. This is why Allan Silver can say, "According to Smith the replacement of *necessitude* by commercial society brings with it a morally superior form of friendship, voluntary and based on natural sympathy, not borne of necessity" (1990, p. 1481). For Smith and traditional economic doctrine, the market is civilization but not (and precisely *because* it is not) friendship, disinterested reciprocity, fraternity (Bruni and Sugden, 2008).

The civil-economic tradition dissents from these fundamental postulates of modern economic theory and practice. For the civil-economy school, the market, the enterprise, the economy are *themselves* the place for friendship, reciprocity, gratuitousness, fraternity. Civil economy rejects today's increasingly common notion, taken for granted, that the market and the economy are radically different from civil society and are ruled by different principles. Instead, the economy *is* civil, the market *is* life in common, and they share the same fundamental law: mutual aid. For Antonio Genovesi's "mutual aid" is something more than Smith's reciprocal advantage. For the latter, a contract will suffice, for the former you need *philia*, perhaps *agape*.

Economics as if people mattered – this catchphrase concisely might indicate the research program of civil economy. The leitmotif of this program can be summed up by referring us to the intellectual myth that has characterized modernity. This is the myth of "one": one science, one truth, one discourse, one law. The consequence has been the wrong belief that we can achieve the unity of knowledge only by silencing alternative voices, as if unity meant uniformity. But the truth is that genuine progress – including the advance of knowledge – is always the product of a variety of approaches and viewpoints. And the logic of "one" is something profoundly different from the logic of "unity," which is necessarily constituted by a plurality of positions.

In the end, the reductive course of economic science beginning in the second half of the nineteenth century disarmed critical thought, with results that are now before the eyes of all. The economics profession has a definite responsibility in this: for too long it taught generations of scholars that scientific rigor was inherently aseptic; that research, in order to be scientific, had to liberate itself from all value judgments. The consequences are in plain sight. Axiological individualism – itself a preanalytical assumption, a value judgment and a very strong one at that – has gained the status of "natural" assumption, which means first that it needs no justification and second that it serves as a benchmark against which any other hypothesis concerning human nature "must" be measured. So it should be no surprise that orthodox economics grants the privilege of "naturalness" to individualism and to individualism alone.

I do not believe that we can proceed much farther along this road. To be sure, there is no hiding the snares and pitfalls of the project that civil economy is proposing. To imagine that the necessary changes will not bring with them high levels of conflict would be naive. But it is essential if we are to overcome the whining over the practical irrelevance of economics – whining that only serves those who have an interest in spreading skepticism – and the disenchanted optimism of those who see the restoration of individualistic rationalism in economics as a sort of triumphal march toward the full understanding of the facts and events of the real world.

It seems to me that Foucault's pendulum is swinging back today to the connection between economics and philosophy, and it is easy to see why. During periods of rapid change, like the present, the physical and mathematical disciplines do not have much to offer economic thought. They can give or provide answers, it is true, but they cannot ask the right questions – and that is what economics most needs today. First of all is the question of the nature of man. This, to my mind, is what explains the recent, vigorous resumption of the debate within the discipline on ethical and anthropological themes. And it also explains the visible disorientation of those numerous economists who seem to lament the loss of time-tested certainties, the sort of certainties that only general economic theories can offer. Indeed, for many years now economics as a discipline has been incapable of producing any sort of general theory, just "local theorizing." Perhaps the time has come to really try to search for one.

In the end, civil economy today stands as an alternative to mainstream economics, which sees the market as the only institution that democracy and freedom really need. Civil economy serves to remind us that while a good society is of course the fruit of the market and of freedom, there are also needs, which can be traced back to the principle of fraternity, which cannot be ignored. At the same time civil economy does not side with those who fight against the markets and who see economic action poised in endemic and natural conflict with the good life, who cry out for less growth and for the retreat of the economic dimension from life in common. Rather, the civil-economy approach proposes a multifaceted humanism in which the market is neither resisted nor "controlled" but considered as a moment of the public sphere which, when conceived and experienced as a place open also to the principles of reciprocity and gratuitousness, can build the city (*polis*).

Literature

Atkinson A.B. 2009. "Economics as a Moral Science." *Economica*, 76, pp. 791–804.

Bruni, L. and Sugden R. 2008. "Fraternity. Why the Market Need Not Be a Morally Free Zone." *Economics and Philosophy*, 24, pp. 35–65.

Bruni, L. and Zamagni, S. 2007. *Civil Economy*. Oxford: Peter Lang.

Putnam, R. 2000. *Bowling Alone*. New York: Simon and Schuster.

Silver A. 1990. "Friendship in Commercial Society: Eighteenth Century Social Theory And Modern Sociology." *American Journal of Sociology*, 95, pp. 1474–1504.

Smith A. 1776. *The Wealth of Nations*. Oxford: Oxford University Press (1976 edition).

Part IV
Business Spirituality

35
Spiritual-Based Leadership
Peter Pruzan

Spiritual-based leadership (SBL) challenges and supplements the two primary rationales underlying the theory and practice of management: scientific rationality and economic rationality. Although far from mainstream at present, the concept of SBL is emerging as an inclusive, holistic, and yet highly personal approach to leadership that integrates a leader's *inner* perspectives on identity, purpose, responsibility, and success with her or his decisions and actions in the *outer* world of business – and therefore SBL is also emerging as a significant framework for understanding, practicing, communicating, and teaching the art and profession of leadership in business (Pruzan, 2008).

To remove potential doubts, I underscore that the concept of spirituality underlying SBL is distinct from that of religion (Mitroff and Denton, 1999; Mitroff, Denton, and Alpaslan, 2009). While religion tends to be characterized by its more formal and institutional aspects (rituals, patterns of worship, dogma, belief systems, priesthoods, and sacred texts), spirituality tends to be characterized by its more personal, introspective, and existential qualities – by a search rather than an arrival. Without attempting to provide a specific definition of the concept of spirituality in "spiritual-based leadership," the following are just a few of the ways that business leaders characterized it during an international research project on SBL (Pruzan and Pruzan Mikkelsen, 2007):

- the true core of being within you;
- acting on behalf of the welfare of the totality;
- man's quest into his innate divinity;
- seeing religion as something that has been handed down to you – something external to you, whereas spirituality is something that is within you;

- the manifestation of the perfection that is already there within you;
- a deep inner search for a fuller personal integration with a greater than our narrow self;
- the connection among myself, other people, and the divine;
- realizing a connection to the world – that I am part of the totality and contribute to it;

Thus, in contrast to religion, the concept of spirituality underlying SBL entails a personal, existential search for or experience of meaning, purpose, truth, identity, and interconnectedness that may or may not include a focus on a divine/transcendent/god. And within the context of organized commercial activity, it entails a contact with deeper levels of consciousness that can empower individuals and collectivities to create sought-for futures that are sensitive to the values of those affected by their decisions.

The emergence of SBL

Although there undoubtedly always have been leaders who have performed their leadership from a spiritual basis, until recently theoreticians and practitioners have not found it efficacious to introduce the concept of "spirituality" into their writings, teachings, and self-reference. This is rapidly changing. For example, anthologies (Biberman and Whitty, 2000; Giacalone and Jurkiewicz, 2003; Biberman and Tischler, 2008) present explorative analyses of the relationship between spirituality and business leadership; my own empirical research, carried out among top leaders from 15 countries in six continents, supplements the prevailing, primarily probative and philosophical/theoretical, approaches to spirituality in business with empirical evidence that business leaders can attain success, recognition, peace of mind, and happiness, while at the same time serving the needs of all those affected by their leadership, when they lead from a spiritual basis (Pruzan and Pruzan Mikkelsen, 2007, 2010).

SBL's point of departure is the individual leader's search for meaning, purpose, and fulfillment in the external world of business and in the internal world of consciousness and conscience. It provides a perspective on leadership as a natural expression of the leader's heart, mind, and soul, where the leader draws on her or his deeply rooted basis for understanding and relating to one's own and one's organization's identity, purpose, values, reputation, and success. Spirituality and rationality are thus mutually supportive (Pruzan, 2009a). As such, SBL constitutes a leadership paradigm that transcends national borders, religious belief systems, and organizational ethos.

The emergence of SBL can also be seen as an overarching perspective on other approaches to leadership that have emerged since the 1980s and that are characterized by a focus on concepts such as "business ethics," "values-leadership," "corporate social responsibility," and "sustainability." While these all tend to supplement the more traditional managerial perspective on leadership, whose foundation is an almost religious and often implicit belief that a corporation's *raison d'être* is to maximize its owners' wealth (Pruzan and Miller, 2006), SBL considers ethics, social responsibility, and sustainability not as instruments to protect and promote the classical business rationale but as fundamental goals in their own right.

The context for the emergence of SBL

Unnoticed by most observers of societal and organizational development, an insidious conflict has evolved during recent decades. This conflict is not manifest in the form of violent behavior. Furthermore – and in contrast to military and religious conflicts, terror, hostile takeovers by corporate raiders, strikes, and lockouts as well as legal and political struggles – the conflict referred to does not take place *between* people and organizations but *within* them. The conflict arises when one's decisions and actions are not in accord with one's inner guidance, but are motivated and dominated instead by the ego's orientation toward personal and collective advantage; the focus is on "success" as traditionally portrayed and understood in the outer world: wealth accumulation, prestige, power, "beating the competitors," and so on. Although such a traditional framework for motivating decision-making and action appears to apply to people in general, it is the guiding perspective for business leaders in particular, at least as this is expressed in the content and motivations of university MBA programs or even more clearly in leading business journals and the business sections of major newspapers.

Accompanying this dominating orientation toward the outer world is a reduced focus by our corporate leaders on the inner world, the domain of consciousness, conscience, and the soul or spirit. In some sense, we become blind to our inner guidance, not because we cannot look within but because we see too much in the so-called real world that dominates our focus. As is argued below, the "blindness" of so many of our business leaders can be attributed to two dominating sources of our rationality: science and economics.

Since the "Age of Enlightenment" in Europe in the eighteenth century, science, together with the technologies that resulted from its discoveries, has evolved to the point where it has a quasi-monopolistic patent on "truth"; in particular, this appears to be the accepted paradigm among those with a higher education, including corporate leaders. While organized religion previously enjoyed the privilege of being the patent owner, that entitlement gradually became the privilege of the scientific community. The methods of science are based on a subject–object dualism, where the scientist, employing technologies and instruments that are products of science, has two strong tacit beliefs: (1) that the so-called scientific method is the only way to develop reliable, true knowledge; and (2) that the scientific community is and should be the final arbiter in determining what is true, no matter whether the object of study is black holes, quarks, dinosaurs, health, consciousness, or SBL.

Furthermore, just as geometry is based on a number of axioms, science is structured on a foundation of implicit metaphysical presuppositions and beliefs that cannot be proven via logic or empirical investigation. These include that the physical universe exists externally to and independently of our consciousness; that it is an ordered universe where there is an isomorphic relationship between physical reality and mathematics; that we directly or indirectly (via technologies that amplify our perceptual and cognitive competences) can investigate, measure, and analyze everything; and that via our rational thought processes we can synthesize our observations and analyses into valid and reliable descriptions and explanations of the universe's ordered reality. This does not mean that the presuppositions are arbitrary or unstable, but it does mean that since science rests on a foundation of unprovable statements, science ultimately is a matter of faith (Pruzan, 2009b, pp. 42–44). It is therefore ironic that science, which is predicated on belief, provides methods of investigation, description, and explanation that classify belief that cannot be supported by scientific investigation as superstition or pseudoscience.

The development of science as a method for providing true statements regarding the physical world has been accompanied by a parallel and closely related development in economics as a primary frame of reference for understanding and guiding the decisions and actions of individuals, organizations, and societies. Employing methods that can be characterized as alchemistic, it tends to reduce everything that it can measure (and to disregard what cannot be measured) to units of money (or the abstract unit "utility") such that even the most complicated decision problems – and this applies at the individual, organizational, and societal levels – can and *should* be simplified and transformed into a question of minimizing costs or maximizing returns and measures of welfare. At the same time, it transforms the very foundations for considering and balancing the different stakeholders' values and expectations by transferring them from the domains of politics and morals to economics. Food for thought here is provided by the observation that the development of SBL appears to be correlated with the disclosure of international corporate scandals characterized by the greed and lack of sensitivity of the corporate leaders to how their decisions affect others.

Concomitant with the development in the number, size, and impact of these scandals, other factors have also led to ethical, intellectual, and emotional challenges to the economic rationale that underlies corporate leadership. These include increasing globalization, the development of highly flexible but opaque and unstable international capital markets, and corporate visions dominated by shareholder and personal economic growth in a world characterized by increasing inequalities, tensions and fear. Fortunately, for many a "*Homo economicus*" this has resulted in an awakening awareness that it is possible to be richer and poorer at the same time; that wealth is not automatically accompanied by joy, satisfaction, respect, peace of mind, and love.

The emergence and development of SBL can therefore also be considered a result of corporate leaders' alienation from themselves and from the organizations they lead. Many experience that it has become more difficult to answer (or to even take the time and have the courage to formulate) fundamental personal and organizational existential questions regarding identity and purpose when they as decision-*makers* in expanding corporations lose contact with the many decision-*receivers* – and with themselves. The predominate focus on growth and the resultant increasing distance between those who decide and those who are affected by their decisions result in reduced contact with and sensitivity to an increasingly complex reality that is affected by the behavior of our corporate leaders. Paradoxically, the resulting "blindness" can lead to decisions and organizational structures that are counter-productive even with respect to the aim of growth, and can eventually lead to the disintegration of the organization itself. The statement "growth, for the sake of growth, is the ideology of the cancer cell" does not only apply to biological systems but to social systems as well.

This is closely related to a tendency that is clearly manifested in the present focus on stress in the workplace; while an increasing number of people, and particularly leaders, are becoming addicted to work as human *doings* they also long to be authentic human *beings*. They find it increasingly difficult to live with integrity, such that their values, thoughts, words, and deeds are in harmony, both at work and in their private lives.

At the same time, a growing number of sensitive corporate leaders (as well as thoughtful leadership theoreticians) have realized that ethical and responsible business behavior is vital for an organization's success – using a broad, inclusive, and service-oriented interpretation of the word. Profits are understood by such leaders less as *the* goal, and more as *a* necessary means that can enable the organization to achieve its many diverse goals – such as to be a wonderful place to work for proud, trusting, and empowered employees; to develop, produce, and market products and services of the highest quality; to deliver a satisfactory return to the owners; to be respected as a good "corporate citizen"; and so on.

Transcending and encompassing economic rationality

I know from my research and personal experience that a paradigm of SBL is far from mainstream at present. There is no shared understanding as to its content and form, and it is still in the process of developing its vocabulary (Biberman and Tischler, 2008). If you ask most leaders and management theoreticians, as well as students of business and economics (as I have done over the course of more than 40 years as a professor as well as a business leader early on in my career), why they should be responsible to people other than themselves and the shareholders – why they should embrace values, ethics, responsibility, and sustainability as perspectives on the quality of their decisions – most often, after a pause, you will receive a hesitant answer with little deeply felt conviction: "It pays to do so." But this instrumental perspective on values, ethics, and responsibility reduces them to means serving a higher rationality: economic rationality. The vision of these leaders has been narrowed by their education and what they have learned while climbing the corporate-hierarchical ladder, to the extent that they think, measure, and express themselves using an instrumental economic rationale that suppresses their innate competency for empathy and ignores the competency of organizations to have consciousness – to have values, virtues, and visions (Pruzan, 2001; Pandey and Gupta, 2008).

Therefore the development of SBL can also be seen as an attempt to develop the language and the rationality that are required if leaders are to be able to understand, motivate, and commit themselves to decision-making behavior that can transcend the limitations imposed by an economic rationale. While traditional managerial leadership aims at optimal economic performance, subject to both self-imposed and societal constraints that mandate attention to the well-being of the organization's stakeholders, SBL essentially interchanges the means and the ends. The "why" of organizational existence is no longer economic growth but the spiritual fulfillment of all those affected by the organization, where a major restriction is the requirement that the organization must maintain and develop its economic capacity to serve its stakeholders. In other words, from the perspective of SBL, spirituality provides a framework for leadership that can serve as the very source of an organization's values, ethics, and responsibility (Pruzan, 2004, 2008; Pruzan and Miller, 2006).

Finally, I note that the concept and practice of SBL has become increasingly visible in recent years as the subject of intellectual inquiry in many places throughout the world. A clear indication has been an increasing number of international associations – for example, *European SPES Forum (Spirituality in Economic and Social Life), Spirit in Business, The International Center for Spirit at Work*, and *Spiritual Business Network*, as well as conferences in many countries at some of the world's most highly respected universities and business schools. In addition, a number of academic journals, including the *Journal of Business Ethics, Journal of Management Education, Journal of Organizational Change Management, Leadership Quarterly, Organization, Asian Management Review,* and *Journal of Human Values* have within the last few years published articles or special issues dealing with spirituality in business. Noteworthy is the *Journal of Management, Spirituality, and Religion;* since its first issue in 2004 it *has* published some 100 papers related to the relevance and relationship of spirituality and religion in management and organizational life. Significantly, in 2001 the special interest group "Management, Spirituality and Religion," which stood behind the establishment of the aforementioned journal of the same name, was founded in the Academy of Management, the world's oldest and largest academic management association based in the USA and with members in more than 100 countries. That prompted André Delbecq, former dean of the Graduate School of Business at Santa Clara University, USA, to proclaim: "There are two things I never thought I would see in my lifetime: one was the fall of the Russian empire; and the other was hearing the word 'God' spoken of in the Academy of Management" (Pruzan and Pruzan Mikkelsen, 2007, p. 10).

Literature

Biberman, J. and Tischler, L. (eds) 2008. *Spirituality in Business: Theory, Practice and Future Directions*. New York and Basingstoke, England: Palgrave Macmillan.

Biberman, J. and Whitty, M.D. (eds) 2000. *Work & Spirit: A Reader of New Spiritual Paradigms for Organizations*. Scranton, PA: University of Scranton Press.

Giacalone, R.A. and Jurkiewicz, C.L. (eds) 2003. *Handbook of Workplace Spirituality and Organizational Performance*. Armonik, NY and London: M.E. Sharpe.

Mitroff, I.I. and Denton, E.A. 1999. *A Spiritual Audit of Corporate America: A Hard Look at Spirituality, Religion, and Values*. San Francisco, CA: Jossey-Bass.

Mitroff, I.I., Denton, E.A. and Alpaslan, C.M. 2009. "A Spiritual Audit of Corporate America: Ten Years Later (Spirituality and Attachment Theory, An Interim Report)" *Journal of Management, Spirituality and Religion*, 6, pp. 27–41.

Pandey, A. and Gupta, R.K. 2008. "A Perspective of Collective Consciousness of Business Organizations." *Journal of Business Ethics*, 80, pp. 889–898.

Pruzan, P. 2001. "The Question of Organizational Consciousness: Can Organizations Have Values, Virtues and Visions?" *Journal of Business Ethics*, 29, pp. 271–284.

Pruzan, P. 2004. "Spirituality as the Context for Leadership." In Zsolnai, L. (ed.), *Spirituality and Ethics in Management*. pp. 15–31. London: Kluwer Academic Publishers.

Pruzan, P. 2008: "Spirituality as a Firm Basis for CSR." In Crane et al. (eds), *Oxford Handbook of Responsible Leadership*. pp. 552–560. Oxford: OxfordUniversity Press.

Pruzan, P. 2009a. *Rational, Ethical and Spiritual Perspectives on Leadership: Selected Writings by Peter Pruzan*. Oxford: Peter Lang.

Pruzan, P. 2009b. *Research Methodology*. Unpublished teaching notes for M.Phil. and Ph.D. students, Sri Sathya Sai University, Prasanthi Nilayam, Andhra Pradesh, India.

Pruzan, P. and Miller, W. 2006. "Spirituality as the Basis of Responsible Leaders and Companies." In T. Maak. and N. Pless (eds), *Responsible Leadership*. pp. 68–92. London: Routledge.

Pruzan, P. and Pruzan Mikkelsen, K. 2007. *Leading with Wisdom: Spiritual-based Leadership in Business*. Sheffield, England: Greenleaf Publishing; New Delhi, India: Sage/Response Books.

Pruzan, P. and Pruzan Mikkelsen, K. 2010. *Ledelse med visdom: Spirituelt baseret lederskab i virksomheder*, (revised and translated Danish version of "Leading with Wisdom: Spiritual-based Leadership in Business") Copenhagen: Gyldendal.

36

Deep Leadership in Spirit-Driven Business Organizations

Gerrit Broekstra and Paul de Blot

As in the severe economic downturn of the early eighties, there is again a call for new leadership in the aftermath of the worst financial and economic crisis since the Great Depression of the 1930s. Unlike the eighties it is suggested here that we look towards the East, rather than the West, the origin of the greed-is-good kind of capitalism, for a new paradigm of deep leadership. In October 2006, just before the outbreak of the credit crisis, *Business Week* reported on the apparent emergence of a new type of capitalism, *karma capitalism*, which may not have been such a bad idea after all. Some successful Indian companies, for example, may constitute the cutting edge of this new paradigm of leadership in the business world.

Shallow leadership

Shortly after the economic recession of the early eighties there was a call for new leadership, originating in the United States. Celebrated examples of top managers who had succeeded in rescuing their companies from disaster were Lee Iacocca of Chrysler and Jack Welch, "Neutron Jack," of General Electric. It started the era of *celebrity CEOs*. Not until two decades later, after the debacles of Enron and Ahold among many others, was it recognized that these emperors had virtually no clothes. In the eighties, business-school professors such as Noel Tichy of Michigan (*The Transformational Leader*, 1986) and John Kotter of Harvard (*The Leadership Factor*, 1988) came to fame with their analyses of the essence of the leadership of these CEOs. Their common conclusion was that it started with some kind of vision that, through some strategy and associated policies on the one hand, and some organizational form (structure, systems, human resources) on the other, was transformed into outstanding business performance (Figure 36.1).

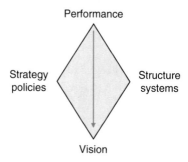

Figure 36.1   Shallow leadership

In a 1988 edition of *Wall Street Journal* management guru Peter Drucker warned in vain against this "leadership rage" of the eighties that promoted "leadership qualities" and particularly "charisma." However, today we still think that this is the way corporate leadership works. More or less out of the blue, the "strong" or "charismatic" CEO envisions a desirable future for the organization that is then "rolled out" and implemented top-down through the hierarchy. It turns out, however, that these visions are, more often than not, strongly influenced by the desired performance and, what's more, are normally expressed in terms of economic growth or shareholder value. That is the meaning of the arrow in the figure: the vision is performance driven. Needless to say, these visions are rather one-dimensional and short-term tunnel visions. Furthermore, performance is compared with that of competitors (benchmarking). As a result these visions and strategies are not very original or authentic, and mostly have a me-too character.

We dubbed this kind of leadership shallow or superficial leadership. It relies on a hierarchy of power, thrives on status and prestige, and induces internally a culture of fear. The inward focus and prevailing egocentrism lead to a relative neglect of the real needs of customers, the employees, and society at large. This shortsightedness and shallowness of business leadership, which has infected the leadership of many other kinds of public and private organizations, have largely contributed, in Fukuyama's terms, to the degradation of whatever high-trust societies were still alive, culminating in today's widespread low-trust societies.

Deep leadership

The essence of deep leadership consists of asking deep questions: Why do we exist? What is our reason for being? What do we really stand for (rather than what do we purport to stand for)? How strong is our organizational spirit? How sustainable is our entrepreneurship? What is our meaning to society? (Broekstra, 2009a). These questions, as significant as they may sound for the future evolution of the organization, have a systematic tendency to be avoided in most boardrooms. The reason is that in-depth probing for answers may lead to the discovery that they are abysmally out of sync with the prevailing organizational policies and practices. These deep questions at the organizational level, directed at uncovering the organizational essence or self, can be viewed as parallel to the central question of self-inquiry at the personal level – *Who am I?* – and can thus be seen as intrinsically spiritual in nature. Interestingly, this spiritual quest for seeking the truth at the organizational level may involve blockages similar to those that may be experienced at the personal level, such as denial and anxiety.

When pursued in depth, the answers to these fundamental questions may produce a so-called *genetic code*, the DNA of the organization, mostly consisting of the mission and values and energy they generate in the organization. On the basis of these, through visioning exercises, a clear and aspiring vision for the future may be produced. This is summarized in Figure 36.2.

The idea behind the Deep-Leadership Model (DLM) is that the energy of people, which is always and everywhere abundantly available in the universe – the universe *is* indeed energy – is being liberated and channeled through a genetic code which is embraced by everyone into a coherent creating of the future. Just as in a laser the energy is amplified into a powerful, coherent bundle, the genetic code acts as a focusing

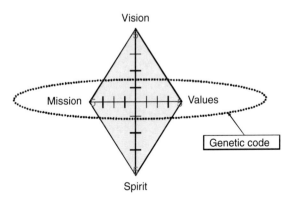

Figure 36.2   Deep-leadership model

lens. This human energy is called the organizational spirit – the origin of all action in organizations. Because of ambiguity or even complete invisibility of a common genetic code the energy level in many organizations is dismally low. But there is also another reason.

Concepts such as mission and values are far from unknown and have even become somewhat worn-out, to the point of having lost any meaning for the organizational members. Most self-respecting organizations have formulated missions and values, "rolled out" across the organization to be subsequently forgotten by everyone. They serve merely as window dressing. They are certainly not living realities that influence daily decision-making and organizational practice. In the DLM the content of these terms changes radically. By persistently asking deep questions, more often than not the answers take a surprising turn, from what is called ego-intentionality to alter-intentionality.

At the human level, if we continue to ask more deeply why some things we do are really important, we eventually arrive at the true nature of human beings, not as independent entities or egos who are primarily busy surviving and comforting their own individual lives, but as spiritual beings who stand in a dependent relationship to other *things* (nature, environment, the planet), other *people* (fellow beings, neighborhoods, society), and *das ganz Andere* (cosmic Unity or the idea that "we are one"). In a similar way, we can apply these three levels of alter-intentionality to the genetic codes, missions, and values of organizations, which above all are communities of humans. And these are more than mere collections of replaceable resources.

The DLM has been developed to give a substance to the new academic discipline of business spirituality. Spirituality in organizations is not something to be startled about. Spirituality is basically the quest for one's true nature, whether individual or organizational. In society at the individual level we can perceive a shift from religionism to spiritualism. The first assumes some anthropomorphic male god who once created the universe but is situated outside it, judges us, and punishes or rewards us accordingly in some afterlife. With rising levels of education the downturn in church attendance is evidence that this (Western) mediæval conception has lost much of its attractiveness. The second rapidly growing development of spiritualism looks for knowledge and experience of "something higher" and liberation within oneself and during one's lifetime. This explains the rising interest in Eastern spiritual traditions.

At the organizational level we may perceive a strong analogy in the shift of the prevailing medievalist adoration of the external, capricious shareholder towards the inner-directed self-inquiry of organizations, that is to say from shallow to deep leadership. This kind of reflection is also a response to the increasing demand for authenticity, internal meaningfulness, external social responsibility of organizations, and ultimately a stronger competitive edge in the marketplace.

Inspirations for the DLM

To underpin its essentially spiritual nature, the DLM is a direct one-to-one mapping of a deep structure of nondual spirituality as developed by the Belgian philosopher and orientalist Ulrich Libbrecht, who some twenty years ago founded the School for Comparative Philosophy at the University of Antwerp. The important concepts of ego- and alter-intentionality have been taken from his work and applied to the organizational context. As part of the genetic code, these concepts inspired the design of a values hierarchy that has been published elsewhere (Broekstra, 2009b).

A second inspiration for the concept of deep leadership came from the well-known and widely accepted distinction made by the Norwegian philosopher Arne Naess between *deep ecology* and *shallow ecology* (Naess, 1973). Shallow ecology has an anthropocentric or egocentric orientation in which humans view themselves as above or outside nature, which is to be exploited as natural resources for human purposes. Deep ecology on the other hand values an ecocentric orientation in which humans are parts of an integrated whole. It values all that lives as constituting an interconnected and interdependent web of life or cosmic unity. Deep ecological awareness is therefore in its deepest essence spiritual awareness, as Fritjof Capra noted, in which the "human spirit is understood as the mode of consciousness in which the individual feels a sense of belonging, of connectedness, to the cosmos as a whole" (Capra, 1996, p. 7). This is a message which nowadays concerns ecologists and economists alike, since both are involved in keeping our house – including the garden – in order ("eco" comes from *oikos,* Greek for house). In essence, deep leadership suggests a similar paradigm shift, as occurred in ecology, from a short-term egocentric to an other- and unity-directed ecocentric approach.

Finally, the concept of deep leadership, reaching deep into the organization, is also an indication of its distributive nature, in the sense that everyone can be his or her own leader, as opposed to the more common hierarchical nature of shallow leadership where a leader is basically defined as someone who has followers. When every employee "owns" the organizational genetic code and carries it in his or her mind and heart, individual decisions and actions always tend to be in the interest of the organizational self, its mission and values. It acts like the DNA in all the cells of the body, enabling its parts a great deal of autonomy and freedom while at the same time preserving its identity and cohesion. We do not have to think all day about keeping our heart going and how the lungs should breathe. Without our awareness, the two stay in tune and adapt automatically to changing circumstances. In other words, the concept of deep leadership also contributes to a more egalitarian rather than hierarchical ethos in organizations, which enhances a deeper sense of meaningfulness and an organizational spirit of oneness. Furthermore, the more these embedded genetic codes are meaningful for the employees – that is, the more alter-intentional rather than ego-intentional they are – the more energy is generated and the more the organization as a whole becomes truly spirit-driven.

Azim Premji, (also known as" the Bill Gates of India"), CEO of the Indian IT-services powerhouse Wipro Ltd ,expressed Wipro's strength as "the depth of its leadership." Its first principle is to "select the right people, give them the right environment, and then don't get into their hair" (*Business Week* 2003). Quite appropriately, the strongly alter-intentional genetic code of Wipro, which is deeply embedded and continuously kept alive to provide the "right environment," is called *The Spirit of Wipro*. Acting within the framework of the genetic code, the autonomy and freedom of all employees to unleash their creativity and entrepreneurial energy are strongly enhanced.

Another interesting example from the nonbusiness world is the centuries-old organization of the Jesuits. Ignatius de Loyola started this organization in 1540 with seven members and it has now grown into one with 25,000 members who are working all over the world on a diversity of projects and in universities and business schools. Its genetic code is defined by the alter-intentional concept of "better service" to humanity, which is kept alive through the so-called Spiritual Exercises. Through this living concept of better service, anchored at the level of being, the autonomy and freedom of the members are strongly enhanced, thus creating a powerful network of friendship and action.

When an alter-intentional genetic code is thus ingrained in the hearts and minds of all employees as a living reality, action in organizations becomes the organizational parallel of the age-old adage of the *Bhagavad-Gita: Yogasthahkuru karmani* – established in *Being*, perform action (*Doing*). In this case, you do not have to worry about the outcome or results of the action. The action naturally becomes *right action*.

All energy goes into the action, rather than spending energy thinking about performance. Clearly this is in complete contrast to the performance-driven activity of the Shallow-Leadership Model. As the *Gita* tells us, detached from the results, all actions thus become spontaneous and are supported by nature. This is entirely in tune with what all mental coaches tell their sports clients who want to improve their performance: "Don't even think about the results; relax and put all your energy into your action."

From Being to Doing

It may be noted that in the DLM the organizational vision is the end-point of a recalibration of the organizational genetic code, rather than the starting point for action as in the Shallow-Leadership Model. Since the DLM is concerned with the organizational self or Being, the question remains how the level of Doing is reached. This can be easily accomplished symbolically by connecting Figures 36.1 and 36.2 in such a way that the vision becomes the hinge point (Figure 36.3).

It is to be noted that now both vision and performance are spirit-driven, as indicated by the arrows, while leadership has achieved depth. Strategy and organization have attained an authentic identity, internal

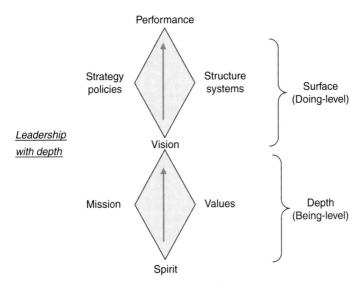

Figure 36.3 Being and Doing in organizational context

cohesion, and meaningfulness. If leadership lacks depth, because the lower diamond no longer sparkles but has disappeared in the organizational mud, the organization will be characterized by disorientation and lack of spirit, which in turn is compensated for by a hunger for power and status. Selfishness and greed are only natural results of this dismal state of affairs. If Western companies could swallow their pride, it might not be such a bad idea to look for examples of spirit-driven organizations of Indian companies such as Wipro, Infosys, and the Tata Group. Apart from their long-sought-after characteristics such as entrepreneurship, innovativeness, and a deeply ingrained ethos of service, they have genetic codes with a relatively strong emphasis on alter-intentionality. The Tata Group's mission, for example, as part of their "leadership with trust" credo, is illustrative but rarely seen in the West: "to improve the quality of life of the communities we serve." They also practice what they preach: a considerable part of the Tata Group's profit goes to charitable projects.

The Spirit of Wipro

From its modest start in 1946 as a western Indian vegetable-oil-products company, "high ethics" was always considered the strongest asset in going forward at Wipro, "bringing it more business, better employees with more muscle tone, more pride, more self respect" (Harris, 2007). Headquartered at Bangalore's Silicon Valley and having grown exponentially into a global IT-services giant during the past decade, late-2005 Wipro felt that its genetic code was, for the third time, due for reassessment (Hamm, 2007). Almost half of the 60,000 employees responded to a survey about both the relevance of the then-current genetic code and about the future one. This was followed up by a series of focus groups and one-on-one interviews across the organization. The final proposal was not adopted until after a thorough review by the employees. Needless to say, this more or less democratic procedure generated intense commitment to the final outcome: The *Spirit of Wipro*. To proceed from *Being* to *Doing,* this was followed up with a visioning exercise to produce a vision as expressed in the above figure, which in turn became the basis for the usual managerial exercise of designing strategy and so on.

   Steve Hamm, in his eye-opening book about Wipro, the *Bangalore Tiger,* emphasizes that all this is in no way "icky navel gazing," as we are very inclined to say in Western companies where negative past experiences with defining missions and values have turned out to be more cosmetic than anything else and have made employees very skeptical about them. Wipro also makes sure that its genetic code is truly lived out in day-to-day decision-making and organizational practices. Its three main components – determination to win, acting with sensitivity, and unyielding integrity – are meaningful, living realities for all Wiproites. In a business world characterized by strong centrifugal forces, clearly, when the code is anchored in everybody's genes as it were, each employee can be his or her own leader. As such, energy is liberated without losing overall focus and coherence.

Conclusion

It should be noted that the concept of deep leadership as defined here is entirely in tune with the way organizations operate effectively and efficiently as complex adaptive systems (CAS), as studied in complexity science. In a similar way, these natural systems operate from a shared genetic code or program that normally contains a surprisingly small number of rules or heuristics, as exemplified in biological systems such as ant colonies and beehives – which, by the way, have no leaders or managers whatsoever. The concept of leadership has lost its meaning in such biological organizations where each member is her own leader. However, each individual member has been endowed with a genetic code that guides daily action and that has been honed by millions of years of evolution.

Similarly, anthropologists tell us that modern man, *Homo sapiens*, for more than 99 percent of his time on earth has lived in egalitarian societies that were for all practical purposes without leaders. Since one can take the ape out of the jungle but not the jungle out of the ape, as the well-known primatologist Frans de Waal often says, would-be leaders or upstarts nonetheless are strongly resented or downright oppressed. Somehow this important social innovation of the egalitarian ethos has been lost in our hierarchical times where power, prestige, and greed have become dominant features.

Given the present-day not-so-positive public opinion about the leadership capabilities in a business world in crisis, the message of this paper is that companies in the West would do well to practice deep leadership. They need to recalibrate their genetic codes towards a higher degree of alter-intentionality and, more importantly, to make them a living reality in their organizations. In this way they can become truly spirit-driven organizations of empowered people, respected guardians of a sustainable planet, and profitable players in the marketplace.

Literature

Broekstra, G. 2009a. *Deep Leadership: The Secret of Right Action at Times of Uncertainty.* Ten Have (in Dutch).

Broekstra, G. 2009b. "The Spirit-Driven Organization as a Prime Source of European Competitive Advantage." In LukBouckaert and Jochanan Eynikel (eds), *Imagine Europe: The Search for European Identity and Spirituality.* pp. 89–101. Antwerp: Garant."Business Lessons from Wipro's Chief," *Business Week,* October 8, 2003.

Business Week 2003. "India's Tech King," Business Week, October 13, 2003.

Capra, F. 1996. *The Web of Life.* New York: Doubleday.

Hamm, S. 2007. *Bangalore Tiger: How Indian Tech Upstart Wipro is Rewriting the Rules of Global Competition.* New York: McGraw-Hill.

Harris, J. 2007. Transcript of a radio interview "From Scratch" with Azim Premji, July 3, 2007.

Naess, A. 1973. "The Shallow and the Deep, Long Range Ecology Movements: A Summary," *Inquiry,* 16, pp. 95–100.

37
Transformation Management

Ronnie Lessem and Alexander Schieffer

In this chapter we explore the specific potential of an enterprise to engage meaningfully with the transformational capacity embedded in a particular societal culture. We shall further illustrate how such an engagement can become a key source of knowledge creation and innovation. We distinguish, as such, between a process of engagement within a particular culture and that between diverse cultures. While the first addresses the recognition and activation of the cultural force within a society, and thereby relates to the local identity of a social system, the latter demonstrates the relevance of meaningful cocreation between the local and the global.

Local cultural forces

Where does the transformation of a social system begin? Is there a place where it takes root, ignited by a spark that sets it in motion? That spark, for us, is lodged within local soil, nurtured and nourished by centuries of knowledge and practice. We refer to this as a local cultural force, or indeed "soul" force, which is often critical to initiate a transformation process. It provides the indigenous cultural force of origination for prospective social innovation that is promoted through subsequent cocreation.

We perceive these cultural forces, moreover, as archetypally resonating within human beings in general. However, each world region, each organization, each individual resonates most with one particular such soul force, while the others are less prominent.

Transformation Management, for us a further evolution of leadership (personal) and management (impersonal) towards the "transpersonal," encourages individuals, organizations, *and* societies (hence

305

transpersonal) to reconnect with the innermost cultural forces rooted within their given context rather than tapping primarily into external, transformative ones (Lessem and Schieffer, 2009).

We now traverse the globe, and what we have termed the "four worlds," to study four examples of indigenous cultural or soul forces, from "Southern" African Ubuntu to "Eastern" Japanese Kyosei, from "Northern" Nordic Näringsliv to "Western" Anglo-Saxon Individuation. Figure 37.1 provides an overview of this journey. We shall start, as is invariably the case in our approach to transformation, in the South.

Ntu and Ubuntu (Southern Africa)

We begin in southern Africa where much of our work is based, with dynamic "Ntu" and stabilizing "Ubuntu," the first more closely connected with nature and the second with culture.

The German anthropologist and African devotee Janheinz Jahn, in his seminal book entitled *Muntu: African Culture and the Western World*, describes *Ntu* as being a universal force amongst the Bantu peoples throughout sub-Saharan Africa (Jahn, 1991). It is the point from which creation flows. From *Ntu* comes *Muntu*, a force endowed with human and more-than-human intelligence. *Kintu* embraces those things that cannot act for themselves and involves plants, animals, minerals, and such. Space and time constitute *Hantu*. It is the force that localizes every motion spatially and temporally, for everything is in motion. *Kuntu* is a modal force, such as beauty or laughter. A key component of *Kuntu* is rhythm. In every expression of African culture, meaning and rhythm are intertwined. Rhythm, for Senegal's president, the philosopher-poet-Leopold Senghor, is the architecture of being, the inner dynamic that gives it form, the pure expression of life force. Rhythm is the vibratory force that grips us at the root of our being. It is expressed through lines, surfaces, colors, and volumes in architecture, art, sculpture, and painting; through accents in poetry and music; through movements in dance. Rhythm turns all these concrete things toward the light of *Ntu*.

The attitude of seeing people not as themselves but as agents for some particular function, either to one's advantage or disadvantage, is, for the late Steve Biko, foreign to the African (Biko, 2004):

> We are not a suspicious race. We believe in the inherent goodness of man. We enjoy man for himself. We regard our living together not as an unfortunate mishap warranting endless competition amongst us but as a deliberate act of God to make us a community of brothers

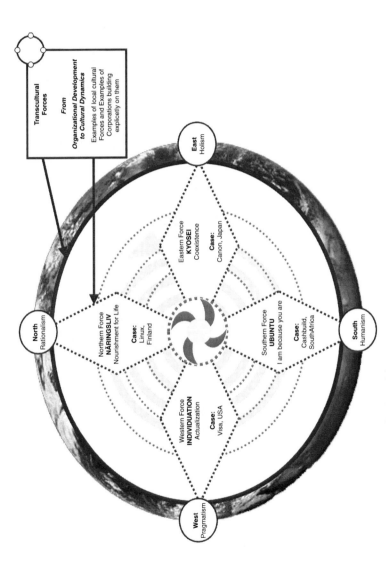

Figure 37.1 Examples of cultural forces

Transcultural Forces

From

Organizational Development to Cultural Dynamics

Examples of local cultural Forces and Examples of Corporations building explicitly on them

East
Holism

North
Rationalism

South
Humanism

West
Pragmatism

Eastern Force
KYOSEI
Coexistence

Case:
Canon, Japan

Northern Force
NÄRINGSLIV
Nourishment for Life

Case:
Linux, Finland

Southern Force
UBUNTU
I am because you are

Case:
Cashbuild, SouthAfrica

Western Force
INDIVIDUATION
Actualization

Case:
Visa, USA

and sisters jointly involved in the quest for a composite answer to the varied problems of life. Hence in all we do we always place man first and therefore all our action is usually joint and community oriented. Nothing then dramatises the eagerness of African[s] to communicate with each other more than their love for song and rhythm. Music in the African culture features in all emotional states. When we go to work we share the burdens and pleasures of the work we are doing through music. In other words, for Africans, music and rhythm are not luxuries but part and parcel of our way of communicating. Any suffering we experienced was made more real by song and rhythm. The major thing to note about our songs, moreover, is that all African songs are group songs.

Most Ubuntu thinkers therefore formulate their views in terms of "a person is a person through other persons," or, "I am because you are." In this way human dignity gains a central place and seems to be related to both morality and nationality. In fact, it is such Ubuntu, in the field of leadership and management, that is now reaching out to the world, as illustrated by South African Parliamentarian Mfuniselwa Bhengu's latest book on *African Economic Humanism* (Bhengu, 2010).

As we move from the South to the East the cultural forces change.

Kyosei (Japan), Taoism and Confucianism (China)

We have identified Kyosei as a transformational force coming from Japan. A concise definition of the term would be "living and working together for the common good." As such it is both dynamic and stabilizing in its overall effect.

Kyosei is still very much alive in current Japanese culture, as can be seen in the case of the Japanese multinational Canon (Kaku, 1997). The company states that "[t]he Corporate Philosophy of Canon is Kyosei" and translates the term into "[a]ll people, regardless of race, religion or culture, harmoniously living and working together into the future," and the company adds reflectively, "Unfortunately, the presence of imbalance in our world – in areas such as trade, income levels and the environment – hinders the achievement of Kyosei." We now turn from Japan to China, philosophically if not economically.

The dynamic natural and cultural force underlying such Kyosei, originally coming from neighboring China, is nature-bound Taoism, converted in Japan into Shintoism. The stabilizing one is Confucianism, which prevails throughout the Far East. It is indigenous Confucianism, moreover, that is forging links with the exogenous West, and vice versa. The term "Confucian dynamism," for example, something of a misnomer in our terms, has seemingly served to characterize the recent economic and technological development of the Asian tigers. We would argue, conversely, that such Eastern dynamism comes from Taoism, which has been left behind, so that Western capitalism – Canon, as we shall see, somewhat excepted – is required to take its place.

For the twentieth-century Chinese writer and philosopher Lin Yutang (1998), Confucianism is essentially decorous, reasonable, and correct; in our terms, it represents a stabilizing force. The slightly rebellious, and dynamic in spirit, look to Taoism. Confucianism, through its doctrine of propriety and social status, stands for culture and constraint; while Taoism, with its emphasis on going back to nature, does not believe in human restraint and culture. Confucianism is essentially an urban philosophy, whereas Taoism is rural. It is therefore unsurprising that in China it is the rural areas that are being left economically behind, because Taoism has not been renewed. Confucianism is fundamentally realism and has little room for fancy and imagination. Taoism stands for the world of wonder and mystery that Confucianism fails to provide. There is a classicism (Confucius) and a romanticism (Laotse) in any nation. The latter stands for the return to nature: the rural ideal of life.

Fung Yu-Lan, a contemporary Chinese philosopher, has also highlighted the seminal part played by Laotse and Confucius, albeit set alongside several other Chinese philosophical streams (Fung, 1998). For the Taoists, when the development of anything brings it to one extreme, a reversal to the other extreme takes place. So, one can argue, Chinese communism gave rise to capitalism, and Western capitalism is giving rise to environmentalism. Everything involves its own negation. This was one of the main theses of Laotse's philosophy, undoubtedly inspired by the movements of the sun and moon and the movements of the four seasons, to which farmers must pay particular heed: "When the cold goes the warmth comes, and when the warmth comes the cold goes." And again, "[W]hen the sun has reached its meridian it declines, and when the moon has become full it wanes."

This has also provided the basis for the golden mean, favored by Confucianists and Taoists alike. Taoism and Confucianism differ, however, in that they are rationalizations of different aspects of the lives of the farmers. The Taoists maintained that the highest achievement in the spiritual cultivation of the sage lies in the identification of himself with the whole of nature, that is, the universe. A great part of Confucianism is the rational justification or theoretical expression of the social system associated with rural life. Because of the latter predominating over the former, Confucianism naturally became the orthodox philosophy, and remained so until the invasion of industrialization from modern Europe and America changed the economic basis of Chinese life. Confucianism, then, emphasizes the social responsibilities of man, while Taoism recognizes what is natural and spontaneous in him. These two trends of philosophical thought historically complemented each other, exercising a sort of balance of power: a balance between the static and the dynamic, in the same way that the North encompasses alternating institutional forces. However, today in China, if not in the Far East in general, such a balance has been lost, which is why Western capitalism is required to balance out "state order," or indeed Confucian values. The North, for us, embodies yet another "soul force."

Näringsliv (Sweden/Scandinavia)

The Nordic notion of Näringsliv is most prolifically represented, today, in Sweden and in Finland. It is in fact commonly used in Sweden as the term for business and commerce and can be found, for example, in the name of the Confederation of Swedish Enterprise, *SvensktNäringsliv*, or in *E24 Näringsliv*, a Swedish online business newspaper, based in Stockholm. Translated, it stands for "nourishment for life."

The Näringsliv Project – initiated some years ago by the US-American Institute of Noetic Sciences – was one of a number of initiatives intending to tap into the ancient wisdom underlying the notion of Näringsliv. They stressed the potential of Näringsliv serving as a new guiding image, most especially relating to business' role in society (Edvinsson, 1997):

> During times of fundamental social transformation, the emergence of a new guiding image can lead societal evolution by providing a direction for creative innovation and change. A compelling core image can act almost like a magnet, creating a powerful pull toward the future. The Swedish core image of business as närings liv, nourishment for life, may have the potential to lead and empower individuals and organizations who are exploring new ways to design their lives and work ... *The metaphor of business as nourishment for life is evocative in several respects. It is simple and elegant. Since most of us already have an intuitive hunch about what provides nourishment in our own lives, it is an effective guide for reflection and decision-making.* It can also serve as a bridge to our common future, connecting our concerns and commitments with those of others in practical and relevant ways.

In our own terms, and from a Northern perspective, such Näringsliv combines the natural dynamic of life itself with the balancing force of business in the environment.

In the West it is the individual more than the nation that counts, which leads us to individuation.

Individuation (USA/Western Europe)

We understand "individuation" here as a process whereby components of an individual, an organization or a society are integrated into an indivisible whole. The term has been used by psychologists, sociologists, philosophers, and theologians and has been variously defined by different scholars, including Sigmund Freund, Carl Jung, and Erik Erikson. It usually refers to the individual and his or her development, but we maintain that it is ultimately also of relevance for organizations and societies in the sense that the last two need to provide the context and soil for progressive individuation. The typical Western conqueror of nature, continually extending the Western frontier, can be seen, preeminently, in this individuating guise.

For American psychotherapist Daniel Levinson, the process of individuation involves events–activities–outcomes being woven into an encompassing design. Recurring themes in various sectors of one's life and work – and by extension within organization and society – help to unify the overall patterns of the tapestry. Such a life course is potentially transformative, if not de-formative or indeed con-formative, and thereby alternates between structure-building and structure-changing. An individual, organizational, or societal life structure, therefore, consists of a series of alternating stable (structure-building) and transitional (structure-changing) periods.

The primary task of every stable period is to build a life structure, which provides for individual and institutional integrity. You or your institution must ensure key choices form a structure around them and pursue values and goals within that structure. A dynamic, structure-changing period terminates the existing life structure and creates the possibility for a new one, indeed, a new expression of individuality. The primary tasks within every such transitional period are to question and reappraise the existing structure, to explore various possibilities for change in the individual or collective self and world, and to move towards commitment to the crucial choices that form the basis for a new life structure in the ensuing stable period.

The first task for the dynamically youthful individual – or analo-gously, the young organization or society – is to move out of the young world, to question the nature of the adult world and to modify or ter-minate existing relationships with persons and institutions. The second task is to take a preliminary step into the formative young-adult world, to explore its possibilities, to imagine oneself or itself as a participant in it, to consolidate an initial adult identity, and to make and test some preliminary choices for adult living. Whereas the first task involves a process of structure-changing, the second is a process of structure-building.

Only those of us in maturity who have in some way taken care of things and people – and who have faced the triumphs and disap-pointments that come with being originators of products and ideas – develop what Levinson terms ultimate "self-integrity." Such integrity, he maintains, is the individual or organizational self's accrued assur-ance of its investment in order and meaning, as part of a world order and grounded in spiritual depth. It is an acceptance of our own per-sonal or collective cycle as something that had to be. Such a mature person, organization, or society would know that all human integrity is at stake in the one style of integrity in which we personally or col-lectively partake. Our own life or culture is wrapped up in everyone else's. The absence of integrity and the danger in this stage is a source of despair. The lack or loss of integrity is signified by the fear of indi-vidual, institutional, or societal death, as if lives or cultures were to take no account of anyone or anything of significance. The integrity of old age thus contributes to the possibility of exploration in the youthful stage.

To the extent that there is a lack of individuation, there is ossifica-tion.

The danger of ossification

We explored in some depth what comprises the core of a society – if not also an organization or a person – the indigenous cultural soil that makes each unique. We examined, first at a societal level, typical forces, both dynamic and stabilizing in the four respective worlds of South, East, North, and West. For us, each of these forces provides their soci-eties, as well as the respective enterprises and individuals, with trans-formative potential. Such potential is constituted of both dynamic cultural forces, closely aligned with natural processes, and stabilizing ones, closely aligned with societal structures.

These cultural forces, altogether, constitute the local soil (nature and culture) and the core of our particular kind of contextualized transformation process. Each such force holds two concurrent forces: one dynamic and outer-directed, allowing a society or an individual or organization to reach out transculturally beyond its boundaries and build bridges with other sources of knowledge; and the other stabilizing and inner-directed, providing the community, institution, or person with a soul. Like twin helixes of the DNA molecule, these forces constitute an essential transformational "undertone."

Many societies become intrinsically caught up in a static survival mode that is overly bound by tradition. From an ecological perspective, they become vulnerable to ossification. Extrinsically, and often in parallel, they are overtaken by the pursuit of the "modern," because that is what is expected of them. In the one case they are unduly constrained by their heritage, and in the other they lose touch with it – in both cases bypassing their potentially unique contributions to the world. In fact, and all too often, a society, or indeed an individual or organization, is caught between these two inauthentic states, as they might be called, displaying signs of a kind of societal schizophrenia.

In such a case, one "lesser developed," indigenous, and often rural society will be dominated by another exogenously "more developed" and often urban one. It will exist, therefore, in a no man's land between tradition and modernity, the indigenous and the exogenous, rural and urban, self and other. Holding on to some of its traditions, literally for dear life, such a society may discard other traditions in the course of copying the simultaneously admired and despised dominant power.

Conclusion

We began this chapter by asking how transcultural forces build upon prior transformational flows to establish the foundations for Transformation Management. The cultural force that we described, underlying a society, community, organization, or individual – linking body and spirit, heart and mind – lies in a dualistic inner-directed and outer-directed movement. The inner-directed movement is that of reaching into the depth of the local identity and celebrating the uniqueness implicit in every identity. But this inner movement is incomplete on its own. In order for it to fulfill its transformational and transcultural potential, it depends upon the outer-directed movement that reaches and makes contact with the other. Without the outer-directed force, societies and organizations either ossify or lose their vitality to exogenous forces. *Each individual and community, organization and society has a unique core, or soul force, to which it must remain faithful, as well as help to evolve.*

Literature

Biko, S. 2004. *I Write What I Like*. Cape Town: Picador Africa.

Bhengu, J. 2010. *African Economic Humanism*. Farnhham: Ashgate-Gower.

Edvinsson, K. 1997. *Intellectual Capital*. New York: Palgrave Macmillan.

Fung, Yu-lan. 1998. *Selected Philosophical Writings*. Beijing: Foreign Languages Press.

Jahn, J. 1991. *Muntu: African Culture and the Western World*. New York: Grove Press.

Kaku, R. 1997. "The Path of Kyosei," *Harvard Business Review,* July-August 1997.

Lessem, R. and Schieffer A. 2009. *Transformation Management*. Farnham: Gower-Ashgate.

Lin, Yutang. 1998. *My Country and My People*. Beijing: Foreign Languages Press.

38
Mindfulness in Business

Sharda Nandram and Margot Esther Borden

Mindfulness, an ancient spiritual practice adapted for modern times, builds quality and strength of character along with an enlarged scope of vision; business, the epitome of the material plane, represents core material needs – but crass materialism, greed, and planetary and human destruction can follow in their wake. In what ways are these two apparent opposites related? Where do the two worlds, spirit and matter, meet?

Mindfulness is increasingly studied in brain research. Due to its adaptability to a Western, nondenominational mindset and scientific proof of positive effects on practitioners, it is increasingly applied in such disciplines as psychology, education, and recently also in business. Mindfulness is developed through simple and easy-to-use practices and philosophical teachings that benefit practitioners on a multidimensional level. On a personal level, it gives us insight into ourselves and our attitudes and brings more objectivity and self-mastery to our lives. On an interpersonal level, practitioners develop compassion, understanding, and an ability to see and accept others as they are. On a spiritual level, it brings greater understanding and connectedness to the bigger picture and to the underlying meanings and drives in life. It leads to peace of mind and congruent actions.

Although mindfulness builds personal mastery and greater congruence on the human level, its spiritual potential is not to be ignored. Gaining a sense of the infinite nature of consciousness and a connection to the Divine, in whatever form we personally or culturally wish, engenders inner transformation that changes our lives in deep and lasting ways. Bringing spirituality into business gives companies a higher vision to which they can align their strategies and actions.

With the current challenges faced by the business world, whose shortcomings and errors are having undeniable repercussions in all aspects of society and the planet, mindfulness provides a powerful tool for change.

Business leaders are among the most influential members of our society on a local and planetary level. Mindfulness gives decision makers the power to engender a transformation, a core shift, in their attitudes, behaviors, and vision with reference to themselves, their employees, and society. This chapter will explore mindfulness and its multidimensional benefits for individuals, the organizations they work in, and society. We will explore the ways in which mindfulness leads to attitudes and actions that transform people's lives and livelihoods. Finally, we will discuss how mindfulness can be implemented in business.

What is mindfulness?

Mindfulness is a broad concept that has two primary approaches, Western and Eastern. Our Western mindset is predominantly macrocosmic; we are interested in understanding our minds, behavior, attitudes, surroundings, and society at large. A Western approach to mindfulness therefore focuses on understanding and optimizing the mind's functions to help individuals achieve success and "happiness." We are focused on "learning to switch modes of thinking... and on "information processing... rather than on meditation" (Weick and Sutcliffe, 2006). In the academic literature, mindfulness has been variously defined as an aspect of emotional intelligence, a cognitive ability, aspects of personality, processes of drawing novel distinctions, a state of inner consciousness in which one is aware of one's thoughts and actions moment by moment, an open awareness of the moment, and the process of becoming whole. Mindfulness helps us become aware of our habits and develops openness, patience, security, satisfaction, and trust. Mindfulness helps people make increasingly refined distinctions in their perceptions. In turn this leads them to see the limits of perceiving things in singular categories and even of categorizing itself (Weick and Sutcliffe, 2006. p. 517.)

Here, we are approaching a more universal aspect of mindfulness coming from age-old Eastern spiritual tradition (Borden and Shekhawat, 2010). The East traditionally holds a more microcosmic worldview, which translates to an interest in man's inner relationship to himself and to his spiritual or universal core. An Eastern view holds that our relationship with the world around us is a reflection of our relationship to our Self.

We define mindfulness as a state of mind involving heightened, more detailed, and more objective awareness of self, others, and life situations. It leads to understanding the outer self and discovering and aligning the axis of our consciousness to our inner Self. It brings to light root attitudes and beliefs: the fears, doubts, and weaknesses that are the source of our egotism and incongruence. It also unveils a sense of meaning and objectivity in our experiences and allows us to harness our greatest potential. Ultimately, practitioners develop the power to see themselves with greater lucidity and navigate in their inner and outer worlds with greater self-mastery. On a deeper level, mindfulness develops love, forgiveness, gratitude, equanimity and ultimately, a grasp of the infinite nature of consciousness. First-hand experiences of these more subtle levels of perception engender deep core shifts in the practitioner's perception of himself. This leads to a transformation in attitudes and behaviors in all areas of life: personal, interpersonal (family, work, etc.), and spiritual.

This section has provided an overview of the different definitions of mindfulness, Eastern and Western. This reflects each culture's understanding of who we are and what gives our lives meaning. It also demonstrates the adaptability of mindfulness to both Eastern and Western models. Both approaches help individuals to purify their tools of perception, make more objective decisions, develop emotional mastery, and enlarge their understanding of who they are, what their lives are about and, therefore, how to act in the world and at work.

How is mindfulness beneficial to business?

Western business models focus on managing and developing outwardly. Eastern thought teaches us that what is outside is but a reflection of our relationship to our inner self. Therefore, being a mindful manager starts with oneself. Starting with the personal level, mindfulness develops greater self-understanding, self-mastery, and objectivity and helps individuals to develop their competences, their authentic characteristics and identify and learn to work with their shortcomings nonjudgmentally. It helps employees cope with challenging tasks and relationships in the workplace. Mindfulness helps individuals learn about and accept who they are with all their strengths and weaknesses. Nonjudgmental acknowledgment of our weaknesses and shortcomings gives us the key to gaining mastery over them and transforming them into strengths. Mindfulness helps employees develop constructive attitudes and facilitates the unleashing of their creative potential. Mindful entrepreneurs have more objectivity, which makes them better equipped to assess and work with the challenges and opportunities at the core of their ideas and visions. On the interpersonal level, mindfulness gives business leaders a clear picture of organizational dynamics and their team's role in the organization's performance. Employees in a mindful environment work collaboratively, with an understanding of how they complement other team members to achieve their respective work goals. On the spiritual level, leaders, entrepreneurs, and employees gain a deeper perspective on their drives and motivations in the various aspects of their lives.

Mindful employees are a highly desirable asset (Joyner and Lardner, 2008) because they enhance both soft and hard performance in areas such as safety, health, productivity, and sales.

Studies find that businesses with a mindful approach have an increased ability to manage the unexpected and avoid catastrophic mistakes (Baker, 2007; Coutu, 2003). Joyner and Lardner (2008) found that a high level of mindful organizing among front-line employees improves innovation, quality, and efficiency. Carrol (2007) explains key principles of mindfulness that help leaders to develop it in the hectic and stressful situations at the workplace.

Studies have been done on the benefits of mindfulness in the areas of: safety and risk (Joyner and Lardner, 2008); communication in cockpit crisis situations (Krieger, 2005); innovation in IT (Swanson and Ramiller, 2004); and prevention and management of burnout (Narayanan and Moynihan, 2006).

Levinthal and Rerup (2006) found that conscious or mindful, and automatic or less-mindful, processes are both needed in organizations. They stated that interruptions trigger a sequential switch from less-mindful to mindful processes, and suggest that organizational processes blend the two forms of cognition and behavior on an ongoing basis.

There is a conflict between mindlessness and mindfulness. Mindlessness focuses on the role of continuity to preserve accumulated experience, whereas mindfulness stresses the importance of novelty to respond to change and unique circumstances. In line with this thinking, Levinthal and Rerup mention that mindfulness can engender extra costs whereas less-mindful, routinized behavior is effective in economizing on scarce attentional resources.

Mindful businesses are more likely to reevaluate their past practices constructively, be alert, open and seek new ways of behaving. Mindful business is more likely to have innovative ideas, while mindless business is dominated by a culture of overconfidence, self-sufficiency, detachment from the environment, internal ignorance (Rerup, 2004), and lack of drive to innovate.

Mindful leadership

Mindfulness helps leaders develop their communication skills, relationships with others, and overall personal development. The mindful leader

- perceives failures as opportunities to learn. Failure provides an ideal opportunity to undertake an analysis of the entire system in order to grow, build resilience, and seek creative solutions. It is not a source of recrimination. When business failure has a stigma attached to it, many potential opportunities are lost. In this scenario when business leaders fail, they often pay the price by getting fired. Taking the time to reflect on and learn from failures produces greater individual and organizational maturity and better long-term results by harnessing hidden opportunities.
- focuses on and anticipates problems on the front line, where the work really gets done.
- sees things as they are, not as he or she wants to see them. In order to keep their organizations in touch with the realities of the business world, the leader is careful not to oversimplify his or her views or strategies.
- tends to be charismatic and influential. Langer (1989) concluded that leaders who are perceived as genuine are also seen as charismatic and influential.

White (2008) concluded that mindfulness helps leaders develop the capacity to control mental and physical responses, better manage requirements of external environments, and provide comprehensive insight into the requirements of social systems. These have an impact on leadership relationships, understanding diversity, team development, sense-making, professional development, and personal growth.

How can businesses bring mindfulness into their practice?

There are different approaches to mindfulness in business. It needs to be adopted on all levels of the organization in order for it to be congruent and therefore requires support at the organizational level. Mindfulness can be brought into organizations through individual or group meditation classes, mindfulness training, coaching sessions, and workshops. Keizer and Nandram (2010) explore a model of mindfulness-based coaching that is effective for assessing and transforming individuals' behavior, thoughts, feelings, and beliefs. They find that starting from the mental level is generally most effective in the workplace. They use a "mental-fitness" tracker to develop the awareness that contributes to success and happiness in life. This is followed up by one-on-one and group coaching sessions. Mindfulness training with individuals provides a space for introspection, gaining a life overview. and reevaluating priorities. With business leaders, it opens the way to building smoother-functioning, optimized organizations that are congruent with respect to self, society, and nature. At the organizational level, greater objectivity and understanding of self and others leads to more harmonious and collaborative relationships.

A mindfulness session in the corporate environment involves gathering participants in a quiet space where they can sit comfortably, either in chairs or on floor cushions. The technique varies according to teacher and context but the aim is simply to bring their awareness fully into the present. This can be done by focusing on breathing, on a candle, or on the *hara* (an area below the navel that relates to groundedness or finding one's "seat"). At the start, participants will find their minds more or less active and unruly. As the inevitable thoughts arise, they are instructed to bring their focus gently back to the object of focus. Over time, one learns to suspend the mind, hold the attention, let the thoughts and sensations come and go from the field of attention but not get involved in them. With time, the practice deepens. As the mind slows down, it becomes easier to distinguish the subtle attitudes that are otherwise indistinguishable in our thoughts and sensations. With practice, it is possible to distinguish the true nature of all that crosses the mind and to choose not to "engage" but simply to watch peacefully. Peak moments occur when a life issue or area of struggle comes to light. Mindfulness develops self-mastery, compassion, discernment, detachment, broader and deeper understanding of self and other, and a multitude of other qualities and capacities.

McKee et al. (2006) applied mindfulness to help leaders eliminate the Sacrifice Syndrome, a vicious cycle leading to mental and physical distress and burnout. This syndrome arises from stress caused by a combination of responsibility, constant self-control and role demands. Leaders facing this syndrome are in dissonance, and their state negatively affects their coworkers. McKee and associates take leaders on a journey to renewal that involves change of habits and patterns; awareness of body, mind, heart and spirit, and their roles as leaders. Table 38.1 demonstrates their road map to well-being. Consistent practice of these steps establishes trust and helps create an environment that

Table 38.1   The road map to well-being

Step 1: *Habits and practices*
Do I act in accordance with my values?
Am I the leader I aspire to be?
How am I managing the stress of my current situation?
How do my key people feel?
Are we in sync?

Step 2: *Articulate and believe in a hopeful future*
Optimistic outlook: we can impact our environment and achieve goals.
Hope has a positive impact on the brain and the hormones, giving more
positive perception.
This slows breathing, lowers blood pressure, strengthens the immune system,
and engages the parasympathetic nervous system.

Step 3: *Compassion*
Compassion begins with curiosity about other people.
Being open to one another enables us to face tough times with creativity and
resilience.
Empathy enables us to connect with people and to understand what moves
them.
It helps us to get things done and to deal with stress.
It helps us build relationships with others.

---

incites proactive feedback, nurtures authentic relationships, and fosters
reliable followers (McKee et al., 2006).

The practice of mindfulness essentially helps individuals to develop
greater awareness and objectivity. We have successfully used this
approach in the form of guided mindfulness exercises to help business
leaders explore work-related points such as ethical issues, relationship
issues, and even larger points such as strategy and vision (Table 38.1).

Conclusion

Mindfulness has the potential to contribute toward personal and organizational transformation. Allotting space and time for mindfulness
practices in the work environment, at work-related meetings, breaks,
and at motivational gatherings improves organizations on all levels.
Mindfulness helps individuals develop their qualities and fine-tune
their perceptions, resulting in smoother work relationships, win-win
reasoning and actions, and greater happiness and fulfillment. On a
spiritual level, the deeper and broader perception of self, other, society, and nature have the power to transform the very axis on which we
think and act in our business and personal interactions.

As interest in mindfulness grows, due to its simplicity and the benefits and vision gained by this nondenominational approach to spirituality, the business world will require an increasing number of professionals trained to teach mindfulness theory and practice.

Based on the literature we conclude that mindfulness has been defined in different ways and explored in terms of its capacity to help individuals cognitively, emotionally, and spiritually. Researchers in management should be aware that while mindfulness provides all-round positive benefits, less-mindful behavior also has relevance and meaning. Further research will ideally focus on the impact of both and should not treat them as a dichotomy. Future scientific research can gain from a standardized, and ideally multidimensional, definition of mindfulness. This would facilitate research to determine the impact of mindfulness on business leaders and their organizations.

Literature

Baker, L.T. 2007. *The Relationship between Mindfulness, Strategic Decision Process and Small Business Performance.* Dissertation Abstracts International.

Borden, M.E. and Shekhawat, P. 2010. "Buddhist Practices and Principles and Their Place in Management." In S. Nandram and M.E. Borden (eds), *Spirituality and Business: Exploring Possibilities for a New Management Paradigm.* 2010. Heidelberg: Springer Publications.

Carroll, M. 2007. *The Mindful Leader: Ten Principles for Bringing out the Best in Ourselves and Others.* Boston, MA: Trumpeter Books.

Coutu, D.L. 2003. "Sense and Reliability: A Conversation with Celebrated Psychologist Karl E. Weick." *Harvard Business Review.* April 18, 2003, pp. 84–90.

Joyner, P. and Lardner, R. 2008. "Mindfulness: Realising the Benefits." *Loss Prevention Bulletin*, 201, pp. 22–27.

Keizer, W.A.J. and Nandram, S.S. 2010. "Transformational Coaching." In S. Nandram and M.E. Borden (eds), *Spirituality and Business: Exploring Possibilities for a New Management Paradigm.* 2010. Heidelberg: Springer Publications.

Krieger, J.L. 2005. "Shared Mindfulness in Cockpit Crisis Situations: An Exploratory Analysis." *Journal of Business Communication*, Vol. 42, no. 2, pp. 135–167.

Langer, E.J. 1989. *Mindfulness.* USA: Perseus Books.

Levinthal, D. and Rerup, C. 2006. "Crossing an Apparent Chasm: Bridging Mindful and Less Mindful Perspectives on Organizational Learning." *Organization Science*, vol. 17, no. 4, pp. 502–513.

McKee, A., Johnston, F., and Massimilian, R. 2006. "Mindfulness, Hope and Compassion: A Leader's Road Map to Renewal." *IVEY Business Journal.* pp. 1–5.

Narayanan, J. and Moynihan, L. 2006. "Mindfulness at Work: The Beneficial Effects on Job Burnout in Call Centers." *Academy of Management Best Conference Paper*, 2006. OB, H1.

Rerup, C. 2004. "Variations in Organizational Mindfulness." *Academy of Management Best Conference Paper*, MOC, B1.

Swanson, E.B. and Ramiller, N.C. 2004. "Innovating Mindfully with Information Technology." *MIS Quarterly*, Vol. 28, no. 4, pp. 553–583.

Weick, K.E. and Sutcliffe, K.M. 2006. "Mindfulness and the Quality of Organizational Attention." *Organization Science*, vol. 17, no. 4, pp. 514–524.

White, B.B. 2008. *Mindfulness within the Organizational Context: A Premise for the Intrasubjective Being*. Dissertation Abstracts International. Section B: The Sciences and Engineering, vol. 69, (1-B), p. 731.

39
Voicing Meaningfulness at Work

Marjolein Lips-Wiersma and Lani Morris

"To be human is to search for a meaningful life." It's all very well to say this, but how do we attend to meaningful living? How do we stay in charge of our ability to make a conscious choice to live a meaningful life? How do we recognize when life is not meaningful, and then, what can we do about it? How can we share our search for meaning with others while retaining our unique identity? These questions have urgency because they relate to so many experiences and decisions in our working lives. In this chapter we describe a framework (Lips-Wiersma and Morris, 2009) that has been used in ten years of action research and has been peer-reviewed by our academic colleagues. We have found that using this framework enables people to have conversations about what is deeply meaningful in the workplace.

In the following almost casual remarks we can hear both a complaint and a desire for meaningful work: "During this change process I find myself increasingly saying, 'This is pointless.'" Or, "We talked about objectives, but these are no longer related to the reasons why we, as employees of this organization, chose to work here in the first place." Or, "Our work is scheduled in such a way that everyone now takes their breaks in their offices, but somehow I don't seem to be able to say at a meeting that I simply miss people's company." Or, "I wanted to talk about my 'passion' but another person immediately said, 'Why talk about passion? Are you not simply saying you approach your tasks in a professional manner?'" These examples were said in the space of one day (by a colleague, a person we mentored, a friend, a spouse) and show that when we listen for it, questions of meaningfulness arise in regard to almost all aspects of work.

The extent to which we find and lose meaningfulness goes to the heart of being human and therefore has profound effects. However, as we can see from the comments above, the search for meaning is often voiced in a negative manner, which reinforces the feeling of powerlessness and can easily drain collective energy. If we find ways to attend to meaningfulness consciously we can be fully human: energy is released, and engagement becomes a naturally constructive way to respond. As Frankl (1969) notes, each person is questioned by life and each person answers for his or her life. When we take conscious responsibility for creating meaning, we achieve coherence between our inner and outer lives through acts of commitment. When we do not take responsibility we are condemned to a state of boredom, discontent, and impotence.

The domain of workplace spirituality (WPS) has from its very outset defined itself in relation to meaningful work. For example, Biberman and Tischler write that the domain is defined by the question of "[w]hat it is to be human, to search for a sense of meaning, purpose, and moral guidance for relating with self, others, and ultimate reality" (Biberman and Tischler, 2008, p. 74). Similarly, Neck and Milliman (1994) define the domain as being concerned with the process of finding meaning and purpose in our lives, and Vaill (1991) notes that spirituality is the feeling individuals have about the fundamental meaning of who they are, what they are doing, and what contributions they are making. At present it is assumed that once we get some misunderstandings about the role of spirituality-versus-religion in organizations out of the way, it will somehow become magically possible to discuss meaningfulness at work. However, as we can see from the quotes above, speaking about what is deeply meaningful to us – while it might be the most important thing we do to honor our humanity – is very hard to do, and to do well, in current organizational life.

Voicing what matters in current organizational life

Spirituality is a new term that is gaining acceptance, and with that, power. It offers a way to signal the importance of profound issues that have been suppressed under the discourse of efficiency and effectiveness. "Spirituality" provides a flag around which people can gather and begin to articulate alternative worldviews. In doing so, it provides a place from which a movement can be created that influences social, political, economic, and working life.

When we speak we draw the attention of others to issues and ideas of concern to us. Yet, as can be seen from the examples above, this is not always easily done, and when it is done it is not always done in ways that actually make a difference. Discourse, as Foucault says, is a power to be seized, and what is "permissible" to speak about changes, and reflects shifts in power when it does. A powerful discourse has the ability to influence our individual lives and our institutions. It has the power to shape the future. Much is at stake. Therefore it is important to think deeply and rigorously about how a new discourse is framed and voiced. In the emerging discourse on spirituality in the workplace it is important to work clearly through and articulate the underpinning philosophy and worldviews and to think about the possible impact on others – both positive and destructive – as well as the organizational and social implications.

Spirituality versus religion in organizations

The domain of WPS has made substantial attempts to distance itself from the term "religion" in order to gain acceptance in academic and applied management discourse. This distancing is usually done in a manner that elevates spirituality above religion and that saddles religion with everything that is harmful. For example, religion has been referred to as partisan and negative (Biberman and Whittey, 1997), dogmatic (Mitroff, 2003), and divisive (Giacalone and Jurkiewicz, 2003). Spirituality on the other hand is seen as free from the past, and therefore from any stigma that attaches to "religion" as a term. It is seen as inclusive in that it seeks to identify common ground and principles, democratic in that it leaves individuals free to choose their own beliefs and practices, and free from the corruption revealed in some of the practices of those involved in religion. It is a new term in cultures passionately committed to the new and very ready to discard the old.

There are however several concerns with this split. *First*, it does not accurately represent the experience of many human beings who do not view religion and spirituality as separate entities. Nor does the distinction pay any attention to those who have no spiritual belief at all. Thus, while WPS insists on recognizing the whole person, it dismisses the possibility for religious or agnostic expression and hence seems to dismiss the possibility for wholeness for many (Hicks, 2002). *Second*, the creation of a split between inclusive spirituality and exclusive religion ignores the role of power in organizations. Spirituality and religion can *both* (intentionally or unintentionally) be imposed on others by those in positions of power towards purposes that do not benefit all (Lips-Wiersma, Lund Dean, and Fornaciari, 2009). Just as we have had experience with religious bullies, we can similarly encounter spiritual bullies. *Third*, while it is argued that spirituality is "an inclusive term, covering all pathways that lead to meaning and purpose" (Tacey, 2003) in relation to day-to-day living, we do not speak in abstract terms but in terms that, whether religious or spiritual, specify distinct worldviews which may not agree with each other (Hicks, 2002). We speak, for example, in terms such as "God," "keeping the Sabbath," "in the next world," "what is meant to be," "all life is sacred." These are terms that all reveal different worldviews. In the splitting of "spirituality" from "religion," the worldviews of the authors are also often ignored. Many who are part of the emergent discourse of spirituality are strongly committed to specific religions, yet do not make their own assumptions and dogmas visible in their theory building, teaching, or consulting practices (Lips-Wiersma, 2003). The problem that goes to the heart of this paper is that the spirituality-versus-religion debate does not identify *how* we can speak about what deeply matters to us in ways that are respectful of *every* human being within the organization and in ways that enable us to collectively reclaim our humanity in organizational life.

In order to move beyond the spirituality-versus-religion debate, the task is not to promote a single spiritual framework but to create a structure and culture in which leaders and followers can respectfully negotiate religious and spiritual diversity (Hicks, 2002). In the next section we identify one such structure that enables respectful negotiation of differences while also identifying our common concern with meaning.

The Holistic Development Model

Appreciative Inquiry says that language is fateful, and that our speaking creates our future. Therefore a first step is to become conscious about the words we use, the questions we pose, the stories we tell, and the models we use to frame the discourse we are in the process of creating. A strong model has real value in an emerging discourse. Good models bring structure and order to new ideas. They are part of the way a new discourse is framed. They express the relationship that the parts have with each other and therefore how things connect, and they put things in right relation to each other. Good models simplify while retaining profound content and unique individual expression. They make that which lies below the surface visible in a way that it can become part of everyday conversation and decision-making. They endure over time and provide consistent value in myriad contexts. We have enjoyed working with one such model over the past ten years (Figure 39.1).

The Holistic Development Model, and the way we work with it, address some important underlying concerns in the religion-versus-spirituality

Examples of diversity in language used to describe similar subthemes
Working Together
"Stimulation from others"; "overcoming shared obstacles"; "team"; "fun"; "mutually motivating"; "feeling 'in kilter'".
Sharing Values
"Recognising – he also thinks that's important"; "shared conversations about values"; "deeper conversation"; "not having to justify everything because there is a common understanding of our values"; "making our values visible in deciding"
Belonging
"warmth"; "being part of"; "being at home among"; "acceptance".

Examples of diversity in world-views (spiritual, religious and agnostic) standing alongside each other in Inspiration
"Io", "God", "Allah", "The world is: all that there is – Buddha"
"My will – God's will"
"Being one with the Divine"
"So deep, so complex, so meaningful, infinite"
"The mystery at the heart of everything"
"Seeking guidance, being open"
"Painting a picture of what is possible"
"Facing what needs to be done and just starting"
"Being with all that is created, mates, nature, beauty"
"My family"

Expressing Profound Knowledge about the nature of being human
E.g. for "Developing and Becoming Self"
I am the source of my being and becoming
Life is my teacher
The glory of God in a person fully alive
To be ready to fulfill my role here
Be the change you want to see in the world
Being a free spirit at my best
(participants did this for each of the elements of the model.)

Making both meaningfulness and meaninglessness in the work-context visible
Creating: "I can still be surprised by what is coming out of my hands, this is highly rewarding" but also "We used to be able to freely offer creative insights and practices. These are now seen as distractions and we self-censure".
Achieving: "When something comes out of my hands that I know to be good, it is a great feeling" but also "It seems we have ground to a halt through all this bureaucracy. I do my work, go through the motions, but no longer have a sense of achievement"
Influencing: "In this role I can actively shape the organization" but also "We had a problem with the new policy, I tried to address it, but my manager blocked all attempts".

Examples of facing Reality
"There is nothing wrong with all of this mission and vision and values stuff itself. However if we are not allowed to articulate where we do not and cannot live up to this, it feels as if we mock something that is really quite profound".
"On the one hand we had these wonderful leadership programs in which we were encouraged to identify our values and live by them. On the other hand, if there was a price increase, no-one would ask how this would affect our poorest customers".

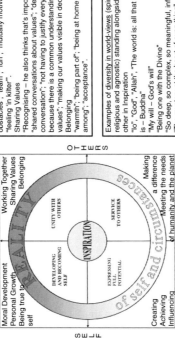

Figure 39.1 Holistic development model ©

debate and put in place some important conditions that help us to have inclusive and respectful conversations about deeper work meanings.

Resonating with profound knowing and the need for participative process

Before we start working with the model in any context, we ask individuals about what they already believe or know about each of its elements and invite them to add additional beliefs that are important to them but do not fit anywhere specifically in the model. Each time we do this, we are struck by the depth of participants' existing knowledge (see top left box in the figure) and their eloquence in expressing this knowledge. Similarly, when participants move around the room and read each other's contributions, they are moved when they recognize their own truth in what others have written as well as the rich diversity of being human. The process encourages a different level of relationship because participants see each other as fellow searchers for meaning.

Experiencing meaningfulness, according to Frankl, is a vital necessity for human well-being but it must be discovered by the individual, not received from superiors. Finding meaning requires effort. Frankl (1959) writes, "At present, instincts do not tell man what he has to do, nor do traditions direct him towards what he ought to do; soon he will not even know what he really wants to do and will be led by what other people want him to do, thus completely succumbing to conformism." The mark of true meaningfulness, therefore, is that it is based on personal discovery and free choice rather than prescription and domination.

The model, and the way we work with it, clearly shows that human beings are already fully engaged with meaningfulness. We consistently find that all participants seek to live meaningfully and are distressed when meaning is lost or absent. It can therefore not be assumed that someone in a position of power knows more about meaningful living than, for example, someone in the warehouse with strong faith and culture who has fostered four children. We argue that it is therefore not the job of the leader, the boss, or anyone else to prescribe meaningfulness, but rather to work with processes that allow for such profound meaning to be articulated by the whole organization/group. The model and the process we use is respectful of the profound knowing of everyone within the organization and makes worldviews visible in a manner that each person can stand side by side in equal humanity.

Addressing universal purposes as well as the diverse worldviews

The model emerged from asking individuals to tell the stories of their working lives and to identify when their deeper work-meanings and their work were and were not aligned. The initial findings were tested through action research on a further diverse sample of 240 participants. Four purposes emerged in all the stories. These are "developing and becoming self," "unity with others," "expressing full potential," and "service to others" (see Holistic Development Model in the middle of the figure). Identifying common purposes has proved to be very helpful in a conversation that can be nebulous or incoherent. It provides the basis for shared meaning and hence purposeful collective action that (because it is intimately linked to personal meaning and language) also engages the hearts of each individual. On the basis of these deep meanings, which have now been made visible, the group decides what to do and stop doing to create more meaningful work. Thus a beautiful balance between inquiry (not dogma) and action is achieved that can naturally go through many cycles of learning.

While common purposes are identified, the model and the way we work with it make it immediately obvious that when we move from the abstract to the concrete, people's underlying worldviews (see left bottom box) and use of language (left top box) are very diverse. Making worldviews visible assists participants in not assuming that all people have the same worldviews that they have, but it also allows them to see that every human being does draw her or his inspiration from somewhere. This makes it easier to have conversations about the differences and similarities of sources of inspiration without making others wrong. This assists us in learning to be skillful in holding peacefully to our views, remaining open to the possibility of change, staying constructive in the midst of clashing worldviews and creating space for those who do not wish to participate in conversations involving spirituality or religion.

At the same time, when individuals can use their own language under "inspiration" it enables those who believe in the transcendent to keep the sacred and mystical visible. This is in contrast to the "inclusive spirituality" paradigm, which has a tendency to ignore the transcendent precisely because this is where differences occur, and hence its application to the workplace has become quite secularized. In such cases, the question arises as to how this in fact differs from other human-centered management techniques (Driscoll and Wiebe, 2007).

Next to worldviews there are also clear examples of differences in language used to describe the subthemes of each purpose. These words range from the deeply personal to language that is more acceptable in the public arena. It therefore allows individuals to consider how much they want to reveal of themselves in public situations that are not always safe. It also allows certain "allergies" to words to be put aside. For example, "I have an intense dislike for the word 'sacrifice'; I think [I'll] use 'helpfulness' instead."

Making meaningfulness as well as meaninglessness visible

As previously discussed, spirituality has been defined as everything that is superior to religion, and this does not properly address diversity. This way of juxtaposing spirituality with religion has also framed spirituality positively, in terms of what might be possible. However our search for meaning also expresses what we long for and currently do not experience (as could be seen from the quotes at the beginning of this paper). It is therefore important to work with a model that makes visible what is meaningless (for examples, see left bottom box). When, as has often happened with culture-management activities, those factors that cause meaninglessness in the first place cannot be articulated, everything that is positive and inspiring is perceived as unreal. When an employee is asked to pretend because she cannot express how her reality is different from the vision statement, for example, it breeds cynicism, which is alienating. Thus, while the individual is by nature deeply concerned about living by values, he has also learned to expect disappointments. As mentioned before, consciously living meaningful lives is hard to do. And hence we become quite skillful at identifying reasons not to have to engage with the harder questions. For employees it is very hard to take responsibility for meaningful living when the organization (or some individuals within it, or the self) silences conversations that identify where the ideal is not lived up to (which is of course a regular and natural occurrence). The model allows us to be present to the reality of our human experience while taking responsibility for the de-energizing, negative, or complaining conversations that often become a default in discussion about meaningfulness. Making reality present through the Holistic Development Model normalizes the fact that we often fall short of our ideals but keep going anyway, and we can do so more meaningfully when we are real.

The experience of meaninglessness can also come from not addressing the relationships among the different purposes. Conversations about what purpose one currently spends the most time in can again highlight diversity in an organization. One person might be at a stage of her career where she has a need to give service to others; another person might be at a stage of his career where he wants to discover and express his full potential. Neither is right nor wrong, but in making these differences clear we can identify that even when there is a common purpose (e.g., to serve the customer/others in the organization), employees might want to acquire different skills and have different roles. Our experience has also shown how one person can stop another from becoming more whole by, for example, having so much need to express the self that the other is forced into doing all the work that "service to others" or "unity with others" requires. Further, it highlights that, at times, whole groups in organizations lose the balance between self and other, or doing and being. For example, this occurs when whole groups of teachers or customer service representatives are close to burnout because they spend too much time on the other and too little time on the needs of the self, or when groups become fragmented when too much time is spent doing things for the customer and not enough on being together. In such cases, even though the nature of the work itself is deeply meaningful, the loss of balance causes meaninglessness. The model therefore supports internal wholeness as well as offering a way of protecting individuals and creating fairness and unity within the larger community.

Conclusion

We have presented the Holistic Development Model as a way to have a grounded discussion about spirituality in the workplace. The structure of this model creates a space that is safe enough for differences to be held and expressed without coercing anyone. At the same time it identifies common purposes and hence a method of uncovering existing connection and agreement while acknowledging the individual journey. While it meets many of the needs and requirements of those involved in the discourse on spirituality, it does not use the term. Instead of saying what "spirit"/"spirituality" is – or is not – it simply focuses on the human need for meaningful living. Meaning is what makes life worth living. It is vital and precious. The rise of "spirituality" as a term gaining acceptance and power in the workplace is a heartwarming and exciting possibility. For those of us passionately concerned about making the most of this opportunity to influence the workplace constructively, we need to ensure that the discourse and all that it means to us is created with thought as well as passion, concern for others as well as ourselves, with practical understanding as well as inspiration, with humor and intelligence as well as faith. We offer the Holistic Development Model as a robust and practical means to furthering this end.

Literature

Biberman, J. and Tischler, L. (eds) 2008. *Spirituality in Business, Theory, Practice and Future Directions*. New York: Palgrave Macmillan.

Biberman, J. and Whittey, M. 1997. "A Postmodern Spiritual Future for Work." *Journal of Organizational Change Management*, vol. 10, no.2, pp. 130–138.

Driscoll, C. and Wiebe, E. 2007. "Technical Spirituality at Work: Jacques Ellul on Workplace Spirituality." *Journal of Management Inquiry*, vol. 16, no. 4, pp. 333–348.

Frankl, V.E. 1959. *Man's Search for Meaning*. New York: Pocket Books.

Frankl, V.E. 1969. *The Will to Meaning*. New York: New American Library.

Giacalone, R.A. and Jurkiewicz, C. 2003. "Toward a Science of Workplace Spirituality" in R.A. Giacalone and C. Jurkiewicz (eds), *Handbook of Workplace Spirituality and Organizational Performance*, pp. 3–28. Armonk: M.E. Sharpe.

Hicks, D.A. 2002. "Spiritual and Religious Diversity in the Workplace, Implications for Leadership." *Leadership Quarterly*, vol. 13, no. 4, pp. 379–396.

Lips-Wiersma, M.S. 2003. "Making Conscious Choices in Doing Research on Workplace Spirituality." *Journal of Organizational Change Management*, vol. 16, no. 4, pp. 406–425.

Lips-Wiersma, M.S., Lund Dean, K., and Fornaciari, C.F. 2009. "Theorizing the Dark Side of the Workplace Spirituality Movement." *Journal of Management Inquiry, Online First*.

Lips-Wiersma, M.S. and Morris, L. 2009. "Discriminating between 'Meaningful Work' and 'the Management of Meaning'." *Journal of Business Ethics*, vol. 88, no. 3, pp. 491–511.

Mitroff, I.I. 2003. "Do not Promote Religion under the Guise of Spirituality." *Organization*, vol. 10, no. 2, pp. 375–382.

Neck, C.P., and Milliman, J.F. 1994. "Thought-Self-Leadership, Finding Spiritual Fulfillment in Organizational Life." *Journal of Managerial Psychology*, vol. 9, no. 6, pp. 9–16.

Tacey, D. 2003. *The Spirituality Revolution – The Emergence of Contemporary Spirituality*. Melbourne: Harper Collins.

Vaill, P.B. 1991. "The Inherent Spirituality of Organizations." Paper prepared for the Academy Of Management meeting, Miami Beach, FL (1991, August 3–7).

40
Multinational Companies and the Common Good

François Lépineux and Jean-Jacques Rosé

The common-good concept has been developed mainly in the context of Western philosophy since Plato and Aristotle, and within Christian theology since St Thomas Aquinas. The idea that the state is the guarantor of the common good at the national level has long prevailed; however, this view is increasingly questioned by the relentless advance of the globalization process, and by the emergence of global risks and threats of all kinds at the planetary level. Quite logically, multinational companies, owing to their huge economic power, to their capacity to influence and to the multiple consequences of their activities, are the focus of much interest among those who strive to devise new ways to serve the common good – and more precisely, the global common good.

From the common good to the global common good

The traditional conception of the common good as the supreme good of the community can be applied to a number of different levels: the family; the organization; the local community; all the intermediate social entities; the nation; and, in its largest extension, the totality of mankind. Could or should multinational companies, then, be concerned about the common good? And about which level of the common good should they primarily be concerned? This question has drawn special attention today, as it arises in the context of a profound societal change characterized by the globalization phenomenon and the spreading of information technology, whose combined effects are driving the world into a new era. With the spread of the global economy, national boundaries tend to become irrelevant for a number of corporations aiming at the world market; multinational companies have become leading players in contemporary society, and exert a great influence in shaping our conditions of life. If it is true that a small number of enlightened business leaders have started to integrate the common good in their corporate policies, it is also true that the combination of multinational companies' considerable power and of their ability to escape national laws represents a threat to the global common good.

That is why this essay will concentrate on the *planetary level* of the common good – that is, on the *global common good*, which can be characterized as *the supreme good of humanity as a whole*. Although very general in its essence, this concept can be approached through a variety of means, tangible and intangible; for example, peace among nations, scientific knowledge, philosophical works, artistic heritage, biodiversity, a healthy climate, the quality of life, and shared economic prosperity. All these elements represent as many conditions, aspects or partial expressions of the global common good, which exceeds and includes them in its universal perspective. In particular, following Riccardo Petrella (2000), it may be said that the global common *good* embraces two general categories of common *goods* (plural): those related to the means of *existence*, such as access to water, energy, and healthcare; and those which enable *coexistence* between all members of the world community, such as freedom of information, cultural diversity, or civil and political rights.

The thesis of Velasquez

In a thought-provoking article published in 1992, Velasquez has provided a stimulating basis for the discussion of the relationship between international business and the common good. Striving to determine whether or not companies that are operating in a competitive international environment have any obligations to contribute to the common good, he examined the problem in the light of the realist objection, which holds that in the case of non-repeated interactions without signaling mechanisms, and in the absence of a third-party authority that can enforce compliance with the principles of morality, individual agents – such as multinational companies – have no moral obligations on the international scale.

Velasquez (1992) derives from his analysis that it is not possible to make the claim that multinationals have a moral obligation to pursue the global common good, since if some multinationals decided to contribute to the common good in the highly competitive arena of globalization while others refused to act likewise, the former would put themselves at a significant disadvantage, and this decision would negatively impact their profits. The reasoning would be different, he argues, if interactions between multinational companies were repeated, and if signaling mechanisms did exist, so that each player could be informed of the other's intent to cooperate; in that case, the players would mutually enforce their cooperative agreements, and no third-party enforcer would be needed. But these conditions, he says, are not met.

In Velasquez's view, what is needed to change this "no-moral-obligation" situation is the establishment of an international authority capable of ensuring that all agents contribute to the global common good: this is, he suggests, the necessary and sufficient condition for moral obligations legitimately to be demanded from multinational corporations worldwide. However, there seem to be some weaknesses associated with his demonstration and with his conviction that a third-party enforcer would be powerful enough to drive all international business actors toward the global common good.

Theoretical counterarguments

In his paper, Velasquez (1992) insists that interactions between multinationals are not repeated and signaling mechanisms do not exist – hence the need for an international institution that can enforce compliance with the principles of morality. However, in the real world, multinational corporations *do have repeated dealings* with one another on the global scale; and in repeated interactions, each player is able to retaliate against another that fails to cooperate in such a dealing, so that the costs of noncooperation can make cooperation the most rational strategy for the rest of the game. In addition, *signaling mechanisms do exist that enable multinationals to express their willingness to cooperate,* notably through the channel of planetary networks, such as the Global Compact or the World Business Council for Sustainable Development, or through the endorsement of international declarations of principles such as, among many others, the OECD Guidelines for Multinational Enterprises.

In another respect, the international authority called for by Velasquez can only be created by states. But how can so many distinct governments agree to set up an international agency to regulate the supply and use of global common goods? Instead of supporting the establishment of a supranational entity devoted to this mission, it is more likely that many states will choose to free-ride, and that they will thwart the others' efforts to find durable collective solutions to transnational problems, pressing though they may be. The national interests involved are too remote from one another. Each country or group of countries (e.g., G7 or OECD countries, emerging countries, or less developed countries) is very likely to defend its own interests, as evidenced by the negotiations on the global warming issue at the Copenhagen summit. As a result, the creation of the agency might prove difficult.

But, let us suppose the problems stated above have been solved, and this international authority dedicated to the global common good exists, with a large number if not all nations involved in it. How can we be sure that this agency will effectively serve the global common good and not distort its original mission? Can we be sure that a global entity of that kind will never become either a petrified and crippling bureaucracy, or the tyrannical instrument of a dangerous ideology, instead of being effective and responsive to the critical problems of the time? Experience shows that corporations willing to keep doing business as usual are very efficient in protecting their vested interests, and that their lobbying efforts can be successful against laws designed to promote the common good.

Constraining regulations versus voluntary policies

Let us now assume this agency exists and effectively serves the global common good. How can we imagine that it will be able to force all multinationals to behave morally? In fact, an agency of that kind exists already in the form of the United Nations, which was created, among other reasons, to promote and maintain peace among nations; but over more than sixty years it has failed in many instances to put an end to international conflicts (though it has also been successful in some cases). Why should we then believe that the creation of a new supranational institution would drive all large economic actors suddenly to start to cooperate in a common search for the common good, as if by the wave of a magic wand? It is doubtful that it would ever be possible for any external authority to force all agents – whether individuals or corporations – to behave morally. On the contrary, human history and all spiritual traditions buttress the idea that the only authority that can surely drive an individual to respect moral rules – including those beyond the scope of laws – is an internal authority: his/her conscience, his/her *inner voice*.

The pursuit of the common good is not only a matter of abiding by current laws; it essentially relies on a *personal attitude, a voluntary commitment and a freely chosen ethics*. Therefore, there are good reasons to believe that an important motivation that would lead multinationals to seek the global common good is the rising awareness of corporate leaders and managers, in tandem with the hypothetical constraints imposed by a third-party; these two motivations, the internal and the external, are complementary. It is certainly not absurd to consider that multinational companies can – and should – *voluntarily* contribute to the global common good, even if consumers, stakeholders, and civil society exert mounting pressures on them to act likewise.

Many examples can be observed of wise corporate leaders, who pay attention to the demands of their multiple stakeholders, and who behave in ways that further the common good. The fast development of the corporate social responsibility (CSR) movement since the mid-1990s, illustrated by the mushrooming of business-led networks such as Business for Social Responsibility (BSR) in the US, or CSR Europe in the EU, arguably supports this assumption; and in the financial arena, the socially responsible investment (SRI) trend is also gaining momentum worldwide, as exemplified by the launch of the Principles for Responsible Investment (PRI) by Kofi Annan in April 2006.

This does not mean, however, that new global institutions are not needed. International law and supranational organizations are necessary to enforce rules for the global economy – a statement already made by Peter Drucker in 1997. It is the mission of governments and entities such as the newly formed G20 to establish rules that will improve the course of globalization, and notably to set higher standards in the social and environmental areas. The safeguard of nature and the fight against poverty are *also matters of political will and courage.* Governments have proved their ability to regulate business in the interest of the common good on a national basis through legislations regarding worker safety, child labor, toxic waste, and affirmative action programs. States should now negotiate appropriate international agreements and enforce compliance with the new regulations; obviously, more constraining laws in the social and environmental fields would help alleviate the negative side effects of globalization and improve the condition of the *"bottom billion."*

Multinationals and the global common good are interdependent

Besides, other determinants are likely to drive multinational companies to take the global common good into account. For instance, it is clearly in the interest of corporations to respond to society's expectations in a *proactive way,* before new, constraining regulations are imposed on their actions. More importantly, corporations – and, in particular, multinational companies – exist and flourish thanks to a legal and institutional system that ensures ownership rights and the security of business transactions. The market mechanism itself is an institutional arrangement agreed upon by society in the name of the public interest; the very possibility for corporations to pursue their private good originates in the concern for society's common good. Therefore, *it can be said that multinationals bear a responsibility to support and promote the global common good, since this is a condition of their perpetuation.*

This statement is also obvious when it comes to the environmental degradation of the Earth; the biosphere, which is the physical basis of life, is deteriorating at a rapid pace. In particular, *global warming is a growing cause of concern;* it has many effects, including the melting of glaciers and polar ice caps, the reduction of ocean salinity, animal species losing their habitats, and an increasing number of people trying to cope with the rise of the sea level. For more than twenty years already, scientists from all around the world have worked together within the Intergovernmental Panel on Climate Change, and have reached a consensus: *climate change is a reality and it is caused by human activities.* The question is not anymore about the *existence* of global warming but about its *magnitude:* by the end of the twenty-first century, will the average temperature at the surface of the Earth have risen by 2°C, 4°C, or 6°C?

Desertification; deforestation; the depletion of natural resources; the pollution of soil, atmosphere, water, etc., are other facets of the environmental devastation. *Biodiversity is vanishing:* the "Millennium Ecosystem Assessment," a major UN report released in March 2005, has confirmed that 60 percent of the world's ecosystems are degraded by a variety of causes. The economic activities of man have already caused irreparable damage to the Earth; *in many respects, thresholds of irreversibility have been crossed.* Ecologically harmful activities, far from being reduced, are still increasing; as a result, the negative ecological impact can only worsen in proportion. *What is at stake today is nothing less than the very possibility for future generations to live on this planet in the long run.* The only way to solve environmental plagues is to change our energy-intensive way of life into an *environmentally friendly lifestyle;* in this regard, both consumers and multinationals have a great role to play.

The construction of a global social contract

Multinational companies can – and should – also promote and support the global common good by reducing extreme poverty, since globalization has entailed the rise of social inequalities to unprecedented levels, aggravating the divide between the richest countries and the less developed ones that are unable to join the movement, and widening the income disparities in almost every nation (Bauman, 1998). *The gap between the North and the South continues to widen:* of a global population of more than 6 billion people, approximately one-fifth, or 1.3 billion, live on less than $1 per day, and nearly half live on less than $2 per day. This means that in spite of decades of economic development, prosperity has not filtered down to the poorest, and that a situation of "economic apartheid" (Mofid, 2003) is prevailing both among and within countries. These figures show that the invisible hand *does not* ensure an efficient allocation of available resources, the successful matching of supply and demand, and the optimal functioning of markets. Consequently, *the attainment of the common good is far from being automatic,* and globalization cannot but induce a reflection on the responsibility of large business actors in this regard.

The TINA doctrine, according to which "There Is No Alternative" to the continuation of business as usual, is increasingly challenged by the constellation of civil society movements that have been expressing contrary views since the Seattle meeting of the World Trade Organization in 1999. Moreover, detractors of global capitalism argue that its extension *undermines cultural diversity by eroding local cultures,* which are important components of the global common good. The alignment of lifestyles on the Western standard generates a threat to cultural identities. Globalization conveys a danger of uniformity: Georg Ritzer (1996) uses the word *"McDonaldization"* to point to the homogenization of society throughout the world. Alter-globalists underline that the goods and services we buy or use, from cars and computers to water and medicines, are more and more provided or controlled by a small number of corporations, thereby endangering democracy. A world in which materialism and selfishness have replaced real human ends such as self-realization and the pursuit of happiness, they say, is not desirable.

But numerous issues now call for global solutions, and the extent to which any state can act independently is diminishing; new forms of global governance are yet to be developed. The reality of the global village questions the significance of national boundaries; as globalization entails the moving up to the universal level, *a new social contract is under construction on a worldwide scale.* In order to be more effective, *the provision of global common goods requires the cooperation of various actors in the spheres of government, business, and civil society* (Kaul, Grunberg, and Stern, 1999). Pioneering multinationals and not-for-profit organizations (social sector and government) are already developing partnerships to that end, and such collaborations often provide fruitful outcomes for all the parties.

Of these multi-stakeholder cooperative schemes, many could be mentioned but we have selected two:

- The United Nations Global Compact – now the world's largest corporate citizenship and sustainability initiative, with over 8,000 participants (including businesses and other organizations) in 130 countries around the world – with a special reference to the Globally Responsible Leadership Initiative that has been developed within it;
- The Fair Labor Association, which brings together constituent groups such as universities, civil society organizations – including local NGOs and trade unions – and corporations (Adidas, Asics, Knights Apparel, Nike, Patagonia, Puma, etc.), and whose mission is to improve working conditions in factories around the world.

Literature

Bauman, Z. 1998. *Globalization – The Human Consequences*. London: Polity Press and Blackwell Publishers.

De Bettignies, H.-C. and Lépineux, F. (eds) 2009. *Business, Globalization and the Common Good*. Oxford: Peter Lang Academic Publishers.

De Bettignies, H.-C. and Lépineux, F. 2009. "Can Multinational Corporations Afford to Ignore the Global Common Good?" *Business and Society Review,* vol. 114, no. 2, pp. 153–182.

Drucker, P. 1997. "The Global Economy and the Nation-State." *Foreign Affairs,* vol. 76, no. 5, pp. 159–171.

Kaul, I., Grunberg, I., and Stern, M. (eds) 1999. *Global Public Goods: International Cooperation in the Twenty-First Century*. Oxford: Oxford University Press.

Mofid, K. 2003. *Globalization for the Common Good*. London: Shepheard-Walwyn.

Petrella, R. 2000. *Le bien commun : éloge de la solidarité*. Brussels: Labor.

Ritzer, G. 1996. *The McDonaldization of Society*. Thousand Oaks, CA: Pine Forge.

Velasquez, M. 1992. "International Business, Morality, and the Common Good." *Business Ethics Quarterly,* vol. 2, no. 1, pp. 27–40.

41
Corporate Conscience
Kenneth E. Goodpaster

Institution-building is one primary form of humankind's sharing in the continuing work of a Creator; it is a kind of "co-creation." But each institution must – in its own way – advance human dignity and the common good. Thus we are called not only to build institutions, but to impart moral sensibilities to the institutional "work of our hands."

The idea that corporations or other institutional forms might have "consciences" – analogous to the consciences of individual persons – is an idea that has been explored at length in the literature of corporate ethics (Goodpaster and Matthews, 1982; Goodpaster, 2007). I have myself been one of its principal exponents, despite skepticism from certain quarters about the implications of such a view for individual responsibility in the corporation.

In his classic *Leadership in Administration,* Philip Selznick (1957) describes institutional *character,* drawing upon an analogy between individual personality and organizational development:

> The study of institutions is in some ways comparable to the clinical study of personality. It requires a genetic and developmental approach, an emphasis on historical origins and growth stages. There is a need to see the enterprise as a whole and to see how it is transformed as new ways of dealing with a changing environment evolve.

This idea – that organizations are in many ways macro-versions (projections) of us as individuals – is as old as Plato's *Republic.* The general principle at stake is not only about the descriptive *meaningfulness* of corporate moral attributes, but also about the *normative* responsibility of leaders to give shape to corporate conscience. Indeed, this responsibility is called for by what we might call the *co-creative imperative*.

Moral projection principle

It is appropriate not only to describe organizations and their characteristics by analogy with individuals; it is also appropriate normatively to look for and to foster moral attributes in organizations by analogy with those we look for and foster in individuals (Goodpaster, 1997a, p. 432). Harvard's Lynn Paine refers to this transfer of attribution as the "moralization" of the corporation: "Through this process…companies have come to be regarded, at least implicitly, as moral actors in their own right. As such, they are presumed to have not only technical functions, such as producing goods or generating profits, but also moral attributes, such as responsibilities, aims, values, and commitments" (Lynn Paine, 2003, p. 98).

Exploring the analogical predication of human traits to institutions need not entail careless anthropomorphism. The study of business has been enriched by exploring the parallels between individual psychology and the attributes of organizations. Lawrence and Dyer (1983, pp. 262–263) make this point persuasively in their classic *Renewing American Industry*:

> In talking about organizations as learning systems we do not mean to suggest that they have human properties. Organizations do not think, do not learn in a literal sense. Only people do. It is true, however, that members of an organization can not only learn as individuals but can transmit their learning to others, can codify it and embody it in the standard procedures of the organization. In this limited sense, the organization can be said to learn.

The unified cultural norms that guide the decision-making of organizations or institutions are intelligible independently of the consciences of the individuals who participate in the corporation as employees – even if those individuals are essential (and they are) for the realization of the unified culture of the corporation. As Lynn Paine (2003, p. 145) put it:

> A company, as a moral actor in society, has commitments, values, and responsibilities, such as duties to its lenders or contractual obligations to its customers that are distinct from those of its individual

members. These corporate responsibilities survive even when a company's individual members and agents change.

Institutional leadership

There are three "practical imperatives" that anchor the moral agenda of institutional leadership: orientating, institutionalizing, and sustaining shared values. The first two involve placing moral considerations in a position of salience and authority alongside considerations of profitability or strategy in the institution's mindset. The third imperative (sustenance) has to do with passing on the spirit of this effort in two directions: to future leaders of the organization, and to the wider network of organizations and institutions that make up the social system as a whole (Figure 41.1).

Leaders who seek to orientate, institutionalize, and sustain ethical values in their organizations – to be architects of institutional conscience – often employ mission statements, codes of conduct, ethics officers, executive development seminars, incentive and reward systems, recruitment and promotion practices, employee training programs, and various other forms of communication. As with individuals, organizational character formation can lead to a fundamental revision of an organization's understanding of *success*. Leaders must inevitably confront Charles Handy's fundamental question: "Whom and what is a business for?" And his answer fits well with these reflections on co-creation (Handy, 2002):

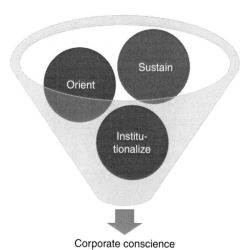

Figure 41.1   Imperatives of institutional leadership

The purpose of a business...is not to make a profit, full stop. It is to make a profit so that the business can do something more or better. That "something" becomes the real justification for the business.

That "something" must in the end contribute to the unfolding of a spiritual design in creation as communicated through what philosophers have called the natural law. The task of the institutional leader is to provide a *memory* function that is rooted in the *ultimate* mission and purpose of every institution – to appreciate human dignity and to advance the common good.

Institutional leadership, then, is an extraordinary vocation rooted in co-creation, whether or not the leader herself or himself embraces this spiritual interpretation. But as we know, the history of organizations is too often *not* a history of cooperation with God's plan. Why is this and what are its implications? We might recall what theologian Michael Novak wrote 30 years ago: "Whether to treat big corporations as potential vessels of Christian vocation or to criticize them for their inevitable sins, Christian theology must advance much further than it has in understanding exactly and fairly every aspect of corporate life" (Novak, 1981).

The failure of institutional leadership

Over the last half century, we have seen organizations manifest dysfunctional behavior from Watergate to Wall Street – and from the career crashes of inside-traders like Ivan Boesky to literal crashes, such as those of NASA's space shuttles *Challenger* and *Columbia*. We have seen some of the most reputable names in American business implicated in questionable behavior: General Electric, Sears, H.J. Heinz, Prudential Insurance, Microsoft, Enron, Arthur Andersen, WorldCom, Lehman Brothers, and the list goes on to include companies in Europe and Asia as well.

I have elsewhere labeled the mindset that lies behind this kind of behavior *teleopathy – the unbalanced pursuit of goals and objectives –* and I have identified its symptoms as fixation, rationalization, and detachment (Goodpaster, 1997b, 2007). The organizational manifestation of teleopathy is illustrated nicely in a story from poet David Whyte's book *The Heart Aroused*. Whyte attributes the story to a friend of his named Joel Henning:

> The idea, issuing from the boardroom, was to offer tempting prizes and outlandish financial rewards to the one department in the

company that could achieve the highest level of growth over the following financial year. Before long it became evident that one particular department had it completely sewn up, and Jim Harrison, the vice president in charge of that area, was the hero of the occasion. By the end of the following financial year his department had doubled its income; no one else came even close to the seductive figures appearing on his reports to the president. Harrison was sent back and forth across the country to give speeches and talks at all the company plants. The toast of the company, by the middle of the following year he had been disgraced and fired. ... The success of Jim Harrison was based on the neglect of every constituent part of the system except the one order programmed from above to improve profitability. Rather than being educated into the broad needs of the business, he was manipulated to produce one result at all costs. In his turn he reflected back to upper management an almost Biblical parable of their own narrow vision. Achieve this, his department had dropped all its education and training programs, stopped all new hiring, cut its research and development to the bone, and instilled the chill atmosphere of a police state onto the office floor. In the second year Harrison's department lost money at a greater rate than any other department. His people were leaving in droves despite the glittering prizes of the previous year, he had trained no one to replace them, and there were no new products appearing on the horizon for them to sell. (Whyte, 1994, pp. 270–271)

This story indicates how business life, like political life, can foster a culture in which destructive behavior is actually *incentivized*. We could add scores of similar stories based on well-researched case studies of business organizations. Enron was fixated on hiding balance-sheet debt. Arthur Andersen was fixated on maintaining lucrative consulting clients. NASA was fixated on its launch schedule, possibly compromising safety. Mortgage bankers were fixated on short-term subprime lending incentives.

What Michael Novak might call the *sins of corporations* seem to have at their root something that spiritually is at the root of the sins of individual persons as well: the fashioning of golden calves out of misplaced devotion, the substitution of inferior gods for a genuine Higher Power. And when some managers discover that their idolatrous pursuits do not deliver the Promised Land, instead of saying "We will settle for less!" – they are apt to say "Let's try that again, just in case it will work the next time!" And the repetition becomes habit-forming.

It holds out the fraudulent promise of extracting the infinite from the iteration of the finite – fulfillment from the accumulation of the insufficient. But it always ends with the melancholy meditation: "Is that all there is?"

Is there a way to reduce the sins of leaders and the sins of corporations; a way to recover our co-creative compass in a culture of counterfeit measures of success? Jim Loehr and Tony Schwartz (2001) offer an insightful path:

> The inclination for busy executives is to live in a perpetual state of triage, doing whatever seems most immediately pressing, while losing sight of any bigger picture. Rituals that give people the opportunity to pause and look inside include *meditation, journal writing, prayer,* and *service to others.* Each of these activities can also serve as a source of recovery – a way to break *the linearity of relentless goal-oriented activity.*

These considerations suggest two prescriptions for organizational leaders – the architects of corporate conscience and culture – prescriptions that are straightforward, but challenging: (1) help your organization to be mindful of tendencies toward *fixation,* misplaced *organizational* cravings based on illusory measures of success; and (2) encourage employees to avoid *rationalization* and *detachment,* to be *aware* of gaps between the ethical talk and the ethical walk – and reward them for finding ways to narrow such gaps.

Conclusion

The widely quoted article, "The Parable of the Sadhu" (McCoy, 1983), describes a Wall Street executive who lost his sense of humanity on a Himalayan mountain-climbing expedition. He left a holy man, a sadhu, to die on the slope. Later he lamented, "Why were we so reluctant to try the lower path, the ambiguous trail? Perhaps because we did not have a leader who could reveal the greater purpose of the trip to us."

This essay has explored the natural institution-building tendencies in the human spirit as a response to a co-creative vocation. And just as our creation as persons is at once ontological and moral – so too, our co-creation of institutions must confer both social reality and corporate conscience. Our institution-building must maintain a line of sight to a larger plan. We must seek leaders who can reveal to their organizations "the greater purpose of the trip."

Literature

Goodpaster, K. and Matthews, J. 1982. "Can a Corporation Have a Conscience?" *Harvard Business Review*, May-June 1982.

Goodpaster, K. 1997a. "Moral Projection." In P.L. Werhane and R.E. Freeman (eds), *Blackwell's Encyclopedic Dictionary of Business Ethics*. Oxford: Blackwell Publishers.

Goodpaster, K. 1997b. "Teleopathy." In P.L. Werhane and R.E. Freeman (eds), *Blackwell's Encyclopedic Dictionary of Business Ethics*. Oxford: Blackwell Publishers.

Goodpaster, K. 2007. *Conscience and Corporate Culture*. Malden, MA and Oxford, UK: Wiley-Blackwell.

Handy, Ch. 2002. "What's a Business For?" *Harvard Business Review*, December 2002.

Lawrence, P. R. and Dyer, D. 1983. *Renewing American Industry*. New York: The Free Press.

Loehr, J. and Schwartz, T. 2001. "The Making of a Corporate Athlete." *Harvard Business Review*, January 2001.

Lynn Paine, S. 2003. *Value Shift*. New York: McGraw-Hill.

McCoy, B. 1983. "The Parable of the Sadhu." *Harvard Business Review*, No. 5 (September–October).

Novak, M. 1981. *Toward a Theology of the Corporation*. Washington, DC: American Enterprise Institute.

Selznick, P. 1957. *Leadership in Administration*. p. 141. New York: Harper & Row.

Whyte, D. 1994. *The Heart Aroused: Poetry and the Preservation of the Soul in Corporate America*. New York: Doubleday.

Part V

Good Practices and Working Models

42
The New Role of Business in Society

Olivier F. Williams

What is the role of business in society? This essay argues that we are in the midst of a major paradigm shift in our understanding of the purpose of business and that this new understanding holds much promise for business being a significant force for peace in our world. Examples of what companies are doing and why they are doing it will be provided. What we are seeing is the emergence of a view of the firm as a socially responsible political actor in the global economy and as an institution that can generate not only material wealth but also wealth that nourishes the full range of human needs, or what some call spiritual capital (Williams, 2008).

Neoclassical economics asserted a strict division of labor between the private and public sectors. Governments are charged with providing public goods and dealing with the challenges of social justice, while collecting taxes to pay for these services. If the people are not pleased with the way elected politicians establish priorities and mediate interests, they can vote them out of office. Business, on the other hand, has another task: to produce goods and services at a reasonable price while returning on investment. Business has made tremendous progress not only in the quantity of goods and services available to the public, but also in the public's quality of life. Technology that enables us to enjoy good music, medicines that increase life expectancy and decrease infant mortality, and machinery that humanizes work are only a few of the fruits of capitalism.

The strict division of labor between the private and public sectors is no longer a reality in our time. Under the rubric of corporate social responsibility (CSR), corporate citizenship, or sustainability, companies are taking increasing responsibility for problems in the wider society. At least in practice, there is clearly a change in progress in the way the responsibilities of the private and public sectors are apportioned. Religious social thought has long championed a wider role for business than simply making profit. Catholic social thought expresses this well in the 1991 encyclical of Pope John Paul II, *Centesimus Annus*. A central thesis of this document is that the purpose of business is not simply to make a profit; but rather, that business is a community of persons and that this community can foster development of society as well as people (Pope John Paul II, 1991).

Perhaps the biggest driver of this enlarged role for business in society is the changing expectations of consumers. A May 1999 poll by Globe Scan revealed that two out of three respondents wanted companies to go beyond their traditional economic goals (provide jobs, create wealth, pay taxes, and obey laws) and to help solve some of the problems in the wider society. Called the *Millennium Poll on Corporate Social Responsibility* and based on 25,000 interviews, the poll reported that one in five consumers claimed to reward or punish companies based on their perception of the companies' social performance (Globe Scan 1999). In contemporary business literature, the term "license to operate" is often used to convey the idea that meeting society's expectations is part of the implicit social contract between business and society. Failing to meet society's expectations can result in tough regulation; for example, the Sarbanes-Oxley law, or loss of discretionary power. This may explain why many companies have become proactive in meeting society's expectations; some, for example, by collaborating with NGOs in designing and implementing ethical norms for the global community. Companies, either alone or partnering with NGOs, have taken on numerous projects to assist the poor around the globe.

One of the reasons consumers expect so much of business today is that it has been so successful. Business has been hugely successful in producing goods and services that consumers want, and it has therefore accrued vast economic power. Large businesses, because of their success, dominate our world. For example, General Electric has sales of over $100 billion a year and has over 300,000 employees; IBM has sales of over $80 billion and some 300,000 employees. Of the over 190 nations in the world, very few have government revenues that approach large multinational business revenues. Many argue that business, with its wide array of resources, especially management skills, is uniquely positioned to solve some of the problems of the wider society.

What the companies are saying about their new role

Most companies argue that CSR, corporate citizenship, or sustainability, whichever term they choose to use, is in the interests of business but that participation in these projects is not based solely on a traditional business case. In a 2008 special report in *The Economist*, several business leaders are quoted. Ed Potter of Coca-Cola speaks of a "broad philosophical commitment to sustainable communities." Edward Bickham of Anglo American suggests that "sustainability is a threshold requirement with any competitive gain staying at the margins." Dr. Gail Kendall of CLP Group speaks of the retrofitting of power stations to reduce emissions as having nothing to do with competition in the market: "It is our shareholders and regulators expectations that this is a correct thing to do in the community ... We see it as the right thing to do." Jeffrey Immelt, CEO of GE, in discussing some of the company's projects throughout the world, commented, "The reason people come to work for GE is that they want to be about something that is bigger than themselves. People want to work hard, they want to get promoted, they want stock options. But they also want to work for a company that makes a difference, a company that's doing great things in the world" (Gunther, 2004). Building community and doing great things in the world are goals that flow from the identity and culture of a business; they are intrinsic objectives.

What we are experiencing, under the influence of the wider society, is a broadening of the values of many business people and, hence, a broadening of the values of capitalism. To be sure, this phenomenon is not present in all business, but a growing number of business people want to make a difference. They are asking about ultimate purpose, about what most deeply matters in life, and they want to chart a life plan that draws on the full range of resources of the human spirit. This new focus is what many describe as a focus on spiritual values. From this standpoint, sustainability reflects the connectedness of business with the wider society. Business must not take responsibility for its own activities only but also for some of the problems in the wider society. This wider vision of companies – the belief that doing well and doing good are not opposites – is championed by many management scholars. In *Built to Last*, Jerry Porras and James Collins discuss a number of these "visionary companies" (Collins and Porras, 1994). For example, Merck Pharmaceutical Company has a mission statement which includes that the company "devotes extensive efforts to increase access to medicines through far-reaching programs that not only donate Merck medicines, but also help deliver them to the people who need them." Merck's employees feel good about their company and this has reportedly enhanced productivity and decreased turnover of employees (Merck).

The UN Global Compact

One new initiative to promote and enhance peaceful societies is the United Nations Global Compact. Founded in 2000 by the then Secretary General of the UN, Kofi Annan, the Global Compact is intended to increase and diffuse the benefits of global economic development through voluntary corporate policies and programs. By promoting human rights and labor rights, enhancing care for the environment and encouraging anticorruption measures, the ten principles of the Global Compact are designed to enable more peaceful societies. Initially comprising several dozen companies, the Compact as of 2010 had enlisted over 5,000 businesses and 1,000 NGOs in 135 countries. The objective is to emphasize the moral purpose of business, with member companies setting a high moral tone throughout the world. Ban Ki-Moon, Secretary General of the UN in 2007, expressed the mission well: "Business practices rooted in universal values can bring social and economic gains" (Global Compact, 2010).

The mission of the Global Compact is to foster the growth of humane values in the global society. The underlying insight is that without the values embedded in the Compact – for example, trust, fairness, integrity, and respect for people – global capitalism would eventually lose legitimacy in the wider society. There is much evidence from surveys that people are increasingly losing trust in business. Public trust in business institutions and leadership is at a low level. For example, a survey released in 2009 by the Edelman firm reported that globally only 29 percent trust information about a business provided by the CEO. In the United States only 38 percent trust business to do the right thing (Edelman, 2009). As people come to trust business less and to judge that trusting the behavior of business is risky, there is more pressure for stronger organizational control systems, that is, rules, regulations, and laws. When people perceive that business is not only seeking its private good but also the common good, and that this is embodied in a mission statement and a widened purpose and activity, there is a slow retrieval of trust in business. This retrieval of trust is manifest in the response to some of the endeavors of signatory companies of the Global Compact. Some examples of this may be helpful.

General Electric and Africa

In 2004, General Electric announced a $20 million program to upgrade hospitals in rural Africa. The company had already determined it would not be profitable to operate in these very poor regions of sub-Saharan

Africa but felt that this endeavor could improve the lives of not only rural Africans, but also its own employees throughout the world. The goal was to reduce infant-mortality rates, provide clean water and better access to medical care, as well as to supply energy. Initially piloted in Ghana, GE teamed up with UN Millennium Village Project and expanded its reach to clinics in Sauri, Kenya; Mayange, Rwanda; Potou, Senegal; and Mwandama, Malawi. The company provided not only equipment, but, perhaps more importantly, management skills, so that the indigenous people could be a part of the project, taking ownership and improving the clinics and hospitals. The GE program in Africa has been cited as a good example of how to aid a developing country. Employees of GE are proud to be part of this program (Greenhut and Corcoran, 2008).

Novartis and needs-orientated projects

As both an academic and a business leader, Klaus M. Leisinger has unique qualifications to articulate an insightful position on the changing role of business in society. As the president and CEO of the Novartis Foundation for Sustainable Development, Leisinger notes that there are two quite different strategies that can guide the structuring of corporate philanthropy. One strategy focuses on the poorest of the poor: the needs-orientated strategy. The other focuses on the "upper-middle-class" poor and is designed to create new customers eventually and thus is good for the shareholder in the medium to long term. Leisinger points out that Novartis opts for the needs-orientated approach, not because it will produce future markets, but because it is the right thing to do. It is based on the conviction of senior officers of the company that being a sustainable company, a good corporate citizen, means that they should help those in dire poverty if they can. Novartis has a whole range of programs, from curing millions of leprosy patients, providing better seeds and promoting more effective agricultural practices in sub-Saharan Africa, to educating rural poor on how to keep healthy and prevent disease. Novartis' leaders, following their company values and vision, have taken measures to try to solve some of the world's problems (Leisinger, 2008).

IBM and the common good

IBM starts from the premise that the company will only be successful if the communities where it operates are successful as well. The definition of "success" for IBM, as demonstrated by its philanthropic contributions and employee volunteer-service hours, includes much more than financial donations. IBM includes "sweat equity," enhancing human development through projects that foster a virtuous citizenry. Passing on management skills, better literacy tools for children and adults, and expansion of efforts to improve the teaching of maths and science are just a few of the IBM efforts. IBM employees give over 3.5 million hours of volunteer service each year and the company's annual contribution budget is more than $150 million. All these efforts flow from the company's mission statement and core values, which provide a vision to deliver sustainable value to customers, employees, and investors as well as communities. This vision is summarized well in a 1969 statement of IBM's then CEO, Tom Watson, Jr.: "We accept our responsibilities as a corporate citizen in community, national, and world affairs; we serve our interests best when we serve the public interest. We acknowledge our obligation as a business institution to help improve the society we are part of" (Litow, 2008).

The future challenge and the promise

To be sure, the paradigm shift highlighted in the opening paragraph of this article – the expansion of the role of business to include business as a quasi-political actor helping to shape a more peaceful world – is a work in progress. Much remains to be done! Reviewing the news headlines of any given week provides much evidence that spiritual values are not the dominant values of many business leaders today. Whether it is the catastrophic oil spill in the Gulf of Mexico caused when BP cut costs on safety, or the terrible crisis of 2008 and beyond when greed eroded any semblance of an ethical culture in the financial world, there is much evidence that business as an institution has a long way to go in realizing spiritual values.

Reflecting the dignity of the person created by God, religious social thought attempts to develop a framework for realizing spiritual values in business and suggests several norms to guide a company. These norms include the following: the need for community in a business; the embracement of fair treatment, lack of discrimination and encouragement of diversity; the formation of channels for employee association and participation; the focus on the connectedness of all stakeholders, solidarity; and the development of an attitude of stewardship toward the physical environment.

In order to outline the direction of future developments required to realize spiritual values in business, it may be helpful to reflect briefly on three of these norms: the need for community in business; the focus on the connectedness of all stakeholders, solidarity; and the imperative to develop an attitude of stewardship toward the physical environment.

Community: If spiritual values are to be present in a business, the logic of exchange (giving in order to acquire) must be subsumed under a common purpose and vision that includes realizing not only a private good, for example, profit, but also the common good. Within this framework, certain products would be excluded from a firm embodying spiritual values, for example, pornography, harmful drugs, and some military weapons. Developing a humane community where the person could grow and thrive would be part of the role of business.

Solidarity: Solidarity means that human beings are by nature interdependent. Business, following this norm, would focus on the connectedness between business and society. Activities and policies that direct business to take on some of the problems of the wider society are a clear sign of the presence of spiritual values. This article has highlighted several firms that have appropriated solidarity in their strategic plans and have assisted in solving problems in the developing world both for their own long-term good as well as that of the planet. Answering the call of sustainability – espousing and implementing this vision and common purpose – is part of the imperative of spiritual values.

Stewardship: This norm focuses on how one uses the gifts of creation, including personal talents but especially the physical environment. Sustainable development, with a focus on ecological issues, is highlighted under this norm. Such issues as fuel efficiency, recycling programs, waste reductions, emission reductions, water savings/water pollution reductions, and greenhouse gas reductions are crucial issues for a firm embodying spiritual values. The UN Global Compact has a number of initiatives to protect the environment and promote its protection. Two major projects center on water issues (The CEO Water Mandate) and global warming (The Caring for Climate Project).

The business leadership as a noble vocation

This essay argues that a growing number of business leaders and firms are taking on projects in the wider society to alleviate poverty, protect the environment, and create a more humane world and workplace. This is done not because businesses have caused these problems (although sometimes they have), but rather, because these leaders are thinking and feeling human beings who realize that their organizations might have the managerial talent and resources to act where governments are unable or unwilling to do so. These leaders have a sense of being called upon to make a difference, to make the world a better place for them having been there. This "calling" is often discussed with the term "vocation." This "servant leadership" perceives the interconnectedness among life and all its enterprises, especially business and the environment (Williams, 2003). While it is true that some of this activity is done simply to respond to society's expectations, there are a growing number of leaders who do it because they believe it is the right thing to do.

That business can be an instrument for achieving more justice and peace in our world is the premise of the UN Global Compact, and this essay has tried to outline that possibility. Clearly, some progress has been made. Whether most businesses will come to perceive that the value they might create in society is much broader than that expressed in monetary terms, only time will tell.

Literature

Collins, J. and Porras, J. 1994. *Built to Last.* New York: Harper Business.

Edelman Trust Barometer. 2009. "Business Loses Mandate to Lead; Public Call for Greater Government Regulation Around World." Availabla at: http://www.edelman.com/news/ShowOne.asp?ID=202

Global Compact, United Nations 2010. Availabla at: http://www.globalcompact.org

Globe Scan 1999. Availabla at: http://www.iblf.org/docs/MillenniumPoll.pdf

Greenhut, M. and Corcoran, B. 2008. "General Electric and Corporate Citizenship: Improving the Health of the Poor in Africa." In Oliver F. Williams (ed.), *Peace Through Commerce.* pp. 349–366. Notre Dame, IN: University of Notre Dame Press.

Gunther, M. 2004. "Money and Morals at GE." *Fortune*, November 1, 2004.

Leisinger, K.M. 2008. "Stretching the Limits of Corporate Responsibility." In Oliver F. Williams (ed.), *Peace Through Commerce.* pp. 199–238. Notre Dame, IN: University of Notre Dame Press.

Litow, S. 2008. "IBM and Corporate Citizenship." In Oliver F. Williams (ed.), *Peace Through Commerce.* pp. 336–348. Notre Dame, IN: University of Notre Dame Press.

Merck & Co., Inc., Whitehouse Station, NJ, USA. Availabla at: http://www.merck.com.

Pope John Paul II. 1991. *Centesimus Annus*, 35.

Williams, O.F. 2008. "Responsible Corporate Citizenship and the Ideals of the United Nations Global Compact." In Oliver F. Williams (ed.), *Peace Through Commerce.* pp. 431–452. Notre Dame, IN: University of Notre Dame Press.

Williams, O.F. 2003. "Introduction." In Oliver F. Williams (ed.), *Business, Religion, and Spirituality: A New Synthesis.* pp. 1–28. Notre Dame, IN: University of Notre Dame Press.

43
Self-Assessment and Improvement Process for Organizations

T. Dean Maines

The *Self-Assessment and Improvement Process* (SAIP) is a method that enables organizations to appraise and enhance their performance on issues of ethics. By adapting techniques taken from Total Quality Management (TQM), it extends a venerable spiritual and moral discipline – the examination of conscience – from the realm of the individual to that of the firm. The SAIP transforms ethical principles into a systematic inventory of questions. Responding to these questions and scoring their answers allows leaders to identify where vital moral values have been integrated within their organization's operations and where this integration is tenuous or lacking. Applied at regular intervals, the method helps an organization develop as a moral agent, bringing its performance into greater conformity with recognized standards for ethically responsible conduct.

In 2007 the University of St Thomas (Minnesota) founded the SAIP Institute, to promote the method's development and its application within for-profit and not-for-profit enterprises. The SAIP method serves as the basis for several distinct assessment tools. One of these, the Catholic Identity Matrix (CIM), has been recognized as a best practice for Catholic healthcare systems within the United States (Catholic Health Association, 2009; MacMillan, 2008).

Foundations of the method

The SAIP method integrates insights from multiple fields: corporate ethics, spirituality, and TQM. Its underpinnings include the principle of moral projection, the practice of conscience examination, and the organizational self-assessment process developed by US-based Baldrige Performance Excellence Program.

359

In Book II of *The Republic,* Plato notes that there are respects in which an organization may be considered an individual person writ large. Ethicists have employed this parallel to assist their investigations into the nature of organizational morality. Their approach utilizes the principle of moral projection, which states that it is appropriate to look normatively for and foster within organizations moral attributes that are analogous to the moral attributes we find and foster within individuals (Goodpaster, 1997). This principle suggests that organizations possess a faculty analogous to the moral conscience of the human person, that is, a *corporate* conscience. This faculty shapes how an organization pursues certain goals (profitability, market share, competitiveness, etc.) by accounting for its moral obligations to groups and individuals who are affected by its decisions and activities. Furthermore, it falls to an organization's leaders to create and cultivate corporate conscience. They do this by undertaking three tasks: *orientating* the firm toward particular moral values; *institutionalizing* those values within its operations; and *sustaining* the values over time, making them an enduring part of the organization's identity (Goodpaster, 1989).

The principle of moral projection undergirds the SAIP, insofar as the method seeks to nurture corporate conscience. Specifically, it assists leaders with the task of institutionalization, that is, embedding moral values within the policies, processes, and practices that shape how their firm performs its work. The SAIP method also builds on the parallel between the person and the organization by extending to the latter a discipline that individuals have used for centuries to aid their moral and spiritual development: the examination of conscience. An examination of conscience is a periodic, systematic review of one's deeds, words, and thoughts for the purpose of determining their conformity with or departure from a set of moral standards. This review helps individuals identify aspects of the moral life where they are flourishing, as well as particular faults. By drawing attention to opportunities for improvement or areas where remediation is required, the practice of conscience examination catalyzes the person's growth or renewal as a moral agent.

Historically, the examination of conscience has been linked closely with the quest for unity with God. For example, within the early Christian community it emerged as a way of helping the faithful develop attitudes and behaviors consistent with the life and teachings of Jesus. Over time the practice became increasingly differentiated and formalized, to support a set of distinct yet related ends: a general examination, to promote growth toward Christian perfection; a particular examination, to avoid a specific fault or acquire a specific virtue; and a preparatory examination, for the sacrament of penance. After the Fourth Lateran Council established the rule of annual confession and communion in 1215, short manuals appeared in order to assist penitents with this third exercise. These texts provided penitents with a structure and process for reflecting upon their lives in light of standards such as the Decalogue, thereby helping them determine the type and number of sins they should confess. Similar frameworks may be found today in Roman Catholic prayer books; they frequently take the form of a structured series of questions organized by commandment (Regan and Wall, 2003).

The SAIP method creates an organizational analogue to these frameworks. It does this by adapting the approach to organizational self-assessment pioneered within the Baldrige Performance Excellence Program. The Baldrige program was launched in 1987 under the auspices of the US Department of Commerce; it seeks to aid the competitiveness of US companies by helping them upgrade the quality of their products or services. As part of its work, the program developed a self-assessment approach that firms can apply to appraise and enhance their operations. The Baldrige self-assessment process converts criteria for performance excellence into a systematic array of questions. By answering these questions on the basis of empirical data and then evaluating the responses using a set of scoring guidelines, leaders can measure to what degree the fundamental drivers of product or service quality are present within their company's operations. The appraisal facilitates the identification of specific opportunities to improve the organization's performance and leads to concrete efforts to address these opportunities.

Modeled after the Baldrige self-assessment, the SAIP method also entails answering questions using empirical evidence, scoring these answers, identifying operational strengths and weaknesses, and implementing improvement initiatives. However, the requirements addressed by the two approaches differ in nature. The questions in the Baldrige self-assessment help a firm evaluate how well it has integrated principles of TQM within all aspects of its activities. In contrast, the questions arising from the application of the SAIP method – like the queries considered in a personal examination of conscience – are rooted in moral standards. Answering this systematic inventory of detailed questions reveals to an organization's leaders the extent to which *ethical* principles have been integrated throughout its operations.

The Catholic Identity Matrix

The SAIP method is flexible and may be employed with a variety of ethical precepts. When used in conjunction with principles that serve as a shared normative standard for an industry, it can provide firms in this sector with a common way to evaluate and improve their performance as moral agents. The CIM is an example of a process that functions in this manner. The CIM illustrates how assessment tools that utilize the SAIP method are structured and applied.

The CIM is intended to help Catholic healthcare executives strengthen the identity of their institutions, specifically their identity as entities that continue the healing mission of Jesus and serve as ministries of the Roman Catholic Church. An initial version of the CIM was developed and tested during 2006 by Ascension Health, the largest Catholic and largest not-for-profit healthcare system in the United States. In 2007 Ascension Health entered into a collaborative partnership with the SAIP Institute. The CIM subsequently was modified to incorporate the SAIP method, building upon an earlier effort to adapt this approach for use within Catholic healthcare (Brinkmann et al., 2006).

The CIM helps a health system or hospital assess the degree to which it has integrated six principles for Catholic healthcare into its operating policies, processes, and practices. These principles include practicing solidarity with the poor; providing holistic care (i.e., care that attends to the physical, psychological, social, and spiritual dimensions of the patient); demonstrating respect for human life and dignity; building a community of work characterized by participation and mutual respect; supporting the common good and stewarding resources effectively; and acting in communion with the Church. The formulation of each principle draws upon a range of sources, including directives issued by the US Catholic bishops and Catholic social teaching. The principles also reflect the core commitments of the Church's health ministry, as viewed from the perspective of Catholic healthcare executives (Giganti, 1999).

The heart of the CIM is an assessment matrix formed by juxtaposing the six principles with a maturity framework. The maturity framework identifies six tasks an organization must address to implement a principle effectively: reflecting the principle in the organization's mission, strategy, and critical operating policies (planning); reinforcing the principle through performance management and compensation systems (alignment); establishing documented processes that incorporate the principle into relevant work procedures (process); ensuring employees have the skills, knowledge, and abilities necessary to execute these processes and improve them over time (training); and establishing metrics to determine whether processes are functioning correctly (measurement) and yielding desired outcomes (impact). The result of this juxtaposition is a six-by-six assessment matrix (Figure 43.1).

Each cell within the matrix contains a question or series of questions. These lead a system or hospital to consider how well it has addressed one of the six tasks for a given principle, and to corroborate its performance with data. Figure 43.2 displays two example questions from the matrix. The first is drawn from cell 1.3, which is created by the intersection of the principle of solidarity with the poor with the process stage of the maturity framework. This question asks the organization to outline its procedure for creating initiatives that address the most pressing healthcare needs of the poor living in the communities where it operates. To do this, the organization first must articulate how it understands the term "poor," that is, the criteria it employs to determine who within its service area should be considered underprivileged, marginalized, or vulnerable. It then must outline the process it uses to identify and prioritize the healthcare requirements of these individuals, and how it moves from the identification of needs to the planning and implementation

	Planning	Alignment	Process	Training	Measurement	Impact
Solidarity with those who live in poverty	1.1	1.2	1.3	1.4	1.5	1.6
Holistic care	2.1	2.2	2.3	2.4	2.5	2.6
Respect for human life and dignity	3.1	3.2	3.3	3.4	3.5	3.6
Participatory community of work and mutual respect	4.1	4.2	4.3	4.4	4.5	4.6
Stewardship	5.1	5.2	5.3	5.4	5.5	5.6
Act in communion with the church	6.1	6.2	6.3	6.4	6.5	6.6

Figure 43.1   Catholic identity matrix

Cell 1.3: Solidarity with the poor/Process

How does the organization develop and implement healthcare programs focused upon the most urgent needs of those who live in poverty in the communities it serves?

Cell 2.5: Holistic care/Measurement

What are the current levels and trends in meaures of patient satisfaction with emotional and spiritual care?

Figure 43.2   Sample questions from the Catholic Identity Matrix

of programs designed to supply these necessities. In this way, the question prompts the organization to consider how its operating processes concretely address the moral aspiration of solidarity, and whether there are gaps in these procedures which impede it from doing so effectively, efficiently, and reliably over time (Figure 43.2).

The second question is taken from the measurement cell for the principle of holistic care (cell 2.5). It requires the institution to provide evidence indicating that its patients believe they receive care that suitably addresses dimensions of health and well-being beyond the physical. To answer this question, the assessing unit must determine how it evaluates this aspect of patient satisfaction. It also must produce data that substantiate current satisfaction levels and how those levels have varied through time, that is, whether the metrics are improving, deteriorating, or holding steady. Examining such information allows an organization to determine whether the processes it has established to address the patients' affective and spiritual needs are functioning as they should, or whether the available evidence suggests they require modification.

Answering all the questions within the matrix allows the assessing unit to create an evidence-based, qualitative profile of its current efforts to put into practice the moral aspirations articulated by the six principles. This qualitative portrait is complemented and extended by a quantitative evaluation. By comparing its answers to the scorecard for a given cell, an organization can make an informed judgment about where its current achievements place it on a progressive six-level scale of performance (Figure 43.3). This permits a numeric score to be assigned to each cell in the matrix. By comparing scores from cell to cell, an organization's leaders can detect areas of relatively strong and weak

Score	Measurement and impact
0%–5% 1	No results are reported on holistic care
10%–25% 2	Limited results are reported on holistic care, but no trend data are available.
30%–45% 3	Performance on holistic care measurers is below comparative benchmarks and trends are unfavorable.
50%–65% 4	Performance on holistic care measurers is below comparative benchmarks but some trends are favorable
70%–85% 5	Performance trends on holistic care measures are positive, and the organization is at comparative benchmarks.
90%–100% 6	Performance trends on holistic care measures are positive, surpass comparative benchmarks, and are top quartile in the industry.

Figure 43.3 Sample scorecard: cell 2.5 (holistic care/measurement)

performance. This comparison suggests where improvement is necessary to better align the organization's conduct with the six principles. Furthermore, the information gathered by answering the questions within the matrix assists with the formulation of initiatives targeting specific improvement needs.

Consistent with both the periodic nature of a conscience examination and the requirements of the SAIP method, the CIM is not intended to be a one-time event. Rather, it is reapplied at regular intervals, ideally once improvement initiatives launched in light of the tool's previous use have generated results. Repeated application of the CIM enables the assessing unit to judge the effectiveness of its ongoing efforts to better align its performance with its professed moral values. Over time, use of the CIM helps a firm establish and sustain a discipline of continuous learning on organizational ethics, thereby fostering its growth as a moral agent.

Method benefits

Use of the CIM yields a set of tangible benefits for Catholic healthcare systems and hospitals. The advantages provided by other assessment tools that employ the SAIP method are similar. Most prominent among these are a realistic, data-based understanding of how well an organization has integrated a set of ethical principles within its operations, and the detection of areas where this integration is incomplete or lacking and thus requiring remediation. Another benefit is enhanced awareness and management control. Executives typically are not cognizant of all the facets of their firm's operations to which a given principle may be applicable; however, the CIM, like other SAIP-based assessment processes, allows them to unearth such activities systematically. The CIM thereby helps leaders exercise more comprehensive control over their organization in the moral realm, promotes greater congruence between the firm's actions and its stated ethical principles, and reduces the risk of unethical (and potentially illegal) conduct. The CIM can also strengthen employee engagement. Staff surveys suggest that many employees join Catholic healthcare institutions because they are attracted to the moral aspirations and commitments these organizations espouse. By enabling them to operate with greater moral integrity, the CIM helps create an organizational climate conducive to greater employee loyalty and improved morale.

Because the CIM uses principles that have emerged from a specific religious tradition, it helps us see how the SAIP method can assist the spiritual growth of those who work within organizations where the method is applied. This assistance comes as a byproduct of its primary purpose, that is, fostering corporate conscience. In short, the CIM catalyzes organizational conditions that permit employees to collaborate with God's work in history more readily and with greater effectiveness.

The CIM nurtures corporate conscience within a Catholic healthcare institution by helping it "interiorize" six moral principles. These principles point toward the divine purpose the institution is intended to advance in the world, namely, Christ's mission of radical healing. Using the SAIP method to promote a richer, fuller connection between these standards and operating policies, processes, and metrics, the CIM helps the institution become a more efficacious vehicle for this mission. It also creates an organizational setting that enables executives, physicians, nurses, pharmacists, clerks, and janitors alike to more easily contribute their talents to Jesus' ministry to the ill in body, mind, and spirit. The enhanced alignment fostered by the CIM aids the advance of God's kingdom at the institutional level by helping an organization carry this ministry forward more effectively. It assists the kingdom's unfolding at the level of the individual by facilitating a deeper unity between employees and their Creator, by creating circumstances which allow each person more effectively to muster and apply his or her professional skills and personal industry in support of God's activity in the world.

Organizations and individuals alike are imperfect, and one hesitates before too easily identifying the efforts of either with divine purposes. In this vein, the SAIP method makes two salutary contributions to a spirituality of co-creation. First, it reminds us that aligning moral aspiration and action is a task never fully accomplished. The SAIP method suggests that one way to address this perennial challenge within a firm is through a discipline of systematic, data-based assessment – the ongoing, sustained practice of examining the corporate conscience – an approach that sees facts as friendly and treats evidence as a potential source of insight into how moral standards might be better woven into operations. Second, through its focus on broader systems – the policies, processes, and practices that influence how individuals perform their jobs – the SAIP method underscores the organizational context of personal labor. Our work can serve as a means of sanctification, a way of growing closer to God; however, for weal or woe, it is shaped by the conditions under which it is carried out. Integrating moral principles into a firm's operations not only promotes the organization's moral integrity, it also has the potential to create an environment more conducive to employees' spiritual growth, one that allows them to better harmonize their labor with the labor of God.

Literature

Brinkmann B., Maines, T. D., Naughton, M. J., Stebbins, J. M., and Weimerskirch, A. 2006.
"Bridging the Gap." *Health Progress*, vol. 87, no. 6, pp. 43–50.
Catholic Health Association of the United States 2009. "By their fruits you will know them: Mission assessment and measurement" (Online). Available at: http://www.chausa.org/mission/
Giganti, E. 1999. "Living Our Promises, Acting on Faith." *Health Progress*, vol. 80, no. 6, pp. 52–55.
Goodpaster, K.E. 1989. "Ethical Imperatives and Corporate Leadership." In K.R. Andrews (ed.), *Ethics in Practice: Managing the Moral Corporation*, pp. 212–228. Boston: Harvard Business School.
Goodpaster, K.E. 1997. "Moral Projection, Principle of." In P.H. Werhane and R.E. Freeman (eds), *Blackwell Encyclopedic Dictionary of Business Ethics*, p. 432. Malden, MA: Blackwell.
MacMillan, D. 2008. "The Issue: Checkup for a Catholic Nonprofit." *Business Week* (Online). Available at: http://www.businessweek.com/managing/inter-active_case_studies/
Regan, J. and Wall, J.B. 2003. "Conscience, Examination of." In B.L. Marthaler (ed.), *New Catholic Encyclopedia*, 2nd edn, vol. 4, pp. 147–148. Detroit, MI: Gale.

44
Edgewalker Organizations
Judi Neal

An Edgewalker Organization is an organization that seeks to be on the leading edge, is curious about what is emerging just over the horizon, supports creativity and innovation, and nurtures the human spirit. The organization develops collective methods of knowing the future. It encourages risk-taking. The leaders understand how to use vision, imagery, and inspiration to paint a picture of a desired future. Employees are imaginative, empowered, and know how to create what has never been created before.

The Edgewalker Organization has great diversity in its leaders and employees. Differences are valued to a much greater degree than in a traditional organization, simply because Edgewalkers are curious and always wanting to learn about other people's worldviews.

There are five different orientations that people can take in an organization, and these affect the extent to which the organization can truly be on the leading edge. These five orientations are as follows:

1. Edgewalkers
2. Flamekeepers
3. Hearthtenders
4. Placeholders
5. Guardians

Each of these will be defined, and then we will look at the implications for organizational culture and performance. These orientations are based on two factors: (1) *Relationship to Time*, and (2) *Relationship to Change*. The Relationship-to-Time factor is a continuum between focus on the past and focus on the future. The Relationship-to-Change factor is a continuum between being closed to change and being open to change.

Edgewalkers

Edgewalkers are people who walk between worlds and have the ability to build bridges between different worldviews. They have a strong spiritual life and are also very grounded and effective in the everyday, material world. Edgewalkers are much more orientated towards the future than to the past, to the degree that they can sometimes run roughshod over tradition and can close their ears to what has worked in the past. They are also high on the change continuum, with a basic philosophy of: "If it ain't broke, fix it anyway."

They are restless and always seeking newness and change. For this reason they can sometimes be difficult to manage, especially for a traditional manager. The Edgewalker may be more focused on his or her creative ideas than on what is most needed in the organization.

A company called Yankee Gas had an interesting approach to valuing its Edgewalkers. They asked their leaders to identify the people in their work units who were "radicals and rebels" and invited these people to be a part of a group that could provide advice and guidance to the organizational leadership. Most organizations tend to suppress people who have radical or unusual ideas, but this forward-thinking and creative organization actually valued and listened to people who would normally be on the fringe.

Flamekeepers

Flamekeepers are those people who keep the original vision and values of the organization alive. They are like the Olympic torchbearer, keeping the flame lit at all costs; or like the keeper of the flame in a temple: one who keeps the sacred candles lit morning, noon, and night.

The Strategic Programs Division of Xerox in Rochester, New York, was the first organization to create a truly green "zero-to-landfill" copying machine, the Document Center 265DC. The organization went through a massive six-year cultural change to support the development of a whole new series of products. In order to support their larger vision of a culture that focused on people first, they created the Council of Wisdom Keepers. A nominating committee selected sixteen people, two from each of the eight functional groups.

The role of the Wisdom Keepers was to walk around taking the temperature of the cultural-change program, to serve as ombudsmen, to cut red tape when necessary, and to catch anything significant that might be falling through the cracks. Some of their official responsibilities included the following (Ott, Kelly and Hotchkiss, 1997, p. 235):

1. to support the company with wisdom previously gained, in both engineering and human dimensions,
2. to hold both people and the vision of the products to the highest ideals and standards,
3. to advocate the well-being and quality of life of all company employees, and
4. to convene from time to time as they see fit to bring issues of importance to the attention of the appropriate people.

Flamekeepers are focused on what is best about the past and on preserving the core values of the organization. At the same time, they are open to change and are willing to look at how the organization can build on what has been developed in the past. They may not be your biggest innovators, but once they see how a new product, service, or strategy fits with the core values and aligns with the vision of the founders, they will be the biggest supporters of change.

Hearthtenders

Hearthtenders are the people who get the day-to-day work of the organization done. They are the ones who keep the home fires burning when the Edgewalkers are out scouting new territory. They keep things running smoothly and are committed to a sense of family in the organization, and to creating a "home-away-from home" atmosphere in the organization. Hearthtenders are the ones who remember people's birthdays and who enjoy the organizational-milestone celebrations. They are the ones who think of creative ways to celebrate accomplishments and to bring people together.

They enjoy working on continuous improvement and, if given half a chance, will have creative ideas about how to improve the workflow in their areas or better serve customers.

Hearthtenders are in the middle of the model in Figure 44.1. In time orientation, they tend to be focused on the present, and they are moderately open to change. These people are generally satisfied with their jobs and with the organization, and are happy to keep things the way they are unless someone has an idea on how to make their work more streamlined and less stressful.

Janice Tarasevich is a Hearthtender manager at Sennheiser USA. Janice's department takes orders and works with the sales department to make sure that customers get what they have ordered in a timely manner. She wanted her team members to better understand the whole sales process so she sent her staff members out in the field with sales reps and to trade shows. This allowed them to develop better relationships with people that they would normally only interact with on the phone. Her focus is on efficiency and positive relationships.

Hearthtenders serve a very important function in the organization by providing stability and by keeping systems running smoothly. Depending on the climate and culture of the organization, Hearthtenders could move into any of the other quadrants. If you are trying to create an organization that is more values-driven and more innovative, you will actively want to find ways to help Hearthtenders become more future-oriented, thus moving them into the Edgewalker orientation, or more past-oriented, thus moving them into the Flamekeeper orientation. Often Hearthtenders are Edgewalkers or Flamekeepers in disguise, and can be encouraged to be more change-oriented if they are listened to, supported, encouraged, and rewarded.

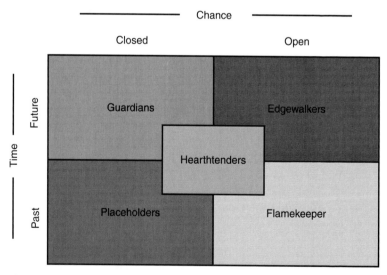

Figure 44.1   Organizational orientation

Placeholders

In contrast to Edgewalkers, who tend to be rare, just about every organization has Placeholders. Tom Brown (2006) defines Placeholders as the people who are holding back organizational progress and innovation. These are the people who see boundaries instead of possibilities, who are focused on the past instead of the future, who use up resources instead of looking at renewal, and who value doing over dreaming. They are the ones who want to employ as few people as possible in contrast to the leaders who engage all of humankind and look for ways to grow the enterprise.

Placeholders are primarily motivated by fear and ego. They are risk-averse because they are afraid of losing whatever they have. They feel they can't afford to fail, and so they get frozen in place, fighting mightily to keep things the way they are. They will give lip service to change, but they will follow any words of support with statements such as:

- You have to show me where the money will come from.
- Let's put a committee together, and I want a report in three months.
- Where else has this been done?
- How can you prove that we'll be successful?
- Corporate will never go for it (or Human Resources, or Management, or the union, or someone else who can be the bad guy).

Placeholders do have a tremendous amount of organizational memory, and perhaps even some wisdom. A Placeholder is, in many ways, like a pessimistic, angry, cynical Flamekeeper. Probably at one time they deeply believed in the vision and values of the organization and perhaps had their faith and ideals trampled on one too many times. So they retreat into their protective shells and long for the past. And they try to block any new initiatives that move them even further from their idealized past.

It takes a tremendous amount of work, a high level of interpersonal skills, and spiritual intelligence to deal with Placeholders. If you are trying to create more of an Edgewalker culture in your organization, you are likely to create even more fear in Placeholders unless you find a way to deal directly with their motives for being naysayers. From a spiritual perspective, it's important to remember that there is good in every person, and if you are in a change-agent role, you will want to find a way to unleash that goodness in your Placeholders.

Programs that increase self-awareness, focus on values, and help people to rediscover their inherent sense of service and higher purpose can be very successful for those at lower levels in the organization. One-on-one coaching, whether it is with a professional coach or with a competent boss, can also help Placeholders to be more open to change, particularly if they can be shown that they will have some influence on the new direction.

But if your top leaders are Placeholders, your organization is essentially stuck in the mud. Edgewalkers and Flamekeepers will eventually leave out of frustration, and you will be left with people who keep the machinery running but who have forgotten the higher purpose and mission of the organization.

Guardians

There are people in organizations who tend to be future-oriented, but unlike Edgewalkers, they have fear and foreboding about what might happen next. They *have a strong sense* of protectiveness and a predilection for preventing problems. In my early work on Edgewalkers, I called them "Doomsayers." The Merriam-Webster Online Dictionary (2006) defines a Doomsayer as "one given to forebodings and predictions of impending calamity." Even more than Placeholders, they can be a tremendous drag on organizational energy if they are strongly fear-based. These folks are not just "the glass is half empty" folks, they are the "glass is broken, the water is going to stain everything, and I'm probably going to bleed to death" folks. They are very concerned about the future, but they always predict the worst possible calamity and then spend their time preparing for doomsday. Or else, in their fear, they just get paralyzed and helpless. At healthier levels, they are the ones who can see what might go wrong and can gently alert the right people to make changes that will keep the team or organization moving ahead.

Typically Guardians get pretty marginalized in organizations, because leaders don't like to hear potential bad news, and they can be seen as complainers. They tend to gravitate towards jobs like safety, environmental engineering, cost accounting, auditing, and other jobs that by their nature focus on what is wrong. The goal of these kinds of jobs is to prevent serious problems from happening and to handle a crisis quickly if they do. Many people in these professions handle the prevention work and the crisis work in a calm and professional manner.

Some Guardians, however, are prone to drama as a way of alerting people to the things they see that others don't see. They get themselves into a vicious cycle. When they see a potential problem emerging, they do whatever they can to get the attention of people who can do something about it. Often this includes using strong emotion to express their concern. Guardians also use exaggeration to get their point across. Because so many things seem like a crisis to them and because they tend to exaggerate and blow things out of proportion, they may become like the little boy who cried "Wolf." Coworkers can become immune to their cries of alarm, and then, when there is a real emergency, no one believes them.

Like Placeholders, Guardians are change-averse. But their resistance to change is based on a belief that the future holds danger. Their theory about the world is that it is not a safe place, and you have to protect yourself at all costs from bad things happening. And as Jack Gibb said, our theories create our reality (Gibb, 1978). So if the least little thing goes wrong, they are able to say: "See, I told you." They tend to ignore all the things that go right most of the time, and if you point that out to them they say: "Well, we've been lucky so far, but just you wait."

Guardians are very difficult to change. However, if you are creating an Edgewalker Organization, you will have to find a way to deal with them, because their negative and fearful energy can be so contagious. Do anything you can to help them develop a more positive relationship with the future. They are already future-orientated, but it is a fear-based orientation. If you can help the Guardian to understand how he or she creates his or her own reality, you have gone a long way towards transformation. Once they can begin to accept that there may be other *ways* to think about the future, you are on your way towards moving Guardians to either the Hearthtender quadrant or even the Edgewalker quadrant.

Appreciative Inquiry is a wonderful process for beginning to open up the consciousness of the Guardian. They often find it very difficult to shift their thinking in this way, but it is possible. When I offer workshops, I often build in a one-hour or two-hour vision quest in nature as part of the process. This kind of experience can also be very helpful to the Guardian. Nature is a gentle teacher about the future.

Basic guidelines for organizations

Here are some actions you can take to begin to create more of an Edgewalker culture in your organization:

1. Assess your organization in comparison to others in your industry. Are you on the leading edge, in the middle of the pack, or a laggard in terms of innovation, creativity, and risk-taking?
2. Decide as a management team if you would like to be more on the leading edge than you currently are.
3. Evaluate your current mix of Edgewalkers, Flamekeepers, Hearthtenders, Placeholders, and Guardians. Does this need to change in order to meet your strategic and cultural objectives?
4. Identify and benchmark Edgewalker organizations. Visit them and talk to leaders and frontline workers. Find out what makes the organization tick. Discuss what you learned with your management team and make decisions about actions you can implement.
5. Study the organizations that have received the International Spirit at Work Award. Attend the annual International Spirit at Work Awards conference to learn from the CEOs and executives of the organizations that have received the award.[1]
6. Explore training programs, hiring practices, reward practices, and other human resource systems to see what can be done to shift people with Placeholder and Doomsayer orientations to Hearthtender, Flamekeeper, and Edgewalker orientations.
7. Don't forget that nature is our best teacher. Plan a vision quest for your top team, then schedule one for everyone else in the organization.

Look for the gifts

I remember a cartoon from years ago that pictured a little boy delightedly shoveling out a stall full of manure. When someone asked him why he was so happy about his shoveling, he replied: "With all this dung in here, there's got to be a pony somewhere!"

Sometimes being an Edgewalker can feel like you are up to your neck in horse manure. Being an Edgewalker is a hard path to walk, but it has many rewards. It is always exciting to break new ground and explore new frontiers. And you meet so many interesting people on the way! You are never bored, and no one would ever accuse you of being boring. But more than anything else, you have the opportunity to make a positive difference in the world.

If you are trying to create an Edgewalker Organization, it is helpful to understand the different orientations that people have towards time and towards change. And like the little boy in the stall, it is valuable to look for the gift in each of these orientations. When you focus on people's strengths, and what they bring to the organization, what you focus on will grow.

"What the caterpillar calls the end of the world, the master calls a butterfly" (Richard Bach).

Note

1. Details about the International Spirit at Work Award and case studies about the honorees are on the Association for Spirit at Work website at http://www.spiritatwork.org.

Literature

Brown, T. 2006. *Anatomy of Fire*. Lexington, KY: Management General, e-book retrieved from http://www.anatomyoffire.com, April 23, 06, chapter 2, p. 3.

Gibb, J. 1978. *Trust: A New View of Personal and Organizational Development*. Los Angeles, CA: Guild of Tutors Press.

Merriam-Webster Online Dictionary 2006: retrieved from http://www.m-w.com/cgi-bin/dictionary?va=doomsayer on April 23, 06.

Ott, R., Kelly, C., and Hotchkiss, M. 1997: *LAKES: A Journey of Heroes*. Webster, NY: Xerox Corporation and Living Systems.

45

The Economy of Communion

Luigino Bruni and Tibor Héjj

The *Economy of Communion* (EoC), the model of the *Focolare Movement*, may provide a solution to integrating spirituality and the economy. In the EoC, entrepreneurs are inspired by principles rooted in a culture different than what prevails in conventional practice and theory of economics. We can define this "culture" as a "culture of giving," which is the antithesis of a "culture of having." Since the inception of the concept almost two decades ago, it has been developed from an idea to a proven practice: it is a project involving hundreds of companies spanning five continents and numerous industries and countries, and it has attracted the interest of scholars and economists alike.

The concept

For many, the economy is only a necessary (though rather negative) aspect of life, and it is something separated from our faith. Yet a modern and sustainable way of sharing goods and decreasing poverty could be accomplished through enterprises with different goals than those aligned to the neoliberal principle of focusing purely on the benefit of the owner.

Rather than concentrating on the need to make businesses more ethical or more humane, the EoC is based on the need to do our part to build a more just world, one where fewer people are forced to live in often inhumane conditions. This is why it cannot and should not become a corporate-social-responsibility project. It did not come about to renew businesses, but to renew social relations.

The EoC is an economy-based approach to gift and community, between which a close relationship exists. A study of the origins of the word *community* by Roberto Esposito shows it as a derivative of *communitas*, from *cum-munus* (reciprocal gift). The key word that best explains the nature of a *gift* is reciprocity. The free gift, which is the experience we all associate with a beautiful and good life, requires that we take turns playing the roles of giver and recipient. It requires that he who receives a gift feels capable of reciprocating, of finding himself in the condition of being able to respond on a basis of substantial equality.

Unreciprocated giving creates imbalance, disorder. Human societies have always preferred symmetry, and the market´s great power is based on a symmetrical exchange of equivalent values (or at least the perception of this). Giving is a way of acting inspired by gratuitousness, by a search for the good in the other, for the common good. The reciprocal aspect of giving is not, in its basic relational structure, substantially different from the phenomenon of economic exchange appearing in cultures much later in respect to ritual giving. In the history of cultures, between giving and the market there was a difference in degree (of measuring equivalents, of the timing of giving and receiving, of the allowed sanctions) but not in nature. It is possible, in theory and practice, to join contract and gift, gratuity and market, *eros* and *agape*. This is the basic challenge of the EoC.

The charismatic principle of economy

A few great figures have had an effect on the economic sphere, such as St Benedict and St Francis. Only a few charisms have had an impact on the economic thought of their own time. Monasticism, we know, gave rise to the economic lexicon of the commercial revolution in Europe around the first millennium. The Franciscans, in their own way, brought about the first real school of economic thought (Ockham, Duns Scotus), which in turn developed the categories necessary to interpret the city-state society and, subsequently, Renaissance society. But the charism of unity is not only a product of economic works (among them the EoC) – it has also inspired theoretical reflection in the field of economics, in the same way that St Benedict and St Francis did in their day. The novelty of the experience of the EoC is essentially a cultural and theoretical novelty; in other words, the novelty of the EoC can be understood on a wider cultural horizon than the praxis of business allows.

An economic proposal starting from the poor

The original intuition of the EoC was launched in May 1991, just after the newly published social-justice encyclical by John Paul II, *Centesimus*

Annus. At that time, Chiara Lubich, founder of the Focolare Movement, visited the city of São Paolo in Brazil. Whoever arrives in that metropolis is confronted with a scenario that powerfully symbolizes the potential contradictions within capitalism: a forest of skyscrapers surrounded by a savannah of slums. EoC arose as a response to this experience of the suffering of humanity – a humanity that is increasingly able to master technology and produce wealth but has not yet been able to overcome misery.

Within a few days of that trip to São Paolo at the end of May 1991, what has come to be known as the EoC was born: businesses managed by means of a new culture (the "culture of giving"), where profits would be put into communion with the aim of demonstrating an example of humanity "with no-one in need," which has since become a model for many.

The three-way sharing of profits became the first practical proposal of the EoC: (1) one part of the profits would be reinvested in the business in order to develop and create new jobs; (2) the second part would be used to create the new culture, which would inspire women and men who were capable of incorporating communion into their lives; and (3) the third part would go directly to the poor so as to bring them fully into the dynamic of communion and reciprocity. This three-way sharing of profits is a "pre-economic" intuition, since it represents neither a new juridical form nor an organizational business model, nor a measurable technique, but rather a vision of the economy and society. Besides being concerned with growth, communion-based businesses are also directly concerned with culture, need, and poverty. For these businesses, profit is regarded as the means rather than the end of entrepreneurial activity, as the profit is put into communion. Thus the EoC is a project for a more just and fraternal humanism.

The natural mission of traditional business is to create jobs and produce products, goods, and services. In the normal course of events, the redistribution of wealth is not prevalent in business (even if it cannot be totally excluded: there are taxes, but also salaries). Instead, the EoC consists of traditional businesses that are invited to go beyond their "normal" social functions or "vocations."

An economy derived from charism

The EoC expresses a given spirituality, a charism. The Focolare Movement – a lay movement within the Catholic Church while still receptive and open to other denominations, religions, and even nonbelievers – began in 1943 in Trent, Italy. There are a few characteristics found in many social experiences that come about as a result of charisms.

The first characteristic: The experiences that come about as a result of charisms affirm the primacy of life over theory. They are therefore popular experiences, always coming about through praxis and never as a result of experts or professionals sitting around a table. This first dimension is very evident in the EoC. Faced with the spectacle of misery and unequal distribution, Lubich's proposal was for immediate action, based on a few intuitions (essentially, the sharing of profits in "three thirds"; industrial estates inserted into the small towns of the Movement; and "we are poor but many"). She left it to life to indicate how to proceed one step at a time. There are many projects to "fight poverty" that are promoted by institutions. In the charismatic economy, such as the EoC, life precedes the theoretical reflection that always accompanies it, because life is denser with truth than theory (which serves life inasmuch as it comes from life and is nourished by it).

The second characteristic: These experiences come about as a response of life to the problems of specific people. While crossing the city of São Paolo, Lubich was struck by the thought that there were people of the Movement, members of her family, in those favelas. The EoC came about for them; it did not come about in an abstract but in a practical way. It is always something vital, alive, rather than a humanitarian project to build a better world.

The third characteristic: These charismatic experiences call into question the idea of wealth and poverty. Here St Francis serves as a paradigm. After his conversion he returned from his journey to Spoleto and immediately threw away the proceeds of his business, now understanding that the true goods are others: the choice of poverty became his new wealth. More generally, every time a charism arrives in economic history, it calls into question the concept of "goods." It says that true goods, "good things," are not those commonly understood as such: money, power, success. A charism, especially a great charism, turns the ordinary vision of things and goods on its head.

The fourth characteristic: This effectively summarizes the preceding ones – a charismatic experience is the gift of "different eyes," which enables us to see beautiful things in the problems we face. For example, when Mother Teresa of Calcutta spoke of the poor, she loved to repeat: "Do not call them problems, call them gifts." As the EoC came about

through a charism – the charism of unity – it shares all of these characteristics that can be found in all experiences of charismatic economy.

Goods and poverty

There are some significant differences between the spirituality of St
Francis and that of the Focolare. St Francis points to poverty above all
as a way to sainthood – freedom from goods so as to attain the Good
with a capital G: God. Lubich proposes the same radical choice with
respect to goods, but puts them in communion with the others in a
view of unity.

The charism of unity, moreover, allows us to understand that the
forms of misery have a lot to do with relationships, and far less to do
with merchandise than is commonly thought. People succumb to misery (as individuals, but also as communities or peoples) when relationships are broken. This aspect has a lot to do with the EoC. When the
profits from business are given to help those in need, the first form of
assistance is the offer of a close relationship and reciprocity. The first
cure for poverty is the relationship itself. Before material help is given, a
relationship, communion, and proximity are established with the poor
person. The true cure starts there, and without this "first," no help is
effective from the perspective of communion. The cure for every form
of poverty is first and foremost a healing of relationships: interpersonal, political, institutional, and environmental. Before any material
assistance is given, the most important intervention is to revitalize the
communion of goods in the local community, and only then can concrete initiatives to assist be engendered. This way of working is, among
other things, in line with the principle of subsidiarity in Catholic Social
Doctrine.

Project implementation

An example of the implementation of the theory of the EoC is the experience of a cluster led by Proactive Management Consulting Ltd (PMC)
in Hungary. The cluster consists of entrepreneurs who have sought to
combine alignment with the market environment, multiple bottom-
line value creation and sustainable cooperation between for-profit and
nonprofit entrepreneurship into a business cluster. The companies are
sovereign entities, sometimes even competing with each other while
running joint projects. They utilize the so-called *Holistic Stakeholder
Value Matrix* (a management tool developed by Tibor Héjj, and based

on the theory of the EoC) both within their own organizations as well as through supporting a nonprofit entrepreneurship within the cluster. The synergy of competences spread throughout the cluster aims at benefiting all stakeholders. The companies and employees have given their money and time to support needy people, communities and various causes for many years, in order to influence positively the lives of people and communities in their immediate and broader environment, jointly or individually, through business activities performed during normal working hours or outside.

The theory behind the operation of the enterprise presumes that human beings can have an identity on one of three layers: by moving "upwards," there is a clear trend from an egocentric, individualistic approach toward a "community-centric," altruistic one (Figure 45.1).

The *physical layer* is connected to skills and capabilities. It is an action-oriented aspect measured by the physical output of an individual, as an individual, and based on self-interest. On the *intellectual layer*, the mind and emotions are considered and measured – it is concerned with relationship to others. The intellectual level is based on information exchange and therefore consists of institutionalized incentives: cooperation based on interest. We consider the *spiritual layer* as the highest level in this hierarchy: it is based on and linked to the transcendent and means being alignment – even, as a goal, united – with God. It means going above the level of financial return to satisfy our own and others' needs, and self-fulfillment becomes a form of giving.

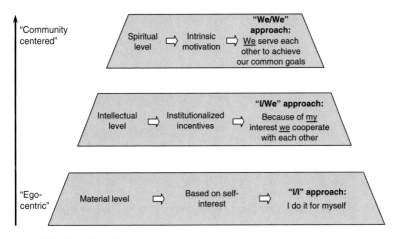

Figure 45.1 Levels of identity

Stakeholders / Layers	Owner/ Shareholder	Managers, Employees	Customers	Vendors, Creditors	Society	Future generations	The poor
Spiritual							
Intellectual							
Physical (material, financial)							

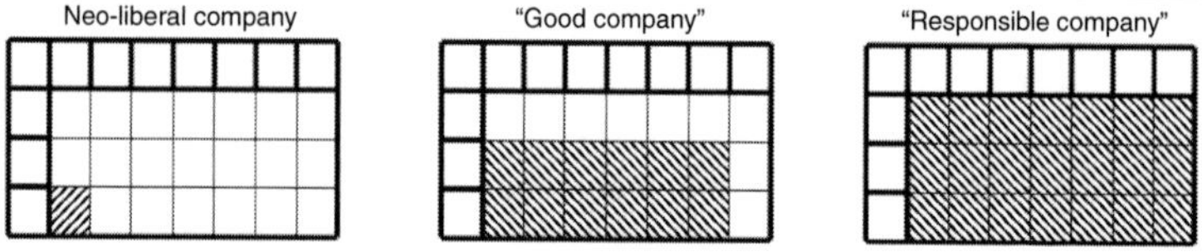

Neo-liberal company　　　　　　　"Good company"　　　　　　　"Responsible company"

Figure 45.2　The Holistic Stakeholder Value Matrix

All this implies that managers can think and act on three levels, depending on from which level their driving forces derive. We believe the ideal leader is a professional with a spiritually driven personality. This community-centered approach forces us to switch from the shareholder approach to a holistic stakeholder approach (i.e., from a profit focus to a concentration on the authentic "common good"), which involves the participation not only of owners and managers but a range of other stakeholders as well, including – according to the Christian approach of the Focolare – the poor of the community. By combining the three layers (material, intellectual, spiritual) with the broadest stakeholder approach, we end up with the Holistic Stakeholder Value Matrix (Figure 45.2).

The Stakeholder Value Matrices of the different approaches (neoliberal, "good company," "spiritual company") proportionately expand their targeted fields as business becomes about more than profit. The aim of an entrepreneur committed to the EoC is living entrepreneurship *as* a Christian. This means that instead of increasing individual wealth, profits serve the sustainable growth of the company, the support of those in need, and the development of people ready to live their lives with this mentality. Therefore, a certain proportion of resources (professional capacity) and revenue at PMC is used for supporting underprivileged persons or groups. This support is realized on different levels, such as through donations, both in civil and in social fields; "time-donations," or providing expertise for the benefit of nonprofit organizations; support for our own colleagues within the companies; and the support of the underprivileged (by job creation), within the framework of our nonprofit organization, Sunflower Ltd, whose mission is to employ the underprivileged and to support others in finding jobs at other companies. This employment rehabilitation consists of preparing and assisting the complete reintegration value chain of the disadvantaged (mostly disabled) in the labor market – in this way rehabilitation becomes, beyond the existential aspect, a developer of humanity as well. Within the "work teams" on which it is based, both improvement and community are realized and experienced.

Thus, keeping the rules of the free market in place, while complementing them with such principles, results in the formation of a practice where the goal is modified: it becomes more complex, and more to the point, relations become different. This approach makes it clear that the economy can augment the possibility of living a balanced spiritual life, and doing business may become a tool that takes us nearer to God.

Conclusion

The EoC is not an experience defined by philanthropists or great entrepreneurs, who give their superfluities to the poor without questioning their own lives without becoming brothers or sisters in equal standing with the "poor" they are helping. The EoC businesses are really an economy of communion even when they have no profits to give, but instead are working in, and producing, a culture of fraternity. Today the economy and the market have a vital need for communion, happiness, relational goods, and goods of gratuity. By remaining faithful to its vocation day by day, the EoC is increasingly capable of producing these typical "goods." Unity with God and thinking in terms of community – in our case, in our cluster and in the Focolare Movement – this is the essence of the EoC.

Literature

"Description of the Economy of Communion." Available at: http://www.edc-online.org

Bruni, L. 2006. *Il prezzo della gratuità*. Rome: Città Nuova.

Bruni, L. 2008. *Reciprocity, Altruism and Civil Society*. London: Routledge.

Bruni, L. and Zamagni, S. 2007. *Civil Economy*. Oxford: Peter Lang.

Esposito, R. 1998. *Communitas*. Turin: Einaudi.

Héjj, T. 2004. "The Economy of Sharing." In Laszlo Zsolnai (ed.), *Spirituality and Ethics in Management*.Dordrecht: Kluwer.

Héjj, T. 2006. "Holistic Stakeholder Value Matrix at Spiritual Companies." Presentation at the conference: *The Good Company – Catholic Social Thought and Corporate Social Responsibility in Dialogue*, Rome, Italy. (Available online

   at: http://www.stthomas.edu/cathstudies/cst/conferences/thegoodcompany/
   GoodCompanyPapers.html)
Héjj, T. and Héjj, R. 2008. "Socially Responsible Clusters in Theory and Practice."
   Workshop presentation at the conference: *The Collaborative Enterprise: Creating
   Values for a Sustainable World*, 2008 June, Bocconi University, Milan.
Pope John Paul II. 1991. *Centesimus Annus*. Encyclical Letter. Available online
   at: http://www.vatican.va/holy_father/john_paul_ii/encyclicals/documents/
   hf_jp- ii_enc_01051991_centesimus-annus_en.html
Szűcs, E. 2007. "Burst of Creativity." *Budapest Business Journal*, 1509 (15/09).
   Available online at: http://bbjonline.hu/index.php?id=22351&bbjissueid=612
   &issuename=1509%20(15/9)

46
Ethical Branding

Mike J. Thompson

The notion of ethical branding emerged in Europe in the 1980s. It accompanied the emergence of ethical consumerism, which represented a segment of less than 5 percent of consumers in western markets (but significant enough to those NGOs and church-based organizations calling for a fair deal for developing world farmers in particular, and for fairer supply chains more generally). The fair-trade movement, exemplified by Max Havelaar (Switzerland) and the Fairtrade Foundation (UK), began to gain media coverage for their claims that brands, and coffee brands in particular, were exploiting farmers in the developing world. In 1998 the Ethical Trading Initiative was formed in the UK as an alliance of mainstream corporations, trade unions and NGOs, with the intent of improving transparency and the protection of human rights in company supply chains through adopting the "Base Code." The early fair-trade brands campaigned for social justice, animal welfares and the promotion of natural substances in the production of groceries (e.g., Gepa), beverages (e.g., Café Direct), chocolate and ice cream (e.g., Green & Blacks and Ben & Jerry's), textiles and handicrafts (e.g., Traidcraft and Gepa), and cosmetics (e.g., The Body Shop).

Ethical aspect of brands

Until recently such ethical brands were regarded as niche brands with limited consumer appeal and were explicitly developed with an ethical campaign at their heart and dependent upon the ethical convictions of their entrepreneurial founders. More recently, however, such brands have been regarded by marketing professionals as "challenger brands" to mainstream brands in the same category. They have also attracted the investment attention of multinational corporations, who offer the potential to upscale trade and distribution networks whilst maintaining the ethical intent of the brand. Innocent, the UK fruit-smoothie manufacturer, which markets itself as being socially and environmentally "friendly," sold a minority stake to Coca-Cola in 2009 in order to fund expansion but without relinquishing any control in the production practices that are associated with the brand, according to Innocent. In the case of Ben and Jerry's, The Body Shop and Green & Blacks, the acquisitions were made *in toto* by their respective multinational parent companies.

Ethical branding has received scant attention in the marketing literature (Fan, 2005, p. 341). However, a number of studies have been carried out by business ethicists into the emergence of ethical consumerism and brands (Smith, 1990; Fan, 2005; Murphy et al., 2005). Marketers and business ethicists have explored the idea that marketing practice might evolve to become a societal "good" in general (Kotler, 1972; Levy and Zaltman, 1975). But ethical branding is a distinct subject area and a subset of both ethical marketing and of brand management. Ethical marketing sets out the moral challenges inherent in the marketing discipline and the ethical frameworks by which marketers might complete values-based judgments. Brand management relates to both preserving the distinctive characteristic and "personality" of a brand and evolving it through innovation and communications to maintain competitive advantage. The foundation for ethical marketing is that wider society expects marketers to consider the moral implications of their actions for other people and society (Brenkert, 2008, p. 51). It would be expected that the majority of brand owners desire that their brands be considered as ethical: ethical behavior is normative whereas unethical brand behavior risks the censure and the sanctions of society. As Brenkert (2008, p. 39) has pointed out, marketing is a value-laden activity that falls within the moral arena. An ethical brand should not harm the public good; instead it should contribute to, or help promote, the public good. (Fan, 2005, p. 342). In this sense, ethical branding applies to the practice of ethical-brand management by all brand owners.

However, the notion of the ethical brand has been formulated around specific and additional commitments made by a brand to society and its environment in a more proactive way than has historically been the case for mainstream brands. These ethical commitments may be grouped into four business areas, each with activities that may be regarded as discretionary and distinctive by comparison with the product's or brand's mainstream competitors:

Product attributes: nontoxic substances, "pure" ingredients, fair pricing, "environmental friendliness," and intrinsic worth to society.

Supply chain and manufacture: care for all those involved in the supply chain; employee welfare, discrimination, human rights, and "fair pay."

Corporate citizenship: community action, societal engagement, and charitable donations.

Communications: truthful claims.

Local/national sourcing: physical proximity of the product of the brand to the consumer, "homegrown" produce and the reduction of "food miles" (the measure of food and beverages transportation distances).

Popular marketing publications appear to have been ahead of marketing academics in the discussion of ethical branding and frequently without the apparent need to define terms. The usage of ethical-branding language has tended to refer to fair-trade or "green" products or brands. The language used to describe the meaning of an ethical brand is frequently confusing and lacks distinctiveness from the wider ideas of sustainability and CSR. "Ethical consumerism" is readily interpreted by marketers as "green consumerism." In 2007, a UK marketing magazine, for example, interpreted a survey on ethical consumerism almost exclusively in terms of "consumers who are going green." A further example is provided by Ethical Brand (International), a web-based organization which promotes the "Ethical Brand Licence" and offers it as a licence to applicants who commit to ensure that their enterprises are "adequately enabled and supported to do the right thing." This is further amplified in their definition of ethical brands:

> Ethical Brands recognise their environmental, economic and social responsibilities because they respect the interests, needs and concerns of their stakeholders. They are genuinely committed to doing the right thing and their commitments are independently monitored and verifiable.(http://www.ethicalbrand.com/home)

There are two difficulties with this kind of generalist definition. Firstly, the triple-bottom-line definition employed here is more properly understood as relating to sustainability without a clear connection to "ethical." Secondly, such a definition is likely to be claimed by all brands rather than just "ethical" brands.

The sustainability agenda has recently become a strong primer for ethical branding as its claims relate both to issues of social justice in the way people throughout the supply chain are treated and also to the environmental claims which require moral considerations. The underlying moral imperative of sustainability is the claim that it is morally wrong for the current generation to devastate the environment and economy because future generations of people will suffer loss or harm. So-called "green ethics" has force but not because the environment *per se* is a moral agent. The moral argument against environmental degradation is that people depend on the environment for their life and well-being, and because humankind has the responsibility to steward the environment and all living beings for the Common Good.

Corporations that communicate messages that help them to be "seen to be green," without a thoroughgoing commitment to sustainability, are now regarded by savvy consumers, ever-watchful for corporate "greenwashing," as being hypocritical and ethically flawed. The larger "corporate targets" find themselves under attack by campaigning NGOs, who are usually afforded greater authority than a corporation because of their higher levels of social capital. Corporations may find themselves being reported for making misleading or untruthful marketing claims on websites such as the Greenwashing Index (www. greenwashingindex.com). Where the opportunity presents, NGOs or activists report questionable eco claims to regulatory authorities. The corporation is then required to give an account of its actions on non-economic grounds, whilst NGOs lay claim to the grounds for social and ethical imperatives.

Marketing is essentially a creative and innovative business practice that can embrace responsibility and consumer concern for its social and environmental practices in a way that differentiates and adds value for consumers. The charge frequently leveled at marketers with respect to ethically related marketing campaigns is one of "greenwash," a public relations stunt with no valid content or commitment to the claims. However, if marketers give rigorous attention to the extent to which they can avoid their products having any negative effects on people or the environment, and develop concepts that are tested with key opinion leaders and stakeholder experts as well as consumers, the opportunity to gain competitive advantage through ethical-branding initiatives becomes clear. In the UK, Marks and Spencer followed extensive research and consideration of their social and environmental responsibilities by launching their Plan A campaign in 2007. The campaign very quickly gained high media visibility, and customer impact significantly improved sales during 2007–08. A simple marketing device has been created through which Marks and Spencer can continue to launch fresh creative executions around the basic sustainability theme, such as: "Look behind the label", "Love Food Hate Waste" and "Wanted – Your Old Clothes. Reward £5."

The legal and ethical challenges to McDonalds Restaurants in the US and the UK in 2003 resulted in the re-creation of the McDonalds brand to blunt the McDonalds' association with unhealthy food and unhealthy children. Confronted by an advertising ban in the UK, McDonalds committed to use advertising to teach children how to achieve healthy lifestyles through a balanced diet and exercise. At the annual conference of the Society for British Advertisers, McDonalds UK CEO, Light, argued:

> We do not need less communication to children: we need more. If we want to educate children to eat right and be active, we need effective marketing communications that are responsive and responsible.

McDonalds overhauled its menus and launched a "healthy happy" campaign, with the tagline "It's what I eat, it's what I do" highlighting fruit and vegetables. In the UK, McDonalds launched a website called *Make Up Your Own Mind* to promote the transparency of its practices and operations.

The overarching marketing claims made by these businesses were simplified to being "right" and "good" in their relations to the society and the planet. In consumer-language terms, simple phrases such as "doing the right thing" (Marks and Spencer) and "doing good" (McDonalds) convey the key elements of ethical branding but require deeper internal substantiation and accountability to provide external and internal assurance that integrity is being practiced and not just claimed.

Ethical branding verification

Over the past decade, there has been a proliferation of agricultural verification and certification organizations responding to the growing demand for more environmentally friendly sourcing combined with agronomic support to farmers and, in the case of fairtrade certification, assurance on the social and educational needs of farming communities in developing countries. One such organization is the Rainforest Alliance, an independent NGO, with expertise in verifying the quality of the agronomic and sustainable farming practices of companies such as Chiquita (bananas), Kraft (Kenco Coffee brand), Costa Coffee and Nestlé

Nespresso (AAA coffee brand). The contract that such companies enter into with the Rainforest Alliance is based on a commitment to practice and be held accountable for a development process which includes

- reduction in water pollution;
- reduction in soil erosion;
- removal of "dangerous pesticides";
- protection of wildlife habitats;
- reduction in waste;
- water conservation;
- improved profitability and competitiveness for farmers; and
- greater collaboration between farmers and conservationists.

The role of responsible marketing is to innovate products and communicate their value through branded frameworks and communications. Increasingly supply-chain sustainability innovations, such as water and carbon "footprinting," are being utilized in marketing communications. The Rainforest Alliance has developed a "ladder of credibility," which sets out the headline steps that show the lowest claim for credibility such as claims with no verifiable substance ("greenwashing"), through steps towards the independent verification and certification of sustainable-sourcing practices. When external monitoring, verification, and certification processes have been embraced in a holistic way, a corporation may justifiably look to find differentiated value propositions for its customers and stakeholders. To maintain integrity, a brand's value proposition and the claims created around an ethical or sustainable supply-chain program need to keep in step with the credibility that the company has earned through independently assessed and benchmarked standards.

Integrity is a moral consideration and a moral commitment, and the principles of morality are normative and relational between the brand owners through their agents (the marketers) and to the consumer.

The character of the marketer

Whilst legal and ethical frameworks assist moral considerations, decisions about brand claims and promises are made by marketers and brand managers as moral agents. George Brenkert (2008, p. 8) has clarified the nature of moral agency for marketers:

> an effective morality will set standards, subject to reason and evidence, by which people can and should behave. The upshot is that

morality is neither simply a matter of opinion, nor irrelevant to marketing. Though too many marketers don't always do what they morally ought to do, this does not itself make morality (or the ethics of marketing) irrelevant.

Such a morality is ultimately grounded in the character of the marketer and the ethical maturity of those guiding organizational decision-making. Moral decision-making, in developing an ethical or sustainable dimension to brands, requires endogenous moral consideration. But this is contentious territory in a worldview dominated by calculative rationality and objective decision-making that largely overshadows notions of substantive moral judgment.

Seeking to understand and account for what the "right" action is by brand owners and marketers is not only found through internal Kantian-type discussions on rights and responsibilities. The conversations that surround a decision to be more transparent in marketing communications might emerge from senior management convictions regarding the kind of people they want to become in taking such an action. The marketer has responsibility with other moral agents to make judgments about the ethical nature of the marketing mix and the brand communication.

Marketing transactions include meeting legitimate human needs, providing choices and serving customers and consumers well. In the pursuit of genuinely serving the customer, and acting justly towards its suppliers, marketing might be regarded as a "social practice" in the sense that Alisdair MacIntyre gives the term: social negotiations in which the virtues are cultivated "not at as an impersonal measurement of costs and benefits, but as an index of the access to relative power within the negotiating processes of different groups" (MacIntyre 2006, p. 120). In a handbook explicating spirituality as a vital human resource to business, it is appropriate to consider the extent to which ethical branding as a social practice calls forth a marketer's spiritual resources. I refer to spirituality here in the sense of the desire for meaning that connects the individual with all living beings (and God for some) and a "source of quality for the individual and society" (Lozano and Ribera, 2004, p. 178). A growing body of literature explores how spirituality in business is operationalized through an emphasis on ethical values, servant leadership, a sense of humility, and a sense of higher purpose (Whetstone, 2001; Pruzan and Mikkelsen, 2007; Thompson, 2008). However, most brand owners make no spiritual claims for their social initiatives, except where "spiritually based" motivations may still be present in marketers and might be defined as:

1. a recognizable contribution towards the Common Good;
2. a genuine commitment towards quality and excellence beyond the product alone;
3. a concern to avoid misleading customers and consumers;
4. a cultivation of direct relationships with stakeholders beyond what is economically required; and
5. signs of trust being fostered in relationships between the brand owner/corporation and wider society.

This "latent spirituality" might be recognized from time to time when marketing creativity is engaged with the dilemmas facing society that are aligned with the brand's distinctive audience. The negotiations involved internally and with stakeholders externally are the ethical engagement of a brand's managers. Questions and debates on transparency, environmental impacts, and on socially responsible sourcing and investment enable a brand's managers to convey ethical attributes to their brands. The brand "becomes ethical" to the degree to which it actively engages in social practice. The conversations of social practice begin with brand owners and brand managers recognizing the nature of their moral agency or what we might call the "inner voice." This inner voice, as the source of our moral agency, has been variously termed the *Moral Sense* or *Sentiment* or the *Voice of Nature* or *Moral Imagination*. Such a voice brings a counterbalance to the reification of *Homo economicus*, and calls for businesses as spheres of social practice to account for their role in society. Ethical branding involves reflecting before acting and conversations about "doing the right thing." It will involve a consideration of all living beings and the responsibilities to the "other," however distant the "other" may be from the challenges of contemporary marketing management.

Literature

Brenkert, G. 2008. *Marketing Ethics*. Oxford: Blackwell.

Fan, Y. 2005. "Ethical Branding and Corporate Reputation." *Corporate Communications*, vol. 10, no. 4, pp. 241–350.

Kotler, P. 1972. "What Consumerism Means for Marketers." *Harvard Business Review*, May–June, pp. 48–57.

Levy S.J. and Zaltman, G. 1975. *Marketing, Society and Conflict*. Englewood Cliffs, NJ: Prentice Hall.

Lozano, J. and Ribera, R. 2004. "New Chance for Management." In L. Zsolnai (ed.), *Spirituality and Ethics in Management*. Dordrecht: Kluwer.

MacIntyre, A.C. 2006. *The Tasks of Philosophy*. Cambridge: Cambridge University Press.

Murphy, P.E. et al., 2005. *Ethical Marketing*. Upper Saddle River, NJ: Prentice Hall.

Pruzan, P. and Pruzan Mikkelsen, K. 2007. *Leading with Wisdom: Spiritual-Based Leadership in Business*. Sheffield: Greenleaf Publishing.

Smith, C. 1990. *Morality and the Market: Consumer Pressure for Corporate Accountability*, London: Routledge.

Thompson, M. J. 2008. "The Practice of Spiritual Dynamics in Business." In L. Zsolnai (ed.), *Europe-Asia Dialogue on Business Spirituality*. Antwerp: Garant.

Whetstone, J. Thomas. 2001. "How Virtue Fits within Business Ethics." *Journal of Business Ethics*, vol. 33, no. 2.

47

Fair Trade Movement

Zsolt Boda

The Fair Trade movement seeks to address the problems of disadvantaged and small-scale producers in the underdeveloped countries by providing market access to their products through trading partnerships. The Fair Trade movement is backed by ethically conscious consumers, who are ready to pay a higher price for products that improve the well-being of marginalized producers as well as their communities. The Fair Trade partnership provides better trading conditions, higher prices, and a continuous relationship with the producers; it also ensures that human rights and environmental concerns are respected, and that children are not exploited in the production process. Fair Trade is a well-established and fast-growing alternative business model to the mainstream way of economizing and trading. It uses a different set of values and objectives than traditional trade, institutionalizing solidarity and putting people and their well-being, as well as the preservation of the natural environment, before the pursuit of the profit.

Fair Trade principles and practices

The World Fair Trade Organization (WFTO) prescribes ten Standards that Fair Trade organizations must follow in their day-to-day work and carries out monitoring to ensure these principles are upheld. These standards, which describe the basic Fair Trade principles and practices, are as follows (see www.wfto.com):

Standard One: *Creating Opportunities for Economically Disadvantaged Producers.* The organization supports marginalized small producers, whether these are independent family businesses, or grouped in associations or co-operatives. It seeks to enable them to move from income insecurity and poverty to economic self-sufficiency and ownership. The trade supports community development.

Standard Two: *Transparency and Accountability.* The organization is transparent and accountable to all its stakeholders and respects the sensitivity and confidentiality of commercial information supplied. The organization finds appropriate, participatory ways to involve employees, members and producers in its decision-making processes.

Standard Three: *Trading Practices.* The organization trades with concern for the social, economic and environmental well-being of marginalized small producers and does not maximize profit at their expense. Fair Trade buyers, recognising the financial disadvantages producers and suppliers face, ensure that orders are paid on receipt of documents and according to the attached guidelines. An interestfree prepayment of at least 50% is made if requested. Where southern Fair Trade suppliers receive a prepayment from buyers, they ensure that this payment is passed on to the producers or farmers who make or grow their Fair Trade products. The organization maintains longterm relationships based on solidarity, trust and mutual respect that contribute to the promotion and growth of Fair Trade.

Standard Four: *Payment of a Fair Price.* A fair price is one that has been mutually agreed by all through dialogue and participation, which provides fair pay to the producers and can also be sustained by the market. Where Fair Trade pricing structures exist, these are used as a minimum. Fair pay means provision of socially acceptable remuneration (in the local context) considered by producers themselves to be fair and which takes into account the principle of equal pay for equal work by women and men.

Standard Five: *Child Labour and Forced Labour.* The organization adheres to the UN Convention on the Rights of the Child, and national/local law on the employment of children. The organization ensures that there is no forced labour in its workforce and/or members or homeworkers.

Standard Six: *NonDiscrimination, Gender Equity and Freedom of Association.* The organization does not discriminate in hiring, remuneration, access to training, promotion, termination or retirement based onrace, caste, national origin, religion, disability, gender, sexual orientation, union membership, political affiliation, HIV/Aids status or age.

Standard Seven: *Working Conditions.* The organization provides a safe and healthy working environment for employees and/or members. It complies, at a minimum, with national and local laws and ILO conventions on health and safety.

Standard Eight: *Capacity Building.* The organization seeks to increase positive developmental impacts for small, marginalised producers through Fair Trade. The organization develops the skills and capabilities of its own employees or members.

Standard Nine: *Promotion of Fair Trade.* The organization raises awareness of the aim of Fair Trade and of the need for greater justice in world trade through Fair Trade. Honest advertising and marketing techniques are always used.

Standard Ten: *Environment.* Organizations which produce Fair Trade products maximize the use of raw materials from sustainably managed sources in their ranges, buying locally when possible. They use production technologies that seek to reduce energy consumption and where possible use renewableenergy technologies that minimize greenhouse-gas emissions. They seek to minimize the impact of their waste stream on the environment. Fair Trade agriculturalcommodity producers minimize their environmental impacts, by using organic or low pesticide use production methods wherever possible.

History of Fair Trade

Alternative or fair trading was started after the Second World War by committed individuals as well as humanitarian and/or religious organizations such as Caritas, Oxfam, Hivos, and Tear Fund, with the aim of advancing the capacities of the most disadvantaged communities in the developing world to allow them to enter the international markets and raise their revenues.

The Fair Trade movement remained a rather marginal phenomenon for several decades, supported by NGOs and characterized by a very limited reach to consumers. In 1969 the first store referred to as a Third World Shop was opened in the Netherlands. When in 1994 the Network of European World Shops (NEW!) was established, 2,500 shops were already participating in the network (DeCarlo, 2007). These shops sold crafts and other Fair Trade products, but at the same time they built awareness and mobilized citizens for trade campaigns.

Two other steps exemplify the development of Fair Trade. *First,* in the mid-1980s new companies such as Max Havelaar and Equal Exchange were founded with the aim of distributing Fair Trade products in ordinary stores, to bring those products close to consumers. The logos of those companies helped consumers differentiate the Fair Trade products from the ordinary ones. The idea of a generally accepted label was then put into practice in 1997, when FLO – Fairtrade Labelling Organization – was founded. Now FLO sets, implements, and controls the standards of Fair Trade and authorizes the use of the Fair Trade logo to those producers and traders that comply with the standards. *Second*, since the beginning of this century several commercial companies and retail chains have initiated their own Fair Trade labels or have acquired the certified Fair Trade logo for some of their products. Examples include Starbucks (US), Procter and Gamble (US), Tesco (UK), Marks and Spencer (UK), Carrefour (France), and Nestlé (Switzerland). While some observe this trend with suspicion, and worry that Fair Trade may lose its original spirit, it is also true that this development brought Fair Trade products as close as possible to consumers, and it has certainly contributed to the fact that Fair Trade has been growing by 30–60 percent per year for the past ten years – a pace of growth never experienced before (Moore, 2004; Krier, 2008). Sales on the Fair Trade market are estimated at nearly 3 billion euros. Two-thirds of the sales are realized in Europe, although the American market has also been growing rapidly in the past years. The most important Fair Trade product is coffee, followed by other agricultural products such as cocoa, tea, fruits, and rice. Handicrafts and industrial products constitute a small fraction of the Fair Trade market.

Besides ethical and humanitarian commitment, political ideas have also been informing the Fair Trade movement. The UNCTAD (United Nations Conference on Trade and Development) introduced the slogan "Trade not Aid" in the 1960s. However, the existing trading system was thought to disfavor the developing countries. According to the economist Raul Prebisch (who was the first secretary of UNCTAD), developing countries are threatened by the deterioration of their terms of trade; therefore, they cannot enjoy the benefits of free trade; and given their reliance on exports of commodities, developing countries need protection or preferential treatment to achieve industrialization and to break the vicious circle of underdevelopment (Prebisch, 1950). The ideal of a more equitable global economy was clearly expressed during the UNCTAD conferences of the 1960s and summarized by the document of the New International Economic Order (NIEO), adopted in 1974 by the UN General Assembly. The claims for a fairer trading regime were partly granted when in 1968 the USA finally accepted the rules of the Generalized System of Preferences (GSP), which were added to the rules of the freetrade regime known as the GATT (General Agreement on Tariffs and Trade). Under the GSP industrialized countries were to grant tariff preferences to developing countries on a nonreciprocal basis. However, such preferences were voluntary, not mandatory, and granted unilaterally. Several sectors and products (such as textiles, oil, etc.) were excluded from the GSP; therefore, it did not play an important role in fostering exports from poor countries.

The 1990s, marked by the unchaining of economic globalization, represent the victory of the freetrade dogma. The defining event is sometimes taken to be the signing of the Marrakesh Convention, the closure of the Uruguay Round, and the foundation of the World Trade Organization in 1994. This was also the year when many developing nations began to adopt free trade policies. However, the unraveling globalization has provoked vivid academic and political debates about its social and environmental effects (Korten, 1995; Klein, 2000). Free trade, being a constitutive element of economic globalization, has been thoroughly scrutinized and criticized by globalization critics; and the concept of fair trade has been reintroduced in both academic and political discourse (Barratt Brown, 1993; Bhagwati, 1996).

NGOs, committed people, and conscious consumers have made the Fair Trade movement big – following the idea that if we cannot change the rules of the game, we should start another game. The aforementioned development of mainstream companies introducing their own Fair Trade labels should also be seen as a reaction to growing globalization and corporate criticism. Critical attitudes about the reality of globalization and the role of multinational companies in it certainly fuel the increasing consumer interest in Fair Trade. Fair Trade is considered to be a model for sustainable consumption, and recently even mainstream consumer-protection organizations, such as Consumers International, have published on the topic (see Boda and Gulyás, 2006).

An ethical analysis of Fair Trade

Let us turn now to the normative-analytical interpretation of the fairness conception expressed by the Fair Trade movement, which is best understood in the light of John Rawls' theory of justice.

Rawls' political philosophy is about justice in a society: "For us the primary subject of justice is the basic structure of society, or more exactly, the way in which the major social institutions distribute fundamental rights and duties and determine the division of advantages from social cooperation" (Rawls, 1971, p. 7). He argues that, in the hypothetical condition of the original position, behind the veil of ignorance, the social contract that society would agree on would consist of two principles of justice. The first embodies the libertarian view that all should have equal and maximal liberties; while the second states that "[s]ocial and economic inequalities are to be arranged so that they are both: (a) to the greatest benefit of the least advantaged, consistent with the justsaving principle, and (b) attached to offices and positions open to all under condition of fair equality of opportunity" (Rawls. 1971, p. 302).

Part (a) of the second principle is the oft-quoted difference principle, which demands the evaluation and comparison of entire institutional structures from the point of view of the worst-off persons. Although Rawls himself did not apply this principle to international society, we may argue that, especially under the conditions of globalization, the idea of international society and the need for justice in global institutions are legitimate concepts and concerns. Now, following the difference principle, international institutions and rules are to be arranged so that they are of the greatest benefit to the least-advantaged people of the least-advantaged countries; or at least that they are of greater benefit to the least-advantaged countries than to the developed ones. That is, in the light of the difference principle, international trade is fair if its institutional structure is arranged so that it maximizes or at least increases the benefits for the poor countries and their people.

From another perspective we may also argue – following the point made by Koslowski (1996, p. 72) – that fair trade is a distinct case of an ancient fairness principle: "To each his own" (*suum cuique tribuere*). "According to the natural right tradition from the Roman *Corpus Iuris* up to Thomas Aquinas, fairness is the permanent attitude, supported by will and directed by prudence, to give each his own, especially his rights." Koslowski argues that fairness always implies a fair equalization of interests; the gains of trade should not be accumulated on one side only. Using the language of business ethics, we might argue that fair trade implies taking into consideration the interests and values of different stakeholder groups. The consumers as stakeholders have a moral right to get good quality products for a fair price; the competitors have a moral right to expect that the principles of fair competition be met by everyone. However, employees also have a moral right to be treated properly; local communities and also nonhuman beings have a moral right to assume that the integrity of their living environment will be respected. And while international trade agreements have devoted considerable space to dealing with the rules of fair competition and making possible quite strict national consumer-protection policies, the moral rights of people (workers and local people) and the natural environment are not taken into consideration by the international trading institutions. Proponents of fair trade argue that this lacuna should be filled; trade will be fair if, and only if, it is based on activities which – using Koslowski's term –"equalize" the interests of each affected party.

Fair Trade and spirituality

Analysts agree that the birth and success of the Fair Trade movement would not have been possible without those "mission-driven" enterprises that uphold alternative ideas and practices based on social, ecological, and place-based commitments (Raynolds, 2009). Although Fair Trade is a kind of market mechanism, its roots and spirit are distinct from the mere profit motive. Many of the founding figures of the movement have been motivated by religious faith, and several religious organizations played an important role in launching the movement. For instance, Ten Thousand Villages is now one of the US's largest Fair Trade organizations; it has its origins in the late 1940s, when Edna Ruth Byler, a volunteer of the Mennonite Central Committee – a relief, peace, and development organization of the Mennonite church – visited Puerto Rico and was introduced to impoverished seamstresses (DeCarlo, 2007). Forty years later Max Havelaar, Europe's most popular Fair Trade company, was cofounded by a Dutch priest, Frans van der Hoff, working in Mexico (Rozen and van der Hoff, 2001).

But apart from the strictly religious aspects, fair traders have been motivated by inherent ethical commitments and caring attitudes towards the poor in distant countries. They have identified themselves with those in need, nurturing an existential feeling of solidarity.

Studies prove that Fair Trade consumers are also primarily motivated by ethical commitments (Shaw, 2005). They are ready to pay a higher price for Fair Trade products in order to help the small producers and their communities in developing countries. The act of buying transcends its strictly commercial nature and becomes an expression of solidarity.

While producers are certainly attracted by the possible economic gains of joining the Fair Trade network, some findings indicate that intangible benefits might be equally important (Murray et al., 2003; Jaffee, 2007). Training and educational opportunities contribute to better production and management practices; running and organizing a cooperative enhances the feeling of community and belonging; the increased rewards of work strengthen self-esteem and political conscience. The quality of life may improve, and autonomy might be fostered at both individual and community levels.

Fair Trade thus represents a system of economizing that transcends itself: the flow of resources is accompanied by a flow of transcendental forces and energies nourished by moral feelings and ethical commitments.

Literature

Barratt Brown, M. 1993. *Fair Trade: Reform and Realities in the International Trading System*. London: Zed Books.

Bhagwati, J. 1996. "The Demands to Reduce Domestic Diversity among Trading Nations." In J. Bhagwati and R.E. Hudec (eds), *Fair Trade and Harmonization: Prerequisites for Free Trade? vol.1: Economic Analysis, vol. 2: Legal Analysis*. Cambridge, MA, London: The MIT Press, vol. 1, pp. 1–40.

Boda, Zs. and Gulyás, E. 2006. "The Ethical Consumerism Movement." *Interdisciplinary Yearbook of Business Ethics*, pp. 141–153.

DeCarlo, J. 2007. *Fair Trade*. Oxford: Oneworld Publications.

Jaffee, D. 2007. *Brewing Justice: Fair Trade Coffee, Sustainability and Survival*. Berkeley and Los Angeles: University of California Press.

Klein, N. 2000. *No Logo*. New York: Alfred A. Knopf.

Krier, J-M. 2008. *Fair Trade 2007: New Facts and Figures from an Ongoing Success Story* Culemborg: DAWS.

Korten, D.C. 1995: *When Corporations Rule the World*. West Hartford: Kumarian Press.

Koslowski, P. 1996. "Ecology and Ethics in the Economy." In F.N. Brady (ed.), *Ethical Universals in International Business*. pp. 58–80. Berlin, Heidelberg, New York: Springer,

Moore, G. 2004. "The Fair Trade movement: Parameters, Issues and Future Research." *Journal of Business Ethics*, 53, pp. 73–86.

Murray, D., Raynolds, L.T., and Taylor, P.L 2003. *One Cup at a Time: Poverty Alleviation and Fair Trade Coffee in Latin America*. Fort Collins: Fair Trade Research Group, Colorado State University.

Prebisch, R. 1950. *The Economic Development of Latin America and Its Principal Problems* New York: UN.

Raynolds, L.T. 2009. "Mainstreaming Fair Trade coffee: From Partnership to Traceability." *World Development*, vol. 37, no. 6, pp. 1083–1093.

Rawls, J. 1971. *A Theory of Justice*. Cambridge, MA: Harvard University Press.

Roozen, N. and van der Hoff, F. 2001. *L'aventure du commerce equitable. Une alternative à la mondialisation*. Paris: JCLattès.

Shaw, D. 2005. "Modelling Consumer Decision Making in Fair Trade." In R. Harrison, T. Newhol, and D. Shaw (eds), *The Ethical Consumer*. pp. 137–154. Sage.

48
Ethical Banking

Frans de Clerck

The values-driven approach of *ethical, sustainable, social, alternative, development, or solidarity* banking and financial institutions provides space and tools for more reflection, consciousness, and responsibility in the use of money. Greater consciousness is a prerequisite in the constant search for quality of life, not only for oneself but for all life. This is true for material matters as well as cultural and spiritual ones. And it leads to taking initiative and responsibility individually, locally, and globally, because we are now more interconnected than ever and compelled to collaborate rather than compete.

Profoundly nontransparent financial processes in global financial markets, and a fundamental lack of responsibility in traditional banking's investment and lending activities, have led to a global financial crisis.

For decades now, ethical-banking pioneers have contested converting a large part of traditional banking into high-profitability/high-risk activities on a "too big to fail" scale. These pioneers offer a different approach based on human values, participative ways of organizing, social responsibility, and transparency that together aim at enhancing the overall sustainability of our society. And they have developed sustainable business models that generate decent profits.

At the same time there has been a growing wave of interest from *civil society*, the so-called *cultural creatives* (Ray and Anderson, 2000)and *social entrepreneurs* (Elkington and Hartigan, 2008) who focus on a type of banking that includes human development, ecological constraints, and economic fairness (People, Planet, Profit).

Nongovernmental organizations (NGOs) have been calling for mainstream financial institutions to implement more socially and environmentally responsible lending policies. They encourage commitments to sustainability: to avoid lending to organizations that actively do harm, to behave responsibly, to be accountable and transparent, and to create sustainable markets and sustainable systems of governance. They have also called for financial institutions to advocate better regulation. These efforts have enjoyed some success. The links and partnerships that ethical banks build with NGOs and civil society are empowering participation in society.

But, for ethical bankers, this pressure is not enough. Additionally, they develop innovative banking models integrating basic values, socially innovative work practices, and a substantial contribution to the common good. "They point the way to the kind of financial decision making which moves above and beyond pure self interest" (Achim Steiner, UN Under-Secretary General and Executive Director, UN Environment Programme [UNEP] at the Global Alliance for Banking on Values constitution meeting in 2009).

Ethical banking might be seen as a methodology, a way of transforming mainstream banking. But, paradoxically, these efforts often demonstrate the impossibility of integrating ethics into institutionalized banking culture.

Over the last twenty years the traditional banking sector has made some progress. It has managed and distributed ethical investment funds, introduced corporate-social-responsibility measures, applied social and environmental reporting guidelines, financed renewable energy, explored and in some cases invested in microfinance, and developed environmental risk assessment in its lending. More than 500 asset owners and investment management firms have accepted the *"Principles for Responsible Investment"* (UNEPFI, 2006), showing they are willing to include environmental, social, and governance (ESG) issues in their investment analyses and decision-making processes.

Some of the traditional cooperative and savings banks have rediscovered their roots and are paying more attention to their social missions.

A worldwide movement of genuinely ethical banks has emerged precisely because traditional banking's progress has been so limited. In particular, it has failed to integrate essential values and ethical principles within organizations and into their structures, market activities, and profit strategies.

The values underpinning sustainable banking are integrated into the institution's mission, internal organization, and business processes – including communication and stakeholder partnering, and networking.

When these elements have worked effectively together ethical banks have been successful in

- delivering social-finance products and basic financial services;
- financing community-based development initiatives and social entrepreneurs;
- fostering the development of sustainable and environmentally sound enterprises;
- fulfilling human-development potential including poverty alleviation; and, importantly,
- generating a triple-bottom line for People, Planet, and Profit (profit as a means to an end, not the end in itself).

The shared values of these institutions are:

- using money as a tool for enhancing the quality of life through human, social, cultural, and environmental development;
- assuming responsibility for the long-term impact of their efforts on their interdependent environment and communities; and
- incorporating transparency, trust, clarity, and inclusiveness in delivering their products and services. (From the Global Alliance for Banking on Values Charter)

It is clear that this type of banking offers concrete, grounded financial solutions. It benefits excluded and underserved people and sectors. At the same time it invites its stakeholders (clients, coworkers, partners, shareholders, etc.) to reflect on the bank's, and their own, capacity to contribute to a qualitative and meaningful life for individuals, communitie and the planet. The values underpinning this work imply a search for human development by connecting individuals to stimulate and help each other in this process with an attitude of interest, respect, and tolerance.

In banking, *transparency and clarity* are key tools for stimulating these processes and moving above and beyond pure self-interest. They show people what is being done with their money. They also demonstrate to social entrepreneurs that these banks understand the entrepreneurs' capacities and motivations, highlighting that they have the active respect and support of savers and investors, as well as the responsible bankers organizing the process.

Another tool is *multiquality savings, lending, investment, and gift money* with its ability to link people and create interest (*inter-esse* in Latin).

This is radically different from the role of money in traditional banking – where the bank creates an nontransparent technical screen between savers and lenders, where risky market dealings account for a large part of profit and loss, and where a fundamental goal of the business is to make money with money without taking meaningful account of ethical or social concerns. This approach sees the ethical neutrality of the bankers as a value in itself, whereas the commitment to human values inherent in actively ethical banking, which is reflected in financing sustainable projects, contributes to responsible decision-making with a long-term impact on society. These qualitative processes create trust, a value that has largely been misused in the financial industry.

The influence of values like human, social, cultural, and environmental development; social cohesion; responsibility, and trust – combined with specific tools and specific forms of internal organization – is not limited to a material impact on the lives of savers, lenders, and bankers. Money also has the potential to free capacities and put talents that promote quality of life to work. It also has the potential to diminish or even destroy those capacities or prevent talents from developing when money is invested in harmful projects. At its most negative, money can stimulate the darker side of our souls and result in greed and abuse of power. The professional banker can either be subsumed within the technical-financial machinery or choose to take personal responsibility and use the financial infrastructure from a healthier, human-development perspective.

It is clear that money affects human beings. Having it can be as harmful as not having it. An addiction to money, just as a lack of money, can lead to loss of personal identity and human dignity and may hinder human development.

This is why a private-banking arm in ethical banks can be a tool to freeing money from a single focus on the highest financial return. Ethical banks make money flow so it can be sustainably invested or donated. In this sense, these institutions help individuals to connect with their higher selves, liberating them from the fear of losing something that is not essential in their own lives, but could become a useful tool in other people's.

Microfinance demonstrates how powerful this can be in practice. It contributes to poverty alleviation, sweeping away practical obstacles to a decent living and creating cultural, spiritual, and social wealth.

Pension funds that apply ethical criteria in their investments, and ethical investment funds can also change the way senior management in conventional companies address important social, environmental, and ethical questions. The banker's special position in society needs some clarification. Through their lending and investment, in particular, business bankers ought to have a perspective on society's needs and opportunities. Their economic research departments and operational units follow economic and financial trends in general, and sector developments in particular. Access to this information and experience in the real economy normally lead to balanced lending and investment decisions. If conventional bankers chose to include ethical principles and criteria in their work, as their ethical equivalents do, they could direct lending and investments to the areas that profit society most: to community building and to a healthy environment at respectable risk/return ratios.

Because of the unique position of banks, and the existence of a public control system regulating their activities, they have an extended social responsibility and a duty to address the "organization of bad behavior." Following the financial crisis, government bailouts using taxpayer money allowed the banking industry's responsibilities to become much more visible. However, the moral imperative behind this new spirit of responsibility is still not widely recognized by individual bankers themselves. This reflects a deeper ethical and moral uncertainty that has grown out of a focus on individualism in modern society. In a negative sense this has led to one-sided self-interest, greed, abuse of power, and to institutionalized irresponsible behavior.

Josef Ackermann, Deutsche Bank CEO and chairman of the Institute of International Finance (in an interview with *Der Spiegel* and *The New York Times*, in October 2009) stated, "It is a government task to introduce more quality regulation in the banking sector in order to prevent devastating competition. Appealing only to morality in a competitive society does not lead to a solution."

What he did not say was that some modern economic thinking and practice already embraces morality, ethics, and individual and collective responsibility. These build a more effective and inclusive economy based on responsible collaboration rather than on "devastating competition." These are complementary drivers to government-led regulation that apply to the banking sector's special position in society.

Following the 2008–2009 financial crisis there were numerous recommendations from the banking sector to self-regulate, and from the international community to put new international regulations in place. One of the recommendations of the Commission Maas of the Netherlands´ Banking Association was the introduction of a banker's oath, reflecting the Hippocratic oath committing doctors to practice medicine ethically. The banking oath would include several ethical aspects: banking with integrity and carefulness; balancing the interests of stakeholders, including those of the bank adhering specific codes of conduct; not abusing banking knowledge; accepting personal responsibility for society; fostering trust in banking; and honoring the banking profession.

While the introduction of these values provides obvious benefits, it will only work well when the financial institutions themselves reform. They in turn will need to change their internal structures and processes so that greed and pure self-interest cannot thrive.

As long as a more conscious, ethical commitment stays outside mainstream banking there will be no real progress in changing an institutionalized culture that promotes and rewards short-term high risk over long-term sustainability. If nothing else the financial crisis may have created an opportunity for fundamental change. As things stand at the time of writing, evidence suggests that the banking world intends to return to business as usual and the old banking model. A familiar focus on profit maximization via speculative financial-market operations, and financial volume and the repackaging and redistribution of risks to remote third parties, appears to have quickly become the norm again. All of which means these structural and moral deficits could easily lead to the next global financial crisis.

The sustainable-banking world offers a compelling alternative. While they started as small-scale pioneers, the ethical banking and finance movement – including microfinance institutions using small lending programs aimed at poverty alleviation – serves millions of customers from across the world with combined assets of tens of billions USD. Ethical banks finance hundreds of thousands of socially, environmentally, and financially sound enterprises; projects and communities; and partner NGOs and civil society movements. While their size and impact grows substantially, and many have flourished during the financial crisis, they remain relatively small.

This sector, with its new banking models, has developed into an effective human-development movement. It uses money, professionalism, and wisdom, based on respect for human values and dignity and with a sense of interdependence, to create new forms of social cohesion.

This increasingly influential ethical-banking body constantly searches for, and reflects on, the meaning of human and economic value creation. And it puts its findings into practice.

Literature

Bakas A. and Peverelli, R., 2008. *The Future of Finance*. Schiedam: Scriptum Publishers.

Council of Europe 2003. *Civil Society and New Social Responsibilities Based on Ethical Foundations.*

De Clerck, F. 2009. "Ethical Banking." in L. Zsolnai (ed.), *Ethical Prospects.* pp. 209–227. Dordrecht, New York: Springer.

Elkington, J. and Hartigan P. 2008. *The Power of Unreasonable People.* Boston, MA: Harvard Business Press.

Forward S. and Buck C. 1994. *Mannen & Vrouwen & Geld.* Utrecht, Antwerpen: Kosmos-Z&K Uitgevers.

Garson B. 2001. *Money Makes the World Go Around.* New York: Penguin Books.

Guene, C. and Mayo, E. 2001. *Banking and Social Cohesion.* Oxfordshire: Jon Carpenter Publishing.

Jeucken, M. 2001. *Sustainable Finance & Banking.* London: Earthscan Publications Ltd.

Jeucken, M. 2004. *Sustainability in Finance.* Delft: Eburon Academic Publishers.

Kamp, J. 2002. *Klein Geld. Hoe vijftig dollar de wereldverandert.* Rotterdam: Lemniscaat.

Kerler, R. 2000. *Was hat geld mitmirzutun?* Dornach: VerlagamGoetheanum.

Louche, C. 2004. *Ethical Investment.* Rotterdam: Erasmus University.

Mackay, P. 2008. *Geld und Menschenwürde.* Dornach: Lecture Goetheanum.

Ray, P. and Anderson, S.R. 2000. *The Cultural Creatives: How 50 Million People Are Changing the World.* New York: Harmony Books.

Reijngoud, T. 2009. *Het NieuweBankieren.* Utrecht/Antwerpen: KosmosUitgevers.

Scharmer, C.O. 2007. *Theory U.* Cambridge, MA: SoL (The Society for Organisational Learning).

Steiner, R. 1922. *NationalökonomischerKurs.* Dornach: Rudolf Steiner Verlag.

Thielemann, U. and Ulrich, P. 2003. *BrennpunktBankenethik.* Berne: Paul Haupt.

Vigier, J.P. 2003. *Lettreouverte à ceux qui veulent render leur argent intelligent et solidaire.* Paris: Editions Charles Léopold Mayer.

Vandaele J. 2005. *Het Recht van de Rijkste.* Antwerpen: Uitgeverij Houtekiet.

Canal, G. v. 1992. *Geisteswissenschaft und Ökonomie.* Schaffhausen: Novalis Verlag.

Index

411